THE METROPOLITAN CHASE

Politics and Policies
in Urban America

E. Terrence Jones
University of Missouri-St. Louis

Prentice
Hall

Upper Saddle River, New Jersey 07458

Library of Congress Cataloging-in-Publication Data

Jones, E. Terrence (Endsley Terrence)
    The metropolitan chase : politics and policies in urban America / E. Terrence Jones.—
1st ed.
        p. cm.
    Includes bibliographical references and index.
    ISBN 0-13-016641-3 (pbk.)
        1. Metropolitan areas—United States.   2. Metropolitan government—United States.
3. Urban policy—United States.   4. Sociology, Urban—United States.   5. Urban economics.
I. Title.

HT334.U5 J66 2003
307.76'4'0973—dc21

2002025845

VP/Editorial Director: Charlyce Jones Owen
Senior Acquisitions Editor: Heather Shelstad
Editorial Assistant: Jessica Drew
Editorial/production supervision and
    interior design: Mary Araneo
Marketing Manager: Claire Bitting
Marketing Assistant: Jennifer Bryant
Prepress and Manufacturing Buyer: Ben Smith

Cover Art Director: Jayne Conte
Cover Designer: Lisa Boylan
Director, Image Resource Center: Melinda Reo
Manager, Image Rights and Permissions: Zina Arabia
Interior Image Specialist: Beth Boyd-Brenzel
Image Researcher: Sheila Norman
Image Permissions Coordinator: Debbie Latronica

This book was set in 10/12 New Baskerville by Interactive Composition Corporation and was printed
and bound by Hamilton Printing. The cover was printed by Phoenix Color Corp.

DOWNTOWN. Words and Music by TONY HATCH. © Copyright WELBECK MUSIC LTD.
ADMINISTERED BY UNIVERSAL—MCA MUSIC PUBLISHING, A DIVISION OF UNIVERSAL
STUDIES, INC. (ASCAP) International Copyright Secured. All Rights Reserved.

 Prentice Hall

© 2003 by Pearson Education, Inc.
Upper Saddle River, New Jersey 07458

Pearson Education LTD., London
Pearson Education Australia PTY, Limited, Sydney
Pearson Education Singapore, Pte. Ltd
Pearson Education North Asia Ltd, Hong Kong
Pearson Education Canada, Ltd., Toronto
Pearson Educación de Mexico, S.A. de C.V.
Pearson Education—Japan, Tokyo
Pearson Education Malaysia, Pte. Ltd
Pearson Education, Upper Saddle River, New Jersey

TO THE LEADERSHIP ST. LOUIS CLASSES

1986–2002

Contents

PART II: THE EXTERNAL CHASE: COMPETITION AMONG METROS   116

Preface

During the past century, metropolitan regions have become the central place for human activity. Although economic factors have had the most to do with creating and expanding them, metropolises must also govern themselves. Politics—who gets what, when, where, and how—now operates *among* metropolitan areas as well as within them. Metropolitan citizens are simultaneously engaged in two contests. The first is competing with other regions for the highest quality of life. The second is striving within each region for who prospers most. These two contests overlap and interact to form the metropolitan chase.

Understanding and explaining political processes and policy issues within metropolitan regions is daunting. First, it is a work in progress. More than other levels of society, most notably the nation-state, metropolitan areas have only been seriously grappling with regional decisions for the past few decades. They are making it up as they go along. Second, it is confusing. Since there is no single overarching government for any metropolitan area, making decisions involves hundreds of players spread across all three sectors: public, business, and nonprofit. That is why the process is typically labeled "governance" rather than "government," signaling that much of the action extends outside the formal public setting in what is becoming a virtual realm, a civic sphere. Fortunately, the past decade has produced substantial research about the new regionalism. Some has come from the traditional sources: university scholars and independent think tanks. Some has been produced by other institutions within metropolitan regions as they struggle to change. Examples include citizens leagues, metropolitan planning organizations, and ad hoc cross-sectoral task forces. Journalists and other public intellectuals have added to the mix, examining recent developments and speculating about alternative arrangements.

Using a metropolitan perspective and a competitive metaphor, *The Metropolitan Chase* synthesizes this material for the regions within the United States. It provides a scorecard outlining the players within each sector (Chapters 2 through 5) and then analyzes how they interact within several policy arenas (Chapters 6 through 14): economic development, transportation, education, arts/entertainment/tourism, public safety, health, environment, housing, parks and recreation, and taxation. It closes with a discussion of the four overriding issues confronting every region: how to compete economically, how to manage growth, how to counter inequity, and how to govern.

The recommended readings at the end of each chapter are a guide for further exploration. The exercises, labeled "doing it," give students an opportunity to explore how all this plays out in their region. The appendices provide a guide for finding further information from the Internet. Precisely because actions on and knowledge about metropolitan areas is expanding so rapidly, printed statistical data are frequently dated well before they are printed. To stay fresh, to have the latest, one must head for the World Wide Web.

Acknowledgments

All authors owe debts but textbook writers incur more. First, they capitalize on the work of many others. The hundreds of footnotes give each person some recognition for their contributions but, cumulatively, the impact is much greater. The scholarly community is blessed with the talented efforts of an increasing number of researchers studying metropolitan matters.

Second, the University of Missouri-St. Louis has been a splendid setting to learn more about regions. During my thirty-three years at UM-St. Louis, I have had an exceptional group of colleagues, past and present, who have taught me much about metropolitan areas. These include Alan Artibise, Brady Baybeck, Robert Calsyn, John Collins, Scott Decker, Bryan Downes, Andrew Glassberg, Andrew Hurley, the late Jim Laue, George McCall, Daniel Monti, Eugene Meehan, Alvin Mushkatel, Hugh Nourse, Thomas Pavlak, Donald Phares, Neal Primm, and Lana Stein. Most notable are two giants in the field: the late Norton Long and Dennis Judd.

Third, Susan Mason, a talented and dedicated research assistant, did the grunt work in preparing the two appendices, searching through the Internet for site after site. The UM-St. Louis Department of Political Science administrative team, most notably Janet Frantzen and Lana Vierdag, tolerate faculty peculiarities and make our daily lives more productive.

Fourth, Prentice Hall has been a splendid partner. Special thanks to Wayne Spohr, bookman extraordinaire, who first urged me to write the book. As a recovering arts and sciences dean, just returned from fourteen years in administration, I needed the encouragement. Also much appreciated are Beth Gillett Mejia, Heather L. Shelstad, Jessica Drew, and Mary Araneo, as well as Prentice Hall reviewers

Michael Rich of Emory University and Peter Suzuki of the University of Nebraska at Omaha for their comments and input.

Fifth, there is the supportive family. My son and fellow political scientist, Mark P. Jones, has been an inspiration. I dedicated an earlier book, published in 1981, to him, never realizing that he would join the same intellectual tribe. My wife and fellow social scientist, Lois Hauck Pierce, has provided much encouragement and forgone many excursions.

Finally, although I have learned so much about metropolitan politics and issues from the scholarly community, I have absorbed even more from those who are in the trenches. Since 1986, I have had the extraordinary joy and honor of being the principal consultant to the Leadership St. Louis Program. In this role, I spend eighteen days annually with fifty-plus marvelous people: appointed and elected government officials, business owners, corporate executives, law firm partners, nonprofit heads, police chiefs, policy advocates, religious leaders, school superintendents, university administrators, and more. Working with two exceptional directors, Carolyn Losos (1986 to 1998) and Christine Chadwick (1998 to the present), these more than eight hundred leaders have become my friends and my tutors. More than anyone else, they have made this book real and, with deep gratitude, I dedicate it to them.

PROLOGUE

CHAPTER 1

The Metropolitan Century

WHAT'S AT STAKE

Four out of five U.S. citizens live in metropolitan areas. It's where they work and play, where they plant roots and raise families—it's the place they call home. Increasingly, Americans identify more with their metropolitan regions than, say, with their states. Asked where we are from when away from our locale, most of us are more likely to name our metropolitan area—Philadelphia or Atlanta—than to mention our state—Pennsylvania or Georgia. Even the one in five residing outside metropolitan areas, half of whom live in adjoining counties, typically have some psychological connection with the nearest metropolis. The states issue our drivers' licenses but the region captures our identity.

The twentieth century featured a military and economic competition among almost two hundred nation states. These nations fought world wars, endured cold wars, engaged in ideological clashes, competed for economic supremacy. Countries will continue as meaningful global actors in the twenty-first century but they already are ceding center stage to the world's metropolitan regions. What will characterize this century is a quality-of-life contest among areas, a metropolitan chase most of us will pursue.

We will be metropolitan citizens engaged in a peaceful but intense competition. We might shift allegiances a few times during our lives by moving from one metropolis to another, a much easier transfer than relocating between countries but, wherever we land, our personal well-being will be intimately intertwined with that of our metropolitan area. The more people who want to dwell in our metropolis, the higher our property values will be. The more enterprises which aspire to locate there, the greater our economic opportunities. The more tourists who desire to play in our area, the richer our leisure time. The cleaner its environment, the healthier our lives.

As in any contest, all cannot finish first. Although almost all have roots somewhere and most would prefer to stay near their relatives and in familiar settings, Americans have a mobile history and twenty- and thirty-somethings are especially likely to relocate. The metropolitan areas which attract these individuals, especially the more talented, will do better and, conversely, those that lose a disproportionate share of their best and brightest will falter. As the chase persists, some keep score of the current standings. Between 1990 and 1997, for example, among the U.S. metropolitan areas with populations exceeding 1 million, the five having the highest proportion of Americans moving to them were Las Vegas, Atlanta, Phoenix, Austin, and Raleigh-Durham; the quintet experiencing the greatest losses were Los Angeles, New York, San Jose, Miami, and Newark.[1]

Accompanying the competition for people is the contest for capital. Those people committed to each metropolitan area want it to be the most appealing place to invest funds, to keep much of the wealth generated within its own boundaries at home, and to attract support from other regions and, indeed, from foreign countries. They want it to be the hot place to make a buck, the region one finds at the end of the rainbow. They fear their metropolis will develop a reputation as being part of the economic past where no outsider wishes to risk an investment and most of the local capital flees for more lucrative possibilities.

The chase is not just among regions. The same competition which exists across metropolitan areas also occurs within each region. Just because all citizens within a metropolis in principle share in its performance does not mean that it is necessarily so. Even in a prospering region, some can be left behind, not only failing to obtain any dividends from the region's progress but perhaps paying a disproportionate portion for the costs of success. For example, their taxes might have been raised to subsidize a project that benefits most of the community but, for them, just means fewer disposable dollars for their own needs. Despite what many political and civic leaders proclaim when calling for regionwide investments, a rising tide does not inevitably lift all boats.

The competition for residents, businesses, shoppers, and more also proceeds within metropolitan areas. Citizens especially identify with the neighborhoods and subdivisions where they live. They want more of the good things—higher property values, faster transportation, better schools—and less of the undesirable items—taxes, polluted environments, unsafe settings. An expanded airport or a wider interstate or a new landfill might benefit the overall region, but if it borders *your* neighborhood or cuts through *your* municipality or permeates *your* air, you are apt to oppose it. This understandable outburst of localism has even produced its own acronym: NIMBY (Not In My Back Yard). Even the most regional-minded citizen will, at some point, exhibit a touch of NIMBYism. It is always preferable to have someone else pay as much of the costs as possible while you receive as many of the benefits as you can.

The internal contest also has an economic component. Which businesses should benefit from policy decisions? Should downtown retailers get a tax break to shore up that area's decline? Or should the subsidies go to spur growth on the fringe? Should the port be improved first, aiding firms using water transportation, or should the rail terminals receive preference, helping enterprises more dependent on that mode?

The conflicts within regions are typically more intense and more immediate than those between metropolitan areas. Just as siblings often are the most upset when one seems to get more than the other, whether it's holiday gifts as a child or a parent's inheritance as an adult, so too residents in a particular part of a metropolitan area are more worried about whether the folks across town benefit disproportionately or that they may themselves pay more than their share for some public improvement. The external competitors, hundreds of other regions in the United States and thousands around the world, are more diffuse and more remote. Few Cincinnatians wake up at night, worried that Chicagolanders are about to steal what is rightfully theirs. But many Cincinnati residents living north of the Ohio River are likely to want assurance that the Kentucky side will not get the upper hand.

Compounding this internal division is the enormous diversity within most metropolitan areas. Glance into an individual neighborhood or subdivision and folks tend to resemble one another closely: similar incomes, same race, consensus about what constitutes the good life. Look across all of them and one is struck by how much they differ from one another. It is difficult enough to reach agreement among similar entities; when economic class and ethnic heritage as well as geography separate factions, having the region act together is even more challenging.

The external and internal contests overlap, interact, and coexist. Citizens want their metropolitan areas to finish high in the competition with others, both within and outside the United States. This is the interdependency which unites a region's residents and spurs it to develop more effective metropolitan policies. But citizens also want *their* piece of the region—their neighborhoods and their economic sectors—to receive more of the benefits and bear less of the costs. This is the division which animates a region's politics and causes each of its governments, businesses, and nonprofit organizations to fight for their own special interests.

This book is a handbook, an owner's manual, for participating in both aspects of the metropolitan chase within the United States. The remainder of this chapter describes the distinguishing characteristics of modern metropolitan regions. Chapters 2 to 4 portray the major stakeholders—governments, businesses, and nonprofit organizations—while Chapter 5 outlines the civic arenas where these groups interact. The remainder of the book, save for the final chapter, explains the most important policy spheres, some of which bear more on the external contest and others more on the internal competition. The last chapter explores what metropolitan areas are doing to improve regional decision making and performance.

WHAT IS A METROPOLITAN AREA?

Although metropolitan areas are local phenomena, it is the federal government which defines them. The U.S. Office of Management and Budget develops the standards and the U.S. Bureau of the Census collects the data to which the rules are applied. Their concept starts with a core city and adds all the surrounding areas having noticeable economic and social links with it. The overall total population must exceed 100,000, although the New England states have successfully lobbied to have the bar lower (75,000) for them.

The list of areas qualifying for metropolitan designation, called metropolitan statistical areas (MSAs), and their precise boundaries change regularly. First, some cities and their environs pass the population needed and join the group. Since 1995, for example, the new entrants include Auburn-Opelika (Alabama), Corvallis (Oregon), Flagstaff (Arizona), Grand Junction (Colorado), Jonesboro (Arkansas), Missoula (Montana), and Pocatello (Idaho). Second, over time the metropolitan area expands and adjoining counties form sufficient connections, measured by factors such as commuting patterns, to be added to the region. When that happens, the practice is to include the entire county. Figure 1–1 portrays those metropolitan areas having one million or more residents, and Appendix B describes key factors for each of them.

The largest metropolitan regions are termed "consolidated" or "CMSAs." They are so extensive that they include two or more contiguous but distinct metropolitan areas. In these situations, numbering almost twenty, the components are called "primary" or "PMSAs." Examples include the Los Angeles-Riverside-Orange County CMSA which encompasses four PMSAs: Los Angeles-Long Beach, Orange County, Riverside-San Bernardino, and Ventura, and the Cleveland-Akron CMSA which is divided into two PSMAs: Akron and Cleveland-Lorain-Elyria.

To complicate matters even more, two other agencies within the federal government—the Bureau of Economic Analysis (BEA) and the Bureau of Labor Statistics (BLS)—have drawn their maps differently. The BEA has cut the country into 172 pieces, using metropolitan regions as the core but then linking them with the economically connected nonurbanized areas. As a consequence, every county is in one of the BEA's units. The BLS calls its components "labor markets" and the guiding rationale is an area within which people are willing to change jobs without switching residences.

Metropolitan areas come in all shapes and sizes, ranging from Los Angeles and New York, each with more than 15 million inhabitants within the CMSA, to several that just exceed the minimum standards. Much of the time, the discussions in this book will apply most directly to the regions having over 1 million residents. Taken as a group, they contain over half the nation's population and an even greater share of its cultural and economic activity. As Table 1–1 shows, they are found throughout the continental United States but neither Anchorage, Alaska, nor Honolulu, Hawaii, have yet to crack the top bracket.

Because there were no widely accepted definitions of metropolitan areas until after World War II, it is impossible to give precise numbers about trends beyond the past fifty years. The best estimate is that about 40 percent of the nation's population lived in metropolitan areas in 1900. When the federal government implemented the now prevailing definition in 1950, the share was 56 percent, by 1980 it was 75 percent, and now it is at 80 percent. That proportion is expected to inch upward in the decades ahead. While the nation's population tripled over the past century, the fraction living in metropolitan areas went up twice as much, by a factor of six.

FIGURE 1–1   U.S. Metropolitan Areas over One Million Population
Source: 1990 Geolytics

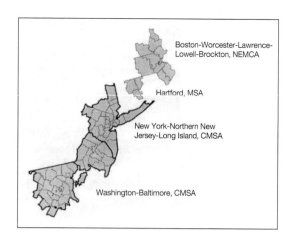

Boston-Worcester-Lawrence-Lowell-Brockton, NEMCA

Hartford, MSA

New York-Northern New Jersey-Long Island, CMSA

Washington-Baltimore, CMSA

Minneapolis-Paul

Milwaukee-Racine

Grand Rapids-Muskegon-Holland

Detroit-Ann Arbor-Flint

Buffalo-Niagara Falls

Boston-Worcester-Lawrence-Lowell-Brockton

Cleveland-Akron

Chicago-Gary-Kenosha

Indianapolis

Columbus

Pittsburgh

New York-Northern New Jersey-Long Island

Philadelphia-Wilmington-Atlantic City

Cincinnati-Hamilton

Louisville

Kansas City

St. Louis

Norfolk-Virginia Beach-Newport News

Memphis

Nashville

Raleigh-Durham-Chapel Hill

Charlotte-Gastonia-Rock Hill

Atlanta

Jacksonville

New Orleans

Orlando

Tampa-St. Petersburg-Clearwater

West Palm Beach-Boca Raton

Miami-Fort Lauderdale

TABLE 1–1   Metropolitan Areas with Population of One Million or More in 1998

Northeast States
  Boston/Worcester/Lowell, Hartford, Providence/Pawtucket

Middle Atlantic States
  Buffalo/Niagara Falls, New York/Northern New Jersey/Long Island, Philadelphia/
  Wilmington/Atlantic City, Pittsburgh, Rochester

North Central States
  Chicago/Gary/Kenosha, Cincinnati/Hamilton, Cleveland/Akron, Columbus, Detroit/Ann
  Arbor/Flint, Grand Rapids/Muskegon/Holland, Indianapolis, Kansas City,
  Milwaukee/Racine, Minneapolis/St. Paul, St. Louis

South Atlantic States
  Atlanta, Charlotte/Gastonia/Rock Hill, Greensboro/Winston Salem/High Point,
  Jacksonville, Miami/Fort Lauderdale, Norfolk/Virginia Beach/Newport News, Orlando,
  Raleigh/Durham/Chapel Hill, Tampa/St. Petersburg/Clearwater, Washington/Baltimore,
  West Palm Beach/Boca Raton

South Central States
  Austin/San Marcos, Dallas/Fort Worth, Houston/Galveston/Brazoria, Memphis,
  Nashville, New Orleans, Oklahoma City, San Antonio

Mountain States
  Denver/Boulder/Greeley, Las Vegas, Phoenix/Mesa, Salt Lake City/Ogden

Pacific States
  Los Angeles/Riverside/Orange County, Portland/Salem, Sacramento/Yolo, San Diego,
  San Francisco/Oakland/San Jose, Seattle/Tacoma/Bremerton

Source: U.S. Bureau of the Census, unpublished data. *www.census.gov.*

Not only are more people living in metropolitan areas, there are also more such regions. At the initial count in 1950, 168 qualified. Today, the number exceeds 320 and has been climbing by one or two per year. Moreover, many metropolitan areas continue to add counties. The St. Louis MSA, for example, consisted of six counties in 1960. Now it has twelve. Over the same period, Atlanta has exploded from five to twenty counties, from 1,723 square miles in 1960 to 5,140 in 1990.

METROPOLITAN AREAS ARE EXPANDING

Metropolitan populations are spreading out over an ever-expanding territory and have been doing so rapidly and steadily since 1950. This process has been most acute in the Midwest and Northeast but examples can occasionally be found elsewhere. In some instances—Cleveland and St. Louis—the central city's population plummeted while suburbia grew. The City of Cleveland, for example, lost over 40 percent of its population between 1950 and 1990 while its suburban residents more than doubled. Others—Atlanta and Denver—posted modest 10-to-20 percent gains in the central cities while their environs mushroomed, sixfold for Atlanta, five times larger for Denver.

There are many reasons why this expansion has occurred but the most straightforward as well as the most profound is that it is the way Americans want it. The contrast with Europe is striking: the City of Paris has over fifty thousand persons per square mile, over four times as dense as, say, the City of Chicago. Six out of seven metropolitan Parisians live within fifteen miles of the central city. The comparable proportion for the New York region is one out of two.

Figure 1–2 shows this trend is continuing since 1990. In the Northeast and parts of the Midwest, the number of central city residents has declined even more

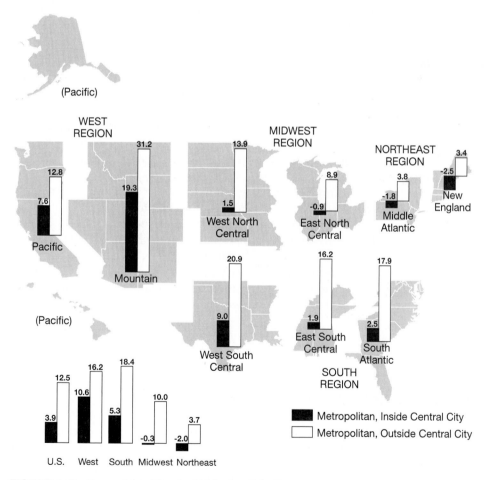

FIGURE 1–2 Percentage Change in Metropolitan Population Inside and Outside Central Cities, by Region and Division: 1990 to 1998

Source: Population Estimates Program, U.S. Census Bureau.

while in the rest of the country, suburban growth clearly outpaces the cities' increases. Only in Texas and the West have central cities prospered and even that is partially aided by many of them having larger boundaries and stronger annexation authority. David Rusk, the former Mayor of Albuquerque, calls them "elastic cities."[2]

This enlargement has also reshaped *what* happens *where* within metropolitan areas. Three figures drawn from Jonathan Barnett's *The Fractured Metropolis* shows what has occurred within the typical region over the past 130 years.[3] Figure 1–3a portrays the emerging city after the Civil War with most of the activity concentrated near the principal waterway and the railroad intersection. Figure 1–3b revisits the same region in 1950, where development had evolved with much of it along one or more corridors where streetcar lines had been built and, then, as automobiles became more prevalent, four-lane thoroughfares had followed. Figure 1–3c depicts the modern metropolis with its many facets—a series of major malls, each anchoring a set of neighborhoods, one or more executive parks with campuslike settings, a post-1960 public university, a new or expanded international airport—all happening over a much more extended area, bisected and later encircled by a network of interstate highways. Metropolitan expansion has had many enablers. Its driving force may be the American thirst for space but other factors have contributed mightily. Most cities began beside a river, lake, or ocean and, for their initial existence, did not stray far from it. Even by 1850, ninety years after its founding, urbanized St. Louis had moved less than two miles from the Mississippi River. But being adjacent to water became less important for many business enterprises and, even for those still requiring large amounts of water, pipes could now transfer it reliably and inexpensively miles from its source.

Manufacturing production became more horizontal and less vertical. Nineteenth-century factories featured four-to-ten story buildings with the raw materials (wool) being transformed into finished goods (suits) in a floor-by-floor process. Henry Ford and the automobile assembly line changed all that. Expansive one-story structures, tens of football fields in scope, became the best way to give the line the space it needed. Such space was easier to find at the edge of the metropolis by clearing a few acres of agricultural land than at its center, where several square blocks would need to be demolished.

As American enterprises became technology-driven in recent decades, it was felt important to provide the scientists and engineers with settings promoting creativity, places which resembled the university campuses from which they came. And suburbia was more likely to have the real estate that looked like a university. It is no accident that Corridor 128 in the Boston region, the Research Triangle in the Chapel Hill, Durham, and Raleigh area, or Silicon Valley near Stanford and between San Francisco and San Jose developed where they did. What was good enough for the techies also seemed appropriate for more conventional white-collar types so they, too, joined the exodus to office parks with a low-rise buildings interspersed on the greensward.[4]

These economic ingredients for metropolitan expansion are secondary, however, to more personal forces. As owning a home on a 6000-square-foot lot became central to the American Dream in the decades following World War II, both free

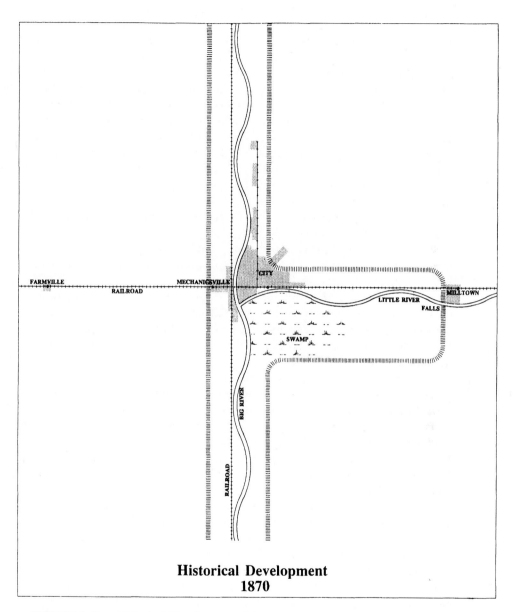

Historical Development
1870

FIGURE 1–3a   Historical Development, 1870
Source: From THE FRACTURED METROPOLIS by JONATHAN BARNETT. Copyright © 1995 by
Jonathan Barnett. Reprinted by permission of Westview Press, a member of Perseus Books, L.L.C.

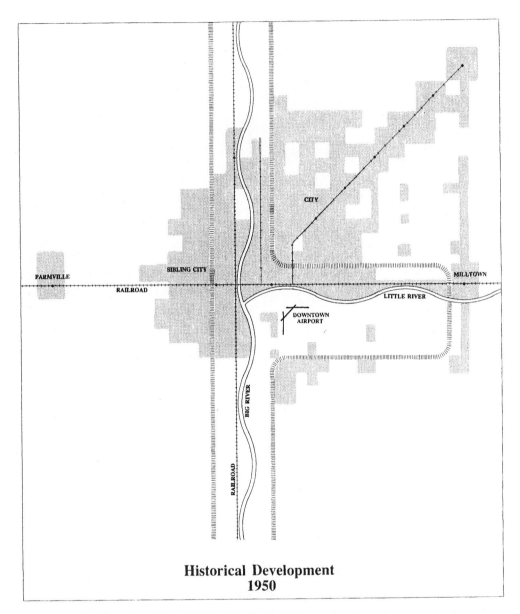

Historical Development
1950

FIGURE 1–3b   Historical Development, 1950
Source: From THE FRACTURED METROPOLIS by JONATHAN BARNETT. Copyright © 1995 by
Jonathan Barnett. Reprinted by permission of Westview Press, a member of Perseus Books, L.L.C.

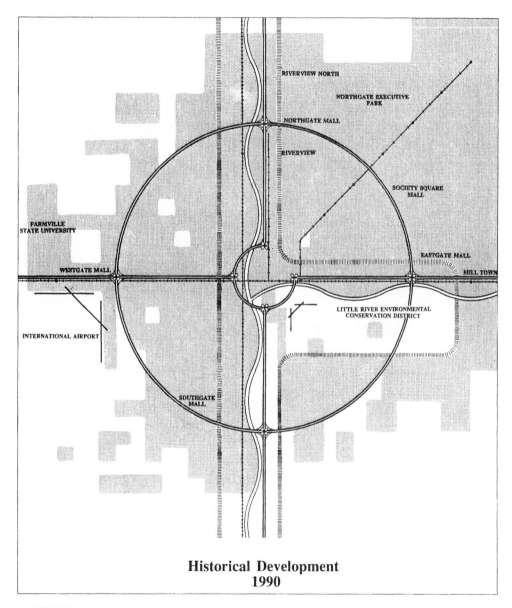

**Historical Development
1990**

FIGURE 1–3c   Historical Development, 1990
Source: From THE FRACTURED METROPOLIS by JONATHAN BARNETT. Copyright © 1995 by
Jonathan Barnett. Reprinted by permission of Westview Press, a member of Perseus Books, L.L.C.

Nortel's Office in the Research Triangle

enterprise and elected officials did their utmost to help more citizens achieve it. The marketplace's chief contribution was the subdivision, changing from the previous practice of building homes one or two at a time to mass producing them in colonies of hundreds. The pioneers were the Levitts, father Abraham and sons William and Alfred, who during the 1940s, 1950s, and 1960s built more than one hundred thousand homes in the New York and Philadelphia regions, creating three separate Levitttowns, one each in New Jersey, New York, and Pennsylvania.[5]

The forced savings created during World War II and the improving economy in the postwar period made owning a home affordable for more Americans. During the peak years for suburbanization, the 1950s and 1960s, the average household's income, after adjusting for inflation, was rising almost 3 percent a year, a rate that meant an almost doubling of earnings during this period.[6] Now the will to buy was backed by the resources to do so.

National elected officials saw the wave of home ownership popularity and chose to ride it. The income tax code already made mortgage interest payments deductible, creating a discount equivalent to a household's national and state income tax brackets. If one's monthly interest payment is $500 and the combined income tax classifications are 30 percent (say 25 percent for the federal return and

Levittown, New York, in 1949

5 percent for the state form), then it is the equivalent, each month, of the household spending $350 and the government's paying the remaining $150. Additional programs, such as Federal Housing Administration loans and the establishment of secondary loan agencies like the Federal National Mortgage Association, made the capital for home purchases cheaper for buyers and safer for investors. For the former, it was a lower down payment. For the latter, it was a guaranteed mortgage.

Moving to the suburbs created greater distances between home and the work site. When the wave of residences preceded the movement of jobs, as was most often the case, workers needed to commute longer distances, typically from suburbia to the central city. When businesses also began to relocate to the suburbs, it often meant going from one part of suburbia to another. While many of the periphery-core trips could be handled by mass transportation—subways, light rail and streetcars, and buses—it was much more challenging to find cost-effective ways to have public transit adapt to a near infinity of crisscross commutes.

No matter. Americans fell in love with the independence provided by the automobile. In 1950, there was one passenger car for every four U.S. residents. Twenty years later, it was one for every two.[7] Cars could go anywhere, anytime, any route. No need to have hundreds going from Point A to Point B to allow efficient use of mass transit. If the nation could move toward one automobile for every worker (as it almost has, except for the poorest 5 percent), then that would handle getting people to and from their jobs.

Again, both business and government did their part to accelerate the automobile revolution. Manufacturers continuously improved production techniques, making cars both more affordable, as a fraction of annual household income, and more reliable. Governments at all levels devoted increasing shares of the public budget to building roads, highways, and bridges, with the national government leading the charge by designing and implementing the Interstate Highway System. They also kept the price of gasoline relatively low through trade policies, industry subsidies, and light-handed taxation. Despite the lengthening journey to and from work in the enlarged metropolis, most Americans seem not to be bothered, more than willing to exchange thirty to sixty minutes alone in their climate-controlled cars with only a radio and CD player for company for the extensive mobility the automobile provides.

In the expanding metropolis, do jobs follow people or vice versa? Probably more the former than the latter. As noted above, businesses have many reasons for preferring a suburban location. Having much of the labor force nearby, especially the highly skilled component, only adds to the attractiveness of being outside the central city. Even if the causal direction runs more toward people first and jobs second, the process is interactive: new residents lure businesses whose jobs attract more inhabitants who in turn are magnets for more enterprises who . . . well the point is clear. Just as the suburban population rose more than 12 percent between 1990 and 1998, a rate more than three times faster than the central city pace, a recent analysis of private job growth between 1993 and 1996 among the ninety-two largest metropolitan areas found that, in four out of every five, suburban jobs grew faster than central city employment and, on average, the suburban rate was about 8 percent higher.[8]

The movement of residents and jobs to the suburbs has sounded the death knell for metropolitan areas with one major core surrounded by a less dense periphery. No longer is most of the economic and political punch located at some geographic nucleus, typically near where the city initially began. Although the rhetoric of "downtown as the heart of the region" still is heard, most often from those with a clear stake in its preservation, the core is now one of several concentrations within metropolitan areas. While in many instances, it remains first among the many parts, it is now accompanied by several other convergences of activity.

These other nodes are often called "edge cities," a term popularized by Joel Garreau.[9] He defines them as places having more than 5 million square feet of office space, over 600,000 square feet of retail space, and including more workers than residents. They have entertainment to go along with the offices and retail stores and, to set them apart from downtowns, they have developed within the last three decades. Examples are numerous: Crystal City in the Washington area, Schaumburg in the Chicago region, Perimeter North in Atlanta, the Galleria area in Houston, and Bloomington in Minneapolis/St. Paul.

With the rise of edge cities, the need for suburbanites to go downtown for either work or play had ebbed. Not only have offices and factories moved to the suburbs, but the trendy restaurants and cinema megaplexes have joined them. Aside from a professional sporting event here and a symphonic performance there—and not even all of those venues remain in the central city—a smaller share of the metropolitan population is making, on average, fewer trips each year to the core. The concentric metropolis has become the polycentric region.

METROPOLITAN AREAS ARE NATURAL ECONOMIES

"The U.S. economy is in reality a common market of local economies, most of them centered on metropolitan areas," note William C. Barnes and Larry C. Ledebur.[10] Although, governmentally, American is a nation of fifty states, they are not natural economic entities. What happens in Erie, Pennsylvania has little more impact on the Philadelphia metropolitan economy than what transpires in Yuma, Arizona. Even though Philadelphia and Erie share a common state, viewed together they do not constitute an interconnected set of enterprises, a single market place where capital and labor interact. While statisticians calculate economic figures for Pennsylvania, the numbers are an artificial aggregate.

But Philadelphia, Pennsylvania, Wilmington, Delaware, and Camden, New Jersey, all connected along the Delaware River and comprising a single metropolitan arena, are an organic whole. People sell their labor and buy goods and services largely within its boundaries. Capital is formed and dispersed primarily inside the metropolis. If one part prospers, the ripple effects are apt to be positive for many other segments within the region. If Dupont expands in Wilmington, its new employees will purchase some of their goods and services in Philadelphia. If a firm in Camden needs a loan to build a new plant, it is apt to approach one of the region's major banks headquartered in Philadelphia.

It is precisely this economic interdependence, along with the growing sense of personal identity, that caused the national government to begin defining metropolitan areas and keeping track of their collective activities. The definitions themselves are primarily rooted in economic phenomena such as the links between where people live and where they work and shop. As Jane Jacobs argued convincingly in *The Economy of Cities*[11] and *Cities and the Wealth of Nations*,[12] metropolitan areas are where most of the nation's wealth is created.

Metropolitan regions are leading players in the global economy. If they were included in the gross national product rankings for the world's nations, thirteen (New York, Los Angeles, Chicago, Boston, Washington/Baltimore, Philadelphia, Houston, Detroit, Atlanta, Dallas, Minneapolis/St. Paul, Seattle, and Phoenix) would finish in the top fifty and forty-seven in the largest one hundred.[13] Within the United States, as Figure 1–4 summarizes, their national shares on key economic factors exceed their 80-percent slice of the population.

Metropolitan areas are especially well represented in the strongest growth sectors. For example, they have 94 percent each of the overall high technology and the

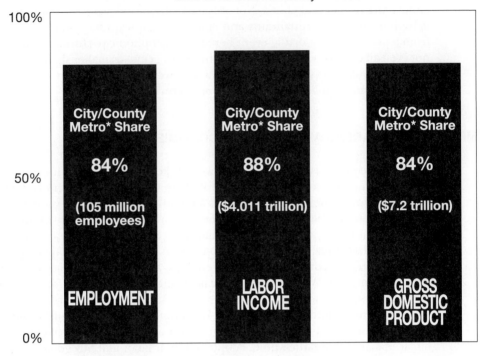

Shares of U.S. Economy —1998

*City/County Metros defined as 317 urbanized areas.

FIGURE 1–4   Metro Areas Generate More than 80 Percent of the Nation's Employment, Income, and Production of Goods and Services
Source: Standard & Poor's DRI, 2000.

business services jobs and 95 percent of those created between 1992 and 1998.[14] As a result, 89 percent of the U.S. economic growth between those two years occurred within them. Since success tends to build on itself, metropolitan regions have become the magnets that attract entrepreneurs wanting to start cutting-edge enterprises, investors with venture capital for these initiatives, and the skilled talent desiring to work for them.

Metropolitan economies, however, are not autonomous. They have far from full control over their own destinies. They exist within the U.S. national economy and the broader global economy, each with its own set of factors. Shifts in federal policies can have significant impacts. The defense cutbacks in the early 1990s, for example, either eliminated or reduced demand for fighter planes assembled in Dallas/Ft. Worth and St. Louis. Squeezing Medicare reimbursements for hospitals will disproportionately harm those areas like Baltimore and Houston with prominent health-care centers. European countries tighten regulations on bioengineered seeds and communities specializing in biotechnology are damaged.

Private sector decisions can also cause overnight changes. A New York-headquartered corporation closes a branch facility in Birmingham, quickly ending employment for hundreds or thousands of workers. A Charlotte bank buys out one in Jacksonville and all the top corporate positions in the Florida city are eliminated. A CEO decides San Antonio would be a better site for the home office than St. Louis and the entire executive suite heads south.

Changes in the market demand, both nationally and globally, also can hit some metropolitan areas disproportionately. A drop in cigarette consumption has special importance for Raleigh-Durham and Winston-Salem. The Asian downturn in the late 1990s hit Seattle hard since it exported airplanes and other goods to that part of the globe. A decline in oil and gas exploration harms New Orleans and Houston, the two areas containing much of that industry.

What goes down for some will probably go up for others. President Kennedy's resolve in the 1960s to have Americans reach the moon within that decade has spawned an entire space industry, much to the benefit of Houston and several Florida metros. The internationalization of fast food has meant much for Chicago, headquarters for McDonald. Los Angeles, past and present, has benefitted from the global popularity for the entertainment films created and produced there. What is certain is that national public policies here and abroad as well as choices in corporate board rooms around the world, matters over which metropolitan areas have no say and often no advance warning, can and will affect their economic well-being.

GOVERNMENTS: NUMEROUS AND WEAK

Metropolitan areas have lots of local governments. Although averages can be deceiving since the range varies considerably, the typical region averaged 104 governments, up slightly from 99 in 1952, for a total of 33,004 for all regions combined.[15] These fall into two broad types: general purpose (counties and municipalities) and special purpose (special districts, school districts, townships). "General" and "special" capture the key distinction between the two categories. The former carry out a wide range of public activities while the latter confine themselves to one or at most a few distinct functions. The general purpose governments are more visible, as county councils and city mayors receive more media coverage, but the special purpose units are more numerous, overall outnumbering the counties and municipalities by about three to one.

Navigating through this governmental maze is all but impossible, even for the experts. Jurisdictions overlap geographically, creating a crazy-quilt pattern when mapped. Indeed, few are foolish enough to even attempt charting them. It is not as straightforward as larger boxes (one or more counties) containing many smaller containers (municipalities and special purpose governments) such as the fifty states within the United States or counties within a single state. Municipalities are usually within counties but they can cross their boundaries. Some portions of a county are part of a city ("incorporated") while others receive their basic services directly from the county ("unincorporated"). Special purpose districts range from small townships providing, say, street lights for a subdivision, to multicounty authorities responsible, to take one example, for an entire region's mass transportation.

Deciding who's in charge depends on where one lives and what function one is discussing. General purpose government leaders are always directly elected by their citizens but there may or may not be an elected executive. Special purpose governments may have their directors chosen at the ballot box but they might also be appointed by some combination of local and state officials. All this means popular control is uneven within any metropolitan area with many decisions being made by persons once or twice removed from the electorate and located in the shadows from a steady media spotlight.

Local governments are also weak. Iowa Judge John F. Dillon decided in 1868 that local governments are "creatures of the state."[16] This has become known as "Dillon's Rule," giving the judge a prominent place in local government jurisprudence. What it means is that each of the fifty states set the rules for what local governments can do: how they can be created, what powers they can exercise, whether or how they can add territory, and which taxes at what levels they can levy. It is "we the people" who give power directly to the national government and to each of the fifty state governments, thereby making them sovereign entities. As a consequence, it is only the people who can alter the basic rules, the constitutions, which stipulate what these governments can do. Not so with local units. It is "they the state governments" who exercise this authority.

During the century-plus since Judge Dillon handed down his decision, local governments have had only marginal success in freeing themselves from state control. The most common device is known as "home rule," available for some cities in all but two states (Alabama and Vermont) and for certain counties in about three-quarters of the states. Without home rule, state statutes dictate the forms and functions of local units, allowing counties and municipalities either no options or choice among just a few alternatives. With home rule, general purpose governments can write quasi-constitutions, most often called charters, where they develop their own structures and powers, subject to whatever limitations the state might impose. In short, home rule allows municipalities and counties to move from doing only what the state tells them they can do to designing whatever the state instructs them they cannot do. Even with the spread of home rule,[17] however, local governments, general and special, still exist at the state's pleasure.

Why have Americans chosen to have numerous and weak local governments? The answer is part philosophic, part historic, part self-interest. Just as concerns about majority tyranny caused the Founding Fathers to have separate branches, checks and balances, and federalism, so too has the enduring suspicion about governments doing more harm than good prompted Americans to limit the powers given to local government. Liberty is the premier value in the United States and even the governments closest to home and easiest to oversee are threats to personal autonomy. Limiting their powers and scope protects individualism.

The historic element has three components. In most states, counties were formed at or near the time a state became part of the union. For most, this was in the late eighteenth or nineteenth century. Counties administered essential public functions: recording deeds, conducting elections, assessing property, probating estates, operating jails. In an era when traveling was difficult, that meant the county seat needed to be accessible which, in turn, required a proliferation of counties. In the twentieth century, as metropolitan areas expanded, they encompassed more counties. Although, in principle, states could combine counties, they have not done so nor are they likely to take such action.

The second historic factor is incremental incorporation. State laws typically made it easy for areas to become municipalities. As people moved outside the central city, there was a gradual but steady growth in the number of small cities. No one stepped back, anticipated the possibility of several hundred thousand additional people over several decades, and prepared in advance a set of fewer but larger boundaries for these new units. Policy making is more reactive and, as a consequence, incorporations happened one at a time.

The third historic element is connected with smaller counties and numerous municipalities. As metropolitan areas became more complex, citizens often wanted some public entity to assume control over emerging policies such as wastewater disposal or public transportation. Since watersheds and transit networks often spanned the boundaries of many general purpose governments, it was easier to have the state government authorize a new special district which overlaid them and encompassed the larger territory.

Self-interest helps create and sustain governmental multiplicity. Combining counties would have called for eliminating one or more county seats. Hundreds of public employees would lose their jobs, elected officials would forego their power, judges would be transferred, and all the private businesses around the courthouse square would be threatened. No state legislature with its political wits about it was likely to take on all that entrenched opposition.

Fueling incorporation, especially in areas adjacent to the central city, was a desire to avoid being annexed by it. Many who left the core for the suburbs were getting away from some undesirable aspect of city life. But their escape was not complete if they stayed in the same county for, under most states' laws, the city could expand its boundaries to include them. The means to avoid that was to incorporate since cities could only annex unincorporated territory. This process feeds on itself. Once the inner ring of suburbs has formed municipalities, when the next layer is inhabited, it has two choices: be annexed by the municipality next door ("them") or incorporate with the folks immediately around them ("us"). More often than not, "us" wins out over "them." This is especially so when the inhabitants of a neighboring municipality come from a lower economic class or have a different ethnic background.

Having local governments which are many in number and limited in authority has extraordinary consequences for metropolitan regions. It means there is no distinctive routine for making metropolitan policies. Ask someone how national policies are established and there is a relatively clear answer. The essentials are in the U.S. Constitution and the explanation for how it all works in any American Government textbook. There is a law-making and rule-making process and, for the most part, the respective roles of the Congress, the presidency, the federal courts, and the bureaucracy are all spelled out. It is never, of course, quite as simple as the textbook describes; thousands of outside forces, from economic interests and elsewhere, seek to influence it. But the basics can be set forth and there is a predictability to the operation.

There is also agreement about where national policy making happens. Most occurs in a small number of government buildings, most located in or near Washington, D.C. If you want to watch federal policy making in action, go to Capitol Hill to observe committee markups or floor debates or watch them on C-SPAN. Yes, there are deals struck inside legislative offices, places where the average citizen cannot go, but even then these bargains will come forward to be voted upon in public.

State government policy making is also reasonably understandable. Tracking it requires more effort: state governments receive less media coverage than the national level, there are no C-SPAN cameras focused on the legislative process, there are fewer textbooks detailing the particulars. Again, though, the state constitutions provide the key fundamentals and the state capitols the primary locations.

Where does one go to observe metropolitan policy making? Who are the actors? What are the rules? The short answers to these three questions are: nowhere, everyone, and unclear! There is no single location, nor even a limited number of sites, where all or most regional decisions are made. There are no overarching sets of elected officials who have the authority to do so, nor are there any private elites who possess either enough resources or sufficient legitimacy to control the larger metropolitan community. There is no ongoing routine for reaching consensus about metropolitan-wide actions. Even those metropolitan areas which have done the most to establish regional public bodies—Portland and Minneapolis-St. Paul most notably—or those which have merged all or portions of their central city and largest county governments—Indianapolis, Jacksonville, and Nashville, for example—have failed to achieve anything close to a comprehensive system. This is what makes the metropolitan chase so challenging for those engaged within it. It is a fluid contest involving players from all sectors carried out at hundreds of locations according to ever-shifting and largely unwritten sets of rules.

Amidst this seeming chaos, however, is a growing need for more metropolitan-wide policies. Looking outward, the quality-of-life competition becomes keener each year. It will be those metropolitan regions which get their act together, which devise a thoughtful strategy and develop the means for implementing it, that will be most likely to prosper. Although luck might shine on some regions for a while, serendipity is not a viable long-term scheme. In all likelihood, the race will be won most regularly by those who prepare best for it. Accomplishing this requires a metropolitan region which has policies promoting economic development, building essential physical infrastructure, educating citizens, fashioning attractive sites for arts and entertainment, securing property and personal safety, protecting health and the environment, producing adequate and affordable housing, preserving open space, and raising enough money to pay for it all—the topics addressed in Chapters 6 through 14.

Looking inward, each of the above issues has its controversial ingredients. Each part of the metropolitan region, be it a governmental entity, a private business, or a nonprofit organization, will compete to have its interests best served by any metropolitan action. Where will a new plant locate, whose tax base will be bolstered, which schools will be improved are all examples of what questions must be settled before a metropolitan initiative can be taken. Although not every interest must be on board before the regional ship sails, threatening too many entities can delay its departure so long that any subsequent action loses much of its impact.

Moreover, as metropolitan areas become more complex, each apparently minor decision is more apt to have regional consequences. What might in earlier times have been a self-contained policy—a stoplight on the principal street in a suburban municipality—might now have unforeseen repercussions on traffic patterns across a wider spectrum. A series of residential zoning rulings reached independently by several municipalities might, cumulatively, reduce the potential for the region's having an adequate supply of affordable housing. How, if at all, are local preferences blended with regional needs in arriving at policies for and within metropolitan regions?

DIVIDING THE METROPOLIS: INCOME, RACE, ETHNICITY

Adding to the external challenges of having metropolitan areas involved in unified actions and complicating the internal struggles within regions is that, for a variety of reasons, metropolitan residents tend to be segregated by income, race, and ethnicity. Even when there are no forces contributing to keeping people apart because of their economic class, the color of their skin, or the origin of their ancestors—and such factors certainly do operate—most people still live near folks similar to them. Complicating matters further are recent trends. For the most part, segregation is either increasing or remaining constant. The metropolitan pot is not melting.

Scholars use two statistical approaches—the dissimilarity index[18] and the isolation index[19]—to track segregation trends. The dissimilarity index measures the proportion of a group (poor, black, etc.) which would need to relocate to have an equal proportion in each subarea within a metropolitan region. For example, if a region has 20 percent poor, then the index would be at its lowest possible value, zero, when each component had 20 percent poor. It would take on its highest possible number, 100, if every poor person lived in an all-poor neighborhood. The isolation index takes the average member of any group (a rich person, a white person, etc.) in a metropolitan region and measures the proportion of his or her neighborhood's population having the same characteristic. If every rich person lives in all-rich neighborhoods, the index reaches its maximum value of 100. In this situation, rich people only interact with their own economic class. Typically, census tracts—the Census Bureau's definition of small area within a metropolitan region—are the units for these segregation analyses. The average tract has between 2,500 and 8,000 inhabitants.

When people still traveled by foot or through horsepower, it was difficult for the rich and the poor to put much residential distance between themselves. But intra-metropolitan rail transportation made possible "streetcar suburbs"[20] linking downtown workplaces with suburban homes for the upper class in the latter parts of the nineteenth century and, following World War II, automobiles and interstate highways created the potential for even greater divisions between, on the one hand, an expanding middle class and the already "arrived" and, on the other, the impoverished.

This capacity for economic segregation has become a reality in many regions. A recent analysis[21] of the 100 largest metropolitan regions finds that the index of dissimilarity for those below the federal poverty level is 36.1, meaning slightly more than one-third of the poor persons would need to move into higher-income neighborhoods in order to achieve an equal distribution of incomes within subareas. This number is up 11 percent from 1970, indicating that the economic sorting out is intensifying. The same study pinpoints the isolation index at 21.0, signifying that the typical poor person lives in a neighborhood where 21 percent of the people are below the poverty level, an increase of 9 percent since 1970. Economic segregation is more acute in the older metropolitan areas in the Northeast (Hartford is 52.8, Philadelphia 47.9) and Midwest (Milwaukee is 55.1, Detroit 50.1) and less a factor in the South (Orlando is 27.2) and West (Portland is 27.1, Las Vegas 28.5).

Another way to look at income differences is to determine how many neighborhoods are becoming what can best be described as slums, places where the isolation index is 40 percent or higher. Such areas, according to Paul Jargowsky's observations, "tended to have a threatening appearance, marked by dilapidated housing, vacant units with broken or boarded-up windows, abandoned and burned-out cars, and men 'hanging out' on street corners."[22] As of 1990, 2,886 metropolitan census tracts qualified for this category, about double the number in 1970. They contain over 8 million residents, about half African American and one-quarter each white and Hispanic.[23] These tracts, of course, are not scattered randomly across the metropolitan landscape. Instead, they cluster in the central cities and, increasingly, the inner suburbs. In doing so, they become core constituencies for some governmental units and somebody else's problem for the remainder of the local jurisdictions.

Although the United States is a country of many colors, it is the stark contrast between African Americans and whites that has and continues to create the greatest gulf. For more than three-quarters of its history, most African Americans were either enslaved or, after the Fifteenth Amendment and before the 1960's civil rights legislation, subjected to legal segregation. It is a legacy that lives on, especially in housing patterns within metropolitan areas.

When scholars first systematically measured black-white residential segregation in U.S. metropolitan areas in the 1960s, they found high indices of dissimilarity, with scores in the 80s and 90s being quite common.[24] This was not surprising with all the formal and informal race-based discrimination as well as severely limited African-American buying power.

Several developments between the 1950s and the 1970s should have cut residential segregation considerably. The African-American middle class grew, increasing their purchase options. Federal legislation forbade housing discrimination, initially by public agencies such as the Federal Housing Administration and ultimately

in private sales and rentals with the Civil Rights Act of 1968. Most state and local governments enacted fair housing legislation. Overt racial attitudes declined with the proportion of white Americans saying they had a right to keep blacks out of their neighborhood dropping from over one-third in the 1960s to less than one-tenth by the late 1970s.[25]

Yet residential segregation persists. The 1990 index of dissimilarity for African Americans is 73.0 for the metropolitan areas having more than 1 million population, according to an U.S. Census Bureau analysis. Six regions—Buffalo, Chicago, Cleveland, Detroit, Milwaukee, and New York—have scores above 80. The index is slightly lower but still relatively high, 63.8, for those regions with between 500,000 and a million inhabitants. It declined 5.5 percent between 1990 and 2000, but most of the change was caused by a few blacks moving into formerly all-white areas and, for the most part, Midwestern and Northeastern regions remained highly segregated.[26]

Why does segregation endure in most metropolitan areas? The largest contributors are, first, differences in black-white preferences about neighborhood integration levels and, second, real estate search patterns. Surveys of whites and blacks in metropolitan areas like Detroit[27] reveal that, for African Americans, the favorite racial mix for a neighborhood is about 30 percent black, 70 percent white: enough African Americans so that they feel comfortable, more Caucasians to insure clout in a majority-white society. Whites are untroubled with a black share under 20 percent but, once it rises much above that, they are reluctant to move into a neighborhood. Combining those two preference patterns creates an anti-integrationist dynamic: just as a neighborhood becomes most attractive for African Americans, passing 20 percent on its way to 30, it loses appeal for whites, with few wanting to enter. The result: African Americans flock to the area, even sometimes paying a premium for housing while whites avoid it. The more blacks who move into the community, the less desirable it is for whites and the outcome over time is an all-black neighborhood.

The second and compatible explanation is that the real estate market is not a racially neutral arena. There is still ample evidence that many real estate agents steer clients to areas dominated by their respective races[28] and that, to a lesser extent, African Americans also have a more difficult time obtaining mortgage financing.[29] The practices are not as overt and widespread as they were decades ago, but controlled experiments where whites and blacks with similar economic backgrounds seek the same housing regularly uncover statistically significant discrimination. The social isolation within the two races—blacks interacting largely with blacks and whites with whites—augments and perpetuates segregation. Each race tends to seek housing guidance from among its own members who, understandably, usually refer them to neighborhoods where that race prevails.

Stable racially integrated suburbs and neighborhoods do exist even within metropolitan areas having high dissimilarity index scores. Examples include Oak Park (Chicago), Shaker Heights (Cleveland), University City (St. Louis), Vollintine-Evergreen (Memphis) and West Mount Airy (Philadelphia). But they are the classic exceptions which support the rule. On close analysis, it requires a rare combination of factors to create and sustain such communities. These include an appealing housing stock, local pride in being diverse, and community organizations which promote integration.[30] Even in these situations, the racial makeup is often a set of largely black blocks bordering a group of nearly all-white blocks, each block comfortable having the other race nearby, rather than most of the blocks being a blend of African American and Caucasian.

African Americans constitute more than 10 percent of the residents in about two-thirds of the metropolitan areas with more than 1 million inhabitants while Hispanics are more than a tenth in approximately one-third of these metropolitan areas. The major concentrations, 20 percent or more, are in Los Angeles, Houston, Miami, Phoenix, San Antonio, and Austin. The 1990 dissimilarity index for Hispanics in the million-plus regions is 53.6, well below the 73.0 for African Americans. For metropolitan areas between 500,000 and 1 million, the index drops slightly to 47.0 Despite being somewhat less segregated than are African Americans, Hispanics share with blacks being located in the same neighborhoods regardless of their socioeconomic status. Upper and upper-middle income blacks and Hispanics are more likely to be living near persons of their own race or ethnicity than beside white individuals with similar incomes.[31] This is less likely the case for Asian Americans although their dissimilarity index for the 1-million-or-more-population regions is 42.3, not that much lower than the score for Hispanics. Those with Asian origins exceed 10 percent of the population in just three of the large metropolitan areas, all of which are in California: Los Angeles, San Diego, and San Francisco.

Most of us think of the immigration era in the United States as part of the nineteenth and early twentieth centuries. Those were indeed times when a steady stream emigrated to this country. But after a mid-century lull, less than 100,000 a year in the 1930s and 1940s and about 300,000 annually between 1950 and 1980, the pace has quickened to over three-quarters of a million a year, close to the numbers arriving a century ago.

Although the flow of immigrants has returned to earlier levels, its composition differs. No longer are most from Europe and, indeed, only about one out of seven originate there. The principal sources are the Balkans and the former Soviet Union. One out of three come from Asia (China, India, the Philippines, and Vietnam are the major sources) and one out of four emigrate from Mexico. As a consequence, they are contributing to the rapid growth rate in the Asian and Hispanic shares of the population, adding to the further racial and ethnic diversification of America. Immigrants account for almost one-third of the increase in the U.S. population during the last decade.

Similar to those who came before, these new Americans are disproportionately settling in metropolitan areas, especially the central cities. What had begun to disappear from much of urban life in the United States, the distinctively ethnic neighborhood featuring restaurants and other small retail shops catering to the recent arrivals, is now reemerging in many metropolitan areas. As that happens, it adds still another dimension of geographically based differences within the regions.

A COMMON DESTINY?

That metropolitan populations are often separated by income, race, and ethnicity—divisions which are then frequently encapsulated with different governmental jurisdictions—raises the question whether the metropolitan area's parts need to act as a whole. Does the prosperity of an edge city, on balance, improve the entire region? If a central city's downtown deteriorates, will there be any noticeable effects on the suburbs? Are metropolitan areas win-win, lose-lose affairs where all or most components—neighborhoods and sectors—share in each other's victories and suffer through each other's defeats? Are these regions the geographic equivalent of a human organism, where no part can long survive if another is seriously ill?

The prevailing consensus, constructed mainly on statistical analyses of economic data over one or two decades, is that the answer to these questions is largely yes: central cities and suburbs are interdependent, at least when it comes to economic well-being, according to a study of seventy-eight metropolitan areas by Ledebur and Barnes.[32] Between 1979 and 1989, 82 percent of the regions had their suburban and central city household incomes move in the same direction while just 18 percent went in opposite ways. In a later review of their own work as well as that of other scholars, they conclude that "the evidence strongly suggests that the economic fates and fortunes of cities and suburbs are inextricably intertwined."[33]

What is less clear is who is the chicken and who is the egg. Do central cities form the economic core with the ripple effects felt in the suburbs? Or is that the way it used to be and now suburban development is the engine driving the metropolitan region? Although this dispute frequently flares up in political circles as downtown interests argue that they matter most and suburbanites contend they are now in the metropolitan saddle, most regional economists consider the debate is overshadowed and made moot by the larger point: each depends on the other and both are simultaneously cause and effect.

Public opinion on mutual dependency is more mixed. A 1998 survey of the Cleveland metropolitan area found that while 90 percent agreed that "problems in the region's big cities affect all communities, not just these cities," that did not mean that all were willing to chip in to correct them: 41 percent overall and larger portions in the suburban counties agreed that "people in large cities like Cleveland, Akron, and Lorain should solve their own problems [and] people in the suburbs and rural areas should not be expected to help."[34] A similar item in a 1999 St. Louis regional poll revealed that 32 percent overall and again somewhat higher fractions in the suburbs concurred that "people in places like the City of St. Louis and East St. Louis should solve their own problems and not expect the people in the suburbs and rural areas to help."[35]

This presence of a sizeable minority and perhaps, at times, a modest majority opposing the better-off suburbs assisting the financially challenged central city makes life difficult for elected officials outside the core. Although their active involvement within the region and their familiarity with the economic ties might lead them intellectually to support regional initiatives, their constituencies, the ultimate judges about whether or not they stay in office, want to be reassured that their interests are not being sacrificed and that their leaders' eyes stay on the local ball.

NOTES

1. Howard J. Wall, "'Voting With Your Feet' and Metro-Area Livability," *The Regional Economist*, 4, no. 2 (April 1999), pp. 15–18.
2. David Rusk, *Cities Without Suburbs* (Washington: Woodrow Wilson Center Press, 1993), p. 9.
3. Jonathan Barnett, *The Fractured Metropolis* (New York: Harper Collins, 1995), pp. 99–105.
4. Robert E. Lang, *Office Sprawl: The Evolving Geography of Business* (Washington: The Brookings Institution Center on Urban and Metropolitan Policy, 2000).
5. Kenneth T. Jackson, *Crabgrass Frontier* (New York: Oxford University Press, 1985), pp. 234–38.
6. Anthony Downs, "The Challenge of Our Declining Big Cities," *Housing Policy Debate*, 8, no. 2 (1997), p. 371.
7. Jackson, *Crabgrass Frontier*, p. 163.
8. John Brennan and Edward W. Hill, *Where Are the Jobs? Cities, Suburbs, and the Competition for Employment* (Washington: Brookings Institution, 1999), pp. 2–6.
9. Joel Garreau, *Edge City* (New York: Doubleday, 1991).

10. William R. Barnes and Larry C. Ledebur, *The New Regional Economics: The U.S. Common Market and the Global Economy* (Thousand Oaks, California: Sage, 1998), p. 5.

11. Jane Jacobs, *The Economy of Cities* (New York: Random House, 1969).

12. Jane Jacobs, *Cities and the Wealth of Nations* (New York: Random House, 1984).

13. Standard and Poor DRI, *U.S. Metro Economies: The Engines of America's Growth* (Washington: U.S. Conference of Mayors and National Association of Counties, 1999), Chart 1.

14. Standard and Poor DRI, *U.S. Metro Economies,* Charts 6 and 8.

15. G. Ross Stephens and Nelson Wikstrom, *Metropolitan Government and Governance* (New York: Oxford University Press, 2000), p. 19. These numbers are based on the 1957 and 1992 Censuses of Governments.

16. *City of Clinton v. Cedar Rapids and Missouri Railroad Company,* 24 Iowa 455 (1868).

17. For the latest update, see Dale Krane, Platon Rigos, and Melvin Hill, eds., *Home Rule in America* (Washington: CQ Press, 2000).

18. The index of dissimilarity was developed by Otis Dudley Duncan and Beverly Duncan, "A Methodological Analysis of Segregation Indices," *American Sociological Review,* 20, no. 2 (1955), pp. 210–17. It was first applied on a wide scale to urban patterns by Karl Taueber and Alma Taueber, *Negroes in Cities: Residential Segregation and Neighborhood Change* (Chicago: Aldine, 1965).

19. Douglas S. Massey and Mitchell L. Eggers, "The Ecology of Inequality: Minorities and the Concentration of Poverty, 1970–1980," *American Journal of Sociology,* 95, no. 5 (March 1990), pp. 1153–88. See also Stanley Lieberson, *A Piece of the Pie: Blacks and White Immigrants, 1880–1930* (Berkeley: University of California Press, 1980).

20. Sam Bass Warner, Jr., *Streetcar Suburbs* (Cambridge: Harvard University Press, 1962).

21. Alan J. Abramson, Mitchell S. Tobin, and Matthew R. VanderGoot, "The Changing Geography of Metropolitan Opportunity: The Segregation of the Poor in U.S. Metropolitan Areas, 1970 to 1990," *Housing Policy Debate,* 6, no. 1 (1995), pp. 45–72.

22. Paul A. Jargowsky, *Poverty and Place: Ghettos, Barrios, and the American City* (New York: Russell Sage, 1997), p. 11.

23. Jargowshy, *Poverty and Place,* p. 16.

24. Karl Taueber and Alma Taueber, *Negroes in Cities;* and Amos H. Hawley and Vincent P. Rock, eds., *Segregation in Residential Areas* (Washington: National Academy of Sciences, 1973).

25. Howard Schuman, Charlotte Steeh, and Lawrence Bobo, *Racial Attitudes in America* (Cambridge: Harvard University Press, 1985), pp. 59–61.

26. Edward L. Glaeser and Jacob L. Vigdor, *Racial Segregation in the 2000 Census: Promising News* (Washington: Brookings Institution Center on Urban and Metropolitan Policy, 2001). Also see *Ethnic Diversity Grows, Neighborhood Integration Lags Behind* (Albany, New York: Lewis Mumford Center, 2001).

27. Reynolds Farley and others, "Continued Racial Residential Segregation in Detroit: 'Chocolate City, Vanilla Suburbs' Revisited," *Journal of Housing Research,* 4, no. 1 (1993), pp. 1–38; and Douglas S. Massey and Nancy A. Denton, *American Apartheid: Segregation and the Making of the Underclass* (Cambridge: Harvard University Press, 1993). For a slightly less pessimistic analysis, see David M. Cutler, Edward L. Glaeser, and Jacob L. Vigdor, "The Rise and Decline of the American Ghetto," *Journal of Political Economy,* 107, no. 3 (June 1999), pp. 455–506.

28. John Yinger, "Housing Discrimination Is Still Worth Worrying About," *Housing Policy Debate,* 9, no. 4 (1998), pp. 893–927; also see Michael Fix and Raymond J. Struyk, editors, *Clear and Convincing Evidence: Measurement of Discrimination in America* (Washington: The Urban Institute Press, 1992).

29. John Goering and Ron Wienk, eds., *Mortgage Lending, Racial Discrimination, and Federal Policy* (Washington: Urban Institute, 1996).

30. Philip Nyden and others, "Neighborhood Racial and Ethnic Diversity in U.S. Cities: Conclusion," *Cityscape,* 4, no. 2 (1998), pp. 261–69.

31. Mario Sims, *A Comparative Analysis of High-Status Residential Segregation and Neighborhood Concentration in Five Metro Areas, 1980–90* (Ann Arbor: University of Michigan Population Studies Center, 1998). The five areas were Chicago, Los Angeles, Miami, New York, and San Francisco.

32. Larry C. Ledebur and William R. Barnes, *All In It Together: Cities, Suburbs, and Local Economic Regions* (Washington: National League of Cities, 1993). See also Hank V. Savitch and others, "Ties That Bind Central Cities, Suburbs, and the New Metropolitan Region," *Economic Development Quarterly,* 7, no. 4 (November 1993), pp. 341–57.

33. Barnes and Ledebur, *The New Regional Economics,* p. 42.

34. *Citizens Rate the Region* (Cleveland: Citizens League Research Institute, 1998), p. 39.

35. *St. Louis Metropolitan Area Survey* (St. Louis: East-West Gateway Coordinating Council, 1999), p. 7.

SUGGESTED READINGS

CISNEROS, HENRY G. *Regionalism: The New Geography of Opportunity.* Washington: U.S. Department of Housing and Urban Development, 1995. The former HUD Secretary and Mayor of San Antonio gives his views in an essay on why metropolitanism is central to the nation's future.

DOWNS, ANTHONY. *New Visions for Metropolitan America.* Washington: Brookings Institution, 1994. One of the country's premier theorists assesses a range of metropolitan issues.

GARREAU, JOEL. *Edge City.* New York: Doubleday, 1991. Defines, identifies, and discusses the emerging economic concentrations outside traditional downtowns.

JACKSON, KENNETH T. *Crabgrass Frontier: The Suburbanization of the United States.* New York: Oxford University Press, 1985. The definitive study of how the United States has become a suburban nation.

JARGOWSKY, PAUL A. *Poverty and Place: Ghettos, Barrios, and the American City.* New York: Russell Sage, 1997. Systematically analyzes the causes and consequences of poverty neighborhoods.

PEIRCE, NEAL R. *Citistates: How Urban America Can Prosper in a Competitive World.* Washington: Seven Locks Press, 1993. The country's leading metropolitan journalist calls attention to the new metropolitan reality, complete with case studies of several major regions.

DOING IT

Competing effectively in the metropolitan chase requires thinking strategically. This demands a careful assessment of how one's part of the metropolitan area compares to its counterparts as well as how the entire region stacks up against the others. This process is typically called an environmental scan or a strengths/weaknesses/opportunities/threats (SWOT) analysis. Here is how it works:

1. Take one part—a suburban municipality, an inner-city neighborhood, or an exurban county—of a metropolitan area and list its relative strengths, weaknesses, opportunities, and threats. What assets does it hold and what does it do especially well? How can it build on them? What are its deficits and where is its performance subpar? How can it correct them or, at a minimum, do a better job of coping with them? What trends are emerging which create opportunities for it? How can it best take advantage of them? What threats loom in the not-too-distant future? What actions should the community follow to guard against them? In conducting this examination, the comparison groups should be other communities within the same region.

2. Now apply these same questions to the entire region, comparing and contrasting it with other metropolitan areas.

3. Finally, what are the compatibilities and conflicts between the local and regional environmental scans? Do the region's opportunities and threats, for example, coincide with the local community's? What might the latter contribute to helping the region either exploit an opportunity or address a threat? Or does a possible beneficial opening for the region in itself present a threat for the local community? If so, what might either side, regional or local, do to soften the conflict?

PART I

THE METROPOLITAN SECTORS

Three sectors—public, business, and nonprofit—capture essentially all the activity within any metropolitan area. Acting singly, none of them has enough independent clout to determine what policies a metropolitan area initiates, adopts, and implements. Instead, all must participate, albeit not always as equal partners, to produce policies for the region.

One normally looks to the public sector, to governments, to make decisions which affect the entire community. They possess the legitimacy to assume this role. Only governments have a democratically satisfying answer to the question: Who put you in charge? The people, they can reply, with their votes. But, as Chapter 1 describes, local governments are too fragmented and too weak to control metropolitan matters unilaterally.

In the free market U.S. economy, businesses, taken collectively, bring remarkable resources to the metropolitan setting. They contain deep reservoirs of financial capital and extensive assemblies of human talent as well as the entrepreneurial skills and the profit incentive to make tomorrow more lucrative than today. Although they have these assets along with an enormous stake in the metropolitan economy and the policies which influence it, both directly and indirectly, businesses rarely dominate America's metropolitan areas. Businesses are more preoccupied with making profits than with producing policies, their involvement in public decision making is more episodic than persistent, they lack the democratic legitimacy possessed by governments, their leaders are often uncomfortable in openly political settings, and, within the business sector, there are often internal divisions about public priorities.

The nonprofit sector supplies much of the social infrastructure which gets things done within communities: social service agencies, faith-based organizations, hospitals, private educational institutions, and the like are woven into the metropolitan fabric. Few claim that nonprofits possess the bulk of the power within regions nor even that they are the equals of governments and businesses. Nonprofits typically depend on private donations and governmental grants for much of their revenues and that alone creates a dependency on the other two sectors. But not much happens in producing policies within metropolitan areas unless they are included in the mix.

An essential fact about governing metropolitan areas is that all or most of the action does not occur within any one of the three sectors. Producing regional policies, be it those aimed at enhancing one's competitive position vis-à-vis other metropolitan areas or those intended to settle conflicts within a region, is a collaborative venture requiring partnerships, some one-time and others more enduring, among some combination of governments, businesses, and nonprofits.

That is why it is useful to think of a fourth sector, the civic sphere. It becomes the place, more a conceptual process than an actual location, where the three sectors interact. Only a few entities—councils of governments and citizens leagues are examples—spend the bulk of their existence within the civic sector. The others come and go as needs arise. But since, as Chapter 1 points out, metropolitan areas have no capitol, no building on a hill symbolizing governance for the entire region, they must invent a sector where partnerships are formed, deals are struck, bargains are made—all determining how the metropolitan chase plays out.

CHAPTER 2

The Public Sector

WHY LOCAL GOVERNMENTS?

Forming local governments is not always easy but that has not prevented Americans from creating about 70,000 counties, municipalities, special districts, and townships as well as almost 14,000 school districts.[1] Nothing speaks more directly to this nation's desire to keep control close to home. Even within metropolitan areas, by definition more densely populated, there is about one local government, excluding school districts, for every 1,000 residents.

Why so many? The counties and municipalities—the general purpose units—have the power to zone, a tool which can and is used to determine who can live and do business within their boundaries. States gave them the power to zone, and the courts, both state and federal, have allowed them to interpret this authority broadly.[2] By deciding how their land is zoned—residential or commercial, open space or industrial, large lots or small, high rise or one story—cities and counties can include some activities and exclude others. Requiring that each home must be on a three-acre lot, for example, coupled with a requirement that there can only be one inter-related family per unit, is a straightforward way for a municipality to decide that it will only have high-income residents. Zoning is the primary means people use to regulate their surroundings and, because they need a general purpose government, preferably a municipality, to employ zoning, they create them.[3]

Citizens also use general purpose local governments to regulate other aspects of everyday life.[4] They want some level of order (the degree varies by town) in the world immediately around them. Speed limits, stop signs, traffic lights, and street patterns manage the ebb and flow of vehicles in the community. Yard and building regulations dictate what needs to be done when and how to property and thereby influences the city's ambience. Public health ordinances monitor food services while construction permits determine how a structure can be erected or modified. To enforce all these regulations, the governments employ police officers and specialized inspectors.

Americans also look to both general and special purpose local governments to provide collective services. Although their first instinct is to go it alone, using the market economy to buy and sell goods and services individually, there are many items produced by and through governments. At the local level, these include airports, education, fire protection, libraries, parks and recreation, public transportation, streets, trash collection, sewage disposal, and water.

There is a dizzying array regarding which local governments furnish what public goods and services within any metropolitan area, and it would take a complex scorecard to detail every particular. Some special districts, as their name implies, confine themselves to one or two functions such as public transportation and sewage treatment. Municipalities have anywhere from a handful to a potful of services and, within many metropolitan areas, there is tension and overlap between them and the counties on who is responsible for what. Counties, in addition to dispensing local services, also administer state functions such as recording deeds and probating estates. All these public goods and services must be financed, typically on a pay-as-you-go basis. State laws usually require local governments to have balanced budgets and, in addition, limit the amount of debt they can incur. As a consequence, metropolitan citizens end up paying a variety of taxes and user fees to their municipality, their county, their school district, and usually several special districts.

Democratic processes, especially elections and fixed terms of office, potentially enable citizens to determine what they want their local governments to do. How focused the zoning? How strict the regulations? Which services at what levels paid for in what manner? The extent of democratic control and accountability, of course, varies substantially, and few universal statements can be made about how it plays out in practice. It is easier to comprehend and participate in municipal matters and, to a lesser extent, county affairs than in the often more technical and usually more distant special district activities. In addition, municipal and county leaders are always elected directly while appointed boards govern many special districts. But participation measured by, say, voting, is lower in local elections than in state and national contests and, for the latter, the turnout has been under 50 percent even in presidential years.

LOCAL GOVERNMENTS AS ENTREPRENEURS

Local governments in today's metropolitan areas are not just the zoners of land, enforcers of regulations, providers of services, and collectors of taxes. As competition for who gets what has intensified within regions, they have become players in the fray.[5] In growth metropolises, the race is for which unit benefits the most. In steady state regions, it is a zero-sum game: if one municipality is to improve, it will be at the expense of others. In declining areas, it is a contest for survival.

Think of a municipality or county as a business. Chief among its assets is the land it occupies. It has a monopoly—by definition it is either the only city or county—over this territory. But the land is also an anchor for the local government since, unlike a private business, it cannot shift locations. If a firm has problems, it can at least consider moving elsewhere within the metropolitan area or even transferring to another region. Not so a general purpose local government. Its boundaries constitute the hand it has been dealt and consequently the one it must play. With few exceptions, it cannot expand or contract its territory.

Local governments compete within one or more of four metropolitan markets: residents, shoppers, workers, and firms. All jurisdictions want residents, preferably the more affluent. Accelerated demand for property raises the price. That helps both the individuals who own it but also benefits the local government. Property which is worth more either generates additional revenues (the same property tax levy applied against a higher assessed valuation) or enables tax reductions (a lower rate against the increased assessment). Conversely, if demand slackens, prices drop, revenues decline, and a downward spiral begins toward a new and lower equilibrium.

In addition to vying over residents, all but the very wealthiest municipalities and every county also compete for some type of economic activity. Attracting shoppers from outside the boundaries yields increased sales taxes, recruiting daytime workers makes some type of job tax possible, getting a firm to transform a vacant lot into a warehouse strengthens the property tax base.

Special districts are also increasingly competitive but although the goal is the same—more revenues—the game is different. For some entities, the contest is over public dollars. Each district wants its service to be seen as the most essential for the community and, if they are cast in that light, the most deserving for higher tax support. School districts trumpet the importance of education, wastewater sewer plants the need for clean streams, and so forth. Their service is their product, and they want consumers to place it at the peak of the value hierarchy. For other special districts, the competition is not within the public arena but rather with the private sector. A mass transit agency, for example, battles for riders, attempting to get people to make more trips on buses or by rail—and fewer by car.

Not all local governments have awakened fully to the intensity of this emerging entrepreneurial environment. Those who, by luck of location within a region, are doing especially well often do not see the need to prepare for a future that might have a more challenging setting. They find it difficult to imagine that things might take a turn for the worse. But, for example, many suburbs which prospered immediately after World War II are struggling today. There is no reason to expect that today's winners might not be tomorrow's losers if they take the outcome for granted.

Others find it difficult to move from a paradigm where local governments existed primarily to regulate behavior and provide services to a framework where they are also engaged in a competitive struggle. There is a predisposition to do things by the book, the way they have always been conducted. Governments, even small ones, are bureaucracies, organizations with significant inertia. In such a setting, change, however necessary, offers more risks than benefits. Unlike the private sector, where profits flow to the winners, there are often few material incentives to reward successful public entrepreneurs.

CENTRAL CITIES

Strategic Setting

Although central cities are no longer the sun around which all the other metropolitan units revolve, for almost every region they remain the single most meaningful unit. Their overall share of the metropolitan population has dropped from 45 percent in 1970 to 38 percent in 1996 but the aggregate number of residents still rose 12 percent during that period. They have not ridden the wave of the 1990's economic expansion—their job increase between 1991 and 1996 was just 2.8 percent, well behind the national average—but neither have they been swamped; collectively they added almost 700,000 positions, modest growth instead of precipitous deterioration.

These averages do, however, mask some significant declines. Among the thirty largest cities in 1970, eleven lost population in every decade since then: Baltimore, Buffalo, Cincinnati, Cleveland, Detroit, Milwaukee, New Orleans, Philadelphia, Pittsburgh, St. Louis, and Washington. This group was left out of the 1991–1996 expansion, shedding about 70,000 jobs, a 2 percent decline. Being a central city in the Rust Belt is an especially challenging role, and few in this setting have managed to avoid slippage. Even central cities which have been prospering and are blessed with larger and more flexible boundaries—Phoenix and San Antonio are two examples—have struggled to preserve their downtown cores.

Within the metropolitan areas, central cities are fighting to be first among equals. As the centrifugal forces spin residents and jobs toward the periphery, they battle to keep what they have and, ultimately, to reverse the flow. Quality matters along with the quantity. It is the upper- and middle-income residents, the major retail outlets, and the better-paying jobs which have moved away, each taking with them part of the city's revenue base. As cities try to recover from these losses, they are keen on becoming places where people live, shop, and work by choice, not by lack of options. They seek ways to stem the downward spiral, where lower revenues lead to weaker services which in turn encourage more to leave and fewer to enter.

Central cities retain some advantages in the metropolitan chase. They contain the region's origins, sited along and beside the waters that led to the area's founding. They remain the place where the interstates connect and the rapid transit lines converge. The principal media outlets—the daily newspaper, the major television stations—are within their boundaries and, as a consequence, more predisposed to point their spotlight on them. The leading venues—the stadiums and the performing arts centers—are most likely at or near the core, bringing people from throughout the region to their events.

St. Louis's Gateway Arch

Cities, at least potentially, possess a buzz, an air of vitality, that makes urban life distinctive. It is their identity which is most closely associated with the region as a whole. The entire metropolitan area uses their name to describe itself. It is their symbols—an Independence Hall in Philadelphia, a Gateway Arch in St. Louis, the River Walk in San Antonio—which are the bonding icons.

History also enlivens inner city neighborhoods. The housing stock has character, there is a sense of place often absent in the suburbs, sprinkled with an imposing church here and a funky restaurant there. It is space with a past where you bridge time, a romanticism and charm which matures gradually and defies instant creation. Even blocks which have fallen upon hard times, with abandoned housing and unkempt vacant yards, hold a flavor for what has been and a hope for what could be. In the past decade, the new wave of immigrants has begun to provide the human capital for some of these neighborhoods. Between 1996 and 1998, for example, more than 1 million settled in central cities.

As central cities attempt to improve their standing, they confront an internal tension. Which has priority: revitalizing downtown or renewing the neighborhoods? It is a turnaround situation, dollars are scarce, and it is almost impossible to wage a two-front war. It is easier to engage the overall region, including the business interests, in improving downtown. That is the part of the central city they use the most and where, therefore, they still have both a psychological and an economic stake. But the city's voters are most affected by their immediate surroundings and demand that the neighborhoods merit top attention.

As central cities compete for external dollars, most pointedly support from state and national governments, to fund downtown and neighborhood improvements, they are enlisting a new ally: the inner suburbs.[6] Emptying out has come to many municipalities within the ring adjoining the central city's border and the latter's problems have become theirs. Notes a U.S. Department of Housing and Urban Development report, "some older suburbs are experiencing problems once associated with only urban areas—job loss, population decline, crime, and disinvestment [and] . . . the challenges are not restricted to one or two regions of the country but are national in scope."[7] Where these alliances are formed, their initial agenda is to seek state legislation that either deters future growth on the periphery or subsidizes new investments in the core.[8]

Services

Central cities offer a wider array of public goods and services than any other type of local government within the metropolitan area. In addition to police and fire protection, street maintenance and water supply, parks and recreation, and public health, several (Baltimore, Buffalo, Boston, Memphis, Nashville, New York, Washington) operate school systems or the electric utility (Austin, Cleveland, Columbus, Detroit, Jacksonville, Los Angeles, Memphis, Minneapolis, Nashville, San Antonio, San Francisco, Seattle). These cities also control zoning within their boundaries, determining not only the allowable use (residential, commercial, industrial, public) for each parcel of land but also deciding how it is taxed.

The reasons for the breadth and depth of services are both historical and immediate. Since they were often the first public provider and the single largest government during the region's early years, they assumed most of the civil responsibilities beyond those specific tasks assigned to counties by state government. As their populations became more diverse, with immigration in the late nineteenth and early twentieth centuries, they rose to meet the demand for greater services. As their residents became poorer in the last half of the twentieth century, the need for public assistance intensified.

They are significant employers, typically among the top fifty in their region. Although New York City, with 400,000-plus staff, is in a league of its own, a recent analysis of thirty-five large cities found that there is about one full-time-equivalent city employee for every thirty-seven residents.[9] Although this ratio is somewhat misleading, since the work force serves commuters and tourists as well, it demonstrates how extensive central cities are. The fact that they supply so many jobs makes them a valuable commodity for their constituents since, by definition, they are one employer who cannot depart for the suburbs. In return, many cities are using their jobs as leverage to attract and retain middle-class residents, imposing a city residency requirement as a condition of employment.

Central-city governments are under intense pressure to fulfill all their service responsibilities. They have a disproportionate share of the region's poor and, more often than not, an above average fraction of the young and the old, both of whom require more public attention than those between 18 and 65. Their physical infrastructure is also older and takes more labor and materials to keep it in working condition. One-hundred-year-old pipes need repairing more than their twenty-year-old equivalents. But, for most, the revenues are not keeping pace with the needs, and others—local governments elsewhere in the region, states, and the national government—are reluctant to come to the rescue.

Decision Making

Most central cities have a strong mayor-council governmental form, a structure which resembles the separation of powers between executive and legislative branches at the state and national levels. Mayors are chosen directly by the voters, typically for

Philadelphia City Hall

a four-year term, with the elections usually held sometime other than those for state and national offices. They make all or most of the appointments to the executive branch, propose legislation and appropriations to the councils, have some type of veto power and, with a qualification here and there, have the authority to run day-to-day municipal operations. The positions are full-time, with salaries in the high five or low six figures.

Council members are most frequently chosen by district, rather than citywide or at-large. They are usually part-timers, combining their modestly compensated legislative duties with more lucrative endeavors such as practicing law or selling insurance, with either two-year or four-year terms.[10] They possess the city's law-making powers, subject to some involvement by the mayors, but are often at a disadvantage because of limited staff and time conflicts.

Although the early twentieth-century progressive reform movement took overt partisan politics out of most municipalities, a majority of central cities have retained party labels for their candidates. As a consequence, the officeholders consider themselves and are viewed by others as professional or semiprofessional politicians rather than, as is the case for suburbs, citizen volunteers, amateurs fulfilling their civic responsibilities.

Progressivism did strike a few central cities and, as a consequence, they adopted the council-manager form of government. The leading examples include Cincinnati, Dallas, Hartford, Miami, Norfolk, Oklahoma City, Phoenix, Sacramento, San Diego, and San Jose. Under this framework, the elected councils, as a group, select a professional manager to administer the executive branch. These individuals serve at the councils' pleasure and can be removed by majority vote. Individual council members are not allowed, at least by the written rules, to interfere with the manager. They are to set policy and let the manager execute it, although what is clear in theory can sometimes become murky in practice. Council-manager cities do have mayors, but they usually do not act as independent leaders. Instead their role is largely ceremonial, presiding over council sessions and representing the city at public functions. When they do have more formal power or when the weaker ones attempt to translate their informal status into meaningful clout, it creates interesting dynamics between the two executives, one appointed and the other elected.[11]

Central-city mayors bring considerable informal power to their roles. Although few have the thousands of jobs to pass out that their historic predecessors did during the era of patronage and machine politics, they still command more media attention than any other locally elected official. Even when their jurisdiction might have just a modest fraction of the metropolitan area's residents, both local and national media tend to treat them as the regional spokesperson. Newspapers, radio outlets, and television stations give them prominence that adds to their influence, providing them greater opportunity than anyone else, public or private, to set the agenda and shape the discussion.

The mayors are often the preeminent local politicians. Few advance to statewide or national office—a person like Senator Richard Lugar, the former Mayor of Indianapolis, is very much the exception and not the rule—so they invest their political capital at home. The more skilled among them build extensive networks and, like industrious spiders, they weave and reweave their webs. They are on the public job full-time, at the center of communications and in the middle of the action. This grants them a considerable informational advantage over part-time councilpersons, business executives, and nonprofit leaders. In the council-manager cities, the city manager shares some of the knowledge-is-power edge but lacks the access to the media spotlight or to electoral legitimacy.

The council members, most of whom represent separate districts, are focused more on the part than the whole, the slice for their neighborhoods rather the size of the entire pie. They are the front line for constituent complaints, doing their best to get a pothole filled or an alley repaved. In racially segregated cities, where all-black or all-white or entirely Hispanic districts send one of their own to the assemblies, the councils also become the arenas in which the politics of race is most visibly conducted.

URBAN COUNTIES

Strategic Setting

Most of their names—Cuyahoga, Fairfax, Maricopa, Nassau, Wayne—are much less familiar than the central-city labels but, despite this, urban counties have become major players in metropolitan matters. They either contain the central city plus its immediate environs (Cuyahoga for Cleveland, Maricopa for Phoenix, Wayne for Detroit) or they have emerged as a vital entity within their region (Fairfax for Washington, Nassau for New York). Although those containing central cities have not escaped the social and economic decline suffered by those municipalities, their larger territory has cushioned the impact. Those adjacent to the inner cities have been the principal beneficiaries of the post–World War II suburban explosion, first adding residents and then attracting jobs.

By any numerical account, the primary urban county within each metropolitan area is usually the largest single unit of local government. Compared to a region's central city, its largest county will cover more territory, house more people, and provide more jobs. Los Angeles County, for example, has more than twice as many residents and workers as does the City of Los Angeles. So, too, Maricopa County is more than double Phoenix on both factors. As a consequence, an urban county has a stronger revenue base and a greater ability to supply public goods and services to a wider clientele. As metropolitan areas have become more complex and thus require a more regional approach, they become the local governmental unit best able to fill that need.

What the urban counties lack is the central city's visibility. The City of Chicago Mayor is much better known, both within the Chicago metropolitan area and throughout the United States, than the President of the Cook County Board of Commissioners. With media attention and public awareness come clout; playing second fiddle in the press and on television has, in and of itself, kept urban counties from capitalizing on their quantitative status. But recent trends and future expectations

Hennepin County Government Center in Downtown Minneapolis

favor them and, in the years ahead, one can anticipate their role and influence within regions to increase further. For the most part, urban county elected officials realize that the future is more theirs than the central city's, and they are content to use their influence more behind the scenes than through the media.

Along with central cities, the larger urban counties have the most at stake in the competition between metropolitan areas. They understand that their future is closely entangled with that of the larger region and that, especially if the area lags behind others, their local jurisdictions are likely to suffer the most harm. As a result, central cities and urban counties provide much of the resources, both human and physical, for efforts to improve their region's comparative standing, ranging from promotional efforts to attract tourists to enterprise incubators for startup businesses.

Services

States initially formed counties to carry out the administrative and judicial transactions needed in a civilized society. Examples include keeping track of who owns what property, conducting civil and criminal trials, and probating wills. Each county has its courthouse, often on a square, and that was where people went to conduct much of their public business. As states assumed more responsibility for social services such as welfare and public health, many of them also chose counties as the administrative subunits for these functions.

As urbanization expanded beyond central-city boundaries, many counties found themselves responding to demands that they supply municipal services. City residents had become accustomed to having some local government provide police protection, repair streets, and maintain parks. In many cases, the people formed new municipalities, suburban miniatures of the city they had left, and these entities met these public needs. But in other situations, they remained unincorporated and expected the counties to become, de facto, their municipal governments. As a consequence, numerous counties began to transform their sheriff's units into police departments, establish public works departments to build and maintain roads, and establish parks. They became municipalities by default including exercising zoning power for this acreage.

As their unincorporated populations grew, several counties began to offer several of these services to incorporated areas. Many smaller municipalities decided it would be easier to purchase items like police patrols or street repaving from their county government rather than going to all the bother of doing it themselves. The counties liked the idea since it enabled them to make a little money. They had already incurred the fixed costs for, say, repaving machinery and the marginal cost for doing a bit more was modest. They could give the municipality an affordable price and still come out ahead.

As urban counties have built the best balance sheets among the general purpose local governments in their metropolitan areas, they have occasionally stepped forward to bankroll new regional facilities such as sports stadiums and performing arts centers. Although central cities have battled to retain such venues as part of their reason for being, they sometimes lack the tax base to finance them. In such cases, sometimes reluctantly and in other instances gratefully, they have stepped aside and let an urban county assume the responsibility.

Decision Making

Most urban counties have one of three types of governments: commission, executive-council, or council-manager.[12] Commission government, a board of elected officials who exercise both executive and legislative powers, was the prototypical form for counties throughout the United States and, for units outside metropolitan areas, it remains the prevailing practice. Relatively few urban counties retain it with Dallas County (Dallas) and Harris County (Houston) being among the most prominent examples. Most often, one of the commissioners is elected by the entire county and the others are chosen by districts. The dynamics vary by county but the logic of this structure encourages the commissioners to divide up authority, either by territory (I'll be king or queen of my district and let you rule in yours) or by function (I'll take the lead for streets and you can be in charge of the parks).

The council-executive model closely resembles the mayor-council form in central cities. It is the most frequent structure in Midwestern and Eastern urban counties including Cuyahoga (Cleveland), Franklin (Columbus), Montgomery (Washington), Nassau (New York), Suffolk (New York), and Wayne (Detroit). The elected executive, usually chosen for a four-year term and serving full-time, is at the center of command with similar powers to the mayor. Some counties have retained separately elected offices for certain functions—assessor for valuing property or a public administrator for probating wills—and in these cases the chief executive has less than complete control over that branch. Like their city counterparts, council members serve part-time and are compensated accordingly although the average county has fewer council members and thus larger council districts than does the typical central city. This imbalance—executive on the job constantly, legislators there occasionally—tilts the power balance toward the executive. Unlike cities, however, county elections are usually held at the same time as state and national contests, subjecting the candidates to possible ripple effects from those races.

The council-manager form in urban counties also looks virtually identical to its municipal counterpart. A professional county manager is the chief operating officer and the council serves as the board of directors. The council, typically a part-time body, is expected to give the manager wide leeway, including allowing that office to make the key staff decisions. Once they establish basic policies, the manager is in charge. If there is an elected executive, that individual, like the mayor in a council-manager city, is more a figurehead than a powerhouse. Council-manager counties are most common in Western states—all California counties, for example, take this approach—but it is also present in other parts of the country such as Bucks (Philadelphia), Fairfax (Washington), Fulton (Atlanta), and Hennepin (Minneapolis).

As metropolitan areas grew during the first few decades after World War II, many central cities considered merging with the urban county in which they were located. Such combinations, it was thought, would remove political tension, eliminate unhealthy competition among the two units, and allow for a more streamlined and coordinated government. Although tens of proposals moved at least to the talking stage, only four were consummated: Baton Rouge and East Baton Rouge Parish (Louisiana's term for county) in 1949, Nashville and Davidson County in 1962, Jacksonville and Duval County in 1968, and Indianapolis and Marion County in 1970. Each of these consolidated governments adopted a mayor-council structure.

SUBURBAN MUNICIPALITIES

Strategic Setting

Even though most metropolitan area residents live in them, suburban municipalities are among the smaller fish in the region's governmental pond. Although, collectively, America is a nation of suburbs, each separate government is only a minute
fraction of the region. With modest stature comes an inward preoccupation, focused more on the struggle within the metropolitan area than on the competition
outside. Each suburban municipality is jockeying with its neighbors, working to
retain past advantages and secure fresh ones.[13] For them, acquiring a larger share of
the existing pie has a more compelling attraction than making the pie larger.

In this ongoing contest, suburbs sort themselves out both by degree of success
and by how they achieve it. First there are the affluent enclaves, home to the ultra
rich. They have names like Bloomfield Hills (Detroit), Ladue (St. Louis), Lake
Forest (Chicago), and Paradise Valley (Phoenix). Filled with expensive homes on
expansive lots, they maintain their status with strict zoning and police forces which
protect the residents and deter outsiders. They often contain gated places, discouraging all but themselves from driving through or looking around. Their principal
strategy is defense, shielding themselves from the unpleasant aspects of the rest of
the region and preserving the beautiful life.

Next are the upper-middle and middle-income suburbs which have successfully combined desirable residential neighborhoods with one or more revenue-
producing assets such as a shopping mall or an office park. The latter pay enough
taxes to subsidize quality public goods and services to the residents without unduly
upsetting the ambiance. These suburbs also work more to protect what they have
won rather than seeking still additional resources. They cultivate their cash cows,
adding a traffic light here or an additional police patrol there, to keep the revenues
flowing.

At the other of the spectrum are the down-and-out suburbs, victims of economic change and residential flight. Most often located in Midwestern and Northeastern metropolitan areas and sited adjacent to central cities, these inner suburbs
flourished earlier in the twentieth century but now time and events have passed
them by. The manufacturing plants that provided their tax base departed, leaving
abandoned buildings and polluted land. Many residents followed the exodus,
drawn by newer homes in greener locales at the region's periphery. Lacking much
individual political clout or recovery potential, these inner suburbs are starting to
plead their case to governments at all levels, seeking to stop the disinvestment and
reverse the decline.

Then there are all the other suburbs, each pursuing some niche which will
improve its standing. For those fortunate enough to be in growing metropolitan
areas, places like Atlanta or Orlando or Phoenix, this means capitalizing on the region's prosperity. As people, stores, and jobs pour in, their task is to get their share
and then some. For those in steady state or declining regions, the contest is more

keen, with each suburb searching for some niche, some comparative advantage, which will make it more attractive than those around it.

Services

Almost all suburban municipalities supply the basics—police protection and street maintenance—and exercise their zoning powers. They may furnish fire protection and emergency medical services although the smaller ones often either purchase them from an adjoining town or relinquish this function to a special district. Still other services (trash collection is the best example) might be contracted out to one or more private suppliers with conditions and prices set by the suburb.

Even though a service carries the same label—say police protection—its style varies from one suburb to the next. Some prefer police officers who act more like social workers than law enforcers, stopping by a senior citizen's apartment to see windows needing insulating or mentoring youth on the playground. Others want civil enforcers who will insure that building and lot codes are respected and traffic regulations obeyed. Still others want watch guards who will vigilantly monitor who comes and who goes, friendly to residents and stern with outsiders.

One of the ways suburbs compete with one another for residents is through public amenities. Outside of the most wealthy, few people can afford dues to private recreational clubs and facilities and, even if they made this a priority for their discretionary spending, they might be uncomfortable in such ritzy settings. To lure and retain these individuals, municipalities build community centers and skating rinks, soccer fields and volleyball courts, libraries and fitness facilities. Like any rivalry, matters can escalate. Where once a modest swimming pool sufficed, now a water park is required. Although the suburbs may charge a small usage fee for all these items, typically general revenues pick up much of the tab.

The amenity race is most common in middle-class suburbs seeking families with children 18 or under. In such settings, pooling local tax dollars to buy recreation collectively makes sense. Wealthier municipalities typically do not bother with amenities, realizing their residents will purchase items such as country club memberships on the private market. Poorer cities, struggling to stay afloat, cannot pay for these frills, making them even less competitive in the pursuit of residents.

As suburban America has become more complex, many municipalities have found it difficult to go it alone. Although there is no thought of abdicating their autonomy—no one is willing to share zoning authority—they are increasingly willing to cooperate with others on service provision. Why have your own police dispatching system, requiring 24-hour, 7-day staffing, when it might be more efficient to join with a few neighboring municipalities? Why not purchase criminal laboratory tests from the central-city department rather than separately mounting a substandard one? The result is an uncounted and swelling web of interlocal governmental agreements and contracts.

The purest form of this approach occurred in the mid-1950s in the Los Angeles metropolitan area when a newly incorporated city, Lakewood, decided to contract with other governmental units to supply services like police protection and street maintenance rather than providing them itself. This vividly demonstrated that the governmental unit demanding a particular service did not also have to supply that service. In more recent years, municipalities and counties have begun to consider private vendors as well as public entities when they contract externally.

Decision Making

Suburban municipalities tend to be socioeconomically and racially homogeneous. The less diverse the population, the fewer the number of policy disputes. With fewer disputes, government's role is more service provider and intrametropolitan strategist than it is conflict resolver. In this setting, holding elective office is a volunteer activity, a public service; the salaries are token and the time commitment limited.

Most suburbs having more than 10,000 residents use the council-manager form or some variation on it. In its pure form, as already described, councils chose a professional manager to oversee day-to-day activities (see Figure 2–1). Mayors are elected citywide and often serve as the councils' presiding officer but their executive functions are largely ceremonial—they are the cutters of ribbons and the dispensers of keys. In some cases, mayors directly appoint the chief operating officers and, in these situations, their influence is elevated.

Being a city manager or administrator in suburban America is not a secure post. Multiple councilpersons, potentially changing with elections every two or four years, serving part-time, not bashful about expressing their views, can make for an unsettling environment. A manager may choose to stay put, balancing the political forces and creating his or her own base. Then the manager becomes the single most important figure. Others are more mobile, opting to move from one suburb to the next as fortunes change and thereby having less impact on any individual government.

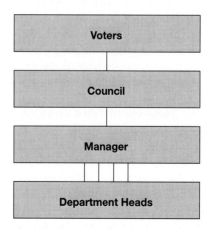

FIGURE 2–1   The Council-Manager Form of Government

Smaller towns often cannot afford a professional executive with a master's degree and a $50,000-plus salary. They rely on the volunteer elected officials to co-ordinate services and use a mix of paid staff and contracts with outside entities to carry them out. This often creates a more amateurish government where reforms in governmental administration are rarely adopted.[14] It also places them at a significant disadvantage in the intrametropolitan contest for residents. With no full-time specialist at the helm, these suburbs find it difficult to modify their policies to adjust to changing circumstances.

Some suburban councils are elected at-large, with all the citizens voting for the entire body, while others are chosen by district, with each segment sending its own representative. At-large councils tend to have less conflict than do district-based bodies. The same majority, presumably sharing similar views, typically picked all of them. Since they have a coinciding constituency, they regularly take a similar approach and, representing the entire city rather than a portion of it, they are more apt to look at overall concerns rather than neighborhood interests.[15]

Although they jealously guard their independence, suburban municipalities do realize that there is sometimes strength in numbers. They often organize a formal group, a league of municipalities, within counties as well as for entire states. These associations both provide information and technical assistance to their members, especially the smaller towns with less well- trained staffs, as well as serve as advocacy groups for municipal interests in metropolitan policy making and the state legislative process.

EXURBAN COUNTIES

Strategic Setting

Exurban counties, those on the outer edge of the metropolitan area, are often conflicted about their relationship with the rest of the metropolitan area. Economic reality, captured in the U.S. Census process which made them part of the region, argues for greater involvement, for the necessity of looking more inward toward the urban core rather than outward toward the rustic surroundings. But there is still much open space, often considerable agricultural activity, and the past frequently has a greater psychological pull than does the future.

The counties' leaders across all sectors tend be drawn from families who have spent many generations in the community. The newcomers, those commuters from the central cities and the urban counties who have by their actions made the exurban counties part of the region, have often yet to become highly involved in local government. The longtime locals are often torn between two contradictory goals. One faction wants to seize the day and capitalize on being at the developmental rim. There is money to be made transforming farmland to subdivisions and building retail outlets for the added customers. The other contingent wants to preserve the counties' rural character, if not totally then substantially, so that its special features can be enjoyed by their children and those beyond.

Services

Exurban counties have fewer municipalities and most of their acreage is unincorporated. County governments therefore supply the basic services—police (often called sheriff), road maintenance, and others—to most of the population in addition to providing the state-mandated operations. They also retain much of the zoning authority and this becomes the arena within with much of the development versus preservation battles are waged.

The breadth and depth of services is distinctly lower than those in urban counties. Less dense populations generate a lower need for many services and there is a lower expectation for what local governments are expected to do. Not only are amenities scarce—few have county parks and recreation programs although their boundaries might include state facilities—but also the ratio of, say, police patrols to number of residents will be less. Even some services—fire protection is one example—might be provided by a blend of volunteer assistance and tax-supported equipment.

Decision Making

Although most urban counties have adopted either the council-executive or council-manager form, exurban counties have for the most part retained the commissioner structure. Depending on a county's size and tradition, these posts may be full-time or part-time. Department heads are less likely to have much formal training, relying instead on materials provided by statewide county associations or university extension services. Exurban county governments, true to their rural heritage, usually take on a good-old-boy-and-girl style which places a premium on social relationships and personal trust.

RESIDENTIAL COMMUNITY ASSOCIATIONS

Strategic Setting

At the bottom of the local government chain are tens of thousands of private organizations that look very much like miniature governments. Most commonly called residential community associations (RCAs), they are mandatory membership organizations for anyone owning residential property for a specified area.[16] When people purchase a house or a condominium within the association's boundaries, the deed will contain language detailing what regulations they must follow, what fees they must pay for which services, and what liability they have for special assessments. They are technically private entities but this legal connection, with deeds enforced by state courts for those disobeying the regulations or becoming delinquent on the fees, gives them a public element.

The RCAs are preoccupied with their own immediate surroundings and view the metropolitan area only as a possible threat to their neighborhood's or subdivision's well-being. As long as there is no outside threat, they mind their own business.

But if some external entity is coming to or near their turf—a new light rail line through their midst or subsidized housing on some adjacent property—then they transform themselves into an intense anywhere-but-here force. When nimbyism—not-in-my-backyard—happens, as often as not some RCA is fueling the fire.

Services

The two most frequent RCA public goods and services are owning and maintaining common ground and the local streets. Under this arrangement, a neighborhood or subdivision can fashion its own tree and shrubbery appearance and not have to depend on a more distant municipality or county government for beautification assistance. With control over the streets, they can limit traffic by closing off certain entrances and regulate speed with metal barriers and other devices. Many RCAs also operate swimming pools, provide ornamental lighting, and maintain sidewalks.

Decision Making

RCAs are governed by elected boards, usually three to six individuals. In some, each residential unit has one vote and, for others, voting is weighted by a property's value or size. There is rarely much competition for these uncompensated posts and sometimes people must be drafted to stand for election. Someone's dining room table serves as the RCAs city hall, with the board members dividing up such unglamourous duties as finding someone to remove the snow, clean the pool, or mow the grass.

SPECIAL DISTRICTS

Strategic Setting

Since special districts concentrate on just one or two functions, their strategy within a metropolitan area is to enhance the demand for whatever it is they do and to spur public opinion to consider their service critical for the region's well-being. Public transit districts promote the convenience of riding the bus, aiming to have their fare revenues rise, and they argue for how mass transportation helps the environment by lowering automobile exhaust emissions, demonstrating how they contribute to the area's quality of life.

Special districts often seek to broaden the perceived need for their operation. Fire protection districts might originally exist to respond to emergency calls and extinguish blazes. Not content to confine themselves to a reactive role, they might expand into fire prevention education, smoke alarm installation, and building inspections. Similarly, solid waste districts will not only operate landfills but also sponsor and implement recycling programs.

In order to prosper, these districts need people either to purchase their services directly, such as buying a subway token, or paying taxes for their operations.

Since special purpose governments overlap with municipalities and counties, they often compete with the general purpose units for the same tax base with each, for example, levying a property tax. In this environment, the districts want their services to stand out above the rest. Moreover, because so many of their functions require large infusions of capital for facilities like wastewater treatment plants, they often need voter support for sizeable bond issues in order to keep their operations modern and efficient.

Services

Excluding school districts, which will be discussed in Chapter 8, there are about 13,000 special districts in U.S. metropolitan areas. The average for a metropolitan area is just over forty, although this number is skewed upward by a few regions which have hundreds; the median number, at latest count, is twenty-three.[17] The most frequent function is fire protection and other common purposes are housing, water, sewers, and flood control. Less routine, but still numbering in the hundreds, are hospitals, libraries, and transportation.

Several of these services—water supply, wastewater collection and treatment, storm water control—are defined by watersheds. In these situations, natural geography trumps general purpose government boundaries and many stream-related services can only be adequately provided if they follow drainage patterns. Special districts are also useful for services requiring significant capital investment and highly trained personnel. It is difficult for small and medium municipalities to underwrite complex and sophisticated equipment and structures and, with a larger jurisdiction, such fixed costs are spread over more taxpayers thereby achieving a better economy of scale. It is also often easier to recruit skilled professionals, such as civil engineers and transportation specialists, to a public unit if it is one or two steps removed from political interference by elected legislators.

Decision Making

There are two generic types of special districts and, to confuse matters, one subset is also called "special district" while the other is termed "public authority." The power to tax is the key difference, with special districts possessing it while public authorities are unable to exercise it. That means the authorities must exist primarily on charging fees to those using their services while the special districts can also impose taxes, which most often are levies on property. Both special districts and public authorities sometimes receive grants and other support from the state or national government. Sewer districts, for example, in the past competed for capital grants from the national government while housing authorities continue to receive both operating and capital assistance from the federal budget.

Special districts typically have elected boards with four years being the most common term of office. All persons residing within the district are eligible to vote in these elections but the turnout rate is quite low, often under 20 percent. Public authorities usually have appointed boards with some elected executive(s) such as governors, mayors, or county executives making the decision. This connection links the board members with the political interests of whoever named them to their posts and, in many cases, they lack the ability to act independently and instead follow their benefactor's instructions.

Most citizens do not participate in their governance and, absent a sensational scandal, the mass media pay scant attention to them. With this limited public oversight, special districts and public authorities are prone to become captive of the narrower interests who most directly benefit from them. These can include the labor unions representing their employees, the contractors who build and maintain their facilities, and the businesses who supply them goods and services. For elected boards, they finance candidates and, with low turnout elections, can make the difference. For appointed bodies, they lobby the selecting executive to name persons sympathetic to their concerns.

TOO MANY GOVERNMENTS?

Some have argued that metropolitan areas have too many governments.[18] This perspective prevailed in the 1950s and 1960s and sparked numerous consolidation efforts, only a few of which succeeded. The case for having fewer governments makes five points. First, and most sweeping, the more governments a region has, the greater the chances that the voices of the smaller parts will win out over the concerns of the larger whole. Public officials will be preoccupied with advocating for their own narrow constituencies, and few if any will speak out on behalf of the metropolitan area. At a time when competition among metropolitan areas has intensified, this handicaps regions.

Second, fragmented governments can be just plain confusing. Say an outside firm wants to locate a business somewhere in the region. More often than not, they will need to go to a municipality for a zoning change, to the county for building permits, and then to special districts for fire inspection and sewer connection. If there were just a single government, then there could be one-stop shopping where all transactions could be conducted.

Third, multiple governments create inequities. As already described, municipalities use their zoning power to decide who can live and do business within their jurisdictions. This leads to striking differences in tax bases and that, in turn, means that some local governments can supply excellent services while others are too strapped to provide even the basics. Instead of having every metropolitan area resident receive equal levels of public goods and services, what citizens get is highly dependent on where they live. Children in one municipality might have access to first-rate recreational facilities and programs while those in the adjoining local government have none.

Fourth, how can citizens have any reasonable chance of keeping their governments accountable when there are so many of them? If, in addition to electing state and national officeholders, residents must keep track of tens of municipal, county, and special district elected officials, being a responsible voter becomes impossible for all but the most diligent.

Finally, having tens and hundreds of local governments is inefficient. If there were fewer but larger units, public services could be produced at lower unit costs. Administrative overhead—police chiefs, city managers, public works directors—would be spread over a greater population. Expensive equipment—a computerized dispatching center, a management information system, a technologically advanced paving machine—would be able to assist more residents.

Where the critics of multiple governments see fragmentation and chaos, its defenders find choice and adaptation.[19] With fewer governments comes sparser options for what packages of public goods and services citizens can purchase. If there were just one government for an entire metropolitan region, then there would be equal levels of public services in each and every neighborhood: one police force with its patrolling style, one parks and recreation department with its leisure preferences, and so forth. Just as consumers have differing tastes in items like food and automobiles, so too they are not all alike when it comes to the quantity and style of public services they desire from their local governments.

Moreover, citizens' ability to select locations within a metropolitan region causes the many governments to compete for them to live, work, and shop within their jurisdictions. This engages the forces of the marketplace and the outcome is a greater public good than would occur if one government had a monopoly. An individual suburban municipality cannot become complacent for fear that it will lose some of its current residents and cease to attract new ones. Americans are also suspicious about concentrating too much power in any single government unit—witness separation of powers, checks and balances, and federalism—and anyone proposing a one-size-fits-all metropolitan government triggers such misgivings.

Even if multiple governments generate inefficiencies, and the evidence on this point is mixed, the multiplicity proponents note that citizens are more than willing to pay a bit extra for, say, easier familiarity with police officers and enhanced control over their enforcement style. Interlocal agreements can be used for more expensive items and, for functions which clearly demand large capital investments, special districts can be formed. They acknowledge that all this leads to service inequities but, for some residents, that is what they want and, for others, larger units—counties, states, and the national government—perhaps can help correct glaring imbalances. Instead of devising some elaborate metropolitan government with unknown consequences, the supporters of many governments suggest letting the many units use devices like interlocal contracts, special districts, and tax-sharing to adapt gradually to changing needs.

As for the confusion about having so many local elected officials, that is essential to avoid governmental tyranny. Having just a few elected officials in charge would be simpler, but the danger of them abusing their authority is too great. Local elected officials, the councilperson from your ward or the suburban municipal mayor, is also quite accessible. Not only can they understand and advocate local interests, but they can help residents navigate the rest of the governmental apparatus.

The larger regional interest being lost in the preoccupation with each unit obtaining its fair share is a legitimate concern, admit those resisting governmental consolidation. But, they contend, having fewer but larger governments is no guarantee that a regional spirit will prevail nor an assurance that those governments will make wiser decisions. Of course, they say, regions must act as regions on many matters, but they recommend accomplishing this through voluntary alliances. They think it more prudent for metropolitan areas to evolve incrementally, joining coalitions in specific situations where they make sense, rather than to transform dramatically, abandoning local autonomy and placing one's destiny permanently in some region-wide government.

The jury of experts remains divided on what type of governmental framework is best for today's metropolitan regions, but few expect any reduction in the foreseeable future and most anticipate that the number of governments will grow albeit at a somewhat lower rate. That means that regionalism through adaptations and alliances, whether it is the best way to do it or the only way to accomplish it, is the present reality.

NOTES

1. These are preliminary numbers from the 1997 Census of Governments. See Stephens and Wikstrom, *Metropolitan Government and Governance*, p. 8.
2. The landmark case is *Village of Euclid v. Amber Realty Co.*, 272 U.S. 365 (1926).
3. Gerald E. Frug, *City Making: Building Communities Without Building Walls* (Princeton, NJ: Princeton University Press, 1999), pp. 143–45.
4. Nancy Burns, *The Formation of American Local Governments: Private Values in Public Institutions* (New York: Oxford University Press, 1994), pp. 8–9.
5. Mark Schneider, *The Competitive City* (Pittsburgh: University of Pittsburgh Press, 1989); and Mark Schneider, Paul Teske, and Michael Mintrom, *Public Entrepreneurs: Agents for Change in American Government* (Princeton, NJ: Princeton University Press, 1995).
6. Myron Orfield, *Metropolitics: A Regional Agenda for Community and Stability* (Washington: Brookings Institution Press, 1997).
7. *The State of the Cities 1999* (Washington: U.S. Department of Housing and Urban Development, 1999), p. iii.
8. Orfield, *Metropolitics*, Chapter 7.
9. Katherine Barrett and Richard Greene, "Grading the Cities: A Management Report Card," *Governing*, 13, no. 5 (February 2000), p. 40.
10. Timothy Bledsoe, *Careers in City Politics: The Case for Urban Democracy* (Pittsburgh: University of Pittsburgh Press, 1993).
11. Over time, many mayor-council and council-manager cities have adopted features of the other type, such as having a powerful chief of staff administrator to provide more professionalism for an elected mayor or giving the mayor more influence within the council to strengthen the executive voice. See H. George Frederickson and Gary Alan Johnson, "The Adapted American City: A Study of Institutional Dynamics," *Urban Affairs Review*, 36, no. 6 (July 2001), pp. 872–84.
12. Donald C. Menzel, ed., *The American County: Frontiers of Knowledge* (Tuscaloosa: University of Alabama Press, 1996).
13. Paul G. Lewis, *Shaping Suburbia: How Political Institutions Shape Urban Development* (Pittsburgh: University of Pittsburgh Press, 1996).
14. Anirudh V.S. Ruhil and others, "Institutions and Reform: Reinventing Local Government," *Urban Affairs Review*, 34, no. 9 (January 1999), pp. 433–55.
15. Susan Welch and Timothy Bledsoe, *Urban Reform and Its Consequences* (Chicago: University of Chicago Press, 1988).
16. *Residential Community Associations: Questions and Answers* (Washington: Advisory Commission on Intergovernmental Relations, 1989). Also see Robert Jay Dilger, *Neighborhood Politics: Residential*

Community Associations in American Governance (New York: New York University Press, 1992); Kathryn Mary Doherty, *Emerging Patterns of Housing, Community and Local Governance: The Case of Private Homeowner Associations* (Washington: U.S. Department of Housing and Urban Development, 2000); Evan McKenzie, *Privatopia: Homeowner Associations and the Rise of Residential Private Government* (New Haven, CT: Yale University Press, 1994); and Donald R. Stabile, *Community Associations: The Emergence and Acceptance of a Quiet Innovation in Housing* (Westport, CT: Greenwood Press, 2000).

17. Kathryn A. Foster, *The Political Economy of Special Purpose Governments* (Washington: Georgetown University Press, 1997), pg. 121.

18. For a summary of these arguments, see Robert L. Bish, *The Public Economy of Metropolitan Areas* (Chicago: Markham, 1970).

19. Vincent Ostrom, Charles M. Tiebout, and Robert O. Warren, "The Organization of Government in Metropolitan Areas: A Theoretical Inquiry," *American Political Science Review*, 60, no. 4 (December 1961), pp. 831–42. For empirical assessments, see *Metropolitan Organization: The St. Louis Case* (Washington: Advisory Commission on Intergovernmental Relations, 1988) and *Metropolitan Organization: The Allegheny County Case* (Washington: Advisory Commission on Intergovernmental Relations, 1992).

SUGGESTED READINGS

BURNS, NANCY. *The Formation of American Local Governments: Private Values in Public Institutions.* New York: Oxford University Press, 1994. Explains how private interests use changes in local government structure to achieve their goals.

FOSTER, KATHRYN A. *The Political Economy of Special-Purpose Government.* Washington: Georgetown University Press, 1997. The definitive work on special districts and public authorities in the United States.

HAMILTON, DAVID K. *Governing Metropolitan Areas: Response to Growth and Change.* New York: Garland Publishing, 1999. Detailed account of metropolitan governmental changes during the past half century.

LEWIS, PAUL G. *Shaping Suburbia: How Political Institutions Organize Urban Development.* Pittsburgh: University of Pittsburgh Press, 1996. An insightful analysis of suburban municipal strategies in the Denver and Portland metropolitan areas.

SCHNEIDER, MARK. *The Competitive City: The Political Economy of Suburbia.* Pittsburgh: Pittsburgh University Press, 1989. Skillfully applies a market perspective to the analysis of suburban municipalities.

STEPHENS, G. ROSS and NELSON WIKSTROM. *Metropolitan Government and Governance: Theoretical Perspectives, Empirical Analysis, and the Future.* New York: Oxford University, 2000. A sophisticated and comprehensive analysis of recent governmental trends within metropolitan areas.

DOING IT

It is a straightforward task to determine where any person fits into the state and national governmental structure. Go to www.vote-smart.org, type in your nine-digit ZIP code, and there are your state and national legislative districts. With just a few more strokes, you can determine who represents you at both levels. It is equally easy to obtain the basic rules of the game, the written constitutions, for a state or the national government.

At the local level, because of having so many governments, matters are more complex. Although, ideally, people should have specific information about their municipality and their county as well as any special districts and public authorities having jurisdiction in their area, extraordinarily few do. So that you can be an exception, compile this material for some address in a metropolitan region. Your directory should answer the following questions for the selected address:

1.   What is the municipality (if any)? What form of government does it have? Who is the mayor (if any)? What is the mayor's term of office? How many members serve on the city's legislative body and how long are their terms? Is it chosen at large or by district? If by district, which council member(s) represent the address? When are elections held for city offices?

2.   What is the county? What form of government does it have? Who is the chief elected executive (if any)? What is the executive's term of office? How many members serve on the county's legislative body and how long are their terms? Is it selected at large or by district? If by district, who represents the address? What other county officials are elected? What are their terms? When are elections held for county offices?

3.   Is the address included in a residential community association? If so, what services does the RCA provide? How many trustees does it have? What are the terms of office and when are they selected?

4.   Identify every special district and public authority providing services to that address. For each one, what is its name? How many persons serve on its board, how are they selected, and what are their terms?

CHAPTER 3

The Business Sector

WHY BUSINESSES ARE INVOLVED

At the abstract level, we can make a straightforward distinction between the public sector and the private or business sector. When communities make decisions collectively, either imposing a regulation, collecting a tax, or supplying a service, that is a public action. When either persons or corporations choose to engage in a transaction with other individuals, exchanging some good or service either for money or other considerations, that is a private deed.

Matters become murkier when trying to capture reality in conceptual categories. All governmental policies have consequences for businesses. Some are advantaged and others handicapped. Locating a fire station means it will be nearer some enterprises, possibly lowering their insurance rates, and it will be more distant from others, potentially increasing their fees. Restricting the size of billboards will harm those firms dependent on that medium but will have no impact for businesses using other means to attract customers. Deciding to tax sales rather than property hurts retail outlets but does not affect manufacturers. Governments set the rules of the game: politics is often defined as who gets what, when, and how. Since rules are rarely neutral, businesses seek to have them work to their advantage.

Beyond this, when private individuals and firms try to make money—and the profit motive is the prime mover in the business sector—they frequently find that government cooperation is required. What business one practices influences which governments are most relevant. Those producing fighter planes or aircraft carriers focus on the national government, the sole U.S. customer for their products. Those building prisons concentrate on state governments, the principal custodian for the million-plus Americans residing behind bars. In each case, the firms follow the money.

What do local governments have that businesses want? For the contest within metropolitan areas, most of the answer revolves around land.[1] Businesses can make money either by exchanging a parcel for cash or by building something on it. Governments regulate land so that its use serves some collective purpose. That means every property in a metropolitan area has an exchange value, its market price in the private sector, and a use value, the local government's preference for what should happen on it.[2] These two values are not always in agreement, and businesses must frequently strive to have local governments change a property's use designation in order to enhance its exchange price.

For the competition among metropolitan areas, businesses have two concerns. First, some have a greater stake than others in having a metropolitan area grow, and those that do will often join forces with the public sector in developing and implementing a strategic expansion plan. Second, since a development scheme can have many options, businesses compete with one another for those which will give their particular enterprise the best return. As regions debate their economic approach, pondering whether, for example, solid state electronics or biotechnology is the most likely route to the promised land and therefore most deserving for public subsidies, firms within each of these two segments are pleading that they should be number one.

LAND AND THE GROWTH MACHINE

Developers is the term most often applied to those attempting to profit from land transactions. For them, the metropolitan area is one gigantic set of parcels and, given the complexity, they tend to specialize. Some speculate in land itself, buying parcels that might be in the path of development. If they either guess right or if they have been able to persuade government to take some action to help enhance its value, say by building a highway interchange nearby, the land's exchange value increases and they sell at a higher price. Others see land as a place to build something: a subdivision of single-family homes, an apartment building, an office complex, an industrial plant. If there is sufficient demand for what they construct, then the price paid to purchase or rent it will cover both the cost of the land and the building as well as provide a profit.

To develop is to deal and, because land has both a private and a public component, the bargaining inevitably includes both businesses and governments. That, of course, is what makes developers active participants in the metropolitan chase. Some deals are driven by developers. They act and government reacts. Others are initiated by governments seeking to attract more interest in their territory. To sample the mix within metropolitan areas, consider four possible land development projects: (1) a new subdivision in an exurban county, (2) an office park in the outer suburbs, (3) a shopping mall in the inner suburbs, and (4) a hotel in the central city.

Exurban Subdivision

Where some see gently rolling countryside, cultivated land or a grazing area at the region's periphery, a developer imagines a subdivision with a few hundred houses. The metropolitan area is growing and demand for single-family homes on spacious lots is high. An elderly couple, both recently deceased, owned the property and had farmed it for all their adult lives. But none of their children saw agriculture as a career and they are eager to have the estate sell the 500-acre homestead. Dollars will be a more liquid inheritance than land. For developers, this is an opportunity waiting to be seized.

If this were entirely a private matter, the transaction would be straightforward. There is a willing seller, the couple's children, and several eager buyers, the developers. All that would be required would be settling on a price. Once that was negotiated, construction could begin. But the exurban county government controls how the land is used. In this instance, it is zoned agricultural. Unless that classification is changed to residential, no homes will arise on what had been fields.

So the negotiations become a blend of public and private. The developers and the couple's survivors need to convince the county government that it is in the public interest to have farmland become houses. They will attempt to persuade the elected commissioners that growth is good, that the homes will generate more property tax revenues, and that their occupants will stimulate retail trade among the local businesses.

The commissioners might be less certain, wishing to protect their county's rural character and resist urbanization. Even if they perceive residential development as inevitable, is this the best deal available? If it is, what conditions should they attach to any rezoning? How much should the developers pay for the impact they will have on county services? In addition to the infrastructure within the subdivision, how much should they pay for, say, widening the road which goes by the property? Should they mandate large lot sizes, ensuring that the new residents will be upscale? If the land is a prime location for development, the county commissioners hold the upper hand and, if they play it skillfully, can make the developers—and ultimately the people purchasing the homes—cover all the direct and indirect public costs spawned by the project.

Suburban Office Park

People have moved to the suburbs, commuting to central city offices is tiresome, green space is in and downtown density out, and talented employees are harder to recruit. If this is the problem, developers have the answer: a campuslike office park in suburbia, close to the upscale suburban communities. This setting will attract both enterprises moving into the region as well as possibly entice some to relocate from the central city.

Scattered amongst the outer suburbs are parcels containing tens of acres, most often land being held by speculators. They may have purchased it five or ten years

The Park Place Office Park, Irvine, California

ago when this part of the region was on the outer edge of development. Now that suburbia has arrived, it is time to cash in on their investment, and they sell the property to an office park developer willing to take the risk that the property can be rezoned from some low-density category, such as single-family homes, to a high-density classification, commercial buildings.

Most suburban municipalities and urban counties are predisposed to accept such a shift. They have discovered that residences and a few retail outlets do not generate enough taxes, especially property levies, to cover the costs of public services. An industrial factory or a set of warehouses would help the tax base but a majority of the local citizens would find them esthetically unacceptable. An office park with appealing structures nestled among landscaped gardens and geese-filled ponds, on the other hand, would pass civic muster, especially since some of the locals would be likely to work there.

Even though the local governments are usually receptive to an office park proposal, they would insist on features that would minimize any negative impacts. Typically, they would have enough leverage to make that happen. As part of the rezoning negotiations, they might limit the buildings' heights, insist on an adequate number of parking places, require the developer to pay for turn lanes and traffic lights, and mandate a minimum ratio of open space to built environment.

Suburban Shopping Mall

As metropolitan areas expand, the exchange value of property on the periphery tends to rise. But in the inner suburbs, especially those with middle- and lower-middle income households, land is not selling for premium prices. If a local government's assessed valuation is stagnant or declining, this cuts into its tax base, reduces its service levels, and makes it less competitive in attracting and retaining residents.

Mall of America, Bloomington, Minnesota

Looking at its assets, the inner suburban municipality notes that it is still located within a densely populated area, with thousands of people within easy driving distance. Each individual household's purchasing power might be modest but, collectively, they constitute an appealing target for, say, chains like Marshall's or Wal-Mart. They can provide the anchor store for the mall, and then other smaller enterprises seeking similar consumers can occupy the remaining units.

A developer notes this potential win-win situation and sets out to broker a deal. The municipality cannot drive a hard bargain. There are many similar nearby suburbs and the market will not support a mall in each one. So, typically, the developer will want the city to go well beyond rezoning. Since, in an aging suburb, no individual tract provides enough space, tens or even hundreds of parcels will need to be assembled for the mall. The municipality will be asked to impose eminent domain, the power to take private property for the greater public good as long as a fair price is paid, to facilitate obtaining the site. That way a few stubborn homeowners cannot stall the project indefinitely, holding out for an exorbitant price.

The developer will also request that the city foot the bill for all the public improvements on or adjacent to the project including light fixtures, sidewalks, and turn lanes. This can be done by having the municipality agree that some or all of the additional tax revenues generated by the venture be dedicated to these enhancements for, say, the first ten or twenty years—a process called tax increment financing explained further in Chapter 14. In sum, it will only be by investing public funds along with the private dollars that the project will proceed.

Downtown Hotel

Unlike the subdivision in the exurban county and the office park in the outer suburbs, where the developer was the pursuer and the government the pursued, the roles are usually reversed for central cities. Just as the inner suburb had to use both its regulatory powers and its taxing authority to entice a shopping mall development, so a central city must step forward in order to make the financial numbers work for downtown developments.

Take a new hotel, for example. As cities compete for conventioneers, having sizable hotels with tens of meeting rooms and a splendid ballroom or two can be decisive. These features are loss leaders for the hotels. It is the sleeping rooms, restaurants, and bars which yield the revenues. So, increasingly, before agreeing to build a convention hotel, a developer will ask the city what it is willing to do to subsidize the project.

In addition to having eminent domain and tax increment financing as lures, cities can also place other inducements on the table. They might agree to float tax-exempt revenue bonds for an adjacent parking garage, removing that risk from the developer. They can often redeploy state or federal grants or tax credits to assist the effort, arguing that a hotel will provide service jobs for low-income households. They might increase the tax on hotel rooms but, at the same time, agree to allocate the extra funds to this initiative.

Marriott Convention Hotel, San Diego

The negotiations become a battle over whose funds are most at risk: private dollars invested by the developer and, perhaps, the hotel chain and public funds allocated both directly by the central city and indirectly through its access to state and national government sources. Developers want to have as little at stake as possible especially in central cities whose futures look less promising than their pasts. Cities see such facilities as critical to their downtown redevelopment efforts, know that public funds must be part of the mix, but are nervous about putting too great a share of their scarce public resources into any single endeavor.

The Growth Machine

All this development activity fuels what has come to be known as the growth machine. Who belongs? Everyone who benefits from land transactions. Besides the developers themselves and the participating governments, that includes real estate brokers, zoning attorneys, home and office builders, construction trade unions, road builders, concrete and lumber firms, banks, mortgage lenders, and more.

In an expanding metropolitan area, the growth machine seeks to accelerate the process, not only riding the wave but propelling it. In a steady state or declining region, it still stirs the land transaction pot. From its perspective, there is more to be gained in the short run—and the profit motive is preoccupied with immediate results—even if there is no net benefit for the metropolitan area. Sponsoring a development at the fringe, even if it means equivalent abandonment at the core, creates demand for all those who gain from the activity. As a result of this dynamic in all types of regions, some variation of the growth machine is part of every metropolitan area.[3]

Because county and municipality decisions, especially on zoning matters, are so central to making money from land deals, developers need more access to local elected officials than any other set of interests. So, not surprisingly, they are the largest single source of contributions to their campaigns.[4] This is especially so for central cities and urban counties where, as is the case at the state and national level, running for office has become an expensive affair. This edge in campaign finance gives the developers an advantage in any controversy framed as growth versus nongrowth.

THE WAR AMONG THE NODES

The growth machine is not monolithic, especially in the larger metropolitan areas. Although some of its members benefit no matter where growth occurs within the region—those supplying materials like bricks, concrete, and lumber being the best example—others have placed all or most of their stake in one of the nodes of development. They are not neutral about where development happens but, instead, want to tilt the process toward their part of the region. The conflict occurs in several arenas, most notably office space, shopping complexes, distribution facilities, and residential housing.

Office Space

Downtowns once dominated the office space market. Companies placed their headquarters and major branch offices there. Then those that served them—the banks, attorneys, accountants, advertising agencies, and so forth—located nearby. Thanks to the technology that enabled towering skyscrapers and high-speed elevators, all this could occur in a relatively small area. Urbanists called it agglomeration but that is just another term for hanging out together.

Skybridge in Downtown Minneapolis

The advent of edge cities and office parks has meant that the businesses which manage downtown buildings and operate the stores which service them no longer have a near-monopoly on what their industry terms Class A space, the kind of offices that prestigious firms want. To contend, they have both organized themselves into downtown associations and partnered with central city governments to fight back. Typically the approach is to use some mix of public and private funds to alter the "look" of downtown by, say, transforming some surface parking lots into small parks with benches, fountains, and statues. Another trend—Atlanta, Cincinnati, and

Minneapolis are examples—is connecting the office towers with above ground walkways, easing the ability to move from one location to another.

The edge city office groups are less political. They think demographic and social trends favor them and their best public strategy is to provide a gentle nudge here or there. They usually confine themselves to urging transportation improvements, such as redesigning a highway interchange or initiating a shuttle service to a light rail station, that enhance access to their buildings. At the same time, however, they are eager to have additional compatible development nearby. The greater the concentration of offices in their specific part of the region, the higher the magnetic attraction for further activity.

Shopping Complexes

Major department stores began downtown. Convenience matters when people decide where to shop and, prior to World War II, being near most of the offices and astride the public transit routes made the most sense. Suburbanization and automobiles changed all that, of course, and now each metropolitan area has numerous shopping malls. Some intentionally seek customers just from their immediate surroundings. If a movie rental store wants to broaden its market, it will open another outlet rather than attempt to get people to come to one place. But others are regional malls or groups of speciality stores (an antique district, for example) hoping to attract clientele from throughout the metropolitan area and, indeed, from outside the region as well. They wish to be a destination, a place where people plan to go to spend their disposable income.

Since retail trade produces both property tax revenues and, in most jurisdictions, sales taxes as well, the governments housing these complexes become allies in their quest for customer dollars. Public funds are often used to promote how enjoyable it is to come consume at our place. Central cities have redesigned parts of their downtown—the 16th Street Mall in Denver, for example—to make it more shopper friendly. As already discussed, municipalities will use tax increment financing and other tools to pay for public improvements, parking lots, decorative street lights, or stylish sidewalks, to enhance a mall or district's appeal. Advocating for this governmental support are both the shopping mall owners and associations representing the stores included in the complex or district.

Distribution Facilities

Metropolitan areas are the hub for storing and distributing an enormous array of products for both households and businesses. Although just-in-time manufacturing, a process where items (for instance, an automobile seat) go directly to a plant (an automobile assembly facility) without becoming inventory in some warehouse, is on the rise, still almost all consumer merchandise and much of business stock must stop someplace in between production and retail sale. The soap factory sends thousands of boxes of detergent to the warehouse where it is subdivided and then sent

Shoppers at Denver's Sixteenth Street Mall

off to hundreds of stores. On a daily basis, companies like Federal Express and UPS ship millions of packages, picking up widely, collecting them at a small number of sites, and then delivering broadly again.

Having warehouses within a local government can be a big property tax producer since both the buildings and the average level of the contents can be taxed as property. Many are therefore eager to furnish what the industry needs so that their jurisdiction becomes one of the handful of distribution sites within the region. Not surprisingly, the requirements include rezoning land, preferably flat, for one-story

A Distribution Facility in Oakland, California

structures covering an acre or more (moving things horizontally is easier than doing so vertically), wide roads for the trucks, and easy access to one or more transportation modes, especially interstate highways but also railroads, waterways, and airports.

Once there are two or more established distribution spots within a metropolitan area, they vie for influence over the future transportation agenda. Which way of spending the next round of infrastructure dollars, typically a blend of federal, state, and local funds, would help each site the most? Those initiatives which would shorten travel time in and out of their area, widening an interstate or constructing an additional bridge, are the ones they and their home governments will fight to have approved.

Residential Housing

Some builders specialize in large subdivisions on previously undeveloped land, usually at the region's periphery. Others emphasize smaller townhome and condominium projects, often in the more established suburbs. Still others stress affordable housing developments in the inner suburbs or the central city. And, finally, some emphasize rehabilitating homes in historic neighborhoods. All want more housing and are therefore part of a growth machine. But because they promote distinctive types of housing in different locations, they are frequently at odds about governmental priorities.

The subdivision developers want few restrictions, be it no limits on destroying trees when they bulldoze the site or at most modest fees to pay for the impact the project will have on other services. For the most part, they are looking for little more from local government than extending the normal goods and services to the new homes, preferably with a minimum of regulations.

All the other builders think the rules have made things too easy for those building subdivisions at the fringe and see themselves at a comparative disadvantage in the housing market. They plead with the older suburbs and central cities to do more to help them, both for greater equity and for reversing the outward migration. Among the requests: be more flexible with zoning requirements, allow higher building densities on smaller lots, discount the property tax bill for the first few years of ownership, urge state and national governments to increase tax credits for historical preservation, provide subsidized mortgages for firsttime homeowners. They might also join forces with these governments to make life more difficult for the exurban builders by, say, obtaining state legislation regulating open space development.

METROPOLITAN EXPANSION

Developers and their growth machine comrades are simultaneously involved in who does what to which land parcel within the metropolitan area and in what can be done to achieve a larger region, one with the added population and jobs which will enhance demand. Joining them in this external phase of the metropolitan chase are other enterprises, especially those whose economic well-being is inextricably connected with the region. These are major firms whose sales are disproportionately within the region and which would find it difficult or impossible to move.

Public Utilities

Although some metropolitan areas supply electricity and natural gas through government, most have publicly regulated but privately owned utilities. Telecommunications, everything from telephone lines to cellular towers, is almost exclusively within the business sector. Even if these firms are part of larger corporations, they have an enormous stake in the metropolitan region. Each has built an extensive distribution network—power lines for electricity, pipes for natural gas, and so forth—to deliver its product. If the region declines, if there are no longer as many industrial plants or residences connected to its grid, then the utility has excess capacity and lower profits. If the metropolitan area remains at its current size, the only way for the utility to make more money is either to make its production more efficient or to increase rates. The former is hard to accomplish and the latter requires government approval, typically at the state level, and is often a political challenge.

The clearest path to a better bottom line is to grow the market. The marginal costs of adding a subdivision or a shopping complex or an office park to the already existing network are modest but, since the going rates can be charged to the new customers, the resulting return is well above average. In earlier times, utilities—especially electric, natural gas, and telephone—often staffed the region's economic development efforts. As government became more involved, they are less often at the top of the hierarchy but they remain active participants in the process, with significant time from top management and meaningful contributions to promotional efforts. Since, with few exceptions, their territory includes all or most of a metropolitan area, they are neutral about where within the region development happens. Anywhere will do.

An Electric Grid in the San Francisco Area

Apart from their commitment to metropolitan growth, public utilities also have a continuing interaction, sometimes pleasant and other times testy, with counties and municipalities. In order to deliver their product, such as electricity or natural gas, they inevitably need local government permission to use public right-of-way for part of their network. Especially with power lines and telephone poles, this can create some delicate negotiations about what goes where. A municipality is concerned about esthetics: underground would be ideal but unobtrusive is second best. A utility is preoccupied with costs: above ground is cheaper and straight lines are simpler. So the negotiations begin.

In most situations, local general purpose governments are also empowered to grant franchises for electricity, natural gas, telephone service, and, in recent years, cellular phones and cable television. In order to do business in these commodities, the city or county must give formal permission which, typically, entitles a firm to exclusive rights for a lengthy time period. For all but cable, all that is to be determined is the price, such as a fixed annual fee or a percentage of each month's billings. The electricity company, for example, realizes that it is the only supplier and that, within reason, the municipality or county has to do business with it. Cellular phone companies, however, compete for tower locations, almost all of which require a rezoning decision.

The recent spotlight on local government-utility interplay has been on the cable television firms. In the 1970s and 1980s, depending on the metropolitan area, two or more companies competed for long-term franchises to provide service within a local government or, in some cases, a coalition of cities. Those contests created their own sparks, with more than a few elected officials indicted for accepting bribes, but the more recent disputes have been about access to the cables used to deliver the television signal. As the Internet has expanded, there is intense demand for ways to transmit enormous quantities of data swiftly and cheaply. Telephone lines, even those which are fiber optic and enhanced, are plodders in the cyberspace age. The cables, already in place, have exponentially higher capacity. But who controls Internet access to the cables? Is it the municipality which awarded the franchise or the company which received it? And should only one company be able to lease the cables for Internet purposes or, like highways, should they be common carriers, available to all at a set price? These issues are being debated and, one by one, resolved in metropolitan areas across the United States. The entire controversy has brought cyberspace to local government.

Mass Media

What the advertising industry calls a mediashed, the territory covered by a daily newspaper's circulation or receiving signals from radio and television stations, corresponds closely with the boundaries of a metropolitan area. Although newspapers charge for their product while radio and television stations distribute theirs free, all make most of their money from advertising. Those rates, in turn, are driven by the number of readers, listeners, and viewers. An expanding region bringing a larger audience is pure profit for an electronic outlet: its signal costs the same whether broadcast to 1 or 10 million. It is close to that for a newspaper since printing one more copy takes just a few pennies. A contracting area, conversely, does not lower expenses but does cut revenues.

This economic dependence on the metropolitan region's vitality presents a special dilemma for its daily newspaper(s). Journalistic tradition calls for critical coverage, telling it like it is, exposing corruption, and highlighting shortcomings. That is why the U.S. Constitution's First Amendment protects freedom of the press, a right interpreted broadly by the subsequent Supreme Court rulings.[5] Such naysaying, however, can damage a region's external image and demoralize its internal spirit, neither one beneficial for helping it expand. As a consequence, newspapers are apt to leaven derogatory comments with good news stories, some of which border on boosterism. The reporters relish being critics but the owners need to be cheerleaders and, at the end of the day, the paper contains some of each.

Radio and television stations are less bashful about the journalistic ethic although the pressure for audience ratings sometimes tempts them to sensationalize, giving prominent play to grisly crimes and sexual peccadillos, neither projecting a positive image. They are more receptive to using both their newcasts as well as other programs, including public service announcements, to promote the region, calling attention to its assets and trumpeting its successes. As a result, growth machine strategies that call for an active publicity effort can usually count on the mass media for enthusiastic coverage delivered at little or no cost.

Transportation Firms

Just as public utilities have massive investments sunk in metropolitan areas, transportation firms from all modes—air, barge, rail, and truck—have placed their corporate bets on certain regions. As the airline industry moved to a hub-and-spoke system, funnelling traffic from many locations through one or a few sites, having passengers change planes at the hubs, and then sending them off on another spoke to their final destination, they learned that this approach is most profitable when the hub location itself generates a significant amount of traffic, where it, in airline terms, is either the origin or destination for the journey.

Since the higher a region's income, employment, and population growth rate, the more origin-and-destination trips, this gives airlines a pivotal stake in their hub region(s). American Airlines worries about Chicago and Dallas and Miami, Delta about Atlanta and Cincinnati and Salt Lake City, Northwest about Detroit and Memphis and Minneapolis-St. Paul, and so on. This has transformed them into metropolitan boosters, placing their names on sports venues and participating in public-private economic development planning.

The rationale is similar, albeit less visible, for the other modes. The railroads have invested in freight yards, the trucking firms in transfer centers, and the barge lines in docking facilities. The greater a region's prosperity, the higher the return on these investments and so they, also, support programs which target economic expansion.

Transportation's joint interest in a bigger region does not inhibit each mode's contesting for what it thinks is its fair share of the public pie. The air, barge, and truck industries are especially dependent on public assistance for airport improvements, port expansion, and highway projects. Although most of the funds for transportation infrastructure come from the national government, it is priorities set by local governments and advocacy by those representing the metropolitan area in Washington which determine how they are allocated. Here, as elsewhere, almost all politics is local.

Banking

Before merger mania invaded the financial industry, with small banks being absorbed by mid-size companies which in turn were gobbled up by mammoth operations, each metropolitan area featured a few financial institutions which derived most of their business from within the region. Although capital now flows globally and, for most metropolitan areas, the banks are branches of mega-corporations like Bank of America, these local affiliates still depend partially on the region for their prosperity.

Banks make much of their money by attracting deposits—checking accounts, money market funds, and so forth—at one price and then lending the money to businesses and households at a higher rate. It is a volume business so more money being generated in a region equals increased deposits equals more loans equals higher profits. All this gives banks ample motivation to participate in the growth machine.

Loans carry the risk that they will not be repaid and, for those made within the metropolitan area, usually a meaningful share of the bank's portfolio, how well the loans perform depends partially on the overall health of the regional economy. Stagnant metropolises not only produce fewer deposits and lower requests for loans, both bad for the banking business, but they also place past commitments more in jeopardy. That is why banks often take the civic lead in helping shore up a slipping downtown or a failing neighborhood.

There is still another reason why banks have shifted some of their investments to low and moderate income areas. In 1977, under pressure from inner city advocates, the national government passed the Community Reinvestment Act (CRA). The earlier Home Mortgage Disclosure Act, enacted in 1975, had required financial institutions to reveal where they were making loans in order to detect whether certain areas were being "redlined," declared too risky for any investments. This was indeed happening and the CRA legislation mandated that banks make an affirmative effort to provide capital to these areas.[6]

LABOR UNIONS

Labor unions are technically membership organizations, not business enterprises. Nevertheless, since they organize people within industries and trades and then bargain collectively with employers about compensation and working conditions, they play an important role in the economic sector. Their business, if one can call it that, is selling human talent. About 12 percent of the U.S. work force belongs to labor unions and the proportion is a bit higher within metropolitan areas.

The construction trade unions—carpenters, ironworkers, pipefitters, and the like—are active in the growth machine. Their livelihood depends on building, especially new projects, and they eagerly participate in efforts to quicken the pace of development. Unions representing workers in industries like automobile assembly or chemical production are less likely to be involved but, along with their trade-craft siblings, most belong to the same umbrella organization, the AFL-CIO, and its metropolitan-level councils are usually included in systemic economic development initiatives.

Labor unions have other interests at stake within metropolitan regions. Local governments draft and enforce codes for both residential housing and commercial buildings. The tougher the regulations and the stricter the enforcement, the greater the need for skilled labor, especially that provided by the craft trades like electrical workers, plumbers, and roofers. For those special districts which are highly unionized or which are ripe for being organized, labor organizations often use both campaign contributions and membership mobilization to dominate the low-turnout elections for the district boards. In a low-turnout election, the norm for special district contests, a low profile but highly coordinated effort can yield effective control of a sewer district or transportation authority.

The strike, withdrawing their members from the work site, is the labor movement's ultimate weapon. Informational picketing, including asking fellow members not to patronize an offending enterprise, is also a hefty part of labor's arsenal. Both have their maximum effect when local police forces are at least neutral, allowing entrances to be blocked and permitting picketers to display signs at visible locations. To insure this evenhanded environment and possibly to shift it to a sympathetic setting, labor unions support local officials, both elected and appointed, who appreciate the movement and its objectives.

BUSINESS EXECUTIVES AS CIVIC LEADERS

Reaching the top in a multinational corporation is an impressive achievement in a capitalist society. From that pinnacle, one is encouraged to take a cosmopolitan view, extending beyond just profits. There is also an expectation that one's leadership talent, having already succeeded in the corporate world, also has something to offer the community. In nineteenth century small-town America, the "city fathers" included the community's small business owners. As metropolitan areas expanded, the city fathers became civic leaders.

Starting in the mid-twentieth century, groups began forming in many of the nation's metropolitan regions. Their membership was almost exclusively businessmen but these organizations shed the business label. In 1963, Banfield and Wilson noted that "the committees were something new in business-government relations—in that they consisted of a few 'big men'—who, far from regarding themselves as special interests, insisted that they served 'the public interest,' often at a considerable sacrifice of private, business interests."[8]

The names reflect this public orientation: the Allegheny Conference on Community Development (Pittsburgh), Central Atlanta Progress, Citizens Council

(Dallas), Civic Progress (St. Louis), Cleveland Tomorrow, Detroit Renaissance, Greater Milwaukee Committee, and the Phoenix 40 (now Greater Phoenix Leadership) are but some examples. Despite the sweeping titles, their memberships are numerically small and overwhelmingly corporate. Most have fewer than one hundred participants and, even when the size is greater (Dallas's Citizens Council, for example, has 250), a smaller executive committee exerts the most influence.[9] The executives are either the chief executive officers of locally headquartered companies or the heads of the branch operation in that region. Although the firms with the greatest stakes in the metropolitan areas, those most devoted to economic expansion, are usually the most active, those heading enterprises whose markets are largely outside their home town, such as an aircraft manufacturer or pet food producer, also join. Calls for either adding business members or diversifying participation are rejected as obstacles to achieving consensus and to acting swiftly.

The initial agenda for these groups was downtown revitalization and a few, most notably Central Atlanta Progress, have retained that emphasis. The others have broadened their geographic scale, now seeing themselves as metropolitan-wide, and have also cast their issue net more widely. St. Louis's Civic Progress, for example, now works in six arenas: education, racial harmony and equality, regionalism, community life, infrastructure, and business climate.[10] Growth machine objectives remain high on the priority list but they are now accompanied by social issues. That has placed the corporate leaders in unfamiliar territory. Economic development comes naturally to them but curing racism and reforming education are more alien. The solutions are murkier, the politics stickier, and the frustrations greater.

The groups operate behind the scenes with minimal publicity and highly controlled access. The region's newspaper publisher belongs to most of them but the reporters are not welcome. When stories about their activities do emerge, they are apt to be either speculative or bland public relations releases. Consensus is prized— public squabbling among corporate presidents would be unseemly—so controversial proposals are often sidetracked. Just as legislators engage in logrolling (you back my bill and I will support yours), so also corporate executives exchange favors, trading help with one pet project for assistance with another.

Because they include so many powerful people with immediate access to the funds and skills inside massive corporations, these groups can make a pivotal difference. If a referendum campaign for a stadium or convention center needs several hundred thousand dollars to persuade the electorate, they can furnish both the advertising talent to craft it and the funds to disseminate it. If a downtown renewal plan requires consultants for its preparation and clout for its implementation, they can do both. If a community cause, say curbing domestic violence, lacks visible sponsors and civic credibility, they can deliver that.

Alone within metropolitan areas, these groups are able to marshal resources swiftly and apply them expeditiously. This monopoly has made them a permanent part of the regional scene. As they reach organizational maturity—the Allegheny Conference is the oldest, formed in 1944, and others like Cleveland Tomorrow date back only to 1982—and as their importance becomes more widely understood, questions about their legitimacy arise. Why should a handful of corporate leaders meeting behind closed doors be such a powerful force in the community? This, in turn, has led to calls for the groups to open their meetings and diversify the membership. Although both steps might bring greater public acceptance, each would also erode the groups' ability to act rapidly.

DOES BUSINESS DOMINATE?

The answer is yes, sometimes, but not as frequently as some allege nor as often as in the past. Taking their intellectual cue from Marxist theory, many have argued that business ultimately rules everything that matters in a capitalist society.[11] Elected officials only appear independent on the surface. A close examination will usually reveal that they are but puppets on a string with their movements controlled by the corporate elite. Capital is the ultimate resource, those in charge of the means of production are at the top of the heap, and everyone else dances to business's tune. Those who think otherwise are naive idealists, according to this point of view.

This perspective has not held up well under close empirical scrutiny. Although business interests often get much of what they are after, seldom does it happen without some compromising with other concerns.[12] The growth machine is not an exclusively business club. Governments belong as well, using tax dollars and public authority on behalf of development. As will be described in the next two chapters, nonprofits and public-private consortia are also involved.

Why does business rarely dominate? Some of the reasons have been enumerated in the introduction to Part I. Businesses are preoccupied with profits and seek political power primarily in those situations where it is a necessary means for achieving that end. If an issue has little economic import, business is apt to take a pass. That is why in community disputes businesses are sometimes at the center of the action and, in other cases, nowhere to be seen. Businesses are aware that they lack a convincing answer to the who-made-you-king-or-queen challenge and are sensitive about public criticism, both because their skins are typically thinner than elected officials' and because open controversy might be bad for sales. Nor is business monolithic within a metropolitan area. There are many growth machines and different businesses may align with separate groups. Some are universal members but others pick and choose.

The biggest obstacle to business rule is that power is now too fragmented. In yesteryear's metropolitan area, where a majority of the people and most of the jobs were in the central city and the largest urban county, business could reign by controlling one or two governments. In some cases, the top corporate leaders accomplished that over a sustained period; the Citizens Council influence over Dallas city government is perhaps the clearest example,[13] and elsewhere they were able to prevail periodically.

Now that regions encompass many counties and numerous municipalities, along with special districts galore, there are hundreds of local governments and thousands of public officials. Getting all or most of them to move in the same direction, assuming it is one they are reluctant to follow, is impossible. With metropolitan

expansion has also come business differentiation. When just a few industries dominated the scene, they along with the standbys—banks and public utilities—found it
much easier to unite on a common agenda than today, when most metropolitan
economies are much more diverse.

NOTES

1. Harvey L. Molotch, "The City as a Growth Machine," *American Journal of Sociology*, 82, no. 2
    (September 1976), pp. 309–30.
2. John R. Logan and Harvey L. Molotch, *Urban Fortunes: The Political Economy of Place* (Berkeley:
    University of California Press, 1987), pp. 1–2.
3. John R. Logan, Rachel Bridges Whaley, and Kyle Crowder, "The Character and Consequences of
    Growth Regimes: An Assessment of Twenty Years of Research," in *The Urban Growth Machine*, ed.
    Andrew E. G. Jonas and David Wilson (Albany: State University of New York Press, 1999),
    pp. 73–94.
4. Arnold Fleishmann and Lana Stein, "Campaign Contributions in Local Elections," *Political Re-
    search Quarterly*, 51, no. 3 (September 1998), pp. 673–89; and John H. Mollenkopf, *A Phoenix in
    the Ashes: The Rise and Fall of the Koch Coalition in New York City Politics* (Princeton, NJ: Princeton
    University Press, 1992).
5. *New York Times vs. Sullivan*, 376 U.S. 254 (1964), for example, requires public officials to establish
    both error and intent when suing for libel.
6. Gregory D. Squires, ed., *From Redlining to Reinvestment: Community Responses to Urban Disinvestment*
    (Philadelphia, PA: Temple University Press, 1992); and Anne B. Shlay, "Influencing the Agents of
    Urban Structure: Evaluating the Effects of Community Reinvestment Organizing on Bank Resi-
    dential Lending Practices," *Urban Affairs Review*, 35, no. 2 (November 1999), pp. 247–78.
7. *Union Membership and Earnings Data Book* (Washington: The Bureau of National Affairs, Inc.,
    1998).
8. Edward C. Banfield and James Q. Wilson, *City Politics* (Cambridge, MA: Harvard University Press
    and the MIT Press, 1973), pp. 267–68. For a more recent perspective, see Rosabeth Moss Kanter,
    "Business Coalitions as a Force for Regionalism," in *Reflections on Regionalism*, ed. Bruce Katz
    (Washington: Brookings Institution Press, 2000), pp. 154–81; and Richard A. Shatten, "Cleveland
    Tomorrow: A Practicing Model of New Roles and Processes for Corporate Leadership in Cities,"
    in *Cleveland: A Metropolitan Reader*, ed. W. Dennis Keating, Norman Krumholz, and David C. Perry
    (Kent, OH: Kent State University Press, 1995), pp. 321–31.
9. *Taking Care of Civic Business* (Grand Rapids, MI: Frey Foundation, 1993), pp. 22–3.
10. *A Vision for Civic Progress* (St. Louis, Missouri: Civic Progress, 1998).
11. At the national level, see C. Wright Mills, *The Power Elite* (New York: Oxford University Press,
    1959). For an application to an urban setting, consult Floyd Hunter, *Community Power Structure*
    (Chapel Hill: University of North Carolina Press, 1953).
12. Susan S. Fainstein and others, *Restructuring the City: The Political Economy of Urban Development* (New
    York: Longman, 1983); Barbara Ferman, *Challenging the Growth Machine: Neighborhood Politics in
    Chicago and Pittsburgh* (Lawrence: University Press of Kansas, 1996); and John H. Mollenkopf, *The
    Contested City* (Princeton, NJ: Princeton University Press, 1983).
13. Darwin Payne, *Big D: Triumphs and Troubles of an American Supercity in the 20th Century* (Dallas, TX:
    Three Forks Press, 1994); and Warren Leslie, *Dallas, Public and Private: Aspects of an American City*
    (Dallas, TX: Southern Methodist University Press, 1998).

SUGGESTED READINGS

EPSTEIN, EDWIN M. *The Corporation in American Politics*. Upper Saddle River, NJ: Prentice Hall,
    1969. After three decades, this remains the most thoughtful treatment of this complex
    and understudied topic.
FERMAN, BARBARA. *Challenging the Growth Machine: Neighborhood Politics in Chicago and Pittsburgh*.
    Lawrence: University Press of Kansas, 1996. Probes the dynamics between business
    motives and neighborhood interests in two major cities.

KANTOR, PAUL. *The Dependent City Revisited: The Political Economy of Urban Development and Social Policy.* Boulder, CO: Westview Press, 1995. Portrays the interplay between economic and governmental interests in U.S. metropolitan areas, arguing that business usually has the upper hand.

LOGAN, JOHN R., and HARVEY L. MOLOTCH. *Urban Fortunes: The Political Economy of Place.* Berkeley: University of California Press, 1987. The classic analysis of land as the centerpiece for much of what happens in metropolitan areas.

MOLLENKOPF, JOHN H. *The Contested City.* Princeton, NJ: Princeton University Press, 1983. A thorough study of development policy in Boston and San Francisco with special attention to the impact of national policies.

DOING IT

To understand development fully, one has to appreciate the art of the deal. Here are two ways to gain some insights into the process where land goes from one use to another, preferably a more lucrative or, in the jargon of planning, its "highest and best" purpose:

1. Identify a land development transaction which has recently been completed in a nearby metropolitan area. Some of the more juicy can be found by scanning press coverage. Check both the major daily newspaper as well as the suburban journals. The latter often devote ample space to describing all the twists and turns of projects in their areas. Using the media coverage, interviews with participants, and public records (they will probably be at the county courthouse), prepare a synopsis of the deal's key components: Who was the seller? How had the seller been using the property? Why did they sell? Who was the buyer? What is the proposed new use for the parcel? What public decisions by which governmental units had to be made in order for the transaction to occur? How controversial were these rulings? Who, if anyone, opposed them on what grounds?

2. Find a piece of property (mininum size: five acres) in a nearby metropolitan area which you think is underutilized. What changes would you make in order for the land to have greater economic value? Why do you think your proposal is a winner? What approvals from which governments would you need in order to implement your plan? What arguments would you use to obtain these endorsements?

CHAPTER 4

The Nonprofit Sector

THE RISE OF THE NONPROFITS

Americans resist expanding government to tackle many of the social needs in a metropolitan area. At the same time, individual actions, what the bumper sticker calls "random acts of kindness," are not enough, especially as communities become more complex. Filling this gap is a hybrid entity, created privately to achieve public goals, that is known as a nonprofit organization. These organizations do many things: revitalize neighborhoods, deliver social services, provide health care, produce art, advocate for social change, and give away money.

How can you identify a nonprofit organization? The species has six distinctive characteristics. Nonprofits are "formally constituted, private as opposed to governmental, not profit-distributing, self-governing, voluntary, and of public benefit."[1] What once was individual charity has become organized, outside the governmental apparatus, restricted from making excess money, allowed to have its own board of directors, dependent on others for financial and human support, and charged with improving the community.

There are about 1.4 million nonprofits in the United States and the typical metropolitan region has several thousand.[2] A majority are outwardly oriented, dispensing some community service like health care or providing some public good such as a theater performance. They are the ones most relevant for matters metropolitan. The remainder are inwardly directed, serving their members. Examples include garden clubs and credit unions. Religious congregations straddle both dimensions, tending both to their members' spiritual lives but, for many faiths, also administering to the temporal needs of a larger clientele.

The nonprofit sector has been expanding at a much faster pace than either the public or business segments. Between 1977 and 1994, the annual growth rate in employees was 3.3 percent for nonprofits compared to 1.9 percent for business and 1.4 percent for government.[3] Excluding religious groups, the number of nonprofit agencies has more than doubled during the past twenty-five years.[4] When a metropolitan area determines that an issue like housing or health care demands more public attention, the responding organizations are more likely to be nonprofit agencies than to be governmental units.

Nonprofits depend heavily on governments, businesses, and individuals. Although many charge for their services—school tuition, hospital fees, and so forth—these payments cover just 39 percent of the costs for the average nonprofit.[5] They require public subsidies and private support to make ends meet. Governments give them tax breaks with local government's primary contribution being an exemption from property taxes. State and national governments are even more helpful. Most nonprofits qualify for tax-deductible contributions, a category known as 501(c)(3), after that part of the federal tax code bestowing such status. For a person or corporation in, say, the 30 percent income tax bracket, this means that the federal government is picking up that portion of the donation. These gifts also qualify for deductions in most states. Governments also make grants to nonprofits and pay them to provide selected services.

Corporations step in with over $5 billion a year.[6] Businesses typically prefer this approach over taxes in fulfilling their community obligations. Not only are the contributions deductible but they can be targeted. Taxes go into a government's general revenue fund and it is the political process, not the corporation, which determines where they are spent. With donations, businesses can decide precisely how and where the funds are applied. If a corporation is a major donor for some nonprofit, it can exercise control over the agency's policy agenda and operating style.

Individuals do their part, volunteering time and contributing gifts. A recent national survey shows that over half of adult Americans volunteer for a nonprofit and more than two-thirds give money to one or more.[7] The cumulative hours translate into the equivalent of more than 9 million full-time employees while the giving totals more than $100 billion, about three-fifths for religious groups and two-fifths for all other nonprofits.[8]

This dependence on just about everybody makes the nonprofit world highly competitive. Even though all of the rhetoric and much of the activity is about serving the community, that only happens if the organization survives. That imperative creates still another set of contests within the metropolitan chase. First, by segment, nonprofits vie: arts organizations for audiences, faith groups for congregations, hospitals for patients, schools for students, and social service agencies for clients. Second, they fight for dollars, with the skirmishes occurring for governmental grants, corporate donations, and individual gifts. Third, they compete for volunteer hours and board members. The former round out the staffing needed to execute the mission while the more prestigious the latter (that is, the corporate CEO is better than an assistant vice president) the greater access to financial support. This ongoing struggle motivates nonprofit agency directors and other top managers to be intensely involved in community life.

The metropolitan area, in turn, relies significantly on nonprofits. About half the nation's hospitals and universities are nonprofits. Although elementary and secondary education is largely a governmental service, with only about one in ten attending private and parochial schools, that fraction is slowly rising. Nonprofits dominate the arts and cultural arena and the delivery of social services.[9] If and when change occurs in many parts of metropolitan life—revitalizing neighborhoods, expanding health care, enlivening the arts, strengthening education—chances are that much of it will happen with and through nonprofit organizations. Without securing their cooperation and engaging their skills, it is difficult to alter a region's well-being. Although the government and business sectors possess more power and their leaders dominate the commander corps in the region, the nonprofits include most of the troops, the rank and file who occupy the trenches and execute the orders. This chapter will consider neighborhood associations, social service agencies, faith-based congregations, advocacy groups, and philanthropic foundations. Arts and cultural organizations and hospitals will be discussed, respectively, in Chapters 9 and 11.

NEIGHBORHOOD ASSOCIATIONS

Strategic Setting

Neighborhood nonprofits represent turf, primarily within central cities. The modern incarnation had its origins in the 1950s, as the inner core struggled with housing deterioration and economic decline. Those neighborhoods suffering the most, as well as some others, became the unwilling victims of progress. Often written off as total losses, mayors and others would designate them for "urban renewal," bulldozing several square blocks of dilapidated buildings ("slum clearance") and replacing them with industrial plants or public housing. As routing decisions were made for the interstate highways being constructed during this period, these downscale neighborhoods became prime targets for being paved over by expressways.[10]

City governments had apparently abandoned them, trading them off for economic development initiatives or federal projects, so these neighborhoods formed associations, often assisted by professional community organizers.[11] Since many were African American, the growth of the civil rights movement in the 1960s brought some political and financial support from the federal government, much of it connected to President Lyndon Johnson's War on Poverty. If these areas had lost their political clout locally, they could at least attempt to recoup some support nationally, seeking funds and programs to help them recover.

Not only had these neighborhoods lost their local political leverage, the private market had also deserted them. The growth machine was ignoring them, failing to invest any new capital and withdrawing maintenance support from existing structures. Realtors were not recommending their neighborhoods, banks were redlining them, commercial enterprises were bypassing them.

The prevailing response to these challenges has been to establish a nonprofit entity, most often called a community development corporation (CDC). Part of its mission resembles a suburban municipality's: retain and recruit residents, attract shoppers, and develop jobs. The other component, since it is not a government itself, is to advocate for more public support, be it from the national, state, or local level.

There are upwards of two thousand CDCs or their equivalents in U.S. metropolitan areas, according to a 1998 census conducted by the National Congress for Community Economic Development. Although that number is not precise, it is considerably higher than the list identified just three years earlier.[12] Not every neighborhood has one nor do they all use the same label. They range from one-person operations to a few with hundreds of employees.

Activities

Housing has become the top activity of most CDCs.[13] This takes many forms: rehabbing structures, managing rental property, generating new units, counseling homeowners and rentors about property maintenance, seeking capital, and everything else needed to sustain the neighborhood's residential stock. When most effective, the approach is comprehensive: sound structures, adequate financing, active promotion, responsible owners or tenants, skilled maintenance. CDCs have learned if one or more of these is absent, housing quality slips. Unless they can stabilize the area's residences, all else will be lost.

The housing thrust links with a social goal: restoring confidence in the neighborhood. These areas have often lost their sense of community. The CDCs organize block parties, neighborhood festivals, and other upbeat events to generate pride and establish personal networks. They implement self-help programs where residents exchange services like babysitting and housecleaning. Externally, they carry the message to lending institutions, media outlets, elected officials, and anyone else who will listen that, yes, the neighborhood went through some tough times but now things are getting better, justifying political backing and economic investment.

Especially when they have experienced success in restoring the residential base, CDCs work on commercial development. Most inner-city neighborhoods once had a thriving retail strip; part of the comeback strategy is to restore it with tools like rent subsidies and joint promotions and, wherever possible, using local residents as owners and employees. If residents must go elsewhere for everyday items like laundry, prescriptions, and fast food, their dollars are helping another neighborhood rather than buttressing their own. The bootstrap approach is to keep those purchases in the immediate vicinity.

Governance and Funding

With their ideological roots in the 1960s, the theory underlying CDCs is that their boards of directors will be primarily local residents.[14] People will empower themselves, taking control of their own destiny and, through the CDC, itself a hybrid public-private enterprise organized as a nonprofit, govern much of the neighborhood's activities. The reality, based more on a few case studies than systematic analysis, suggests that the boards are much less of a factor.[15] Board members, largely from low-income households, lack the discretionary time to develop comprehensive plans. Even if they did, they lack the wherewithal to implement them which, almost by definition for an inner city neighborhood, must largely come from outside sources.

Instead the CDC agenda is driven more by the professional staff, responding strategically to public and private funding opportunities. Acting collectively, CDCs and allied organizations have helped pass legislation in both Washington and many state capitals which either provide grants or tax credits for housing and other projects. As the U.S. Department of Housing and Urban Development, administrator for most of the federal funds, writes and interprets guidelines for this legislation, it simultaneously influences what CDCs will do since, to survive, they need this support.

Banks and foundations, sometimes acting alone but also operating through national consortia, have also become places where CDCs go for money. The largest of these groups is the Local Initiatives Support Corporation (LISC), based in New York City. It distributes hundreds of millions of dollars annually for a wide range of CDC projects. LISC backing is a prestigious stamp of approval and those CDCs fortunate enough to receive it have been able to parlay it into even more investments from other governments and business organizations.

All this means that the CDC staff must be intensely entrepreneurial, both politically and economically. They must navigate state capitals and federal bureaucracies, local banks and national foundations, central city governments and private investors, all while keeping their boards informed and managing the projects already underway. With the demands intense and the pay low, it is not surprising that turnover is high.[16] This instability in CDC leadership weakens its capacity to achieve its potential.

These neighborhood associations' hands-on approach, putting down roots in the area, establishing boards, and rallying the residents often creates an uneasy relationship between them and central city elected officials. Although councilpersons and mayors appreciate assistance in improving their constituencies and applaud the CDC efforts, they realize that these nonprofits have created a separate force for advocating for the neighborhood, an effort which plays out in many public and private arenas. No longer is the councilperson necessarily the one to see if a resident needs something. Perhaps the CDC staff will be more likely to deliver results. When neighborhood associations exist, determining who really represents the area is a much murkier task.

SOCIAL SERVICE AGENCIES

Strategic Setting

Nonprofit social service agencies address social needs that governments do not wish to handle directly, although they may pay part of the expenses, and that businesses think are not profit making. There are many such needs within metropolitan areas, from adoption to youth development, and thus there are hundreds of nonprofits seeking to meet them. Even though a disproportionate share of their energies is aimed at the poor, a group concentrated in the central cities and inner suburbs, their programs and services are found throughout the metropolitan region with many targeted toward middle class households.

Although the desire to serve motivates social services agencies, the wish to survive preoccupies them. To maintain and possibly expand their organizations, they

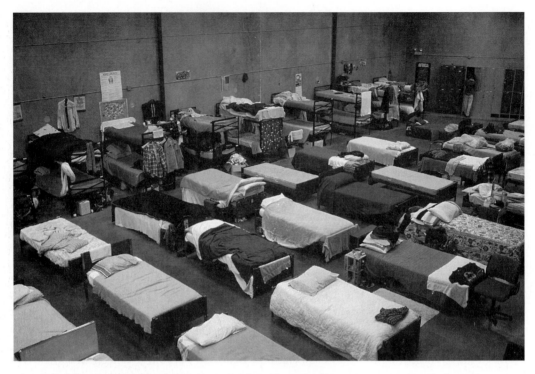

A Homeless Shelter in Contra Costa County, California

vie with their counterparts for community support. This competition occurs both between problems and within them and is carried out largely through the media and within funding agencies. Each attempts to make its part of the human condition the most worthy without disparaging other endeavors. The Humane Society explains how a pet brings meaning to a senior's life, the Girl Scouts stress how their programs transform girls into productive women, the Red Cross emphasizes how it is swiftly there when disaster strikes. Accompanying these messages are compelling photographs: the adoring dog, the freckle-cheeked girl, the rising floodwater. Just as businesses use advertising to place their products in the most attractive light, so too nonprofits strive to position their mission in the best setting.

Within segments, social service agencies stress the same items as private enterprises: innovative techniques (our substance abuse program has the lowest recidivism rate), customer satisfaction (you are valued client and not just a case number), accessibility (call the hotline for immediate attention), and cost-effectiveness (over 90 percent of donations are spent on service delivery and less than 10 percent on administration).

As circumstances change, social service agencies, at least the successful ones, adapt. If a new problem arises, existing organizations will add programs to their portfolios. If enough do not, then nonprofit entrepreneurs will fill the gap, forming still another subset. The emergence of AIDS in the 1980s, for example, spurred the development of agencies to address the special counseling, dietary, health care, and housing needs of those with this condition.

Activities

Even an incomplete list of social service agencies is lengthy: adoption, counseling, day care, disaster assistance, family planning, food pantries, homeless shelters, legal aid, mental health, nonhospital health care, refugee assistance, substance abuse treatment, vocational rehabilitation, and youth development. For some, day care is one example, the agencies often compete with for-profit businesses like Kindercare. For other services, such as disaster assistance, they complement governmental agencies: Red Cross and the Federal Emergency Management Agency (FEMA) are both apt be on the scene of a major flood. And for still others, refugee assistance for instance, nonprofits are essentially the sole provider.

Although there are a few national giants (Boy Scouts, Girl Scouts, Red Cross, and the Salvation Army are the most notable) in the social service field, most of it is highly fragmented. The mergers and acquisitions that have led to concentration within the business sector have yet to affect the nonprofit world. Agencies tend to be small and specialized, usually by the type of problem they address but sometimes by the age group they serve. A mental health organization serves both children and adults but only provides a limited number of programs. A youth development agency, conversely, delivers a wide array of assistance to a single age segment.

This social service fragmentation often leads to calls for enhanced collaboration or outright consolidation. Both public and private funders express concern about duplication of services (does a metropolitan area need ten separate adoption agencies) and excessive overhead (ten agencies have ten executive directors while one agency needs just a single head). Although multiplicity seems inevitable among local governments for reasons discussed in Chapter 2, and competition is prized in the business arena as part of what makes a free market economy tick, competition is not considered a virtue in the nonprofit sector. No matter. Once born, social service agencies resist death—and there inevitably are entrepreneurs with other brilliant ideas for solving problems, creating still more organizations.

Since social services are and will remain scattered by speciality, style, and location across a metropolitan area, anyone needing several types of assistance must approach many agencies. A recovering alcoholic goes one place for his treatment program, another for temporary housing, and still another for emergency food. One-stop shopping is a rarity. So, to address this gap, still other agencies form to help clients navigate their way through the social service maze.

Governance and Funding

Compared to private corporations, the boards of directors for social service agencies "are larger, with fewer insiders, more conflicted and more involved in operations."[17] The twenty to thirty members typically include a range of occupations, with lawyers and accountants for professional advice, wealthy individuals for fundraising assistance, other nonprofit executives for management counsel, and academic specialists for programmatic oversight.

Compensation is psychic, not financial, and most board members have a passion for the agency's mission. Although they share a commitment to the agency's goals, they often disagree about the best means for pursuing them, a condition that both generates disagreements within the board and sometimes between the board and the staff. The boards are self-perpetuating, with the members determining the length of terms and selecting replacements.

Boards define the mission and, increasingly, develop strategic plans to achieve it. They play an active role in raising funds, they hire and sometimes fire executive directors. The latter oversee day-to-day operations and juggle management responsibilities with board relations. Most frequently, the executive director is a professional in the agency's line of work, a psychologist for a mental health unit or a social worker for an adoption bureau. This makes them quite knowledgeable about program delivery but often less experienced in managing an organization, creating still more dependency upon and possible friction with the board.

Although social service agencies are most often portrayed as administering to the needy, only about one-quarter have that as their number one objective.[18] By definition, poor people do not pay their own way. Nonprofits must either be paid by governments or through gifts for servicing low-income residents. This occurs for programs which are politically popular or for recipients who have fundraising appeal. Otherwise, fees must be paid and nonprofits must attract clients who can afford their services. All this means that social service agencies must compete for revenues in three distinct markets: government spending, charitable contributions, and individual fees.

FAITH-BASED CONGREGATIONS

Strategic Setting

Sixty-one percent of Americans say religion is very important in their lives, 68 percent belong to a church or synagogue, 47 percent attend services either every week or almost every week, and 66 percent agree that religion can help answer all or most of society's problems.[19] The nation has almost 300,000 religious congregations with about 200,000 in metropolitan areas.[20] It is difficult to go more than a few blocks without passing by a place of worship.

All faiths compete for followers, each one claiming that *it* offers the best path to eternal salvation. For a minority of these religions, that consumes essentially all of their energies. Their creeds stress preparing for the next life and discourage active involvement in secular matters. As organizations, they opt out of the metropolitan chase. But most Americans belong to faiths which "perceive the here and now of the world as the main arena of God's redemptive activity, and humankind as the primary agent of establishing God's kingdom on earth [and] . . . achievement of a more just and humane society is a high priority."[21] These outwardly oriented congregations, mostly Judeo-Christian in the American context, engage their regions, expressing concern about the public sector's fixation on power and the business segment's pre-occupation with material gain.[22] They seek to emphasize larger concerns: adherence to a moral code, the duty to help others, support for the community.

Activities

Religious congregations strive to shape the public moral code in their regions.[23] On issues such as pornography and hate crimes, they present a relatively united front, speaking out against zoning ordinances which allow strip clubs or adult bookstores near residential neighborhoods and decrying doing harm to people based solely on their ethnicity or lifestyle. But on many questions, faiths differ on what is morally correct. Some believe in gay rights, supporting ordinances forbidding discrimination based on sexual preference, while others consider homosexuality a sin, arguing for regulations which discourage it. Some regard abortion as murder while others place higher value on a woman's right to choose. In these matters, religious congregations are active participants in the debate, rallying around one side or the other, but the contest is as much within the faith community as it is between religion and secular life.

Church of St. Paul & St. Andrew Food Pantry in New York City

Believing that assisting the needy is important for salvation, religions both preach the word, encouraging others to act charitably, and do the deed, sponsoring many of the social service agencies described in the preceding section. They are frequent advocates for allocating more public and private funds for the less privileged. Demonstrations on behalf of the homeless or hungry are apt to include many religious leaders. Within their own faiths, they operate a wide range of human services and health organizations and approximately nine out of every ten congregrations have some involvement in these arenas.[24] Their presence in delivering programs for the needy creates complications, given the First Amendment's establishment clause. Religious-based social service agencies have much to offer but there is ongoing concern that public dollars as well as some private donations be spent only for secular purposes, assisting clients rather than spent on promoting dogma. The congregations often see these two goals as intertwined while the grantors want them to be separable.

Religious congregations emphasize building communities. They frequently are leaders in the alliances to form neighborhood associations, including community development corporations. Older residential areas often have high concentrations of people of a particular faith. Their place of worship, more than any other structure, symbolizes the neighborhood. Its identity and future becomes linked with the neighborhood's. If the neighborhood deteriorates and people depart, it is less likely they will return for services, threatening the congregation's survival. Understanding this, the church or synagogue becomes the center for revitalization efforts, providing space and mobilizing residents.

Working through alliances, sometimes within a single denomination and in other instances across faiths, congregations also seek to develop a greater sense of community within the larger metropolitan region. The most common pattern is for affluent congregations to partner with low-income ones. The religious organizations realize that governmental structures reinforce economic and racial segregation. Redistribution from the better off to those less endowed is not apt to happen through local governments. Nor is understanding between the races likely to improve when there is little or no interaction between groups. By having rich congregations link with poor, white worshipers with black congregants, greater bonding can occur. For these religions, building community, a sense that everyone is their neighbor's keeper and that people are not islands unto themselves, is an article of faith. In implementing that belief within metropolitan areas, these religious consortia work to fashion a more expanded sense of connection, providing a centripetal counterweight to the other public and private centrifugal forces with regions.

Governance and Funding

For most religions, the clergy have more influence than the laity. In the more hierarchical faiths, Roman Catholicism for example, the regional bishops and archbishops are the principal spokesmen. Parish priests can play a significant role, but they must operate within boundaries set by their leaders. In the more decentralized religions such as most of the mainstream Protestant denominations and Judaism, each congregation is largely on its own. The local minister or rabbi establishes the tone and steers the efforts. Here the laity are a greater factor since, if their clergy stray too far from the followers, the congregation is apt to seek another leader.

Priests, ministers, rabbis, and other religious leaders can be potent forces in any debate. In addition to being well-educated and highly motivated, they are much more credible than elected officials and business leaders when they claim to have the community interests as their sole concern. Only they can enlist the blessing and authority of a higher being when arguing on behalf of their position. Given their status, secular leaders are reluctant to attack clergy, giving them even more ability to have their message heard unchallenged.

Religious congregations raise revenues primarily from their own members, spending about three-quarters on internal operations for the congregation and one-quarter on community matters.[25] Since Americans contribute generously to their faiths, this latter amount totals upwards of $20 billion annually. In a metropolitan area with 1 million people, that external commitment translates into about $75 million each year.

ADVOCACY GROUPS

Strategic Setting

Interest groups play a key role in the U.S. political process at the national and state levels and they are also important within metropolitan areas. Political parties are relatively weak, especially at the local level where many elections are nonpartisan. If individual organizations want to have their interests adequately recognized in metropolitan policy making, they must band together with others who share their goals and objectives.

Some metropolitan interest groups are affiliates of state or national organizations such as local chapters of the American Association of Retired Persons or the Sierra Club. Others are home grown with titles, often containing phrases like "Alliance for" or "Citizens for" or "Coalition for." Most are relatively permanent, representing ongoing concerns for segments such as children, the mentally ill, or persons with disabilities. A fewer number come and go, coalescing around a single episode, perhaps an initiative to build a new bridge or an effort to oppose a proposed shopping center.

A majority of interest groups within metropolitan regions avoid characterizing themselves as such. They think they will be more effective if they are perceived as something else, a factor which accounts for the frequent use of "citizens" in their titles. Although the laws and regulations governing the 501(c)(3) organizations permit spending part of their budgets on lobbying without losing their tax deductible status, the fear that too much overt politicking will both threaten this provision and also tarnish their image causes them to prefer calling their efforts "educational" rather than "political."[26]

Activities

Local interest group activity targets both public opinion, especially among the 10 to 20 percent of the population most attentive to metropolitan issues, and metropolitan leadership, including both elected officials in the public sector and corporate executives in the business community. These two objectives interact. Influencing public opinion generates demands that leadership do something and, if top officials are to move ahead, they appreciate efforts to produce a sympathetic audience.

The public opinion ventures focus on the metropolitan mass media. Invisibility is an interest group's nightmare. If there are no stories about the mentally ill in the newspaper or the late evening television news, then those not directly affected by it are likely to forget that it requires public funds and private donations. Effective advocacy groups have a media strategy that includes staged events ("new study shows 28 percent of metropolitan residents suffer from depression") and opportunistic interpretations ("recent killings might have been avoided if there were more mental health funding").

The groups pepper public officials and business executives with information about why their issue is one of the keys to improving the metropolitan region. Often wrapped in scientific language, full of statistics from commissioned studies, these communications stress how, say, helping people with disabilities become more independent will strengthen the region or how, to take another example, lowering air pollution is critical for future economic development. The more aggressive organizations become involved, albeit subtly and at some distance, in recruiting candidates for office and supporting their campaigns. The group's own funds are not used, as that would violate their 501(c)(3) status. Instead, board members will host fund-raisers, inviting the group's constituents to contribute as individuals, or preferred candidates will be invited to address the organization's annual meeting, giving them favorable exposure and implying that they support the group's agenda.

Most advocacy efforts emphasize mobilizing friends and persuading the undecided. Punishing enemies, working for the defeat of an elected official or spreading negative publicity about a corporation, is generally seen as counterproductive, especially in the long run. This is especially the case with the more permanent groups which realize that advocacy never ends, that some skirmishes are lost while others are won, and that today's opponent might become tomorrow's ally.

Governance and Funding

Professional staff drive advocacy strategy with occasional volunteer assistance from board members. The competent interest groups are led by persons who understand media routines, political processes, and civic leadership. These individuals combine a passion for the issue with, typically, past experience working with or for government. Advocacy boards might be as occupationally diverse as social service agency boards, but they share a deep commitment to the issue. As a result, they are more unified behind their executive directors unless, in their evaluation, they are not making enough headway.

Most of the funding comes from membership dues with some occasional assistance from foundation grants. Because contributions are tax deductible, advocacy groups are an attractive financial alternative for issue supporters to advance their convictions. Unlike giving money to a candidate, where there is no tax benefit, the national and state government is subsidizing between 20 and 40 percent of the donation. There are also no limits on the amount given—federal and some state candidate campaigns do have caps—and that makes advocacy groups an appealing place for wealthier individuals. More than a few metropolitan interest groups are bankrolled by one or two families.

PHILANTHROPIC ORGANIZATIONS

Just as elected officials seek votes for political capital and businesses approach venture firms for economic capital, social causes solicit philanthropic foundations for social capital. The politician with a better idea markets it to voters, the businessperson with a new product goes after investors, and the nonprofit organization with an innovative way to improve the community woos a foundation.

There are many available for courting, almost 50,000 in the United States. In 1999, they collectively distributed $22.8 billion and had assets valued at $385.1 billion. Even after discounting for inflation, both giving and endowments have doubled in the past ten years and the absolute number of foundations has increased two-fold in the last two decades.[27] Three types of foundations have special relevance for metropolitan areas: independent, community, and corporate. In addition, another type of giving—federated funding—plays an important role in regional activities.

Independent Foundations

This segment dominates the foundation world, possessing about 80 percent of the assets and distributing over 70 percent of the grants. Theirs are the names—Ford, Kellogg, MacArthur—which come to mind when thinking about large-scale philanthropy. Most have a national or international agenda steering their grant decisions and, in some instances, this plan has a metropolitan component. For example, the Annie E. Casey Foundation emphasizes welfare-to-work programs, the Robert Wood Johnson Foundation stresses health care, and the Pew Charitable Trust civic engagement. In addition, many often pay special attention to the metropolitan areas where they are headquartered such as the Lilly Endowment in Indianapolis, the Ewing Marion Kauffmann Foundation in Kansas City, the Pew Charitable Trust in Philadelphia, the Richard King Mellon Foundation in Pittsburgh, the Danforth Foundation in St. Louis.

There is no universal formula for obtaining funds from independent foundations. Most take an active stance toward giving, seeking recipients willing to go in directions the foundations find desirable. They do not sit back passively, waiting for intriguing ideas to persuade them. This gives them a pivotal role in determining which policy innovations will be tested within metropolitan regions and makes their top officers and program directors a behind-the-scenes influence on policy change.

Although these foundations give multiyear grants, sometimes for as long as five or even ten years, they are reluctant to be obligated indefinitely. They see their contributions as getting a project off the ground and underway, not as a subsidy lasting forever. They will support the invention and the initial application but not the permanent implementation. From their perspective, some other entity—perhaps government or a lower-ranking philanthropy—should pick up the slack after the their risk capital has demonstrated a program's viability.

Community Foundations

Community foundations provide an umbrella under which small and medium donors can use a single organization to manage their contributions and oversee their allocation. A bequest of $1 here and a gift of $50,000 there can be combined into a single entity. Only New York's and Cleveland's have more than $1 billion in assets, but even the modest-sized ones make millions in grants in the larger metropolitan areas. In 1999, as a group, they gave out $1.68 billion.

These donations are much more diversified than those from independent foundations. Some donors remain actively involved in how their gifts are allocated while others let the foundation decide but limit its options to a particular field of interest or one or two organizations. Only part of their portfolio is unrestricted, able to be dispersed according to the preferences of the directors and the professional staff. Even these funds are scattered over a wider range of areas, ranging from the arts to social services.

Corporate executives are overrepresented on the community foundation boards of directors and the foundations frequently have close links with trust operations, a major referral source for donations. But the governance also includes other groups and, in recent years, there has been more concern about race and gender diversity. All this reinforces a giving pattern that, first, can be all things to all people and, second, will not create unwelcome controversy.

Corporate Foundations

Third are corporate foundations, especially relevant for firms headquartered in the region or which have a substantial presence there. Most large private enterprises recognize an obligation to spend a modest portion of their profits on community needs. In 1999, the slightly more than two thousand corporate foundations spent $2.99 billion, much of it within metropolitan regions. Among those giving more than $25 million annually are AT&T, Bank of America, GTE, SBC Communications, UPS, and Wal-Mart.

Prior to the past decade, corporate foundation gifts had a haphazard quality, changing with the predilections of board members and top executives. Much of the funding went to their favorite projects and what was left over was scattered among safe and proven recipients. More recently, corporations have begun to define their foundations as part of the firm's overall strategy and seeking a funding plan that advances the business's goals and objectives. Fannie Mae Foundation, the arm of a leading secondary mortgage corporation, supports housing research, GTE Foundation emphasizes mathematics and science education, and the Wal-Mart Foundation features scholarships in the thousands of communities having Wal-Marts. In addition to these thrusts, the corporate foundations reserve part of their allocations for grants to established institutions such as symphonies, universities, and zoos. Even here, however, the principal criterion is what improves the firm's image, not what does the most good.

Federated Funding

Federated fundraising is when many organizations band together to make a joint appeal for their causes. It might be all the charities within a religious denomination, such as the United Jewish Appeal, or all historically black colleges and universities, working together through the United Negro College Fund, or a group of arts and cultural agencies, making a combined solicitation to support their efforts.

The best known and most widely found federated funding operation is the United Way, comprised of hundreds of chapters. Virtually every metropolitan area has one and, collectively, they raise more than $3 billion annually. They often dominate social-service giving within their regions and have become a de facto metropolitan department of social welfare, deciding which programs and what needs are most deserving.

Corporations and their executives wield significant control over United Ways.[28] They occupy more places on the boards of directors, have many of their subordinates serve as "loaned executives" to help with the fundraising, and oversee the allocation process. From the United Way's perspective, corporations bestow a marvelous

The United Way of America: The Leading Federated Funder

benefit: workplace giving.[29] Instead of having to solicit people over the telephone or in their homes, corporations allow the United Way to make their request on the job site. Even better, corporations offer their employees an easy payment carrot ("we'll deduct a small amount each week from your paycheck"), a civic-minded message ("give your fair share"), and, for middle and upper management, a competitive stick ("leaders in our company are among the most generous in the corporate sector").

United Ways do redistribute wealth. On average, donors have more income than do recipients. But it is establishment-style philanthropy with the civic notables deeply involved in raising the funds and deciding how to spend them. This places social-service agencies wishing to share in the bounty in a subservient posture. They are well advised to have corporate executives on their own boards of directors, giving their organization added linkages to United Way funding but simultaneously extending the corporate reach into the social-service arena. It is also prudent for them to avoid controversial programs and negative publicity, to be seen as part of the solid mainstream rather than a component of the radical fringe. Boy Scouts, for example, prosper while abortion providers languish.

Once a United Way fund has instituted a distribution pattern, it does not change dramatically from year to year. Nonprofit agencies come to expect their annual grant plus a little for inflation, much the same as governmental bureaus anticipate receiving last year's appropriation with a cost-of-living factor. This makes it difficult for an emerging need, AIDS for example, or a new agency with an innovative approach to break into the particular local United Way circle. It happens but modestly and slowly.

NONPROFITS AND THE FUTURE

Although most nonprofits were born within the last century-and-a-half, the nonreligious ones, as organizations, are adolescents or young adults, and their role within metropolitan areas grows steadily. The fact that they are neither fully public nor completely private makes them initially an oddity, but when it comes to doing something collectively at the local level, nonprofits are the primary organizational force.

To date, those becoming nonprofit staff executives have arrived there more by accident than by design. They began as service deliverers and, as their careers evolved and their entity expanded, became agency managers. It is only recently that heading nonprofits has become recognized as a profession, complete with baccalaureate- and professional-degree programs to prepare cadres for their roles.

As that happens, the competition among nonprofits, focused more on who gets what within the region than on the contest among metropolitan areas, will likely intensify. Better trained leaders will be more aggressive and more strategic. Instead of passively waiting for the other two sectors to turn to them for implementing their public and private agendas, they will accelerate their efforts to have government and business increase their support. Although revenue dependence will indefinitely constrain nonprofits and prevent them from being equal players on the metropolitan stage, their stature will mature over time.

NOTES

1. Lester M. Salamon, *America's Nonprofit Sector: A Primer* (New York: The Foundation Center, 1992), pp. 6–7.
2. Virginia A. Hodgkinson and Murray S. Weitzmann, *The Nonprofit Almanac 1996–1997: Dimensions of the Independent Sector* (San Francisco: Jossey-Bass Publishers, 1996), pg. 25. Altering definitions, for example, by counting all the YMCA branches in a community separately instead of treating them as one organization would increase this estimate. The 1.4 million includes religious congregations.
3. Ibid., pg. 3.
4. Ibid., pg. 14.
5. Ibid., pg. 159.
6. Ibid., pg. 81.
7. *Giving and Volunteering in the United States* (Washington: Independent Sector, 1999).
8. Salamon, *America's Nonprofit Sector,* pg. 20.
9. Ibid., Chapters 5 to 9.
10. Alice O'Connor, "Swimming Against the Tide: A Brief History of Federal Policy in Poor Communities," in *Urban Problems and Community Development,* eds. Ronald F. Ferguson and William T. Dickens (Washington: Brookings Institution Press, 1999), pp. 96–97.
11. The organizers' handbook was Saul D. Alinsky's *Reveille for Radicals* (Chicago: University of Chicago Press, 1946). For a recent update, see Mark R. Warren, *Dry Bones Rattling: Community Building to Revitalize American Democracy* (Princeton, NJ: Princeton University Press, 2001).
12. *Tying It All Together: The Comprehensive Achievements of Community-Based Development Corporations* (Washington: National Congress for Community Economic Development, 1995).
13. Sara E. Stoutland, "Community Development Corporations: Mission, Strategy, Achievements," in *Urban Problems and Community Development,* eds. Ferguson and Dickens, pg. 202.
14. Milton Kotler, *Neighborhood Government: The Local Foundations of Political Life* (Indianapolis, IN: The Bobbs-Merrill Company, 1969), pp. 81–87.
15. See, for example, Randy Stoecker, "The CDC Model of Urban Redevelopment: A Critique and an Alternative," *Journal of Urban Affairs,* 19, no. 1 (1997), pp. 1–22; and Rita Mae Kelly, *Community Control of Economic Development: The Boards of Community Development Corporations* (New York: Praeger, 1977).
16. Norman J. Glickman and Lisa J. Servon, "More than Bricks and Sticks: Five Components of Community Development Corporation Capacity," *Housing Policy Debate,* 9, no. 3 (1998), pg. 513.
17. Sharon M. Oster, *Strategic Management for Nonprofit Organizations: Theory and Cases* (New York: Oxford University Press, 1995), pg. 76.
18. Lester M. Salamon, "Social Services," in *Who Benefits from the Nonprofit Sector?* ed. Charles T. Clotfelder (Chicago: University of Chicago Press, 1992), pg. 149. Also see Elizabeth T. Boris and C. Eugene Steuerle, eds., *Nonprofits and Government* (Washington: Urban Institute Press, 1999), Chapter 6.
19. These estimates are from a March 17–19, 2000 survey of a probability sample of 1,024 Americans conducted by the Gallup Organization and reported by them in a March 24, 2000 press release.
20. Virginia A. Hodgkinson, Murray S. Weitzmann, and Arthur D. Kirsch, *From Belief to Commitment: The Activities and Finances of Religious Congregations in the United States* (Washington: Independent Sector, 1988), pg. 7.
21. David A. Roozen, William McKinney, and Jackson W. Carroll, *Varieties of Religious Presence: Mission in Public Life* (New York: Pilgrim Press, 1988), pg. 35.
22. Meredith Ramsay, "Redeeming the City: Exploring the Relationship Between Church and Metropolis," *Urban Affairs Review,* 33, no. 5 (May 1998), pp. 595–626.
23. Elaine B. Sharp, "Culture Wars and City Politics: Local Government's Role in Social Conflicts," *Urban Affairs Review,* 31, no. 6 (July 1996), pp. 738–58.
24. Hodgkinson, Weitzmann, and Kirsch, *From Beliefs to Commitment,* pp. 18–22.
25. Hodgkinson and Weitzmann, *The Nonprofit Almanac 1996–1997,* pg. 11.
26. Bob Smocker, *The Nonprofit Lobbying Guide: Advocating Your Cause and Getting Results* (Washington: Independent Sector, 1991).
27. *Foundation Growth and Giving Estimates: 1999 Preview* (New York: The Foundation Center, 2000). All the foundation statistics in this section come from this document.
28. Eleanor L. Brilliant, *The United Way: Dilemmas of Organized Charity* (New York: Columbia University Press, 1990), pp. 162–68.
29. *The Future of Workplace Giving* (New York: The Conference Board, 1994).

SUGGESTED READINGS

BRILLIANT, ELEANOR L. *The United Way: Dilemmas of Organized Charity* (New York: Columbia University Press, 1990).

CLOTFELDER, CHARLES T., ed. *Who Benefits from the Nonprofit Sector?* (Chicago: University of Chicago Press, 1992). Discusses nonprofit's role in health services, education, religion, social services, arts and culture, and philanthropy.

FERGUSON, RONALD F., and WILLIAM T. DICKENS, eds. *Urban Problems and Community Development* (Washington: Brookings Institution Press, 1999). Essays and commentaries on community development corporations and their housing, educational, jobs, and business initiatives.

KEATING, W. DENNIS, NORMAN KRUMHOLZ, and PHILIP STAR, eds. *Revitalizing Urban Neighborhoods* (Lawrence: University Press of Kansas, 1996). Several case studies on how nonprofit associations have led neighborhood improvement efforts.

SALAMON, LESTER M. *Partners in Public Service: Government-Nonprofit Relations in the Modern Welfare State* (Baltimore, Maryland: The Johns Hopkins University Press, 1995). Essays by the leading scholar on the linkages between nonprofit organizations and the public sector.

SMITH, STEPHEN RATHGEB, and MICHAEL LIPSKY. *Nonprofits for Hire: The Welfare State in the Age of Contracting.* Cambridge, MA: Harvard University Press, 1993. Incisive analysis of the competition among nonprofits in securing public funds for social services.

DOING IT

What is your United Way up to? What are its priorities and how, if any, have they changed during the past five years? Which organizations have broken into the funding flow? What issues and interests do they represent? Who are the members of the Board of Directors? What are their firms or organizations? Who has headed the fundraising drive in each of the last five years?

The answers to these questions will say much about social service trends in your community, what needs are considered important to meet and which merit less attention, as well as who is making the decisions about these matters. The most straightforward way is to obtain this information from the United Way reports, which should be available by contacting their office. The allocations are sometimes published in the major metropolitan newspaper although this practice is not universal.

CHAPTER 5

The Civic Sphere

WHO'S IN CHARGE?

The best short answer to "who's in charge?" in any metropolitan area is "nobody." The search for a dominant source of control, be it a visible governmental unit or a behind-the-scenes business elite, will have a fruitless end. Governments are fragmented and divided, businesses are far from monolithic and are also preoccupied with profits, and nonprofit organizations are immersed within their specific issues and absorbed with financial survival.

If no single entity rules a metropolitan area, how do decisions affecting all or most of the region get made? Which interests using what processes determine what will happen? These questions cannot be answered uniformly for all metropolitan areas but the range of possibilities can be described—going from regions where nobody really means nobody, to those which have a series of ad hoc arrangements, to those with an established set of routines.

Nobody Means Nobody

In some metropolitan areas, each set of interests goes about its own affairs, interacting primarily with those within its own arenas. In the words of Norton Long, it is the "local community as a ecology of games."[1] Financial institutions compete for deposits and loans, churches contest for congregations and contributions, governments for residents and revenues, and so forth. Each game has its distinctive rules, some formal and others informal, and an accepted way of keeping score.

As Long put it, "individuals play in a number of games, but, for the most part, their major preoccupation is with one, and their sense of major achievement is through success in one."[2] Bankers focus on profits, clergy on donations, and politicians on votes. Players cross boundaries to seek some assistance within their own contests. Bankers seek deposits from local governments and elected officials solicit campaign contributions from financiers. But these interactions are occasional rather than routine and motivated by competition within their own primary game more than an attempt to influence the outcome of another's game.

There is no metropolitan game as such. None of the region's interests has such a contest as their fundamental activity. What passes for regional decision making is simply the accidental by-product of the interplay among and between each of the analytically separate but empirically overlapping games being played out upon and within the metropolitan area's territory. Just as the interactions among wildlife and plants in a forest is a natural ecology, unguided by any overriding force, so, too, the interplay among and between economic, political, religious, and other games within the metropolitan region is a social ecology, undirected by any political or economic Wizard of Oz.

"Take us to your leader."

Source: CartoonStock

As metropolitan areas become more complex, regional policy making is rarely a pure ecology of games. The enhanced national and international competition among metropolitan areas has awakened some forces within each region to think, at least some of the time, about what the metropolitan area as a whole should do. Nevertheless, estimates about the amount and scale of regional decision processes are often exaggerated and, within all metropolises, some of the metropolitan outcomes remain the unplanned consequences of interactions among the many games rather than the intended result of a defined policy process.

Ad Hoc Arrangements

Many metropolitan areas are able to separate local issues, such as whether to have a recreational facility in one of its counties, from regional concerns, such as whether to expand the international airport at its current site or instead build a new complex. This local-regional sorting is not always perfect, especially when apparently minor judgments affecting only one part of the region, say locating an industrial plant, turn out to have significant impacts on the whole, such as by pushing the region's air pollution past what the federal standards allow. But for the most part the leaders have learned to identify regional problems and label them accordingly.

What this local-regional distinction has not accomplished is a constant routine for making metropolitan decisions. Any one of the local governments, a county for example, has a reasonably predictable process for deciding whether to add a community center. The formal rules are set out in the county charter and the informal norms, the ways in which the county executive and council members negotiate, is familiar for the involved players. Businesses and nonprofit organizations with a stake in the issue know whom to lobby and when to make their appeal.

For regional issues, the decision-making process mechanism must be designed anew for each topic. There is no constant or even semipermanent way to decide. The policy-making venue changes with each problem and even the same type of issue, education or health care, might be dealt with differently from one year to the next. Nor does the cast remain the same as players come and go, depending on the particular circumstances. Exurban county commissioners might be included in the debate about one regional matter but excluded from the discussion about another, even though both affect their jurisdiction.

Established Routines

On some issues in certain metropolitan areas, regional decision making has become more predictable. This is usually because some combination of public governments, private businesses, and nonprofit organizations has coalesced, succeeded in having its way on some matters, learned that cooperation has advantages for all the involved parties, and developed procedures for sustaining their hegemony. These coalitions are often called "regimes," defined by Clarence Stone as "the informal arrangements by which public bodies and private interests function together in order to be able to make and carry out governing decisions."[3]

When such regimes exist, their major components are usually the largest local governments, the central city and the urban county, and the principal corporations, especially those with a significant stake in the region's economic well-being. Non-profit organizations, if part of the regime, are more likely to be junior partners, benefiting from the regime's agenda and providing it with community support.

The regimes are not monolithic power structures, controlling all or most of what happens in their regions. They are more fluid patterns of cooperation with a core membership and, on particular matters, some more temporary participants. They do not have an unblemished record of success. They never include all the power sources within a region and sometimes they fail to accomplish parts of their agenda. Even if the regime encompasses a majority of the region's political power and economic influence, fragmentation within metropolitan areas enables less robust interests often to keep something from happening. But, over time and on the whole, the regimes win more often than they lose.

Deciding Regionally

During the past forty years, as the need for metropolitan-wide policy making has grown, it occurs more in some places and in certain ways than others in the civic sphere. All metropolitan areas have metropolitan planning organizations which often take the policy lead on issues like transportation and the environment. Two regions—Minneapolis-St. Paul and Portland—have established metropolitan councils that deal with a limited range of policies. An increasing number of regions have formed citizens leagues, nonprofit entities which propose regional policies and advocate for their adoption, and most have established metropolitan-wide leadership programs. Several have initiated visionary processes to develop and implement a regional agenda. Most have been more self-conscious about improving their collaborative skills, drawing lessons from past successes and failures to do a better job of working together. In some regions, state governments have reintroduced themselves into metropolitan policy making, using their ample powers to spur change. The remainder of this chapter will examine these approaches, each part of the civic sphere.

METROPOLITAN PLANNING ORGANIZATIONS

The Beginnings

In the early 1960s the national government decided that greater coordination was needed within metropolitan areas to assure that federal dollars for selected programs were spent efficiently. After the urban vote had provided the narrow margin for John F. Kennedy's presidential victory in 1960, grant-in-aid programs for metropolitan areas were expanded, receiving more funds and covering additional needs.

Concern arose among federal officials that both political conflicts and program duplication might occur if the national government dealt separately with various units within any given metropolitan region. This was especially so for transportation programs but other initiatives, including sewers and water supplies, hospitals, and land conservation, were also involved.[4] Bureaucratic agencies had a structural answer: mandate a clearinghouse, a metropolitan planning organization (MPO), for each region which would screen and coordinate local jurisdictions' applications for various programs. All this culminated in the Intergovernmental Cooperation Act of 1968 and its implementing marching order, Circular A-95 produced by the Office of Management and Budget.[5] Accompanying this stick—if you want federal assistance, obtain MPO approval—was a carrot: federal agencies initially paid for most of the staffing expenses and still cover a significant fraction.

In metropolitan areas already having voluntary associations of elected officials, usually called councils of governments (COGs), they typically became the MPOs.[6] In regions not possessing a council, the newly formed MPO also became, de facto, the council of governments. MPO's governing boards consist of elected officials, usually at least one from every county government within the region, as well as a few from municipalities. Some assign equal votes to each jurisdiction, regardless of its population, while others weight votes by the number of residents.[7]

Influence: Up, Down, Rebound

Flush with federal funding, staffed by capable professionals, and governed by local officials eager for grants-in-aid, MPOs quickly became a major factor in most regions in the 1970s in those policy areas—air quality, housing, transportation, and water quality—where the national government mandated intrametropolitan coordination. Aiding this influence was the MPO's near monopoly on relevant information and policy analysis. Issues like environmental quality and transportation planning are inordinately data dependent and most MPO staffs used their deep familiarity with the subject matter to affect outcomes.

MPOs received a triple blow from the Reagan Administration in the early 1980s, causing their power to plummet. First, many of the grants-in-aid programs coordinated through MPOs were either eliminated or reduced. Metropolitan regions were told, in effect, that they could sink or swim on their own. They should not expect the federal government to fuel their prosperity or salve their wounds. Second, the A-95 review authority was shifted from the national government to each of the fifty states. For the remaining federal programs, it was less necessary to have MPO's blessing. Local counties and municipalities could use their existing relationships with state officials to bypass the MPO. Third, the national government slashed funding for staff, reducing it from 60 to 80 percent of the budget to less than half. Since, at the metropolitan level, MPOs are volunteer associations, this meant they had to ask their constituent governments to make up the difference. Most counties and municipalities refused, staffing levels declined, and policy expertise, a key MPO asset, dwindled.

Fortunes changed when the national government passed the Intermodal Surface Transportation Efficiency Act in 1991. More commonly known by its acronym, ISTEA, and its spoken equivalent ("ice tea"), this legislation made fundamental changes in how federal transportation funds are allocated. First, it allowed metropolitan areas to shift dollars from highways to mass transit and environmental improvement programs rather than having specific amounts in each category. Second, it advocated coordinating transportation planning for all modes (air, rail, road, water) within a metropolitan area. Third, it required broader public participation in the planning process. Fourth, and most relevant for MPOs, it made them the focal point for reaching transportation and environmental decisions within each region. ISTEA's successor legislation, the Transportation Equity Act for the Twenty-First Century (TEA-21), has retained these features and upped the appropriation by over $30 billion annually.[8]

ISTEA's and TEA-21's proponents include environmentalists, who seek to link transportation funding to air-quality improvement, state and local governments, who desire greater flexibility in spending federal dollars, and mass transit suppliers and operators, who want a greater slice of the transportation pie. Highway interests, those who pour the concrete and build the bridges, have been mollified by greater overall support for transportation funding. Even though the highway share is now at risk and could be lower, the larger funding for transportation in general more than makes up for it.

Although ISTEA and TEA-21 has only modestly helped MPOs with their staffing needs, it has made them the center of action for increasingly important transportation and environmental decisions within metropolitan areas. Along with the stricter requirements for citizen involvement, this has raised their policy-making profile and allowed them to reappear as a notable part of the civic sphere.[9] They are the only place where a region's top elected executives meet regularly on substantive matters. Although they come primarily because millions of federal dollars are at stake, debates about highway initiatives and mass transit routes which affect the development patterns within the region, the MPO also provides opportunities to discuss other cross-jurisdictional questions. In addition, their staffs have become the leading specialists on what is happening regionwide on a broad range of issues, collecting and analyzing data, publishing and disseminating reports.

MPOs also have clear limitations. They continue to owe their existence to federal mandates, making them more imposed upon the region rather than springing up from within it. Their staffs have dual governmental masters: national regulations and a local board. To the extent that they must remind the region what the federal government will allow, they are not unlike colonial administrators representing the home country. Their effectiveness is also hampered in some metropolitan areas by being understaffed or by not having a single MPO for the entire region.[10]

METROPOLITAN COUNCILS

City-County Consolidation

As metropolitan areas expanded in the 1950s and 1960s, the initial proposed response toward achieving greater interregional cooperation was to merge the central city with the larger county within which it was located. At that time, typically three-quarters or more of the residents and an even higher share of the economic activity would then be contained within the merged jurisdiction. By combining the two, the surviving unit would encompass most of the metropolitan area. With two exceptions—Minneapolis-St. Paul and Portland—including additional counties within the region was not on the reform agenda.

Between the late 1940s and the early 1970s, approximately fifty consolidation efforts made it to the voter approval stage.[11] Twelve were endorsed and implemented while the remainder were defeated. Only two of the twelve were in larger metropolitan areas: Jacksonville and Duval County (1968) and Nashville and Davidson County (1962). A third major city-county consolidation occurred between Indianapolis and Marion County in 1969 but Indiana's statutes did not require voter approval, and the state legislature could and did take the final action. Earlier (1957), Miami had become part of a municipal federation within Dade County. Louisville and Jefferson County broke the three-decade drought when voters approved their merger in 2000 but, with this exception, no central city has merged with its home county, attempts are rare, and even smaller consolidations are infrequent.[12]

The city-county consolidations generally broadened the area for services like planning, transportation, and sewers and gave more power to the countywide elected executive and legislative council. They avoided heavily redistributive policies where revenues from the more affluent portions subsidized services from the low-income neighborhoods. All tightened the linkage between paying property taxes and receiving quid-pro-quo services and each retained some elements of choice in their service delivery.[13]

As competition among metropolitan areas heated up in the past three decades, the three original city-county consolidators—Indianapolis, Jacksonville, and Nashville—have fared well. All have attracted additional status symbols—each now has a National Football League franchise—and each has had above-average economic growth. The evidence is strong, if not fully conclusive, that the consolidations have made it easier for these regions to devise and execute strategic plans.[14] Nevertheless, as their regions expand, the consolidated government represents a decreasing share of the metropolitan area. Jacksonville/Duval still contains 71 percent of that region's residents, but Indianapolis/Marion is down to 54 percent and Nashville/Davidson to 47 percent. In today's and tomorrow's metropolitan world, it takes more than one county to encompass the region.

Twin Cities Metropolitan Council

Just as the federal government was the impetus for establishing metropolitan planning organizations, the State of Minnesota sparked the formation of the Metropolitan Council of the Twin Cities Area (TWMC). With the state capitol located within the region, interests preferring a more regional approach found it politically easier to use the state legislative route rather than, say, merging counties or combining Minneapolis and St. Paul to achieve their goals.[15]

The TWMC started as a super-planning agency, charged with producing metropolitan policies for the seven-county region. The immediate task was unifying wastewater collection and treatment, and the infant organization met the challenge.

◢◢ Metropolitan Council

The Twin Cities Metropolitan Council Logo

Its proposal to institute a separate Metropolitan Waste Control Commission was implemented, exchanging an ad hoc combination of smaller sewer systems and septic tanks for a single seven-county operation.[16] The TWMC's portfolio also includes transit, parks and open space, housing, land use planning, and tax assessment practices.

Throughout most of its existence, TWMC proposed and other agencies disposed, creating what John Harrigan calls "a bifurcated model," where the TWMC developed metropolitan policies and then worked with special districts, counties, and municipalities to implement them.[17] The state legislation governing TWMC gives it leverage over these other units with a mix of appointing authority, veto power, and funding authorization. As a result, it has been a planning agency with some teeth to make its proposals reality.

In 1994, the TWMC took over the mass transit and wastewater special districts, giving it an even greater role in metropolitan decision making. It "moved the council from a $60-million-a-year regional planning agency, with loose supervisory control over regional agencies, to a $600-million-a-year regional government directly operating regional sewers and transit systems."[18] Unlike any other metropolitan area, the TWMC places under one roof two of the largest special district functions along with much of the region's planning responsibilities.

Despite several attempts to make its governing board an elected body, the TWMC remains an arm of the State of Minnesota. The legislature dictates what it can and cannot do and the governor appoints each of the sixteen members of the board, each representing an equally populated district with the metropolitan area. As of 1994, the governor also has the power to remove board appointees, giving that office even more control over the TWMC. Instead of having locally elected officials run a metropolitan council, it is the governor who simultaneously becomes the chief elected executive for the entire state as well as the power behind the scenes for a major metropolitan entity.

Portland Metro

Like the Twin Cities Metropolitan Council, Portland Metro combines the MPO planning role with special district responsibilities but, unlike it, Metro has an elected board and executive, making it the only regional government entity in the United States where the leaders are chosen directly by the people. Covering three counties (Clackamas, Multnomah, Washington) in the Oregon portion of the Portland MSA, a jurisdiction encompassing about two-thirds of the region's population, it has a seven-member board, picked by district, and an executive elected at large. The contests are nonpartisan and the terms extend four years.

Metro evolved from the Metropolitan Services District (MSD), an appointed body authorized by the Oregon legislature in 1969 and approved by the voters in 1970. Its initial responsibilities focused on watersheds and solid waste and, at the same time, a separate regional transportation agency, Tri-Met, was formed. In 1978, again with state legislative and electoral endorsement, MSD assumed additional responsibilities, most notably the MPO planning function and regional land use planning.[19] On a more revolutionary note, the board (then twelve members) changed from being appointed by local governments to being directly elected, giving it an independent bond with the people rather than an indirect link through other elected officials.[20]

The next step came in 1992 when the electorate approved a home rule charter, expanding MSD's powers and changing its name to Metro. It now continues to do the MPO planning for transportation and land use, manages regional parks and open space, and oversees facilities such as a performing arts center, a sports venue, the convention center, and the zoo. It also directs solid waste disposal and recycling programs and administers the tourism recruitment effort.

These duties alone make Metro one of the two most truly regional governments in the United States but its potential scope far surpasses its current reach. Its charter gives it additional authority, starting with explicitly allowing it to take over the regional transit system. Even more sweeping are the preamble's rhetoric ("to establish an elected, visible, and accountable regional government") and the body's powers, most conspicuously Section 5 giving it jurisdiction over "those matters the council determines to be of metropolitan concern." Although Metro currently relies on earmarked property taxes and fees, the charter empowers it, with voter approval, to impose income, sales, or property taxes. The biggest check is a limitation on taking over any service currently provided by a local government without joint approval from the Metro Policy Advisory Council, a group of county and municipal elected officials, and the electorate.

CITIZENS LEAGUES AND LEADERSHIP PROGRAMS

Citizens Leagues

Metropolitan planning organizations, city-county consolidations, and metropolitan councils are all public sector responses to enlarging the civic sphere. MPOs are universal but their influence is limited, city-county mergers are rarely even proposed any more, and the Twin Cities and Portland metropolitan governments are "widely praised but never copied."[21]

Why has the governmental reform approach to greater metropolitanism lagged during recent years? One reason is that there is often no organized group advocating for more regionalism. Local governments, business interests, and nonprofit organizations each lobby for their own agendas within the metropolitan area, but there are precious few speaking out on behalf of the entire region. After studying several metropolises, Neal Peirce noted that "in place after place we have been struck by the logic of creating some form of region wide citizen organization working for the shared and common good over pressure from special interests and parochial positions of fragmented local governments."[22]

Two metropolitan areas, Cleveland and Minneapolis-St. Paul, have had viable citizens leagues for many decades. Others have been formed more recently such as in Cincinnati, Indianapolis, Jacksonville, Kansas City, Oklahoma City, and St. Louis. Unlike the narrower advocacy groups described in Chapter 4, these groups express interest in a range of issues rather than confining themselves to one or two. Membership is either exclusively or primarily individual-based, open to any regional resident at nominal dues. The leagues are self-governing and independent of associations such as chambers of commerce or MPOs, each of which sometimes has citizen advisory or engagement arms. Membership typically numbers between 1000 and 3000, with well-educated residents heavily over represented.

Their mission statements stress regionalism, policy innovation, and citizen participation. The Minneapolis-St. Paul Citizens League "promotes the public interest . . . by involving citizens in identifying and framing critical public policy choices, forging recommendations, and advocating their adoption" while FOCUS St. Louis's says its goal is "to create a cooperative, thriving region by engaging citizens in active leadership roles to influence positive community change" and that its core values are "citizen involvement, quality leadership, regional perspective, diversity, community consensus, and focused outcomes."

Most citizens leagues employ a task force method, with a group of citizens studying an issue for six to eighteen months, determining both what *is* and proposing what *should be*. The league then issues a report and, within limited organizational resources, works to have its recommendations adopted and implemented. Topics include substantive policy areas, such as crime, education, housing, transportation, and so forth, as well as structural changes like governmental reform and collaborative ventures. The Citizens League in the Twin Cities, for example, urged several of the changes in that area's metropolitan council.

Their public style features compatibility and rationality. Threats for resisting recommended changes are never made. Reports are expected to stand or fall more on the quality of their reasoning, not the extent of subsequent arm twisting. This approach fits comfortably with the members' self-image as reasonable people striving to identify the region's interests. It also avoids embroiling the league in nasty public controversies which might make it seem too partisan and also threaten funding support from foundations and corporations.

As they try to achieve regional policies that serve the greater good, as they see it, the leagues continuously must deal with the tension between engaging a diverse citizenry and proposing meaningful reforms. If they do not broadly involve people, then it is hypocritical for them to wear the "citizens" label and they risk being called elitist. But if they do not produce change on at least some of their initiatives, then they hazard becoming seen as idle debating forums. To date, few critics have challenged their citizenship credentials, despite having membership less than 2 percent of the region's population and unrepresentative of those with lower education or those who live on the periphery, and the leagues have tended to place more emphasis on policy advocacy.

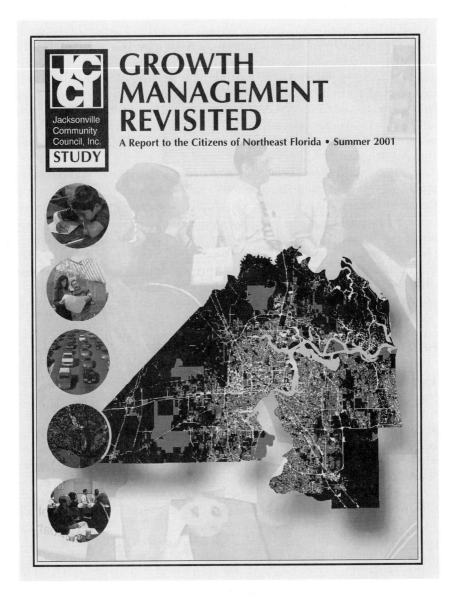

GROWTH MANAGEMENT REVISITED

Jacksonville Community Council, Inc. STUDY

A Report to the Citizens of Northeast Florida • Summer 2001

A Recent Jacksonville Community Council Citizens Task Force Report

Leadership Programs

A vibrant civic sphere requires leaders from all sectors who are comfortable with one another, understand the needs and perspectives of each interest within the region, and have polished skills needed to identify the common ground. To cultivate such individuals, many metropolitan areas have during the past few decades founded some type of regional leadership program, typically entitled Leadership Atlanta or Leadership Charlotte or Leadership Louisville.

These programs convene fifty or so leaders from all parts of the metropolitan area. The list includes elected officials, school superintendents, nonprofit directors, corporate executives, judges, and partners from the major law firms. They go through a year-long program, featuring a mixture of retreats, policy briefings, experiential learning, skill building, and small group discussions. Leadership Atlanta's goals are typical: "grow in awareness and understanding of the challenges and issues facing the community, . . . develop valuable contacts and communications networks within the community, . . . ready the participants for other leadership opportunities."

The aim is to grow a leadership cohort filled with people who can become as effective in achieving regional action as they have been in accomplishing change within their own organizations. In addition, these programs try to raise the participants' consciousness level about the regional implications of their individual unit's actions, identifying and dealing with both the opportunities and challenges of the strain between the internal and external metropolitan chase. They put a personal face on cross-sector regional decision making, attempting to change stark stereotypes for shaded understanding. The year-long leadership experience creates bonds of mutual understanding and trust, essential ingredients for generating regional consensus.

VISIONING AND REGIONAL AGENDAS

There is no shortage of agendas within any metropolitan area. Each government, business, and nonprofit has its goals and objectives, many complete with detailed strategic plans and action steps. Is the regional agenda simply the sum of all these separate priorities? Will the entire metropolitan area benefit even when most of its parts succeed in achieving all or most of their aspirations? Or should there also be some overarching plan which addresses regionwide issues and sets a common vision for the future?

To create such a vision, a few regions turn to existing units. Portland Metro's charter, for example, required it to adopt a "Future Vision," defined as "a conceptual statement that indicates population levels and settlement patterns that the region can accommodate within the carrying capacity of the land, water, and air resources of the region, and its educational and economic resources, and that achieves a desired quality of life." The document, issued in 1995, has a fifty-year perspective. The Atlanta Regional Commission, that area's MPO, housed the Atlanta Vision 2020 initiative conducted in the mid-1990s.

Most metropolitan areas, however, must start from scratch since there is usually no regional entity with the breadth and credibility to spearhead such an effort. An ad hoc organization forms and designs an inclusive process for gathering views from all the stakeholders in the community. The civic leaders behind the initiative fear having any vision labeled as an elitist agenda and set forth into all parts of the region to solicit ideas.

This involves tens of public forums, complete with facilitators, recorders, and flip charts. The grist from these sessions then goes through an analytic mill, with task forces and their subcommittees grinding away in order to develop concrete goals with specific action steps. The product is then assembled into a draft plan which, once again, heads out to public meetings for reaction and refinement. Then, months and sometimes even years after the process began, the visionary agenda is proclaimed.

The prototype for regional agenda-setting was Chattanooga Venture's Vision 2000 conducted in 1984.[23] It is credited with turning the community's attention to its riverfront and its neighborhoods, sparking projects like the Tennessee Aquarium and Tennessee Riverpark as well as creating organizations such as Chattanooga Neighborhood Enterprise and the Neighborhood Network. A 1993 follow-up effort, ReVision 2000, reaffirmed the earlier undertakings and opened up a new environmental initiative which has transformed Chattanooga from one of the nation's most polluted regions to a prime example of a sustainable community.[24]

More recent visioning efforts include Oklahoma City (Central Oklahoma 2020) and St. Louis (St. Louis 2004).[25] The latter's action plan, announced in 1998 after almost two years of deliberations, declares "we'll start acting as a unified region . . . working together to combat youth gang violence . . . emerge as a center for cutting-edge, 21st century technologies . . . Downtown St. Louis will come alive . . . neighborhoods throughout the region will begin to turn the corner . . . kids will have safe places . . . extend health insurance to people not covered . . . clean up our air . . . create a world-class system of interlinking parks and green ways." These visioning efforts give citizens some practice in thinking regionally, raise the sights for what the metropolis might accomplish, and generate civic cheerleading.

COLLABORATIONS

Making decisions through governments or within organizations usually has a formal structure. There are written rules for submitting suggestions, detailed procedures for reviewing them, and a clear understanding about who is in charge. Within a government, for example, only specified individuals can introduce legislation, the deliberative body must have prior notice about such proposals, and a minimum number of votes are needed to approve it. Inside an organization, significant policy changes must move through the chain of command, be screened at several points, and receive final sign-off from someone at the top of the hierarchy. These procedures become routine and predictable. The most apt metaphor is a mechanical apparatus: put the idea in one end, turn the crank, and there is an outcome at the other end: proposal accepted or rejected.

But, as already seen, there is no single machine making metropolitan decisions. Although some such policies are made through structures like metropolitan planning organizations and others might be produced by a handful of the more powerful units within a region, many will require a fluid process, more organic than mechanic. In order to address much of what confronts metropolitan areas, "the task is to create collaborative relationships that cross many sectors" and are "facilitative, based on consensus."[26]

These last two characteristics distinguish collaborations from cooptations. Sets of interests within a metropolitan area often seek to recruit others to push their narrow agenda. The rhetoric is one of cooperation, but that term is operationally defined as "help us achieve our goals" rather than as "what can we do that will benefit all of us equally." Collaboration, instead, is "a mutually beneficial relationship between two or more parties who work toward common goals by sharing responsibility, authority, and accountability for achieving results."[27]

Collaborative decision making at the regional level is in its infancy, and it is unclear whether it will ever be widespread: their "half-life . . . is quite short, most never survive addressing their first regional challenge, and few are ever institutionalized."[28] First and foremost, it requires divergent individuals and groups to trust one another enough to engage in meaningful discussions. National and state legislators, for the most part, learn to bond enough to transform conflict into action but they have the advantage of working together at the same site for extended periods. How can this capacity to act effectively within communities, what Robert Putnam calls "social capital,"[29] be developed across regions, especially larger ones? As Chapter 1 noted, many powerful forces—economic, racial, social—pull groups apart. When each set of interests lives largely within its own part of the metropolitan world, seeing little of others and knowing only what it consumes in the media, stereotypes dominate and divisions deepen. Leadership programs aim to overcome this separation but they touch a minuscule share of the population.

Productive collaborations also require reinventing how communities engage collectively. If political institutions are being bypassed, then there must be some substitute procedures. If seemingly minor items—like where meetings are held, who is invited to attend, and how agendas are formed—are not designed and executed skillfully, then the process fails. Moreover, unlike governmental routines, the decision-making process details must be designed anew with each collaboration, even if some basic principles such as being open and inclusive remain constant. One especially difficult challenge is identifying a neutral convener, an organization and a place sufficiently trusted and respected by all parties that they feel comfortable working with and through it. Citizens leagues, universities, United Ways, and religious alliances are among those attempting to fulfill this role but often they are not seen as completely impartial.

If all those involved in a collaborative effort do not have meaningful access to information, then succeeding is difficult. As Bill Potapchuk notes, "good process is not enough . . . when participants do not have appropriate data to understand the situation, enough information to understand what works and what does not, and a shared sense of the outcome being sought, genuine progress is unlikely."[30] Knowledge is part of power. If only a few have a monopoly on the relevant data, then they can often manipulate the proceedings. Obtaining such information can be a challenge in most metropolitan areas. Although data abound, they are overly scattered and inadequately analyzed.

Constructive collaboration requires a different leadership style. Instead of being out front leading the charge, like a military commander or a corporate CEO, "the primary role of collaborative leaders is to promote and safeguard the process."[31] Several gurus have urged this approach in recent years, each with their own pet terminology.[32] The core notion is that one works and achieves through others. The collaborative leader involves every stakeholder, pushes the deliberations forward, identifies creative solutions for obstacles, and keeps spirits high.[33] At the end, however, the group is the winner and the leader, ever facilitative, has the group take center stage.

From the standpoint of an individual organization, deciding whether to participate in a collaborative venture is a tough call. Should, for example, a successful nonprofit providing affordable housing in a central city accept an invitation to join a collaborative effort to improve housing opportunities throughout the region? Will such an overarching alliance cause funders to forget about the agency and shift some or all of their support to the collaboration? If that happens, will dollars still flow through to the agency? Will the nonprofit retain its autonomy or will it become a branch operation governed by the alliance? Is it worth the time of the agency's staff, especially its executive director, to attend the tens of meetings needed to design and implement the collaboration? If the alliance never gels, are all those hours wasted? What are the incentives to risk so much on an effort whose success is highly unpredictable?

STATE MANDATES

Although local governments, both general purpose and special district, are creatures of the state, the Dillon's Rule principle, the states have wielded their life-and-death authority gently. As long as they did not ask for much financial assistance, states have allowed local units a relatively free hand over land use zoning, service provision, and organizational structure. In the past two decades, as metropolitan expansion accelerates and regional problems accentuate, several states have begun to insert themselves into regional decision making. When that happens, the state policy-making process then becomes part of the civic sphere, another place where metropolitan decisions can be made.

Land-use plans are the most common way for states to try to influence metropolitan policies. Pressured by demands to preserve open space, especially segments which are esthetically attractive such as beaches or environmentally threatened like wetlands, a few states have enacted some type of land-use or growth-management plan. Oregon requires metropolitan areas like Portland to have urban-growth boundaries. Residential, commercial, or industrial development can only occur inside those lines. Responding to its rapid population increases, Florida now requires all its local governments to prove that they can provide services to any new development before approving it.

The most recent state to join the land-use movement is Maryland. In the mid-1990s, it enacted a "Smart Growth" program. This approach relies more on incentives than penalties or regulations. The state told local jurisdictions that it would spend the bulk of its infrastructure dollars in existing urbanized areas and the legislation "prohibits the provision of state funds for highways, sewer and water construction, and housing and economic development assistance" to any projects outside those boundaries.[34]

Georgia is the latest state to enter the metropolitan arena. The Georgia Regional Transportation Agency, established in 1999, has the potential to wield wide power in transportation and land-use policy making. Its board, appointed by the governor, has oversight over transportation funding in the Atlanta region and, under some circumstances, can build and operate a light rail system. It also has veto power over selected local zoning decisions when, in its judgment, it would harm transportation and air quality.[35]

In an attempt to encourage more annexations and fewer incorporations, thereby limiting the number of local general purpose governments, twelve states (Alaska, California, Iowa, Michigan, Minnesota, Missouri, Nevada, New Mexico, Oregon, Utah, Virginia, Washington) have some type of boundary review commission to review such requests.[36] There is little supporting evidence, however, that their existence has had much impact on how governments have evolved within the regions within those states.[37]

Although a 1999 report issued by the National Research Council's Commission on Behavioral and Social Sciences and Education concluded that "state governments . . . have both the responsibility and the authority to bring about change in the metropolitan governance system by changing the legal framework within which local governments operate and the set of incentives they respond to,"[38] to date state involvement is more the exception than the rule. As Stephens and Wikstrom conclude, "most state action in terms of solving local and metropolitan problems tends to be the lowest common denominator: the minimum necessary to alleviate some of the worst aspects of a particular situation."[39]

WHITHER THE CIVIC SPHERE?

The intensifying competition with other metropolitan areas generates the need for more regional decision making. There are more "regional impulses . . . factors that motivate local governments and other interest groups to achieve regional outcomes."[40] That alone would suggest that the civic sphere will expand in the years ahead. It is difficult, however, to predict what form it will take. At this point, it is easier to see the limitations of each current component of the civic sphere than it is to discern the potential.

Metropolitan planning organizations depend heavily on federal authority and funding. Under existing national legislation, their purview is confined more to *things,* transportation and the environment, than to *people,* policies like housing and health care. Although some MPOs have used transit as a link to social issues, such as job commuting for persons in welfare-to-work programs, their planning cannot be comprehensive. In addition, even though their board members are mostly local elected officials, the MPOs have no independent political base.

The Twin Cities and Portland metropolitan governments have been up and going for some time and are widely known among those urging more regionalism. But these reforms apparently can only grow in those two regions' political climates and cannot be transplanted. Setting up other metropolitan councils with powers equal to those of the TCMC or Portland Metro has not even been attempted, much less tried and defeated.

More informal approaches—citizens leagues, leadership programs, visioning initiatives, and collaborative ventures—suffer from that very feature. While there are many success stories, it is ad hoc regionalism. Their limited resources, their sometimes amorphous structure, their fragile existence, and their uncertain legitimacy all circumscribe their influence.

State interventions are sporadic and often heavy-handed. Fewer than half the states have inserted themselves significantly into the civic sphere with most efforts involving land-use and growth management. When states do become more active in metropolitan matters, their sticks often weigh more than their carrots. It is an imposed regionalism, coming down from the state capitol, rather than an emerging regionalism, arising from within the metropolitan area.

So, for the foreseeable future, the civic sphere will remain a sometimes real, other times imagined place where forces converge to determine regional policies. Its shape will be difficult to define and even more challenging to describe. Many decisions with metropolitan-wide implications will continue to be made subregionally. More than most human endeavors, the civic sphere is a work in progress—as each metropolitan area struggles to devise its own ways for making regional policies.

NOTES

1. Norton E. Long, "The Local Community as an Ecology of Games," *American Journal of Sociology*, 44, no. 6 (November 1958), pp. 251–61.
2. Ibid., pg. 252.
3. Clarence E. Stone, *Regime Politics: Governing Atlanta 1946–1988* (Lawrence: University Press of Kansas, 1989), pg. 6. Also see Stephen L. Elkin, *City and Regime in the American Republic* (Chicago: University of Chicago Press, 1987).
4. J. Eugene Grigsby III, "Regional Governance and Regional Councils," *National Civic Review*, 85, no. 2 (Spring-Summer 1996), pp. 53–58.
5. David B. Walker, *The Rebirth of Federalism: Slouching Toward Washington* (Chatham, NJ: Chatham House Publishers, 1995), pg. 274.
6. Nelson Wikstrom, *Councils of Governments: A Study of Political Incrementalism* (Chicago: Nelson-Hall, 1977), pg. 91.
7. Paul G. Lewis, "Regionalism and Representation: Measuring and Assessing Representation in Metropolitan Planning Organizations," *Urban Affairs Review*, 33, no. 6 (July 1998), pp. 839–53.
8. Lisa Wormser, "Two for TEA," *Planning*, 64, no. 8 (August 1998), pp. 10–13.
9. Robert W. Gage and Bruce D. McDowell, "ISTEA and the Role of MPO's in the New Transportation Environment: A Midterm Assessment," *Publius*, 25, no. 3 (Summer 1995), pp. 133–54.
10. David K. Hamilton, *Governing Metropolitan Areas: Response to Growth and Change* (New York: Garland Publishing, 1999), pp. 160–61.
11. James F. Horan and G. Thomas Taylor, Jr., *Experiments in Metropolitan Government* (New York: Praeger Publishers, 1977), pg. xv. Voter rejections of city-county consolidations included Albuquerque-Bernalillo County (1959), Cleveland-Cuyahoga County (1959), Richmond-Henrico County (1961), Memphis-Shelby County (1962), Chattanooga-Hamilton County (1964 and 1970), Tampa-Hillsborough County (1967 and 1970), Charlotte-Mecklenburg County (1971), and Sacramento-Sacramento County (1974).
12. Kansas City, Kansas—not the region's central city—merged with Wyandotte County in 1997 but Kansas City, Missouri remains separate from its home county, Jackson. See G. Ross Stephens and

Nelson Wikstrom, *Metropolitan Government and Governance: Theoretical Perspectives, Empirical Analysis, and the Future* (New York: Oxford University Press, 2000), pp. 53–61.

13. Melvin B. Moguloff, *Five Metropolitan Governments* (Washington: The Urban Institute, 1972).
14. Stephens and Wikstrom, *Metropolitan Government and Governance*, pg. 87.
15. For a thorough account, see John J. Harrigan and William C. Johnson, *Governing the Twin Cities Region: The Metropolitan Council in Comparative Perspective* (Minneapolis: University of Minnesota Press, 1978), pp. 22–38.
16. John J. Harrigan, "Minneapolis-St. Paul: Structuring Metropolitan Government," in *Regional Politics: America in a Post-City Age*, ed. H.V. Savitch and Ronald K. Vogel (Thousand Oaks, CA: Sage Publications, 1996), pp. 213–14.
17. Harrigan, "Minneapolis-St. Paul: Structuring Metropolitan Government," pg. 213.
18. Myron Orfield, *Metropolitics: A Regional Agenda for Community and Stability* (Washington: Brookings Institution Press, 1997), pg. 129. See also Judith A. Martin, "Renegotiating Metropolitan Consciousness: The Twin Cities Faces Its Future," in *Metropolitan Governance Revisited: American/Canadian Intergovernmental Perspectives* (Berkeley: University of California Institute of Governmental Studies Press, 1998), pp. 237–71.
19. Carl Abbott, *Portland: Planning, Politics, and Growth in a Twentieth Century City* (Lincoln: University of Nebraska Press, 1983), pp. 248–66; and Margaret Weir, "Coalition Building for Regionalism," in *Reflections on Regionalism,* ed. Bruce Katz (Washington: Brookings Institution Press, 2000), pp. 130–33.
20. Arthur C. Nelson, "Portland: The Metropolitan Umbrella," in *Regional Politics: America in a Post-City Age*, ed. H.V. Savitch and Ronald K. Vogel (Thousand Oaks, CA: Sage Publications, 1996), pp. 262–63.
21. Harrigan, "Minneapolis-St. Paul: Structuring Metropolitan Government," pg. 206.
22. Neal R. Peirce, *Citistates: How Urban America Can Prosper in a Competitive World* (Washington: Seven Locks Press, 1993), pg. 322.
23. William R. Dodge, *Regional Excellence: Governing Together To Compete Globally and Flourish Locally* (Washington: National League of Cities, 1996), pp. 276–77. Also see Carl M. Moore, Gianni Longo, and Patsy Palmer, "Visioning," in *The Consensus Building Handbook*, ed. Lawrence Susskind, Sarah McKearnan, and Jennifer Thomas-Larmer (Thousand Oaks, CA: Sage Publications, 1999), pp. 557–89.
24. Jim Motavalli, "Chattanooga on a Roll: From America's Dirtiest City to One of Its Greenest," *E*, 9, no. 2 (March-April 1998), pp. 14–16.
25. Jonathan Walters, "Cities and the Vision Thing," *Governing*, 11, no. 8 (May 1998), pp. 32–36.
26. William R. Potapchuk, Jarle P. Crocker, Jr., and William H. Schechter, "The Transformative Power of Governance," *National Civic Review*, 88, no. 3 (Fall 1999), pp. 220–21.
27. David D. Chrislip and Carl E. Larson, *Collaborative Leadership: How Citizens and Civic Leaders Can Make a Difference* (San Francisco: Jossey-Bass Publishers, 1994), pg. 5.
28. See Robert D. Putnam, *Making Democracy Work: Civic Traditions in Modern Italy* (Princeton, NJ: Princeton University Press, 1993), and Putnam, "Bowling Alone: America's Declining Social Capital," *Journal of Democracy*, 6, no. 1 (January 1995), pp. 65–78.
29. Dodge, *Regional Excellence*, pg. 282.
30. William R. Potapchuk, "Building an Infrastructure of Community Collaboration," *National Civic Review*, 88, no. 3 (Fall 1999), pg. 167.
31. Chrislip and Larson, *Collaborative Leadership*, pg. 138.
32. See, for example, John W. Gardner, *On Leadership* (New York: Free Press, 1990) and Robert K. Greenleaf, Don M. Frick, and Larry C. Spears, eds., *On Becoming a Servant Leader* (San Francisco: Jossey-Bass Publishers, 1996).
33. Chrislip and Larson, *Collaborative Leadership*, pp. 138–41.
34. Alan Altshuler and others, eds., *Governance and Opportunity in Metropolitan America* (Washington: National Academy Press, 1999), pg. 84.
35. Alan Ehrenhalt, "The Czar of Gridlock," *Governing*, 12, no. 3 (May 1999), pp. 20–27.
36. Hamilton, *Governing Metropolitan Areas*, pp. 168–69.
37. *Local Boundary Commissions: Status and Roles and Forming, Adjusting, and Dissolving Local Government Boundaries* (Washington: Advisory Commission on Intergovernmental Relations, 1992).
38. Altshuler and others, eds., *Governance and Opportunity in Metropolitan America*, pg. 11.
39. Stephens and Wikstrom, *Metropolitan Government and Governance*, pg. 127.
40. Kathryn A. Foster, "Regional Impulses," *Journal of Urban Affairs*, 19, no. 4 (1997), pg. 376.

SUGGESTED READINGS

ALTSHULER, ALAN, and others. *Governance and Opportunity in Metropolitan America.* Washington: National Academy Press, 1999. Diagnoses of and prescriptions for metropolitan policies and governance from a distinguished panel of scholars and practitioners.

CHRISLIP, DAVID D., and CARL E. LARSON. *Collaborative Leadership: How Citizens and Civic Leaders Can Make a Difference.* San Francisco: Jossey-Bass Publishers, 1994. Outlines skills and techniques required for effective collaboration and gives examples of its application from several metropolitan regions.

DODGE, WILLIAM R. *Regional Excellence: Governing Together to Compete Globally and Flourish Locally.* Washington: National League of Cities, 1996. Identifies, categorizes, and sketches hundreds of regional governance initiatives throughout the United States.

ROTHBLATT, DONALD N., and ANDREW SANCTON, editors. *Metropolitan Governance Revisited: American/Canadian Intergovernmental Perspectives.* Berkeley: University of California Institute of Governmental Studies Press, 1998. Essays on regional governance in Boston, Montreal, Chicago, Toronto, Minneapolis-St. Paul, Edmonton, Houston, Vancouver, and San Francisco.

SAVITCH, H.V., and RONALD K. VOGEL, editors. *Regional Politics: America in a Post-City Age.* Thousand Oaks, CA: Sage Publications, 1996. Updates on metropolitan decision making in New York, Los Angeles, St. Louis, Washington (D.C.), Louisville, Pittsburgh, Miami, Minneapolis-St. Paul, Jacksonville, and Portland.

DOING IT

Here are two ways to probe what regional governance is all about:

1. How would you adapt Portland Metro's home rule charter to another metropolitan area? You can find the charter at *www.metro-region.org/glance/charter.html.* What parts of the charter would you keep? Which segments might you change, what adjustments might you make, and why? Once you have a draft, assess its chances for being adopted. Who might support it and why? Who might oppose it and why? What strategies would you recommend to maximize support and minimize opposition?

2. Identify a working collaboration in a metropolitan area near you. It might be called an alliance, a collaborative, a consortium, or a partnership. The venture should include at least two counties. Education, housing, and mental health are the most likely issues areas for collaborations but they can also be found in other arenas. Using interviews and written materials such as newspaper accounts and organizational records, answer the following questions: How did the collaboration begin? What individuals and groups were initially involved and what others joined later? What motivated the participants to form a collaboration? What did each think they would gain from the effort? What process did they use to determine the collaboration's structure and activities? What were the process's strengths and weaknesses? Which person(s) provided leadership? What made the leadership effective? How well is the collaboration doing today? Does anything threaten its future? If so, what is being done to meet the threat?

PART II

THE EXTERNAL CHASE
COMPETITION AMONG METROS

Metropolitan areas have always competed. The feature performers change with the epochs—Athens versus Sparta, Rome versus Carthage, Paris versus London, New York versus Tokyo—but the contest endures. Two factors make it qualitatively different now: the number of metropolitan areas involved is much higher, hundreds in the United States and thousands around the globe, and the race is more self-consciously intense—a strategic enterprise waged on several fronts.

At the core of the competition is economic well-being. Although humans do not live by bread alone, some measure of prosperity is a precondition for almost everything else. It is difficult to imagine a good life which does not include resources both for basics such as food and shelter as well as amenities like recreation and travel. Although individual households can try to navigate their own way through the market economy, succeeding or failing on their separate merits, most people's fortunes are linked to where they live. It is easier to do well in a booming metropolitan area than in a declining one, to ride with the current rather than to swim upstream.

What must metropolitan regions do to have robust economies? The economist's answer is straightforward: import cheap and export dear. Bring stuff into the metropolitan area at a low cost, do something with or to it which adds value, and then sell it to someone outside the region for a higher price. The difference between the purchase and sales price tags is pure financial gain, an addition to the wealth of a region and at least some of its residents.

The classic prototype for this process is manufacturing. A steel plant imports raw materials such as iron and coal, uses skilled labor and complex furnaces to transform them into, say, girders used for desirable products like buildings and bridges, and markets them throughout the world. For regions like Birmingham and Pittsburgh, steel was a major piece of their original economic development. Automobile assembly, gathering components from many sites and putting them together into a coherent vehicle, is still another example, one which has served well areas like Detroit and St. Louis.

In today's complex economy, traditional manufacturing is not the only way or often not even the primary means for importing cheap and exporting dear. For example, a world-class medical center imports sick bodies from outside its region, applies the talents of health care professionals and medical technology, and in most cases exports cured people. In the process, it keeps the fees for the services it provides, the value it has added to its clients. Moreover, even when the operation fails and the patient dies, the transaction succeeds financially although, if there are too many corpses over the long haul, fewer might patronize it. Metropolitan regions like Baltimore and Houston, housing such health enterprises, benefit from the willingness of people from around the world to come there to find a remedy.

More than any other factor, the sharpened economic competition among metropolitan areas has kindled regionwide decision making both within the governmental arena and between the public and private sectors. As Chapter 1 points out, metropolises are natural economies encompassing all the governmental jurisdictions within them. If each of these governments within a region goes its own way when planning and executing economic development policy, if they work at cross purposes rather than acting together, the chances for external success will be less. Businesses have a direct and immediate stake in economic development and must partner with governments in order to have a fully integrated strategy.

Chapter 6 discusses what economic development strategies metropolitan areas are using to champion their cause. It provides the overall framework for the external chase among regions. But plans alone will not succeed unless some other key ingredients exist. Chapter 7 addresses the first of these, the ability to move people, things, and information swiftly and inexpensively. A region must be able to receive items from other metropolitan areas and deliver them back. This requires a whole array of transportation infrastructure: airports, rail terminals, fiber optic networks, interstate highways, port facilities, and the like. If you cannot get somewhere from almost everywhere else, few will either import or export with you.

People, seen as human capital, also count tremendously in the intermetropolitan competition. In an economy where knowledge matters more than ever and in an age demanding that people update their skills regularly, the need for learning has become pervasive. When value is added, it is typically done by someone who has discovered a better way to do so. Education, once concentrated mostly between ages 5 and 18 and conducted largely through formal institutions, is now done throughout life and in a variety of settings. Chapter 8 examines what metropolitan areas are doing to make their residents, especially those in the work force, proficient.

Beyond economy and infrastructure and learning there is buzz. Humans have become a traveling bunch, eager for fresh ways to enjoy their expanding leisure time. Young adults, especially the more adventuresome, want to live where the action is. To attract both groups, the tourists and the twenty- and thirty-somethings, metropolitan areas strive to create an atmosphere that sizzles. Some regions seem to have it naturally: Boston, New Orleans, and San Francisco are apt examples. Others seek to generate it artificially: the Inner Harbor in Baltimore or downtown developments like Jacobs Field and the Rock and Roll Hall of Fame in Cleveland. Chapter 9 analyzes what metropolitan areas are doing with cultural institutions, entertainment venues, and tourist attractions in the competition for having an exciting atmosphere.

Although Part II stresses the external chase, each of its topics is also part of the internal competition. Where jobs are located, where private capital is invested, what routes highways take, who has access to quality education, and who pays for the buzz are all examples of contentious issues within any region, and these points will be raised as well. The metropolitan chase is a Janus-like venture, simultaneously looking outward to other regions and inward to competing interests.

CHAPTER 6

Economic Development

THE SETTING

The goals of metropolitan economic development policy are straightforward: more jobs, higher incomes, and greater stability. Each additional laborer produces something that, in principle, can either be exported to another region or substituted for something presently imported. That, in turn, brings more income which, through spending and saving, will be shared with others in the region. As the economists put it, these dollars multiply, spreading their impact. The more diversified the jobs and the industries they represent, the greater the metropolitan area's protection from abrupt changes in the global marketplace. No region wishes to have all its economic eggs in a few baskets, no matter how promising they might seem at the moment.

Although the strategies for achieving these ends can be controversial and problematic, there is little debate about economic development having a high priority. As Paul Peterson notes, "it is only a modest oversimplification to equate the interests of cities with the interests of their export industries."[1] For governments, economic activity produces tax revenues to meet service needs. For businesses, especially those within the innards of the growth machine, it raises land values and creates synergism. For nonprofits, it facilitates generating funds from the public and private sector. For the civic sphere, it creates a greater sense of accomplishment.

Having said that, it has only been recently that all sectors, especially governments, have devoted much attention to economic development. Go back three decades and one would be hard pressed to identify more than a handful of local governments which had a unit with "economic development" or a synonym in its title. But since the 1970s, it "has grown from a relatively marginal item on the political agendas of state and local officials to a central—even pivotal—issue among prevailing concerns."[2] The reasons are many but foremost among them was the federal government's decision, starting midway through the Carter Administration (1977–1981) and accelerated during the Reagan years (1981–1989), to lower substantially its subsidies to struggling states and communities.[3] Washington's message to these jurisdictions was clear: You are on your own—don't expect the national government to bail you out!

Each metropolitan area enters the economic competition with its own distinctive set of circumstances and conditions. Some have geographic features—Baltimore's deep water harbor, San Diego's moderate climate, Chicago's central location—which give them a positive edge, while others must cope with the absence of such attributes. Some have been blessed with historic benefits—the national government in Washington or state capitols in Austin and Boston—while others have had to make do without such good fortune. These assets and liabilities become part of the equation as regions plot their economic development strategies.

Geography and history are not always destiny. To draw this lesson, Pagano and Bowman[4] point to two nineteenth-century cities, one hundred miles apart and each on the eastern edge of the Rocky Mountains. The first had geography and history on its side, resting astride the most feasible route between the East and West Coasts,

San Diego Bay Spurred San Diego's Development

a path taken by the Oregon Trail, the transcontinental railroad, and ultimately Interstate 80. The other was adjacent to a chain of 14,000 foot peaks, inhibiting any movement to the west. Most bets would have been on the first area, Cheyenne, but it was the second, Denver, which emerged as the major metropolis on the Rocky Mountains' eastern slope.

It is what metropolitan areas make of their circumstances that determines their economic condition. What can they do to get the edge on their competitors? In what niches can they excel? In earlier times, following Adam Smith's script, this meant devising a comparative advantage and exploiting it. Chicago, for example, had the easiest transportation access to the Midwest's fertile fields. It was less expensive for farmers to ship their livestock and crops there than anywhere else. Once processed in Chicago's meatpacking plants and food processing factories, the products could be shipped by water (Lake Michigan and, via the Chicago and Illinois Rivers, onto the Mississippi River) or rail (it was the largest freight hub between east and west as well as north and south) throughout North America and beyond. In Carl Sandburg's poetic words, Chicago became "Hog Butcher of the World . . . Stalker of Wheat . . . City of Big Shoulders."

In recent times, it has been more difficult for a metropolitan area to sustain a comparative advantage. Factors like skilled labor and key raw materials are more mobile. Location can give a region a temporary edge but others, using sharper technology here or cheaper labor there, can imitate successful models and beat them at their own game. Meatpacking plants, to continue with the Chicago example, relocated to smaller towns even closer to the livestock. Interstate highways provided additional access, rural labor forces worked for lower wages, and one-story plants covering tens of acres were superior to multistory structures in an urbanized setting.

Instead of comparative advantage, economic development strategists now talk about competitive advantage. Harvard Business School Professor Michael E. Porter has pioneered this approach and it is fast becoming conventional wisdom.[5] It instructs regions to identify clusters of enterprises, "geographic connections of interconnected companies, specialized suppliers, service providers, firms in related industries, and associated institutions (e.g., universities, standards agencies, trade associations) in a particular field that compete but also cooperate."[6]

This is a more complex way of interpreting a region's economic makeup. It requires searching for the core of a metropolitan area's economic structure and then specifying all the linkages, forward and backward, associated with it. Take Cleveland and Akron.[7] At the nucleus of their economy lies materials: metals such as aluminum and steel, as well as speciality chemicals like paint and rubber. The region both generates these materials and supports companies which transform them into end products such as automobile frames and plastic windshields. Looking backward along the chain, Cleveland-Akron is also a leading research center on topics like polymer chemistry. With several companies competing in the same industry (e.g., Firestone and Goodrich in tires), the region attracts and retains skilled labor in part because there are several potential employers.

It is more difficult for other regions to play catch up if one achieves a competitive advantage since the challenger must reproduce not just a single industry but an interconnected set of enterprises. If someone is thinking about entering the software sector, it makes more sense to locate in San Jose or Seattle, where computer talent is abundant and research universities specialize in those fields, than in Miami or New Orleans, both of which are below average on these factors. For metropolitan areas lacking a clear-cut competitive advantage, the recommendation is to find some likely pieces of what could be one and then fill in the missing components.

THE STRATEGIES

As metropolitan areas have intensified their pursuit of economic development, they have used a wide array of devices. A recent compilation lists over sixty—and no one claims that the end is yet in sight.[8] The first set of tactics aims at attracting businesses to relocate in the metropolitan area, usually from elsewhere in the United States but sometimes from another country. The second group concentrates on growth from within, helping existing enterprises inside the region to prosper and encouraging entrepreneurs to start new companies. The third focuses on capacity building, making targeted investments within the metropolitan area which will help the economy, often those which will buttress the segment(s) having a competitive advantage.

These three approaches have tended to occur sequentially: relocation prevailed in the 1970s, grow your own became common in the 1980s, and finally coordinated programs have sprung up in the 1990s. But even though they have appeared in three waves,[9] the process has been more addition than substitution so that, currently, metropolitan areas typically do all three, although in differing combinations.[10]

Attracting Businesses

In the days when export industries meant behemoth manufacturing plants, the slang for this approach was "smokestack chasing." It was shotgun salesmanship, panning for prospects, and then putting together a package that would close the deal. As Herbert Rubin summarized it, the strategy was essentially "shoot anything that flies, claim anything that falls."[11]

The relocation toolkit has many instruments. To catch the attention of potential clients, there is often a marketing campaign trumpeting the virtues of doing business in the metropolitan region, touting all its positives and stating that the welcome sign is out for each and every enterprise looking for a better place. Once a firm expresses an interest, the recruiting region assembles a package, doing whatever it can to lower the company's costs if it chooses to move. That might mean selling property at a below-market price, acreage that had been purchased earlier to serve as bait for just such a situation, and pledging that one or more local governments will pay for road and other infrastructure support. It almost always includes some type of tax reduction, such as abating property taxes or dedicating the additional taxes generated by the project for site improvements on the site, the latter known as tax-increment financing. It often involves having a public entity subsidize or guarantee loans for relocation expenses and business expansion.

Similar to someone selling luxury automobiles, relocation professionals tend to have a lot more lookers than takers. As more metropolitan areas became aggressive recruiters, businesses began to play one suitor off against other. After learning about the lucrative incentives their competitors were receiving to move, enterprises which had not even thought about relocating began to explore what could be done for them. More began threatening to migrate, seeing whether a possible departure would trigger a counteroffer from their current home. This lowered the net benefits for many metropolitan regions which began to use part of their incentive kit just to keep current businesses from fleeing.

Another dimension of business attraction occurs when a firm decides to build a new facility with a hefty payroll. When this happens in the contemporary frenzied climate for luring jobs to metropolitan areas, it sets off a bidding war. Companies announce their expansion plans and then sit back, waiting for their regional supplicants. They do not have to tarry long nor do they have to settle for token inducements. When United Airlines, for example, said it wanted to establish another maintenance facility, Indianapolis's winning proposal contained more than $300 million in support.[12]

Business recruitment continues but at a slower pace than in the past. The dream of landing the big one—the hundreds or thousands of jobs that will create headlines, getting economic development officials promoted and mayors or county executives reelected—is still a powerful motivator and the thrill of the chase an intoxicating stimulant.[13] But there is a maturing awareness that the game is not always worth the candle. From a national perspective, especially, there is no net benefit: one region's gain is another's loss. More communities are realizing that there are not that many live prospects at any given time, that if the demand by regions exceeds the supply of relocatable firms then the price to attract them rises beyond acceptable levels, and that the types of firms wanting to change areas are often among the weaker enterprises, seeking governmental subsidies to offset a declining bottom line.[14]

Growing Businesses

During the late 1970s, concerns grew about the limited and episodic payoffs from pursing someone else's companies. Regions realized that, just like successful major league baseball teams blend purchasing free agents with a productive minor league system, metropolitan areas could not grow solely through external acquisitions. They then began redirecting much of the economic development strategy toward a search for what might be done to encourage more business formations within the region.

In the initial stages, many metropolitan areas seized upon federal grants to jump start some aspect of the regional economy. The plainest example was the Urban Development Action Grant (UDAG) Program which was in place from 1978 through 1989. UDAG's rationale was to provide federal loans and grants to private projects which regions put forward as attractive investment opportunities for improving economic conditions. One or more local governments, usually the central city or urban county, served as creative matchmakers, finding a private firm with an exciting development and then, on its behalf, entreating the federal government to pick up part of the tab.[15]

Central city reconversion projects were especially popular. In the many Northeastern and Midwestern regions, UDAG funds were used to transform vacated industrial factories into mixed commercial and residential complexes. In St. Louis, the main train terminal, Union Station, abandoned and in disrepair, became an upscale hotel and festival mall. These ventures created jobs, especially entry-level positions in the retail and hospitality fields, but they were rarely cutting-edge projects. Out-of-towners provided some revenues, staying in hotel rooms and patronizing boutique shops and restaurants, but the remainder was shifted from elsewhere within the region.

St. Louis's Union Station: A UDAG Project

Business incubators are a more local approach with a longer term perspective. It is a big-oaks-from-little-acorns-grow concept with the premise that the acorns need assistance. People with a brilliant idea for, say, building a better mousetrap rarely have all that it takes to convert it into a profitable enterprise. They need sophisticated things like business plans, accounting and legal services, and marketing consultation as well as basic items like space, voice mail, and a copier.[16] If they do not receive them or, for some elements, do not even realize that they need them, what might have been a major success story instead is just another failed venture.

To help small entrepreneurs become big businesspeople, local governments, often in cooperation with chambers of commerce or their equivalent, subsidize some of the start-up costs and facilitate access to the needed services. They purchase and renovate buildings, underwrite office equipment which can be shared by all the occupants, and recruit qualified business and legal consultants and pay part of their fees. Sometimes the incubators are available for all types of enterprises, other times they specialize with manufacturing and technology then being the most common themes. Manufacturing start-ups often need and can share computerized machine tooling, while technology firms require laboratory space and equipment.

Although business incubation is a relatively new approach, the early assessments are encouraging but not overwhelming.[17] Most incubator firms have increasing sales and growing employment. Many have not yet left the nest but some have departed, opening spaces for budding entrepreneurs. The primary challenge to this approach is as much political will as it is business strategy: success will occur over decades, not years, but elected officials must run every two or four years. Will they continue to support a program where the spectacular payoffs will occur, if they do, long after they have left office?

Emerging enterprises also need capital. In the start-up phase, costs almost always exceed revenues, often by an alarming margin. Hundreds of thousands and often millions of dollars must be spent before there is any hope of seeing some financial returns. Most entrepreneurs cannot fund these expenses out of their own ockets. They need loans from patient investors who are willing to gamble that the idea is a sound one and wait a while before having their judgment rewarded.

Venture capital is the standard term for these investments and it is often in short supply. Traditional lenders such as banks and pension funds want to put their funds into secure loans, those with substantial collateral and an almost certain probability of being repaid. Even the Small Business Administration, the federal government's response to this type of capital need, cannot tolerate too high a default rate. What is required is an entity willing to invest in tens of new firms, realizing that most will not ultimately succeed but that the few long shots which do break through will more than make up for the losses. These venture capitalists do not loan money. They purchase an equity interest so that, for the winning companies, they can ultimately sell stock that has hundreds or even thousands times more value over the original price.

Many metropolitan areas lack hometown venture capital firms. Most are located on the East or West Coasts and, while they are willing to explore opportunities outside their immediate vicinity, they are less likely to invest in them.[18] They prefer to place their bets on propositions that can be closely monitored and that is easiest if they are nearby. So many local governments have taken the lead to encourage private investors to form venture capital operations, either as spinoffs from existing financial institutions or as entirely new firms. Using a mixture of civic loyalty ("your community needs your investments") and avaricious appeal ("the potential returns are enormous"), mayors and county executives entreat the lending community to do its part to promote economic development.

Building Capacity

The first two approaches tend to work firm by firm, either luring one from else-where or nurturing one locally. They are also opportunistic, seizing whatever situation seems to offer the most promise at the moment. In contrast, this third method works across one or more business sectors and bases its actions on strategic assessments, often using competitive advantage studies.[19]

This perspective stresses two related concepts: networks and "co-eption."[20] The metropolitan economy should be seen as an interconnected web involving businesses, nonprofits, and governments rather than as an isolated series of individual companies. To improve a region's competitive advantage in, say, plant genetics, the web would include agricultural companies, university researchers, public economic development agencies, and trade associations. On a personal level, the company's vice president for research, the university's top plant scientist, the economic development agency's head, and the soybean association's director would interact regularly—they network.

Co-eption "means that individuals and companies—compete ferociously but collaborate at the same time to create knowledge."[21] The mind set is win-win with enough growth for everyone rather than win-lose, where your gain is my loss. Information about manufacturing techniques, technological applications, and selling opportunities is both valued and, to a large extent, shared. The emphasis is on collaboratively expanding the market for the industry and then competing for shares in the enlarged sector. There is as much commitment to the mission, such as using genetic discoveries to feed a hungry planet, as there is to a particular company's bottom line.

Building capacity in some type of technology has been a common tactic for this strategy. Having observed Boston's electronic boom and San Jose's computer explosion, other metropolitan areas have sought to identify their color on the scientific rainbow. As they embark on this search, the first stop is most often a nearby research university.[22] The Massachusetts Institute of Technology and Stanford University were central to their regions' development, providing both cutting-edge findings and a stream of highly-educated employees.

Before too long, San Diego discovered life sciences at the University of California-San Diego, Pittsburgh robotics at Carnegie Mellon University, and Austin physics at the University of Texas-Austin. In these cases, there are typically the initial pieces of a network already established, perhaps a few connections between professors and recent graduates who have started companies. The challenge then

Carnegie Mellon University in Pittsburgh

becomes expanding the linkages and facilitating communications. This might include raising more funds for the scientific investigations at the university, developing a research park for the emerging companies, and arranging meetings and exchanges among all those involved.

Technology is not always the avenue pursued. A cluster analysis of the Los Angeles region found, to no one's surprise, that the entertainment industry was a key sector employing about 164,000 people. There was no problem attracting creative talent: they flocked to the Hollywood mecca. But there was no plan to prepare and retain the skilled craftspeople needed to build the props, construct the sets, and design the special effects.[23] To make the most of its competitive advantage in entertainment, the Los Angeles region needed to develop and implement a workforce preparation program for these occupations.

In addition to its industry focus, capacity building also looks to what other institutional changes might assist the metropolitan economy. The globalization of the economy has meant more potential business outside the United States. As of 1996, foreign exports in ten regions (San Jose, New York, Detroit, Los Angeles, Chicago, Seattle, Houston, Minneapolis-St. Paul, Miami) topped $10 billion and the annual growth rate is substantial.[24]

Large multinational corporations are already veterans at international trade. With offices at major trading centers like London and Hong Kong, they are fully equipped to sell wherever there is a customer. Smaller enterprises, however, are unfamiliar with all the intricacies associated with doing business outside the United States. From identifying customers to mastering import-export forms, they need assistance.

To internationalize the metropolitan economy, many regions have embarked on a series of initiatives, all aimed at stimulating exports by the local businesses, especially mid-sized and smaller enterprises. Many establish "World Trade Centers," each a franchise of an international nonprofit promoting international business exchanges. They match domestic sellers with foreign buyers, help with processing forms, provide translation services, host foreign visitors, and sponsor trade fairs. Central cities form international families with "sister cities," Phoenix with Grenoble (France) and Chengdu (China) and St. Louis with Stuttgart (Germany) and Suwa (Japan), to establish a more personal foothold. These sibling relationships are then fostered with regular visits by elected local executives and business leaders.

INNER CITIES AND THE POOR

Not everyone is doing well financially in metropolitan America. Even booming regions have residents and neighborhoods that have not shared in the bounty and the lagging metropolises have an even greater share. As Chapter 1 describes, the economic divide has been growing. In addition to being a moral obligation and a social challenge, the unemployed and the underemployed are a drag on intrametropolitan competition. Instead of contributing to the region's productivity, they must be supported by everyone else. They are riding the metropolitan wagon instead of pulling it.

The impoverished residents and derelict areas present a special trial for economic development policy. The rising tide represented by the strategies described in the previous section have only a marginal impact on the poor. Recognizing this, central cities and inner suburbs, often with a dose of federal funding, are experimenting with several fresh strategies. Because poverty is geographically concentrated, most strategies are area based. These include enterprise and empowerment zones, inner-city cluster analyses, and the community development corporations described in Chapter 4. Some, however, focus on individual businesses, with micro-enterprises being the most vivid example.

The national government's hefty involvement in these efforts points out one aspect of metropolitan area politics. Central cities, the most vigorous advocates for assistance, find they have more clout working collectively with the federal government than separately within each region. Their votes are still crucial for Democratic presidential candidacies, and hence they have a receptive audience when a member of that party occupies the White House. The central cities are more isolated within their own regions and states and, consequently, have less ability to persuade those units to redistribute tax dollars on their behalf, although more than half the states also have enterprise zone programs, most modestly funded at best.[25]

Empowerment/Enterprise Zones

The Clinton Administration's Empowerment Zone and Enterprise Community is the latest in a series of federal initiatives to target assistance to hardcore impoverished inner-city neighborhoods. Passed in 1993, it offered up to $100,000,000 in assistance over a ten-year period to each of the six metropolitan regions with the soundest proposals. The winners were Atlanta, Baltimore, Chicago, Detroit, New York, and Philadelphia. The rules were altered to allow two more victors—Cleveland and Los Angeles—and in 1999 fifteen more regions received similar awards. Within each of these regions, the designated zone encompasses upwards of 200,000 people. About 100 other metropolitan areas received much smaller consolation grants which were labeled "enterprise communities."

The program has four principles: "economic opportunity in private sector jobs and training, sustainable community development (with) a comprehensive coordinated approach, community-based partnerships that engage representatives from all parts of the community, and strategic vision for change based on cooperative planning and community consultation."[26] Tax credits and redirecting existing federal programs generate the funding stream, with the goal bringing jobs to the area and targeting them to those living there.

Even though the original round of awards was made in 1994, it is premature to reach any conclusions about impact although skepticism outweighs optimism.[27] Changing process by involving the broader community and devising sensible plans and substance by stimulating economic investment is politically treacherous, programmatically daunting, and immensely time consuming. Even a $100,000,000 carrot over a decade amounts to $50 a year per resident in an empowerment zone with 200,000 residents and, nationwide, less than twenty-five metropolitan regions are involved. According to the critics, it is too few dollars pursuing ambitions that are both too lofty and too diffuse.

Cluster Analysis

From Porter's cluster analysis and competitive advantage perspective, the empowerment and enterprise zone approach has it all wrong. He argues that "a sustainable economic base can be created in inner cities only . . . through private, for-profit initiatives and investments based on economic self-interest and genuine competitive advantage instead of artificial inducements, government mandates, or charity."[28] It is hard-headed business rather than soft-hearted handouts.

While not denying the obstacles in revitalizing the inner city, Porter sees their neighborhoods having four distinctive economic advantages.[29] First, their location places them near certain industries—hotels and restaurants are one example—which require speedy delivery of perishable goods like food. Second, since many retail chains have abandoned these areas, there is pent-up demand for everyday goods and services. The residents may be poor but, collectively, they still purchase a lot of stuff. Third, the neighborhoods are often near the cluster that gives the region its competitive edge and, if they think strategically, they can link their fortunes to that

Microenterprisers Often Sell Their Products at Flea Markets

star. Fourth, the people themselves are an underutilized resource, human talent waiting to be tapped and shaped.

Porter has turned his ideas into his own cottage nonprofit, "The Initiative for a Competitive Inner City," and prepared strategies for several areas including Boston, Chicago, Kansas City, Miami, and Oakland. The Chicago analysis, for example, found all four advantages present in the low-income neighborhoods on the city's west and south sides and identified twelve opportunities, among them linking with the region's extensive transportation sector, locating back-office facilities serving downtown financial enterprises, and expanding retail outlets.[30]

Some find flaws in Porter's approach which, like all proposed policies for revamping the inner city, has yet to succeed on any significant scale. His methodology has been criticized as being "a superficial analysis of urban problems that relies on over generalizations for evidence,"[31] he is charged with having "greatly underestimated the obstacles to revitalization of the inner-city economies,"[32] and for downplaying "the contribution . . . of [some] government programs and [some] activities of [some] local organizations based within urban communities of color."[33]

Microenterprises

Microenterprise programs are virtual business incubators but on a much smaller scale. They target the more motivated and better skilled among the impoverished, seeking those who have an idea for starting their own business, either as their primary livelihood or to supplement their income. Catering, jewelry design, and knitwear are just some of the examples. A recent survey identified over 340 such initiatives in the United States, not all of which are located in metropolitan regions.[34] Almost all are administered by nonprofit organizations with some receiving modest governmental assistance. Examples include Women's Initiative in San Francisco and Working Capital in Boston.[35]

The modal participant is a single mother, often highly educated, who wishes to start some business that she can pursue at home. The programs offer modest financial credit but typically only after an applicant has gone through a business-skills training course. They often form support groups so that the isolation of working as a one-person operation can be overcome with ongoing meetings with entrepreneurial comrades. They are part of a broader social strategy, premised on the belief that enabling poor people to build both economic and social capital is the key to escaping poverty.[36]

As is the case with other bootstrap efforts, microenterprise programs' effectiveness is mixed. A recent analysis finds that they "are unlikely to increase the number who move (from welfare to self-employment) by more than 1 in 100" and that most of these successes already have "above-average assets, education, experience, and skills."[37] Another study of three urban programs concurs that they "do more to help those who exist at the margins of the mainstream economy than those who are completely cut off from the economic mainstream."[38]

THE DECISION-MAKING PROCESS

Governments

Local governments are the centerpiece for economic-development policy making within metropolitan areas but the federal and state governments often participate as well. Federal programs such as empowerment zones are often part of the strategy,

national facilities like military bases and regional offices are attractive targets of opportunity, and U.S. taxes fund infrastructure improvements. On a smaller scale,
states also offer the same array. They also can provide items like workforce training
at local community colleges and tax credits for hiring low-income individuals.

Within the region, most counties and many municipalities have established
economic development units during the past two decades. They might be a separate
department, standing beside more traditional divisions like public works, or the
function might have been added to an existing unit, most typically community development or its equivalent, or it might be a special unit housed within the elected
executive's immediate staff.[39] It has also become commonplace for local governments to form special authorities with more financing flexibility than general purpose units to assist in economic-development policy implementation.[40]

County executives and municipal mayors dominate the elected official contingent on economic-development issues with the local legislatures less involved.
Business leaders, those being wooed and nurtured, want to interact with the boss
and, for them, those are the local governments' elected executives.[41] Working along
with them are a new cadre of public servants, economic-development specialists,
who are more change oriented than most of their governmental counterparts. The
best of these are highly recruited. Just as professional sports teams hope that a
change in coaches will spark success, so also local governments dream that a dynamic public entrepreneur will change their economic fortunes.

The need to coordinate different tiers of government—national, state, and
local—as well as many public entities within the metropolitan region brings an
acute complexity to economic-development decision making. Programs and packages have multiple contributors and all must be aligned for progress to occur. That
is still another reason why executives, who can be more nimble than legislatures, are
out in front.

Public-Private Partnerships

Local governments and the growth machine share a common purpose in expanding the metropolitan economy. They also need each other to achieve this goal. The
public sector cannot unilaterally create jobs except on a very limited scale, and
the private sector almost always needs governmental assistance such as a zoning
adjustment or a highway interchange. This joint aspiration and mutual interdependence has brought them together in a variety of partnerships, some enduring
and others temporary.

Local governmental officials, business executives, and nonprofit leaders have
never been strangers to one another but their acting jointly became more evident
soon after World War II. Downtown redevelopment was most often the stimulus.
Central-city governments saw their office and commercial core threatened by a combination of physical deterioration and suburban expansion. Businesses with a downtown stake knew action must be taken to protect their investment. In the 1950s
alone, such partnerships were founded in Atlanta (Central Atlanta Improvement

Association), Baltimore (Greater Baltimore Committee), Boston (New Boston Committee), Philadelphia (Greater Philadelphia Movement), Pittsburgh (Allegheny Conference on Community Development), San Francisco (San Francisco Planning and Urban Renewal Association), and St. Louis (Civic Progress).[42]

As economic development gained prominence on the local governmental agenda, these initial ventures paved the way for additional cooperative ventures. Business and political leaders had become accustomed to acting together, both sides had a better appreciation for the other's perspectives and contributions, and each year brought more challenges and opportunities. Some were one-time endeavors—Charlotte obtaining a National Football League franchise or Denver building a new airport—while others planned and implemented a cluster-based economic strategy.

These partnerships' strengths are the marrying of government's formal powers and democratic legitimacy with the business community's prestige and financial resources. It is a powerful combination, the kind needed to meet the demands of intense competition among metropolitan areas, and an attractive image, the public and private joining forces to improve the region. But their complex nature also often obscures deliberations and blurs accountability. Unlike policies formed and

Denver International Airport: A Public-Private Partnership

enacted solely within government, where the debate is largely open and the details readily available, the partnership deliberations are usually conducted behind closed doors and the precise terms are difficult to access. It is public policy privately processed.

Conflict

Economic development is less controversial than most public policy issues. Presumably, most will benefit from a larger economy. It is hard to determine if anyone loses when a business relocates in one's metropolitan area or new enterprises spring up there. Indeed, those who do criticize particular economic-development initiatives are often characterized as parochial and anti-community and portrayed as not having the sense to appreciate a great deal.

Nevertheless, dissension sometimes emerges. The primary issue is who pays and who benefits.[43] When governments award tax subsidies to business, it essentially means that everyone else must either pay a little bit more or that some services will be marginally reduced. Although this approach takes advantage of the axiom that policies seeking approval are well advised to generate a few big winners (each of whom will work mightily for adoption) and many small losers (few of whom will find it worthwhile to expend much energy in opposition), a few vocal citizens occasionally protest using the public till to help businesses make more money.

Who bears the cost of economic development has another facet. How should the initial price tag for a new project be divided among the private and public sectors and, for the latter, which jurisdictions within the metropolitan region should pay how much? The first attempt, of course, is to persuade someone outside the region, often the national or state government, to bear much of the burden but, absent that intervention, the bill must be split by the locals. This often leads to an elaborate web of loan guarantees and in-kind contributions almost impossible to disentangle by anyone other than skilled tax accountants.

Many projects also have indirect costs which can cause friction. A stadium or airport or industrial park might, on the whole, benefit the entire region, but it can be a nuisance for those living nearby. For them, the immediate consequences are added congestion and heightened noise. Should they be expected to shrug and bear it or should they be compensated for their discomfort or, for the most acute situations, should they be relocated with a bonus for the significant disruption?

WHO IS THE ENGINE?

Various participants within each metropolitan area vie for being the top priority in economic-development policy. The prevailing label for this status is "engine," as in our unit "drives" the metropolitan economy. If there is widespread consensus about who deserves the engine emblem, then it becomes the sun around which most of the programs revolve. But there is little agreement and an internal competition is waged on two fronts: geographic and sectoral.

Geographic

Central cities contend that they deserve primacy, that no economically healthy metropolitan area can prosper unless it has a viable core. They promote policies that favor inner cities, such as empowerment zones and brownfield cleanups, and public investments which will revitalize downtowns, like mass-transit systems which use them as hubs. They insist that current laws put them at a disadvantage, citing how highway subsidies and mortgage interest deductions favor the suburban and exurban segments, and argue that the metropolitan playing field needs leveling.[44]

Suburban and exurban elements say favoring central cities runs counter to market forces. Most businesses making locational decisions in the past two decades have preferred sites outside the central city for reasons such as more land for low-rise buildings, ample parking lots, and campus settings. The people they want to work at their firms also are more likely to be living in the suburbs. If a metropolitan area places too many obstacles in the way of development at the periphery, they argue, it will only artificially restrict growth and chase businesses to other regions. Instead, metropolitan areas should be talking up the entrepreneurial pluses of their suburban and exurban communities because that is where most of the action is.

This rivalry between the core and the fringe can come to preoccupy a region's attention, inhibiting its ability to compete as a single metropolitan area. Moreover, the evidence is at best mixed about whether growth at the region's edges is the principal culprit in the decline of central cities.[45] An increasing number of metropolises are using some type of public-private entity to offer a unified economic-development approach, providing a coherent umbrella which contains but does not fully eliminate the internal strife.[46]

Sectoral

As competitive advantage has become more prevalent in economic-development strategy, different potential clusters within any metropolitan areas put themselves forward as the key to future prosperity, the sharpest of the possible cutting edges. Since the winning sector will become the regional "darling" for possibly decades to come, being designated as the prodigal child is a handsome prize. Often this becomes a contest between the tried and true, the industries that have brought the region to its current state, and the untested and risky, the dreams which might vault into a higher orbit.

Whichever the triumphant cluster, there is then a battle to decide which is its most fundamental component. This role has especially become a rallying cry for research universities, who claim that is the unending stream of discoveries from their faculties which fuels the engine. Already attempting to occupy the high ground as civilizing forces, they have added economic growth to their reason for being, calling for both public and private contributions to their operations but, in the name of free inquiry, resisting outside attempts to channel their investigations.

Another dimension in the sectoral battles is big versus small, old versus new. The larger corporations claim they merit the most attention. They employ thousands, they purchase millions in supplies and services from local sources, and they bring visibility to the region. What would Atlanta be without Coca-Cola, Detroit without General Motors, or Seattle without Boeing? As the largest egg in the metropolitan basket, they should be number one.

The smaller enterprises, the ones emerging from the incubators having developed without such support, assert that they represent the future. It will be from their ranks that the multinational corporations of tomorrow will arise. Today's leaders have largely plateaued while many of the newer firms have exponential growth rates. Therefore it only makes sense to have an economic-development strategy which will accelerate their flowering.

Finally, infrastructure interests sometimes claim that their facilities are the real engines, supporting not only the top cluster but also the rest of the economy. In coastal regions such as Baltimore or San Diego, the ports are likely to make this assertion. If their capacity is not expanded, then economic deterioration is inevitable. In almost every million-plus metropolitan area, airports attempt to position themselves as the prime mover. They are the mechanism bringing both people and cargo to and from the region. In putting forth these appeals, Dallas-Fort Worth's DFW complex and Chicago's O'Hare Airport are frequently cited as cases in point.

DOES IT MATTER?

Are all these efforts to improve metropolitan areas' economic well-being much ado about little? Are the ebbs and tides in national and global economies so powerful that they dwarf any initiatives taken by an individual region? Is success based more on good luck than sound policy?

After three decades of active economic-development efforts by local governments and public-private partnerships, the evidence that these policies contribute to prosperity is at best skimpy.[47] Wooing firms from elsewhere has had dubious reviews. As noted earlier, regions often overpay to have businesses relocate within their borders, the newcomers sometimes turn out to be not as attractive as they initially seemed; then the whole process triggers a bidding war to keep existing enterprises content to remain.

Breeding one's own businesses with incubators and the like has numerous anecdotal success stories but there are no carefully controlled experiments.[48] It could very well be that most of these firms would make it even if they were orphans, absent the supportive technical assistance. Similarly, as noted earlier, it is too soon to conclude that any of the initiatives aimed at the inner city can make a significant difference.

Cluster analysis is also far too recent to decide whether it holds the key to effective economic-development policy making. It requires thorough analysis before being applied and the techniques for conducting these studies are still evolving. At the moment, it is "an art, not a science" and "as an underdeveloped art, it is not a mechanical process."[49]

In Wolman and Spitzley's words, "why do they [local officials] do it, even though we tell them it does not work?"[50] The short answer is doing nothing is politically riskier than doing something, even if there is scant evidence that action will be beneficial. The electorate will be more sympathetic toward those who have, mimicking Shakespeare, pursued and lost than toward those who did not pursue at all. Moreover, there will usually be victories, if only by chance, and one can only claim credit if some deed preceded them. As long as governments avoid rigorous evaluations of the policy effectiveness, these anecdotal assertions cannot be fully challenged. Less cynically, maybe one or more of these economic-development strategies does indeed hold the answer. A metropolitan area will only know if it tries them. Beyond this, there is general consensus that regions must furnish modern infrastructure, quality education, and attractive amenities. Inadequate transportation, weak schooling, and a dull ambience are definite liabilities in the external chase for jobs and residents.

NOTES

1. Paul E. Peterson, *City Limits* (Chicago: University of Chicago Press, 1981), pg. 23.
2. Peter K. Eisinger, *The Rise of the Entrepreneurial State: State and Local Economic Development Policy in the United States* (Madison: University of Wisconsin Press, 1988), pp. 15–16.
3. Ibid., pp. 67–69.
4. Michael A. Pagano and Ann O'M. Bowman, *Cityscapes and Capital: The Politics of Urban Development* (Baltimore: Johns Hopkins University Press, 1995), pg. xiii.
5. Michael E. Porter, *The Competitive Advantage of Nations* (New York: Free Press, 1990).
6. Michael E. Porter, "Location, Competition, and Economic Development: Local Clusters in a Global Economy," *Economic Development Quarterly*, 14, no. 1 (February 2000), pg. 15–16.
7. This example is taken from Edward W. Hill and John F. Brennan, "A Methodology for Identifying the Drivers of Industrial Clusters: The Foundation of Regional Competitive Advantage," *Economic Development Quarterly*, 14, no. 1 (February 2000), pp. 65–96.
8. Susan E. Clarke and Gary L. Gaile, *The Work of Cities* (Minneapolis: University of Minnesota Press, 1998), pp. 225–232.
9. Ted K. Bradshaw and Edward T. Blakely, "What Are 'Third-Wave' State Economic Development Efforts? From Incentives to Industrial Policy," *Economic Development Quarterly*, 13, no. 3 (August 1999), pp. 229–44.
10. Michael McGuire, "The 'More Means More' Assumption: Congruence versus Contingency in Local Economic Development Research," *Economic Development Quarterly*, 13, no. 2 (May 1999), pp. 157–71.
11. Herbert Rubin, "Shoot Anything That Flies, Claim Anything That Falls," *Economic Development Quarterly*, 2, no. 3 (August 1988), pp. 236–51.
12. Samuel Nunn and Carl Schoedel, "Cities and Airport-Based Economic Development Strategies: An Analysis of Public-Private Deals to Provide Airline Maintenance Operation Centers in Urban Airports," *Economic Development Quarterly*, 9, no. 2 (May 1995), pp. 159–73.
13. Scott Loveridge, "On the Continuing Popularity of Industrial Recruitment," *Economic Development Quarterly*, 10, no. 2 (May 1996), pp. 151–58.
14. Peter S. Fisher and Alan H. Peters, *Industrial Incentives: Competition among American States and Cities* (Kalamazoo, Michigan: W.E. Upjohn Institute for Employment Research, 1998), pp. 7–10. Also see Dick Netzer, "An Evaluation of Interjurisdictional Competition Through Economic Development Incentives," in *Competition among State and Local Governments: Efficiency and Equity in American Federalism,* ed. Daphne A. Kenyon and John Kincaid (Washington: The Urban Institute, 1991), pp. 221–45.
15. Douglas J. Watson, John G. Heilman, and Robert S. Montjoy, *The Politics of Redistributing Urban Aid* (Westport, CT: Praeger, 1994).

16. Mark P. Rice and Jana B. Mathews, *Growing New Ventures, Creating New Jobs: Principles and Practices of Successful Business Incubators* (Westport, CT: Quorum, 1995).

17. Hugh Sherman and David S. Chappell, "Methodological Challenges in Evaluating Business Incubator Outcomes," *Economic Development Quarterly*, 12, no. 4 (November 1998), pp. 313–21.

18. Leon Taylor, "Can City Hall Create Private Jobs?" in *Dilemmas of Urban Economic Development*, ed. Richard D. Bingham and Robert Mier (Thousand Oaks, CA: Sage Publications, 1997), pp. 210–11.

19. Douglas Henton, John Melville, and Kimberly Walesh, *Grassroots Leaders for a New Economy: How Civic Entrepreneurs Are Building Prosperous Communities* (San Francisco: Jossey-Bass, 1997).

20. *Innovative Regions: The Importance of Place and Networks in the Innovative Economy* (Palo Alto, CA: Collaborative Economics, 1999), pg. 5.

21. Ibid., pg. 5.

22. Irwin Feller, "Universities as Engines of R & D-Based Economic Growth: They Think They Can," *Research Policy*, 19, no. 4 (August 1990), pp. 335–48.

23. *Collaborating to Compete in the New Economy: An Economic Strategy for California* (Sacramento: California Trade and Commerce Agency, 1997).

24. Earl H. Fry, *The Expanding Role of State and Local Governments in U.S. Foreign Affairs* (New York: Council on Foreign Relations, 1998), pg. 85.

25. Kala Seetharam Sridhar, "Tax Costs and Employment Benefits of Enterprise Zones," *Economic Development Quarterly*, 10, no. 1 (February 1996), pp. 69–90.

26. Alice O'Connor, "Swimming Against the Tide: A Brief History of Federal Policy in Poor Communities," in *Urban Problems and Community Development*, ed. Ronald F. Ferguson and William T. Dickens (Washington: Brookings Institution Press, 1999), pg. 116. Beginning in the early 1980s and extending through the present, most of the states have also initiated some type of enterprise zone initiative. See Karen Mossberger, *The Politics of Ideas and the Spread of Enterprise Zones* (Washington: Georgetown University Press, 2000), pp. 80–94.

27. See Marilyn Gittell and others, "Expanding Civic Opportunity: Urban Empowerment Zones," *Urban Affairs Review*, 33, no. 4 (March 1998), pp. 530–58; and Noah T. Jenkins and Michael I.J. Bennett, "Toward an Empowerment Zone Evaluation," *Economic Development Quarterly*, 13, no. 1 (February 1999), pp. 23–28.

28. Michael E. Porter, "New Strategies for Inner-City Economic Development," *Economic Development Quarterly*, 11, no. 1 (February 1997), pg. 12.

29. Michael E. Porter, "The Competitive Advantage of the Inner City," *Harvard Business Review*, 73, no. 3 (May-June 1995), pp. 55–71.

30. *Strategies for Business Growth in Chicago's Low-Income Neighborhoods* (Boston: The Boston Consulting Group and the Initiative for a Competitive Inner City, 1998), pp. 7–8.

31. Timothy Bates, "Response: Michael Porter's Conservative Urban Agenda Will Not Revitalize America's Inner Cities: What Will?" *Economic Development Quarterly*, 11, no. 1 (February 1997), pg. 39.

32. Edward J. Blakely and Leslie Small, "Michael Porter's New Gilder of Ghettos," in *The Inner City: Urban Poverty and Economic Development in the Next Century*, ed. By Thomas D. Boston and Catherine L. Ross (New Brunswick, NJ: Transaction Publishers, 1997), pg. 181.

33. Bennett Harrison and Amy K. Glasmerer, "Response: Why Business Alone Won't Redevelop the Inner City: A Friendly Critique of Michael Porter's Approach to Urban Revitalization," *Economic Development Quarterly*, 11, no. 1 (February 1997), pg. 29.

34. *1999 Directory of U.S. Microenterprise Programs* (Washington: The Aspen Institute, 1999).

35. Lisa Servon, "Credit and Social Capital: The Community Development Potential of U.S. Microenterprise Programs," *Housing Policy Debate*, 9, no. 1 (1998), pp. 115–49.

36. Deborah Page-Adams and Michael Sherraden, "Asset Building as a Community Revitalization Strategy," *Social Work*, 42, no. 5 (September 1997), pp. 423–44.

37. Mark Schreiner, "Self-Employment, Microenterprise, and the Poorest Americans," *Social Service Review*, 73, no. 4 (December 1999), pg. 518.

38. Lisa J. Servon, "Microenterprise Programs in U.S. Inner Cities: Economic Development or Social Welfare?" *Economic Development Quarterly*, 11, no. 2 (May 1997), pg. 177.

39. Arnold Fleischmann and Gary P. Green, "Organizing Local Agencies to Promote Economic Development," *American Review of Public Administration*, 21, no. 1 (March 1991), pp. 1–15.

40. Susan E. Clarke and Gary L. Gaile, "The Next Wave: Local Economic Development Strategies in the Post-Federal Era," *Economic Development Quarterly*, 6, no. 2 (May 1992), pp. 189–98.

41. Mark Schneider and Paul Teske, "The Progrowth Entrepreneur in Local Government," *Urban Affairs Quarterly*, 29, no. 2 (December 1993), pp. 316–27.

42. Robert A. Beauregard, "Public-Private Partnerships as Historical Chameleons: The Case of the United States," in *Partnerships in Urban Governance*, ed. Jon Pierre (New York: St. Martin's Press, 1998), pg. 62.
43. Norman Krumholz, "Equitable Approaches to Local Economic Development," *Policy Studies Journal*, 27, no. 1 (Spring 1999), pp. 83–94.
44. Peter Gordon and Harry W. Richardson, "Prove It: The Costs and Benefits of Sprawl," *Brookings Review*, 16, no. 4 (Fall 1998), pg. 24.
45. Anthony Downs, "Some Realities about Sprawl and Urban Decline," *Housing Policy Debate*, 10, no. 4 (1999), pp. 955–74. Also see Peter D. Linneman and Anita A. Summers, " Patterns and Processes of Employment and Population Decentralization in the United States," in *Urban Change in the United States and Western Europe*, ed. Anita A. Summers, Paul C. Cheshire, and Lanfranco Senn (Washington: Urban Institute Press, 1999), pp. 89–148.
46. Linda McCarthy, *Competitive Regionalism: Beyond Individual Competition* (Washington: U.S. Economic Development Administration, 2000).
47. Joseph Persky, Daniel Felsenstein, and Wim Wiewel, "How Do We Know That 'But for the Incentives' the Development Would Not Have Occurred?" in *Dilemmas in Urban Economic Development*, ed. Bingham and Mier, pp. 28–45.
48. Timothy J. Bartik and Richard D. Bingham, "Can Economic Development Programs Be Evaluated?" in *Dilemmas in Urban Economic Development*, ed. Bingham and Mier, pp. 246–77.
49. Kenneth Boytek and Larry Ledebur, "Is Industry Targeting a Viable Economic Development Strategy?" in *Dilemmas in Urban Economic Development*, ed. Bingham and Mier, pp. 190–91.
50. Harold Wolman and David Spitzley, "The Politics of Local Economic Development," *Economic Development Quarterly*, 10, no. 2 (May 1996), pg. 134.

SUGGESTED READINGS

BINGHAM, RICHARD D., and ROBERT MIER, eds. *Dilemmas of Urban Economic Development*. Thousand Oaks, CA: Sage Publications, 1998. Critical analyses, with commentaries, of the various approaches to economic development.

CLARKE, SUSAN E., and GARY L. GAILE. *The Work of Cities*. Minneapolis: University of Minnesota Press, 1998. Empirically grounded and conceptually rich treatment of the economic-development tools used by metropolitan areas both in the United States and abroad.

EISINGER, PETER K. *The Rise of the Entrepreneurial State: State and Local Economic Development Policy in the United States*. Madison: University of Wisconsin Press, 1988. Classic analysis of the origins and implementation of economic-development public policy, describing the transition from supply-side to demand-side programs.

HENTON, DOUGLAS, JOHN MELVILLE, and KIMBERLY WALESH. *Grassroots Leaders for a New Economy: How Civic Entrepreneurs Are Building Prosperous Communities*. San Francisco: Jossey-Bass, 1997. The bible, complete with exhortations and instructions, for taking a strategic and collaborative approach to metropolitan economic development.

DOING IT

Identify a major local governmental economic-development unit in a nearby metropolitan area. If there is one which works on behalf of the entire metropolitan area, use it. Otherwise select one which represents the central city or an urban county.

Based on the agency's documents, newspaper accounts, and interviews with one or more of its top managers, describe its economic-development strategy by answering the following questions:

1. Does it attempt to attract firms from outside the region? If so, what types of appeals are used? What businesses have relocated in the metropolitan area

within the past three years? What incentives were used to lure them? What has been the impact, positive and negative, on the region?

2. What efforts are used to develop local businesses? Does the agency support one or more incubators? If so, what kinds of firms do they house and what support services are provided? What are the principal sources of venture capital? What is the agency doing to raise additional investment funds for promising entrepreneurs?

3. Has the agency sponsored or participated in a cluster analysis for all or part of the metropolitan region? If so, what were the results and what is being done as a result of the study? What other capacity-building initiatives are being encouraged by the agency? Work force programs? Infrastructure improvements? Others?

CHAPTER 7

Transportation

THE SETTING

Productive metropolitan areas must move people and commodities expeditiously and efficiently between themselves and other regions. They must also do so within the boundaries of their own territory. If you cannot fly easily to a metropolis, if it is difficult to export goods by truck or rail or water, if congestion clogs the highways, if workers spend hours daily getting to and from their jobs, if electronic data cannot flow swiftly from one portal to another, then it will lag behind in the external metropolitan chase. Time is indeed money. The less of it spent in transit, the more profitable the enterprise.[1]

Transportation access has always been important. The U.S. metropolitan areas formed during the eighteenth and nineteenth centuries owe their precise location primarily to proximity to key waterways. The coastal cities—Boston, New York, Philadelphia, Seattle, San Francisco, San Diego—are adjacent to expansive deep water harbors. The inland metropolises lie astride one or more major rivers: Pittsburgh where the Allegheny and Monongahela join to form the Ohio, St. Louis near the confluence of the Illinois, Missouri, and Mississippi. More recent metropolitan areas, Atlanta being one example, had their initial spurt stimulated by railroad junctions.

Americans are traveling more than ever. Between 1977 and 1995, the number of daily trips made by the average person rose 79 percent, going from 2.9 to 4.3, with each traveling about forty miles a day locally.[2] The number of long-distance journeys, those one hundred miles or greater one way, increased at about the same rate, 74 percent. As of 1995, the typical person takes about four out-of-town trips a year,

Downtown Pittsburgh: Allegheny and Monongahela Rivers Form the Ohio River

each averaging approximately eight hundred miles round trip. Although the September 11, 2001, terrorist attacks on New York and Washington have lowered these rates, expectations are that they will return to their previous pace.

Automobiles are the preferred mode. About 90 percent of the local trips and 80 percent of the long distance ones are made by car. Bicycles and walking (6 percent) and public transit (4 percent) make up most of the remaining internal trips while airplanes have about 90 percent on the nonauto long-distance journeys. Adjusted for inflation, the cost of travel has dropped between 1977 and 1995, down 17 percent for automobiles and 30 percent for air. More people, increased trips per person, and lower cost have combined to create a transportation outburst.

The nation's businesses are also shipping more cargo. Between 1993 and 1997 alone, tonnage rose 14 percent, about 280 pounds a day for each American. Whether measured by weight or by value, trucks convey well over half of the freight with the remainder divided among rail, water, air, parcel and postal services, and pipelines. Intermodal shipments, those using more than one transit type such as containers moving from barges to truck, are especially on the rise.

Transportation is big business for the nation and for metropolitan areas. Through private expenditures and tax dollars, the nation spends well over $1 trillion annually on transportation facilities and services. The array is staggering: 4 million miles of paved roads, 200 million automobiles and light trucks, 7 million commercial trucks, 8,000 commercial airliners, over 1 million railroad freight cars operating on more than 100,000 miles of track, and much more.

INTERMETROPOLITAN TRIPS

Air Transit

Americans have a longstanding and intense relationship with their automobiles but air transportation is becoming a favored second choice. The number of domestic passenger miles flown has more than doubled during the past two decades while air cargo shipments have tripled. Each day in the United States, about 2 million people take more than 20,000 commercial flights. The nation's four busiest airports— Atlanta's Hartsfield, Chicago's O'Hare, Los Angeles International, and Dallas-Fort Worth International—each handle about 100,000 outgoing passengers daily.

People are not the only ones flying. The overnight shipping industry has revolutionized small package delivery. At Federal Express's massive exchange facility at the Memphis International Airport, each weekday evening witnesses a million parcels arriving from around the country during the late evening, sorted during the early morning hours, and then sent off to their final destination before dawn. UPS, the U.S. Postal Service, and Emery Worldwide have similar operations at, respectively, the Louisville, Indianapolis, and Dayton airports.

As knowledge has become the prime mover for so much of the new economy, it has become more meaningful than ever for people to meet face-to-face. Electronic mail, telephones, and faxes are useful communication supplements, but commerce is still a social endeavor. As such, it works best when words are accompanied by faces, verbal communications by nonverbal ones.

Nor is business primarily conducted within a few hundred mile sphere around any metropolis. The linkages extend around the country and across the world. That means the competitive metropolitan area must be able to send and receive passengers conveniently and speedily with as many other regions as possible. Time spent traveling is not very productive. The money is made once people have arrived. If one cannot readily get to several destinations from a metropolitan area, or many find it difficult to fly to that region, it will lag behind.

The metropolitan areas which do best in the air transit competition have three pluses: hub status, intense fare competition, and a massive airport. The hub phenomenon is a product of the Airline Deregulation Act of 1978. Prior to this legislation, the federal government regulated which routes airlines could serve and what prices they could charge. The companies competed for lucrative routes, using a mix of local, state, and national politicking to advance themselves. The result was a crazy quilt patchwork of point-to-point routes, created over several decades of lobbying.

After deregulation, airlines have been largely free to fly any routes they wish and charge whatever prices they think the market will bear. In order to get the optimal return on their substantial capital investment in planes, the airlines quickly discovered that a hub-and-spoke route system made the most sense. Say a company wants to serve eighty metropolitan areas. If it were to mount three nonstops a day in each direction between every pair, that would require 18,960 flights. But if it identifies a central location, a hub, among the eighty regions and has the same three flights a day each way between the hub and the remaining seventy-nine cities, the spokes, it only takes 474 trips. The flights can be scheduled so that there are brief layovers in the hub city so that traveling, say, from Syracuse to Albuquerque, a four-hour nonstop trip, might only require five-and-a-half hours with a connection in a hub like Chicago or Dallas-Fort Worth.[3]

It is better to be a hub than a spoke. Whether headed for a hub or a spoke, hub residents have nonstop flights. Spoke citizens are usually changing planes unless their business takes them to a hub. Connections take longer, chewing up time, and they raise the chances of travel disruptions caused by bad weather or equipment problems. Hubs also have more international flights. With all the spokes feeding traffic into them, there are a critical mass of passengers to justify wide body plane service to places like London, Frankfurt, and Tokyo. Finally, hubs generate more income for the internal metropolitan economy. As passengers change planes several times a day, bags are transferred, coffee and pizza consumed in the concourses, landing fees paid to the airport—all job and income producers.

It is even more preferable to be a hub for two carriers such as Chicago's O'Hare (American, United) or Dallas-Fort Worth (American, Delta) since that heightens competition and therefore tends to lower fares. If only one airline uses a metropolitan area as a hub, such as Northwest in Minneapolis-St. Paul or United in Denver, it then operates most of the flights from that site. It still must compete for spoke-to-spoke traffic, such as flying from Louisville to Portland through either the Twin Cities or Denver, but it does not need to worry about trips which begin or end at the hub.

In order to handle hundreds of flights, ensuring that most are on time, metropolitan areas need airports with multiple runways which can handle simultaneous arrivals and departures. The leading hubs have at least four strips, each adequately separated so that concurrent traffic can continue even under adverse weather conditions. With tens of thousands of passengers changing planes each day, these airports must also have expansive terminals with subways to ease transfers among concourses and shops and restaurants to make the brief stays more pleasant.

Next best to having two hub airlines is having one of the low-cost carriers enter the market. The most noted member of this maverick group is Southwest Airlines which uses tactics such as no meal service and no seat assignments to minimize expenses and maximize turnaround. When it locates in what had been a monopoly hub, such as with America West in Phoenix or Continental in Cleveland, it forces those carriers to lower their fares on routes served by both airlines.

Metropolitan areas which are not major hubs do three things to enhance their air transit capability. First, they attempt to be spokes to the largest possible number of hubs. That adds to the number of nonstop destinations and, even if connections are still required, it generates more travel options and creates tighter competition. Second, they seek to recruit a low-cost carrier, especially Southwest, to add them to their route system. Third, they do not give up on becoming a hub, entreating one of the airlines to establish a secondary axis at their airport, such as Delta in Salt Lake City or America West in Columbus.

Highways and Rail Transit

People prefer air travel for non-auto trips between metropolitan areas but most of the goods go by either truck or rail. Some bulk commodities, especially grain, often use river barges, and oil and natural gas often use pipelines. Overall, about 60 percent of the freight moves by truck or rail, 20 percent through pipelines, 15 percent via water, and 5 percent by air.[4]

As was the case with airlines, the federal government controlled interstate trucking and rail freight transportation, assigning routes and approving rates, for most of the twentieth century, limiting how much regions could do to improve their access to these modes. But two years after the airlines were deregulated in 1978, the Motor Carrier Act of 1980 and the Staggers Rail Act of 1980 removed many of the governmental controls. Some restrictions remained, more so than exist in the air sector, but the primary effect is similar: trucking companies and railroads are now much freer to adapt to changing market conditions.[5]

For railroads, this meant mergers, combining operations to achieve greater efficiencies which could then be translated into lower rates. The remaining four major rail networks—BNSF, CSXT, Norfolk Southern, and Union Pacific—concentrate much more on transit between the major metropolitan regions, abandoning many of their routes to smaller communities. Trucking companies multiplied, in part to fill this gap, going from 18,000 in 1980 to 49,000 by 1992.[6]

As for air transportation, metropolitan areas vie to occupy central nodes on the rail and highway networks. For rail, Chicago is far and away the big winner as the only large region served by all four top railroads. This makes it an extremely attractive location for industries requiring production components from all parts of the country or wishing to send finished products throughout the nation. The vast rail yards interchanging thousands of freight cars daily also generates many jobs.

Trucks rely primarily on the 46,000-mile interstate highway system. The more interstates a region has, the better placed it is for having efficient and plentiful trucking service. The ideal is to have interstates headed toward as many points on the compass as possible. Among the more favored are Atlanta, with interstates headed northwest and southeast (I-75), northeast and southwest (I-85), and west and east (I-20). Indianapolis is equally well positioned, with four different routes (I-65, I-69, I-70, I-74) coming through its boundaries (illustrated in Figure 7–1).

Another enviable location is astride one of the principal east-west or north-south arteries. Interstate 5 along the West Coast connects Seattle, San Francisco, Los Angeles, and San Diego while its East Coast counterpart, Interstate 95, links Boston, New York, Philadelphia, Washington, and Miami. Interstates 40, 70, and 80 dominate much of the transcontinental traffic, so being along one of them is a plus. Interstate 75, running through the midlands from northern Michigan to the tip of Florida, is still another key route.

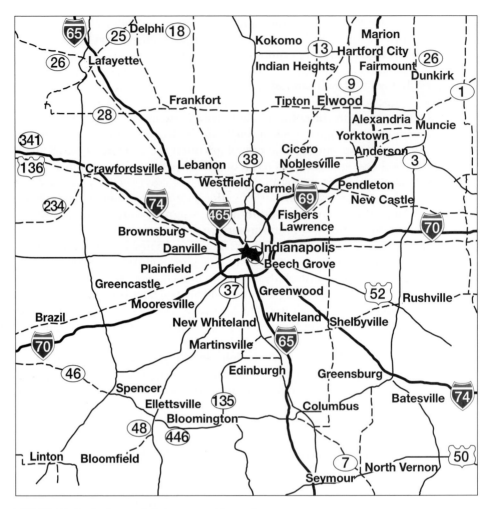

FIGURE 7–1   Indianapolis's Interstate Network

To facilitate truck freight operations, many metropolitan areas have built circumferential interstates: I-285 in Atlanta, I-275 in Cincinnati, I-465 in Indianapolis, I-255/270 in St. Louis. Along or near these beltways are distribution warehouses. This combination means that the eighteen-wheelers do not have to tangle with inner-city traffic. Instead they can pick up and drop off their loads on the periphery, letting smaller local trucks move the cargo within the region.

Since the interstate highway system is essentially in place, with more emphasis on maintaining the current roads than on building additional ones, many metropolitan areas are left with a gap in their network. Birmingham has no direct connection with the southeast or St. Louis with the northwest, to take two examples. Having lost out on the original development of the network, they are still struggling to cope with the consequences and, on occasion, seek to have just a few more routes added.

Once fierce competitors and still sometime rivals, the trucking firms and railroads now cooperate much more than they have in the past, taking advantage of the strengths of each of their modes. Trucks can go virtually anywhere but become more costly to operate over long distances. Trains are limited to where the rails go but become quite efficient as the miles add up. The answer is to combine them, having a truck pick up the cargo, then driving to a nearby rail yard to transfer the trailer or a container to a freight car, then traversing most of the distance by train, and then having a truck retrieve the cargo for the ultimate delivery. This process, termed intermodal transport, has tripled during the past three decades and now accounts for about one-fifth of all rail traffic. Recognizing this trend, metropolitan areas are now revamping their infrastructure to ease the rail-truck and, for river and lake regions, the water-rail-truck connections.

Rail and bus passenger loads account for only 2 percent of the intercity trips and, for most metropolitan areas, are not a serious factor in current regional competition. The principal exception is the Northeast Corridor where the Boston-New York-Philadelphia-Baltimore-Washington link is being upgraded to lower travel times to three hours for the Boston-New York leg and two-and-a-half hours for the New York-Washington trip. This will give this entire megapolis a competitive advantage, offering a speedy and comfortable alternative to air passage and relieving congestion along highway routes.[7] Other corridors considering similar improvements include San Francisco-Oakland-Sacramento-Los Angeles-San Diego, Portland-Seattle, and a Chicago hub with spokes to Indianapolis/Cincinnati, Detroit, Milwaukee, Minneapolis-St. Paul, and St. Louis.

INTRAMETROPOLITAN TRIPS

Automobiles

In earlier times, transportation within metropolitan areas was a much simpler system. The bulk of the jobs were in the central city, with most residents living within a few miles of their workplace. All that was needed for trips to and from employment were roads and public transit links between the many residential locations and downtown and its environs. As for personal trips, most of the frequent destinations—grocery stores, laundries, barber shops—were within walking distance of one's home. Less common journeys, say for a medical appointment or to attend a movie, were also straightforward since doctors' offices and theaters were usually located on public transit lines. Take the trolley to work, walk to the store. Life was simpler.

No more. As Chapter 1 described, the modern metropolis has many employment nodes as well as multiple entertainment locations. What was a hub-and-spoke system up through the twentieth century's midpoint, still often reflected in rail transit networks, is now an intricate web. Some trips still take people from suburb to city but even by 1980 there were more than two trips between suburban points for every one trip between a suburb and a city in metropolitan areas such as Atlanta.[8] No longer could public transit bear much of the intrametropolitan transit load. There were just too many origin-destinations combinations, far more than the number of rail lines and bus routes. In 1945, more than one in three trips were done by public transit. Just one decade later, 1955, the share was down to one in ten.[9] Today, it approaches one in fifty.[10]

Lower residential density and separating subdivisions from retail stores also contributes to the automobile's centrality. The more people spread out in single-family dwellings on large lots and the greater the distance between living quarters and shopping outlets, the more and longer automobile trips are needed.[11] The journey to visit Uncle Wally and the doing of errands at the dry cleaners both require more time and mileage.

So today's metropolitan areas have more automobiles, over 100 million, traveling on approximately 250,000 miles of paved roads and over more than 100,000 bridges. Ninety-two percent of the households have at least one car or truck, with the average residence having 1.8. With a few exceptions, most notably New York, it is difficult to conduct a normal life without owning a vehicle.

The result is heightened traffic congestion. A recent study of sixty-eight metropolitan areas, including most of the nation's largest regions, finds it takes twice as long to get somewhere during rush periods in 1997 as it did in 1982 and, in over half of the regions, delays have more than tripled.[12] In addition, the commuting period is longer, often extending over three hours each in the morning and afternoon.

For the most congested regions—Atlanta, Boston, Detroit, Los Angeles, Seattle, and Washington—the average commuting driver spends over sixty hours a year stalled in traffic, costing several hundred dollars a year in fuel costs alone.[13] Congestion has few defenders. It is a drag on the metropolitan economy since most time spent idling in traffic is not productive. In its more acute manifestations, it creates a damaging impression that a region is just too difficult a place to get around, thereby losing its allure as a place to live and work. Atlanta, for example, has become so concerned about its rising rank among the nation's most crowded roads that it has strengthened its transportation decision-making apparatus.[14] As Chapter 11 will discuss further, it pollutes the air, making the region less healthy and subjecting it to economic sanctions by the national government.

Fighting congestion therefore becomes a top priority for participants in the metropolitan chase. But how? The most straightforward response would be to build more roads—either build entirely new highways or add lanes to existing ones. As the accompanying cartoon portrays humorously, however, many regard this as a slippery slope with only temporary benefits. In the short run, the added capacity lowers travel time but that makes those locations more attractive, stimulating demand to build residences and stores near the route. Within a few years, congestion has often returned to its earlier levels. Even if it were effective, building more roads comes at a high price. The same study of sixty-eight regions estimates that, for the entire group, "it would take an annual addition of 1,087 lane-miles of freeway and 1,432 lane-miles of principal arterial streets each year to maintain current levels."[15]

The Highway Congestion Mantra
Source: Kirk Anderson

Another alternative is to squeeze more out of the existing road network. The most common target is reducing the number of people driving alone. Single occupancy vehicles account for the vast majority of trips, especially suburb-to-suburb commutes.[16] There are an increasing number of programs to encourage car pooling, using public relations outreach to identify potential partners and even subsidizing the purchase of vans, either by employers or governmental agencies. High-occupancy vehicle lanes on expressways, set aside for the exclusive use of vehicles having multiple passengers, have been tried in many metropolitan areas, including Houston, Los Angeles, and Seattle. Their primary drawback is that they free up space in the remaining lanes for additional driver-only cars so that there is no net benefit in traffic flow.[17]

Intelligent transportation systems are another approach. San Antonio, for example, combines cameras on freeway light poles and message boards, all controlled by a central facility, to manage traffic on the region's major arteries, alerting drivers to backups and suggesting alternative routes.[18] New York, Phoenix, and Seattle are also experimenting with this strategy, which requires a significant technological investment and extensive intergovernmental cooperation.

Many economists recommend congestion pricing, charging motorists for driving either on high-traffic routes or at popular times.[19] This is the textbook method for reducing demand. Those who really need such trips will pay while those who can use alternate routes or defer their travel to a less crowded time will do so in order to forego the toll. Recent experiments include an express lane on Interstate 15 in San Diego, and State Route 91 connecting Orange, Riverside, and San Bernardino counties within the Los Angeles region.

Making automobile travel significantly more expensive, especially compared to public transit, would be another alternative to reduce congestion. A bus can carry the equivalent of almost seventy single-occupancy cars and a four-to-eight-car rail transit many times more. But neither imposing higher taxes on cars and gasoline nor increasing subsidies for mass transit is politically palatable. Americans have both an economic investment in and an emotional attachment to their automobiles. Having made that major purchase, they want the personal travel freedom which accompanies it.

Public Transit

Mass transit has had difficulties adjusting to the new metropolitan realities. By definition, rail tracks have fixed routes. They work most efficiently either when there are thousands of people who wish to go between Point A (e.g., Westport, Connecticut) and Point B (Downtown New York City) or when hundreds of thousands of residents, many in high density neighborhoods, live along several points on a single line which also serves major employers and other popular destinations (e.g., Washington Metro's Blue Line whose stops include Ronald Reagan National Airport, Pentagon City, Rosslyn, Capitol Hill, and the RFK Stadium). Such routes still exist but they are largely confined to the relatively few metropolitan areas which combine multimillion populations with compact residential communities.

For most regions, rail is not a viable option unless developed on the premise that if you build a line, people and businesses will then cluster along it. Instead of serving an existing dense corridor, the strategy is to use rail to encourage more concentration. Mass transit then becomes a tool in shaping land-use patterns. The light-rail projects described below often have this goal as part of their rationale, an approach termed "transit-oriented development."[20]

Buses are the universal workhorses of mass transit. They carry about 60 percent of all passengers using that mode and, with the flexibility to adapt their routes to changing conditions and a variety of sizes, every metropolitan area has a bus network. Routes with modest usage can have service scheduled at longer intervals, every half hour or hour, while those with high demand can have buses at more frequent intervals. Increasingly, transit system fleets include both smaller 20–30 passenger units along with the more traditional 60–70 person models. Fares are relatively low, often under $1 per ride, making them financially accessible to the less than 10 percent of the population who depend on mass transit because they do not own automobiles.

Heavy-rail transit—old-timers like Chicago's "El" system and New York's subways and newer versions such as Atlanta's MARTA and San Francisco's BART—partner with the buses in the nation's largest metropolitan regions. These systems use an electrified rail, usually known as the third rail, as a power source. Even though they are confined to fewer than ten regions, their ability to serve high-density routes with short intervals between each train generates about 30 percent of the country's mass-transit journeys. Most of these giant metropolises also have commuter rail, trains running on existing railroad tracks from the exurbs and the suburbs to the central business district during rush hours. Their prices are three-or-more times as high as buses and heavy rail, with their target ridership being upscale workers.

Bus, heavy-rail, and commuter-rail patronage has remained relatively constant in recent years, with buses declining slightly and the two rail modes increasing modestly. Experiencing the most growth is the newest public-transit entrant, light rail, a modern version of yesterday's streetcar. These one-to-four-car units also use electric power, typically drawn from wires running above the right-of-way. Although they still account for less than 5 percent of mass transit trips, their ridership has risen by almost 50 percent during the 1990s.

Metropolitan areas without the density to support heavy rail but wanting to break out of the buses-only brigade, regions such as Dallas-Fort Worth, Denver, Portland, San Diego, and St. Louis, have developed one or more light-rail lines during the past two decades. Despite the modest density along these routes, they have been able to meet or exceed rider projections.[21] The light-rail cars are spiffier, avoiding the downscale images of buses and thereby attracting passengers from a

A Light Rail Train in Portland, Oregon

wider socioeconomic spectrum. Transit systems have also redesigned their bus routes, feeding passengers into light-rail stations to transfer for the longer journey, a process similar to the airlines' hub-and-spoke approach.

Confronted with heightened automobile congestion, metropolitan areas are experimenting with other approaches beyond new light-rail lines in order to have more trips, especially commuter journeys, done by public transit rather than by car. One strategy is to make bus trips faster. Using the model set by Curtiba, Brazil, Miami has built an exclusive two-lane right-of-way, the South Dade Busway, for buses along a major north-south corridor. The capital costs are less than for rail and, in the first two years of operation, ridership has almost doubled.

Another tactic is to use the tax code to induce employers to shift their subsidy for employee parking to support for mass-transit commuting. Instead of paying, directly or indirectly, for places for workers' cars, companies can now pick up the tab for all or part of public-transit passes. Under recent federal legislation, these contributions are tax free to the employee, thereby making public transit more economically appealing.

There is little expectation that all of these strategies to increase public-transit usage will make much of a dent in metropolitan areas' traffic congestion. Although they might help at the margin, shifting thousands of trips from cars to buses or rail, these will be far outnumbered by additional automobile traffic as regions add people and expand their boundaries. As Anthony Downs concludes, "there is no such thing as an easy solution to the traffic congestion problem (and) . . . it is a condition inherent in the quality of modern metropolitan life."[22]

Paratransit

Automobiles and public transit account for the overwhelming proportion of intra-metropolitan trips but there are a few specialized modes for addressing particular niches, each having multiple passengers or users for the same vehicle in an effort to minimize the number of cars on the road. These include shared ride taxis, dial-a-ride services, jitneys, and vanpools. These modes handle small numbers of passengers, usually fifteen or less, and collectively account for between 1 and 5 percent of trips within metropolitan areas.[23]

All these paratransit alternatives identify and collect a small number of individuals interested in going from one place to another or to several locations along the same route in a way that they can use the same vehicle. Shared ride taxis are most common for airport to downtown routes, allowing two or more strangers to divide a single cab. Dial-a-ride vans use a central dispatching service to guide a multipassenger van from one or more pickup points to one or more destinations. They are also used in gathering travelers throughout a region for trips to the airport, such as the SuperShuttle service in regions like Los Angeles and San Francisco, and public-transit agencies increasingly employ them to serve the distinctive transportation needs of persons with disabilities. Jitneys typically follow a fixed route, with minor deviations, using privately owned-and-operated vans to pick up and drop off passengers anywhere along the passage. Vanpools collect employees at their homes in a portion of the region and deliver them to and from their work site.

Car sharing is the most recent innovation in intrametropolitan transit. Modeled after similar programs in Canada and Europe, it allows households located within the same vicinity to share a fleet of automobiles. Instead of one unit/one car, the ratio can be several residences to a single vehicle since not everyone needs an automobile at the same time. The costs are thereby divided among a larger clientele. CarSharing Portland pioneered this approach in 1997 and Seattle's Flexcar joined the movement in 2000.[24]

SPATIAL MISMATCH

As jobs have dispersed to the suburbs and poverty households become more concentrated within central cities, there is a growing breach, a spatial mismatch, between employment opportunities and low-income job seekers.[25] Inner-city residents seeking entry-level positions like janitor or fast-food worker find that most of them are located on the periphery, ten to thirty miles away from their residences. If they do not have an automobile or if their car's condition is subpar, they must rely on public transportation for their commute. For many, even if they have landed a job, the combination of low pay and high auto-insurance premiums makes car ownership prohibitive.

Mass-transit networks, however, are not designed to handle central city to suburban commutes . While the systems typically cover most of the central city and inner suburbs, there are at best sparse tentacles into the outer portions of the region. Even these are primarily express buses or commuter rail lines to help middle- and upper-income suburbanites journey to downtown jobs. There are few routes which go from the inner city to the fringe or, for that matter, from one suburb to another and, even when they do exist, they run infrequently, making for lengthy commutes.[26] Moreover, there is often no service to deliver workers to entry-level night-shift positions, cleaning offices in edge cities or unloading trucks in the warehouses along the circumferential interstate.

The passage of the Personal Responsibility and Work Opportunity Reconciliation Act in 1996, the legislation that mandates that most able-bodied welfare recipients must find jobs within two years or otherwise lose their benefits, has made the situation more acute. One set of public entities—national and state governments—are insisting that those on welfare absolutely must find gainful employment while another group—metropolitan transit agencies—are unable to provide widespread service to get these individuals from where most of them live to where the bulk of the jobs are. Complicating matters further is that many of these low-income job seekers are single parents. This means that the journey from home to job must also often include an intermediate stop each way at a day care facility.[27]

Spatial mismatch is more of a problem for some metropolitan areas than for others. First, and most obviously, it affects larger regions, those where population and employment is spread over a wider land mass, more than smaller metropolitan areas. Second, some central cities, Dallas and San Francisco are two examples, continue to add entry-level posts and therefore nearby economic opportunity for low-income residents. Other downtowns and their environs such as Boston, New York, Philadelphia, and St. Louis have had major drops in the past three decades and, in these cases, suburbs contain the overwhelming share of the openings. Third, some public transit systems including those in Atlanta, Chicago, and Philadelphia are not well structured to meet the challenge.[28] Atlanta, most notably, has essentially no mass transit service to its rapidly growing northern suburbs.

Expanding awareness of and knowledge about spatial mismatch is spawning several attempts to address it. Some public transit systems are experimenting with special bus runs between central city neighborhoods and exurban employment centers, often subsidized with federal funds under the Access to Jobs program. Some outer suburban employers, especially those in tighter labor markets, are dealing directly with the issue, providing van service for their inner-city workers. Still other regions, recognizing that automobiles will remain the dominant mode, are exploring ways to make car ownership and operations less expensive for those moving from welfare to work.

TELECOMMUNICATIONS

People and commodities are not the only things that need to be moved swiftly and efficiently among and within metropolitan areas. As individuals and firms rely more on voice and data communications, those must also be readily available at multiple sites within a region. Not only must corporate executives and manufacturing parts be able to get from here to there, so too must packets of data, typically measured in electronic bits per second, be able to flow freely and smoothly.

The best analogy, albeit an imperfect one, is to water. Regions need huge amounts, and if there is not a nearby river, then aqueducts connecting them to ample sources must be built. Los Angeles, for example, was able to thrive only after it was linked to Northern Californian lakes and rivers. Within metropolitan areas, industries relying on water for production processes must have large conduits coupling them to the liquid network and residences need smaller pipes in order to meet their daily requirements.

As more firms and households depend on electronically transmitted information for their business and personal needs, regions must provide a network for delivering it. It must have some combination of cable (fiber optic, coaxial, or wire), focused beams such as microwaves, and broadcast facilities like satellite sending and receiving dishes, all able to convey huge quantities at lightning speed. The analogy, again, is to the earlier infrastructure systems—electricity, natural gas, roads, sewers—already in place.[29]

For the competition between metropolitan areas, the aim is to be a major switching center on what has become known as the Internet backbone.[30] These are the largest portals, operating at billions (giga) of bits a second. Being on the

Fiber Optic Cable Being Installed in Downtown Austin, Texas

backbone is like having a hub airport or several interstates. It links the region with the other primary players. It means massive data files can move easily into and out of the local business and research computers. It enables telephone call centers handling hundreds of thousands of financial transactions each day. If a region is on the periphery of the information highway, it will lose out in the contest for data-dependent enterprises.

Information coming in and out of a metropolitan area must be distributed to its users. It must be quickly down- and up-loaded into the backbone. This requires significant capacity, the technical term is bandwidth, within the region. At the moment, the premier option is fiber optic cable which has much more bandwidth and considerably higher dependability than older alternatives like coaxial cable (the type used by most cable television systems) or copper wire, the standby of the telephone network. As a result, regions are competing with one another to facilitate the laying of extensive fiber optic trunklines. Just as businesses want to be located near truck, rail, air, and highway links, so too they want to be able to connect to a nearby fiber optic line.

This creates competition within metropolitan areas. As William Mitchell notes, "tapping directly into a broadband data highway is like being on Main Street, but a low baud-rate connection puts you out in the boonies, where the flow of information reduces to a trickle, where you cannot make so many connections, and where interactions are less intense."[31] Not every place within a region can be Main Street. Some will be farther away from a high-speed carrier. If, for example, a printing business increasingly receives text and artwork electronically, and if it lacks a fast connection, then it will lose its market edge since customers will find it cumbersome to send it materials. Having access to data highways is still one more obstacle for revitalizing inner-city neighborhoods and growing minority businesses since, at the moment, they are less likely to have the appropriate information linkages.[32]

WHO PAYS? WHO DECIDES?

Most U.S. transportation policy is based on three principles: the authority to tax and spend for transportation is shared by all governmental levels, those who use transportation facilities should pay for a significant part of their costs, and taxes levied on transportation usage should only be spent on that function.[33] Like any postulates regarding the American political process, there are exceptions here and there, but this perspective—federalism and dedicated funds raised from users—carries the most influence.

Although transportation spending and decision making involves all levels of government—national, state, and local—the units within the metropolitan region are definitely the junior partners. Because the bulk of the money, especially highway funds, is raised through national and state taxes and appropriated by their respective legislatures, they call most of the shots. As they seek support for their airports, public transit, interstate highways, and other transportation facilities, regions must play the game by the federal and state rules.

The national and state governments both reserve the authority to tax transportation usage, either directly through, for example, a ticket fee on airline passengers, or indirectly such as taxing gasoline or tires. Interest groups affected by these levies—the airline industry, automobile driver associations, truckers, and the like—have accepted having their usage taxed if there is a guarantee that the revenues will be devoted exclusively to transportation. Indeed, many states' constitutions expressly forbid spending fuel taxes on anything not directly connected to highways and bridges.

Highways

National and state governments have a longstanding division of responsibility concerning highways. Both participate in planning their routes and in paying for their construction. Both tax gasoline, motor oil, tires, and other related items to fund them. The states build and maintain the highways, even when they carry an Interstate or U.S. designation. The federal government establishes standards such as pavement depth and coordinates planning both within and among the states so that, to take an obvious example, highways connect when they cross state boundaries.

There is no shortage of interest-group support for building more highways. The tens of millions of drivers, the automobile producers, the road builders, and the trucking firms all urge their legislators to spend generously. Over the years, they have created expectations that vehicular transportation is a top priority and that the public sector will respond promptly to its needs. So it does. Currently, the national Highway Trust Fund, created in 1956, disperses about $30 billion a year and states allocate many billions more. For the most part, these amounts are off limits to any other spending objective. They can only be disbursed on road-related items. This means they do not have to compete in the annual or biennial appropriation competition. The decision about how much to spend on roads—and that's quite a bit—has been made for the indefinite future. The only remaining issue is which projects in what states get the money.

Confronted with the willingness of higher-level governments to pick up the tab and acknowledging the breadth of backing for highway construction, metropolitan areas end up doing mostly what their state and national governments want to do. Although acting individually or through their metropolitan planning organizations, local governments *could* veto projects and *could* refuse to accept the national or state funds, that is a nonstarter politically. By and large, it is the state transportation units, through which the federal dollars flow and to which the state resources come, which hold the upper hand.[34]

Public Transit

Building and supporting roads has been accepted as a federal and state responsibility since the early days of the republic. Mass transit, however, largely began as a business initiative, with private firms building and operating the original subways, streetcars, and buses. Gradually, as metropolitan areas became less dense and automobiles more prevalent, companies could no longer make a profit providing transit in urban areas. By the 1960s, most of their operations had been taken over by some governmental entity, most typically a special district or public authority.

That left local governments responsible for subsidizing mass transit. It was no longer a money maker—that is why it had been abandoned by the private sector—and the costs could not be recouped through fares alone. At the present time, for example, the average mass-transit trip requires about a $1.25 subsidy above and beyond the fare. Raising ticket prices would be counterproductive, causing even more people to shift to automobiles and lowering ridership even further.

The subsidy could come from local taxes but given that the federal and state governments were paying for highways, why not ask them to also pick up part of the expenses for public transit? Many state governments, especially those with significant rural contingents, were and are unsympathetic but the large city electoral contribution to the Democratic Party's presidential-support coalition created a breakthrough for federal funds in the 1960s, most notably the passage of the Urban Mass Transportation Act of 1964.[35] Noting that highways had a dependable source from the dedicated Highway Trust Fund, public transit backers sought a similar entitlement—but it was not until 1982 that, in return for supporting a gas tax increase for highways, a small sliver of the money was dedicated to mass transit.[36]

Currently, the national government furnishes slightly more than $6 billion a year for public transit. Most of these funds are designated for capital expenditures, buying new equipment or building new lines. The federal allocations have not expanded nearly as fast as metropolitan aspirations, especially for the increasingly popular light-rail lines. As a result, there is an intensifying political competition from the approximately twenty regions seeking to initiate or expand light-rail lines, causing the federal government to spend moderate amounts across many systems, slowing the overall pace of development in any one metropolitan area unless it chooses to fund it from local sources.

ISTEA/TEA-21

In 1991, the federal government changed the funding rules for metropolitan transportation. As described in Chapter 5, the Intermodal Surface Transportation Efficiency Act (ISTEA) gave regions more flexibility in how national funds were spent, including the ability to shift funds across categories. Highway dollars could be spent on public transit, or vice versa, and either could also go for special programs to lessen traffic congestion or improve air quality. Metropolitan planning organizations (MPOs) are given more authority and enhanced responsibility for coordinating these decisions.

The impact has not been revolutionary—but it has been significant. Between 1992 and 1999, metropolitan areas collectively transferred slightly more than $4 billion from highway to public transit (about $1 out of every $8 eligible to be shifted).[37] Two-thirds of these reallocations, however, have occurred in just six states, California, Illinois, Massachusetts, New Jersey, New York, and Pennsylvania—the nation's most populous jurisdictions, containing some of its largest metropolitan areas.

ISTEA's successor legislation, the Transportation Equity Act for the 21st Century (TEA-21) enacted in 1998, retains the discretionary authority for regions to move funds from one objective to another. Highways are still number one and their political strength remains formidable. But their sacred status has been qualified and their funding exclusivity ended. As a condition of federal funding, regions, acting through their MPOs, must take a more planned and coordinated approach to metropolitan transportation policy making, encouraging additional public participation and incorporating land-use and environmental factors. In short, the national government has linked its funding carrot to a regulatory stick to insist on more regional decision making.[38]

Airports

Metropolitan areas have an easier time finding money to operate and expand their airports. The federal government taxes every passenger ticket and, like the gasoline levies, these go into a dedicated source, the Airport and Airways Trust Fund. That revenue flow, now exceeding $6 billion annually, is more than enough to operate the nation's air-traffic control system and still have almost $2 billion left for airport improvements, a pot eagerly fought over by metropolitan regions. Federal legislation also allows local jurisdictions to impose a head tax on each passenger as long as the proceeds are used for airport purposes.

Even absent federal assistance, airports are money-makers. Airlines pay to land their planes, rent their gates, and lease space for offices and clubs. Passengers pay to park, eat, drink, and recreate. Taxis and shuttle services pay to transport people to and from the terminals. Rental car companies pay for counter space and parking lots. It all adds up to big bucks, enough to cover all the expenses and have something left over for other public services.

Instead of who pays, airport controversies within metropolitan areas focus on where and how the airport expands. As air traffic becomes more critical for regional development, it requires more space. Should an entirely new airport be built, as Denver did in the 1990s? If so, where? Should the existing airport add one or more runways, as is or has been done in Pittsburgh and St. Louis? If so, in which direction should the expansion occur? Should a second or third reliever airport be designated, as is being debated in Chicago? If so, which one in what part of the region? There is near universal support for airport improvements conceptually, but much disagreement over who must tolerate the noise and congestion aggravations.

Intercity Rail and Waterways

Just as private enterprises found urban mass transit to be a losing proposition and started bailing out in the 1950s and 1960s, so too railroads decided that transporting freight was more lucrative than carrying passengers during the same period. To fill the gap, Congress initiated a government corporation, now called Amtrak, in the early 1970s. The aim was for Amtrak's operations to be self-supporting but, with the possible exception of the Northeast Corridor, that has failed.[39] As a result, the national government is providing upwards of $600 million a year in subsidies and some state governments are also contributing. In return, these units are insisting on having a say on which routes receive what service. The federal government, acting through the Surface Transportation Board, also retains some regulatory authority over rail-freight traffic.

The U.S. Department of Transportation is the federal agency involved in all modes except water. For the nation's inland waterways, the U.S. Army Corps of Engineers is in charge.[40] It operates hundreds of locks and dams and maintains navigation channels, paying for these services from both fees charged to barge traffic as well as from general revenues. Although many metropolitan areas, especially those on principal streams like the Ohio and Mississippi, have a meaningful stake in river transportation, they must work through the Corps of Engineers to achieve their objectives.

NOTES

1. Susan Hanson, "Getting There: Urban Transportation in Context," in *The Geography of Urban Transportation,* 2nd ed., ed Susan Hanson (New York: Guilford Press, 1995), pp. 3–25.
2. Unless otherwise noted, all the statistics in this chapter are from the U.S. Department of Transportation.
3. For more on the airline industry's characteristics, see Steven A. Morrison and Clifford Winston, *The Evolution of the Airline Industry* (Washington: Brookings Institution Press, 1995); *Twenty Years of Deregulation: 1978 to 1998* (Washington: U.S. Federal Aviation Administration, 1999); and Morrison and Winston, *The Economic Effects of Airline Deregulation* (Washington: Brookings Institution, 1986).
4. Clifford Winston and others, *The Economic Effects of Surface Freight Deregulation* (Washington: Brookings Institution, 1990), pg. 2.
5. Paul Teske, Samuel Best, and Michael Mintrom, *Deregulating Freight Transportation: Delivering the Goods* (Washington: The AEI Press, 1995). Also see Steven A. Morrison and Clifford Winston, "Regulatory Reform of U.S. Intercity Transportation," in *Essays in Transportation Economics and Policy,* ed. Jose Gomez-Ibanez, William B. Tye, and Clifford Winston (Washington: Brookings Institution Press, 1999), pp. 469–92.
6. Teske, Best, and Mintrom, *Deregulating Freight Transportation,* pg. 71.
7. James A. Dunn, Jr., *Driving Forces: The Automobile, Its Enemies, and the Politics of Mobility* (Washington: Brookings Institution Press, 1998), pp. 129–32.
8. Ronald L. Mitchelson and James O. Wheeler, "Analysis of Aggregate Flows: The Atlanta Case," in *The Geography of Urban Transportation,* ed. Hanson, pg. 133.
9. Dunn, *Driving Forces,* pg. 103.
10. John F. Kain, "The Urban Transportation Problem: A Reexamination and Update," in *Essays in Transportation Economics and Policy,* ed. Gomez-Ibanez, Tye, and Winston, pg. 365.
11. Anthony Downs, *Stuck in Traffic: Coping with Peak-Hour Traffic Congestion* (Washington: Brookings Institution, 1992).
12. *1999 Annual Mobility Report* (College Station: Texas Transportation Institute, 1999), Chapter III.
13. *1999 Annual Mobility Report,* Tables 4 and 7.
14. Alan Ehrenhalt, "The Czar of Gridlock," *Governing,* 12, no. 8 (May 1999), pp. 20–27.
15. *1999 Annual Mobility Report,* Chapter V.
16. Eric I. Pas, "The Urban Transportation Planning Process," in *The Geography of Urban Transportation,* ed. Hanson, pg. 57.
17. Vukan R. Vuchic, *Transportation for Livable Cities* (New Brunswick, New Jersey: Center for Urban Policy Research, 1999), pp. 112–18.
18. Marilyn J. Cohodas, "Roads to Nowhere," *Governing,* 12, no. 9 (June 1999), pg. 62.
19. *Curbing Gridlock: Peak Period Fees to Relieve Congestion* (Washington: National Research Council, 1993).
20. Peter Calthorpe, *The Next American Metropolis: Ecology, Community, and the American Dream* (Princeton, New Jersey: Princeton Architectural Press, 1993).
21. Ellen Perlman, "The Little Engine That Might," *Governing,* 11, no. 11 (August 1998), pp. 36–40.
22. Anthony Downs, "Some Realities about Sprawl and Urban Decline," *Housing Policy Debate,* 10, no. 4 (1999), pg. 970.
23. Robert Cervero, *Paratransit in America: Redefining Mass Transportation* (Westport, Connecticut: Praeger, 1997), pp. 14–23.
24. Richard Katzey, *Car Sharing Portland: Review and Analysis of its First Year* (Portland, Oregon: Public Policy Research, 1999).
25. John F. Kain, "The Spatial Mismatch Hypothesis: Three Decades Later," *Housing Policy Debate,* 3, no. 2 (1992), pp. 374–460; John D. Kasarda, "Industrial Restructuring and the Changing Location of Jobs," in *State of the Union: America in the 1990s: Economic Trends,* ed. Reynolds Farley (New York: Russell Sage, 1995), pp. 215–67; and Michael A. Stoll, Harry J. Holzer, and Keith R. Ihlanfeldt, "Within Cities and Suburbs: Racial Residential Concentration and the Spatial Distribution of Employment Opportunities across Sub-Metropolitan Areas," *Journal of Policy Analysis and Management,* 19, no. 2 (Spring 2000), pp. 207–31.
26. Katherine M. O'Regan and John M. Quigley, "Accessibility and Economic Opportunity," in *Essays in Transportation Economics and Policy,* ed. Gomez-Ibanez, Tye, and Winston, pp. 437–66.
27. Susan Hanson and Geraldine Pratt, *Gender, Work, and Space* (New York: Routledge, 1995).
28. Margaret Pugh, "Barriers to Work: The Spatial Divide between Jobs and Welfare Recipients in Metropolitan Areas" (Washington: Brookings Institution Center on Urban and Metropolitan Policy, September 1998).

29. Stephen Graham and Simon Marvin, *Telecommunications and the City: Electronic Spaces, Urban Places* (London: Routledge, 1996), pp. 278–82.
30. William J. Mitchell, *E-Topia: "Urban Life, Jim—But Not as We Know It"* (Cambridge, MA: The MIT Press, 1999), pg. 19.
31. William J. Mitchell, *City of Bits: Space, Place, and the Infobahn* (Cambridge, MA: The MIT Press, 1995), pg. 17.
32. *The Technological Reshaping of Metropolitan America* (Washington: Office of Technology Assessment, 1995), Chapter 7. Also see Joel Kotkin, *The New Geography: How the Digital Revolution Is Reshaping the American Landscape* (New York: Random House, 2000).
33. Dunn, *Driving Forces,* pg. 33.
34. Bruce D. McDowell, "Improving Regional Transportation Decisions: MPOs and Certification" (Washington: Brookings Institution Center on Urban and Metropolitan Policy, September 1999), pg. 15–16.
35. George M. Smerk, *The Federal Role in Urban Mass Transportation* (Bloomington: Indiana University Press, 1991), Chapters 5 and 6.
36. Dunn, *Driving Forces,* pg. 92.
37. Robert Puentes, "Flexible Funding for Transit: Who Uses It?" (Washington: Brookings Institution Center on Urban and Metropolitan Policy, May 2000), pp. 2–3.
38. Martin Wachs and Jennifer Dill, "Regionalism in Transportation and Air Quality: History, Interpretation, and Insights for Regional Governance" in *Governance and Opportunity in Metropolitan America,* ed. Alan Altshuler and others (Washington: National Academy Press, 1999), pp. 296–323.
39. Clifford Winston, "You Can't Get There From Here: Government Failure in U.S. Transportation," *Brookings Review,* 17, no. 3 (Summer 1999), pg. 42.
40. Arthur Maass, *Muddy Waters: The Army Engineers and the Nation's Rivers* (Cambridge, MA: Harvard University Press, 1951).

SUGGESTED READINGS

DOWNS, ANTHONY. *Stuck in Traffic: Coping with Peak-Hour Traffic Congestion.* Washington: Brookings Institution, 1992. A clearly written and ably argued analysis of why traffic jams occur and how their effects might be handled.

DUNN, JAMES A. JR. *Driving Forces: The Automobile, Its Enemies and the Politics of Mobility.* Washington: Brookings Institution Press, 1998. Excellent study of why automobiles reign along with a thorough consideration of rail alternatives.

MITCHELL, WILLIAM J. *E-Topia: "Urban Life, Jim—But Not As We Know It."* Cambridge, MA: The MIT Press, 1999. Insightful discussion of how telecommunications and computers are reshaping life in metropolitan regions.

VUCHIC, VUKAN R. *Transportation for Livable Cities.* Using examples from around the globe, points out the interplay between transportation policies and the quality of life.

DOING IT

What is the transportation strategy for your metropolitan area or one located near you? To determine this, the first step is to obtain the most recent plans. Sources include the metropolitan planning organization, the public transit agency, and the state transportation department. Websites for many of these can be found through *www.piperinfo.com.* You can also e-mail the Association of Metropolitan Planning Organizations (*ataft@ampo.org*) to identify the appropriate MPO. The American Public Transit Association web site (*www.apta.com*) also has links to most of the MPOs and state transportation units, as well as to the transit agencies.

As you examine the plans, consider the following issues:

1. What is the balance between highways and public transit? How much coordination is proposed between these two modes?
2. What role does growth management have in the transportation planning? Is it an important factor or does it have a low priority?
3. What role does air quality play? Again, is it a major consideration or just an afterthought?
4. Who is going to pay for the improvements proposed in the plan? What are the respective contributions from federal, state, and local governments? What user charges, including tolls, are proposed?
5. How does the plan propose to lessen traffic congestion?

CHAPTER 8

Education

OVERVIEW

Human talent has become the principal dimension in the competition among metropolitan areas. Physical characteristics—access to natural resources, quality of transportation facilities, and attractiveness of geographic setting—still count but they are eclipsed by which region does the finest job educating its residents. As knowledge commands an increasingly consequential role in producing goods and delivering services, as it becomes the largest component of the value added by metropolitan economies, the region possessing the most educated and best trained citizenry is going to finish at the top.[1]

In older manufacturing processes, where brute force and physical repetition were all that was needed to produce most of the goods, a much smaller fraction of the labor force needed to have high educational levels. Most of the workers could earn adequate wages doing menial tasks requiring only modest mental prowess: putting tires on automobiles in an assembly plant, shoveling coal in a steel mill, cleaning bottles in a brewery. Today a majority of jobs require workers to have complex skills. Moreover, as the technological applications accelerate, employees must regularly acquire new capacities. Two decades ago, clerical workers needed only to know about typing, filing, and, perhaps, taking dictation. Now they must master word processing and spreadsheet programs and, on a routine basis, learn still another version of some software package.

Once twelve years of formal education was seen as adequate to prepare most individuals for a meaningful economic position. For many, that number has crept up to fourteen, then sixteen, and now postgraduate degrees have become relatively common. Between 1960 and 1998, the proportion of Americans age 25 and older with high school diplomas doubled, from 41.1 percent to 82.8 percent, while the share of college graduates more than tripled, from 7.7 percent to 24.4 percent. In five of the million-plus metropolitan regions (Boston, Denver, San Francisco, Seattle, Washington), more than one out of nine have postgraduate degrees.

Education has a snowball effect. The more it is happening within a metropolitan area, the more it becomes the norm for existing residents and the greater the attraction for those educated elsewhere to relocate there. If almost everyone from high school is going on to a postsecondary experience, then even the few who might not otherwise have done so are more likely to imitate the majority. Regions with high concentrations of well-educated citizens become magnets for attracting similarly prepared people from outside the metropolitan area.

Education has also become lifelong. No longer can what was obtained in formal schooling between age 5 and the late teens and early twenties suffice for an entire career. Knowledge is developing so rapidly that, to stay competitive, individual workers must continually advance their learning capacities. The race now belongs to the mentally swift. The past prevailing pattern of getting an education, going to work for an organization, and staying with it until retirement is becoming the exception. Today's workers are on their own and, to survive, they must routinely enhance their skills.

Education's contributions to a metropolitan region are more than economic. Citizens are better prepared to enrich community life as volunteers and voters if they have had additional schooling. They are more likely to support cultural institutions and artistic endeavors, more apt to help with youth development programs, more prone to serve on nonprofit boards and governmental committees. They become the leaders in building social capital, weaving the fabric that transforms isolated individuals into cohesive communities.[2]

ELEMENTARY AND SECONDARY EDUCATION

The Setting

When discussions turn to the topic of education, most people automatically think of formal schooling, especially the span between first grade in elementary school and senior year in high school. Completing those twelve years has become a common experience for more than five out of six Americans. It is the period when education is the priority task, the interval when children devote more of their daily lives to learning than to any other activity. The society mandates that, for most of these years, youth must attend school for upwards of 200 days annually and guarantees that it will pay for providing universal education.

In U.S. metropolitan areas, elementary and secondary education is highly decentralized and mainly public. There are upwards of 10,000 public school districts with more than 50,000 individual public schools which serve almost 90 percent of the students.[3] The remainder attend private schools, about three-quarters of which are religious and the rest nonsectarian. More than half of the faith-based enroll-ments are in Catholic institutions. The combined public-private effort is a substantial enterprise: about 40 million students taught by more than 2.5 million teachers with a collective annual operating budget, excluding capital expenditures, approaching $250 billion dollars.

Education has many adult stakeholders—parents, administrators, taxpayers—but classroom teachers are at the heart of the undertaking, the ones who hour by hour and day by day deliver the instruction. Although they often only have marginal impact on state and district educational policies, they control the classrooms and that singular fact makes them a critical element. The teachers may have diplomas galore—more than two out of five have earned master's degrees—but their compen-sation continues to lag behind other occupations with similar educational attain-ment. Compared to their students, they are disproportionately female and white.

Principals are also other key position although their role and influences varies across districts. In most private schools and many public ones, they have consider-able discretion and, more than anyone else, set the direction and establish the tone for what happens in their buildings. Although most teachers are women, men dom-inate the principal ranks within public schools, while there is roughly an even male-female division in private institutions.

With the exception of some of the metropolitan area's central cities, citizens give high marks to their own community's schools but assign much lower grades to those in other parts of the region and elsewhere in the nation.[4] This dismay about the general condition of education has made reform proposals an habitual part of the policy debate at all levels of government. Rare is the gubernatorial contest that does not feature rival claims about who can do the most to improve the schools and, increasingly, presidential candidates have also weighed in on the issue.

Issues

Because it has become conventional wisdom that elementary and secondary educa-tion, at least in the public schools outside one's own immediate community, is either completely broken or partially cracked, there are no shortage of proposals for fix-ing it. *A Nation at Risk,* a well-publicized report issued in 1983,[5] catapulted the need to do something about the schools up on the policy agenda and it has remained there ever since. What has not happened since then is developing a consensus about which reforms make the most sense under what circumstances. Instead, there are competing paradigms for what fulcrum will generate the most leverage for improv-ing learning. Here are the five remedies prescribed most frequently for what ails public elementary and secondary education.

1. Empower the personnel directly involved in the schools and enhance their capacity to make a difference.[6] Give teachers and principals more professional de-velopment opportunities, enable teachers to interact across schools and districts to promote a freer exchange of ideas, raise their salaries to attract and retain qualified people. Decentralize the system, placing more responsibility and authority within

*An Open Letter
to the
American People*

A Nation at Risk:

The Imperative for Educational Reform
A Report to the Nation
and the Secretary of Education
United States Department of Education
by
The National Commission on Excellence in Education

April 1983

A Nation at Risk: A Call for Educational Reform

each school building. The problem, as defined by this approach, is that those at the bottom of the structure have not been given adequate opportunity or status to do their job effectively.

　　2.　Set and enforce stricter standards.[7] State governments should mandate what schools are expected to accomplish. They should implement extensive testing procedures to monitor student progress and hold entire districts and particular schools accountable by publicizing report cards on their performance. Those who fail should be punished, both financially and by threatening to remove accreditation. Students who do not pass muster should be required to have additional instruction, after school or during the summer, and social promotions, almost automatically allowing children to advance a grade, should be eliminated. The diagnosis is that educators have been too lax. Those at or near the top need to impose closer scrutiny and exercise tough love.

3. Introduce competition.[8] Market forces keep private businesses on their toes. If a restaurant or a drug store starts to give shabby service, it knows it will lose customers to its rivals. But public schools have a monopoly over access to education and that means the almost 90 percent who attend them do not have a meaningful option. They can only use free public schools in the districts where they live. Go anywhere else, a public school in another district or a private institution, and they must pay tuition. If parents could shop for public schools like they do for automobiles, the educational suppliers would work harder and more effectively to produce quality education. Alternatives can be provided on a sweeping scale, issuing vouchers which parents could use to purchase education at any public or private school, or on a more limited basis, allowing students to enroll in any one of several public districts. The most recent choice initiative has been charter schools, enabling community groups or sets of educators to establish their own institutions which then qualify for public assistance.

4. Involve the community.[9] This applies the thinking behind the aphorism "it takes a village to raise a child" to K-12 education. For too long, this diagnosis argues, those managing and operating the schools have walled themselves off from the rest of society. Others, most notably the business sector but also sometimes state and local general governments as well as nonprofit organizations, need to be more involved. Corporations should adopt schools, encouraging their employees to assist with the instruction and applying cutting edge technology. Cultural institutions should enrich the curriculum: symphony orchestras with music, theater, and dance ensembles with artistic performance, history museums with archaeology, art institutes with painting and interpretation. Elected officials should be more attentive to the educational mission, using their political prominence to applaud or to prod, depending on the situation.

5. Reshape the curriculum.[10] This remedy takes numerous forms, many at odds with others. Focus on the basics—reading, writing, calculating—and minimize time spent on more peripheral subjects like art or health education. Restructure the school day so that time allotments fit the subject matter and instructional style instead of forcing everything into fifty-minute segments. Lecture less and discuss more so that students learn from each other instead of just from the teacher who, under this scenario, coaches more and directs less. Make learning more experiential with field trips and laboratory experiments because child developmental theories suggest that students move from concrete sensing to abstract thinking. Emphasize problem solving over memorization, in order to make education more authentic for the challenges of adult life. Incorporate values like honesty and respect into teaching so that characters are molded at the same time intellects are formed.

Each of these approaches has its champions, those fervently believing that only if *their* suggestions were accepted and implemented, then there would be enormous progress in educational achievement. But despite all the sound and fury generated by those seeking to reform educational structure or practice, what is most striking is how similar elementary and secondary education remains from one decade to the next.[11] As Frederick M. Hess notes, "reform is the status quo" and "the collective exercise of reform has become a spinning of wheels [as] more and more energy is expended in an effort that goes nowhere."[12]

Governance

State governments and local school districts contend for control of elementary and secondary education with the federal government's role being meaningful but modest. Education is a state responsibility, and it is each state's constitution (Iowa does it statutorily) which pronounces every child's right to a free and public schooling. But, with the exception of Hawaii, states have chosen to execute their educational mission through numerous local school districts rather than by establishing a single statewide system. The typical metropolitan area has tens of these districts and each jealously protects its prerogatives. "Local control" is the mantra of K-12 education.

Most states have their own boards of education, most often appointed by the governor but in one-quarter of the jurisdictions elected directly by the citizens. In a majority of states, these boards hire the chief state school officer although, again, in about one-fourth (not all the same as those choosing boards) this is an elected post. These arrangements put some distance between governors and legislators on one side and the educational boards and executives on the other, giving the latter more autonomy over educational policy than those responsible for state functions like corrections or social services.

Over 95 percent of the local school boards are elected, usually at-large rather than from subdistricts, and the remainder are most frequently appointed by an elected local government executive such as a mayor. These districtwide selections help preserve the belief that educational decision making should speak to the overall good and not to special interests. The boards appoint a fulltime superintendent to direct daily operations.

At both the state and local level, the professional staff, led by the state school chief or the district superintendent, has tended to control what happens.[13] Whether elected or appointed, the board members are volunteers, rarely receiving any compensation beyond reimbursement for expenses. Lacking the information held by the bureaucracy and having other personal and professional obligations, their role is more advocacy and oversight than deciding and implementing.

Until the late 1970s and early 1980s, the individual districts had considerable leeway and local control was largely unquestioned. As concern about educational quality grew with the issuance of reports like *A Nation at Risk,* state elected executives and legislators became more committed to sponsoring programs to improve learning and, concurrently, increased state budgetary support. There is considerable variation across states but, on average, states now contribute slightly more than local districts to annual operations. With additional funding has come enhanced accountability and most states now set learning standards and test student achievement. Local districts often chafe under these regulations but, welcoming the dollars, they strive to comply.

As education has become more prominent on the political agenda, the national government has significantly increased its rhetorical role, with presidents and secretaries of education frequently trumpeting for one or another reform. Although fear of a national curriculum and pride in retaining local control has kept the federal role at the periphery, the temptation to take national grant funds has given federal policy makers some influence with K-12 public education and today about 5 percent of the typical district's budget comes from Washington.

Two interest groups—parents within local districts and teacher unions at all levels—are intimately involved in educational governance. In most metropolitan areas, school board elections are low-turnout contests, held at times other than Novembers in even-numbered years, ostensibly to insulate them from partisan contamination. Paying the most attention are those most affected—parents and teachers—and they therefore wield considerable influence. The two largest unions—the American Federation of Teachers and the National Education Association—are advocates in Washington and the state capitals for more funding and greater teacher autonomy.

Educational governance is not only decentralized but it is also entrenched. State and local interests have been at it for decades and have developed their own set of routines, both within their respective tiers and between each level. This leaves very little room for metropolitan concerns to be expressed and almost no way for elementary and secondary education to make conscious adaptations to improve regional competitiveness. There are no councils of school districts comparable to councils of governments. The linkages between metropolitan governance and K-12 policy making have yet to be built. As a result, there is little connection between metropolitan economic-development goals and the elementary and secondary educational changes which would be necessary to help achieve them.

CENTRAL CITY PUBLIC SCHOOLS

Suburbanites and exurban residents generally give high marks to their local community's schools but are much more critical about public education elsewhere.[14] Part of the reason is that central city schools are seen as performing poorly. Harder data support this perception. In one inner-city school district after another, dropout rates are higher and test scores are lower than their suburban counterparts, often by a factor of two or more,[15] and disruptive incidents are more common.[16] Although occasional stories about a superior elementary or secondary school in an impoverished neighborhood appear in the media, this coverage only emphasizes that such successes are the exception and not the rule. The overall trend is at best stagnant.

This subpar record threatens regional progress. In most metropolitan areas, the central city district is either the largest or among that group. Some are huge: Chicago, Los Angeles, and New York City combined have more than 2 million students.

Nationally, more than one out of five metropolitan public school students is in a central-city district.[17] If their products cannot pass muster, if they are not prepared for a high technology economy, then that weakens a region's economic strength not just currently but for decades to come. If the dropouts turn to crime, as a disproportionate share have done in the past, then weak schools also jeopardize public safety.

The primary cause for the decline in central-city education has been the demographic trends outlined in Chapter 1. As middle- and upper-class residents leave for the suburbs, what remains is an increasingly concentrated poverty population. As Clarence Stone comments, "lower-SES students, despite many significant exceptions, have generally been low academic achievers" and "now [inner city] educators are asked to turn that around, not just in selected instances, but en masse."[18]

Central-city districts are even more hierarchical and centralized than other school systems, with the superintendent holding the most power, more so than the school board. They "determine the shape of the school board's agenda and the amount of information that board members receive."[19] They have been sought as saviors for what ails urban schools but, with an average tenure of three years, rarely is there enough time to implement one or more of the internal reforms mentioned in the preceding section. Having failed to execute a near-instant turnaround, they either resign or are fired. As Hill and Celio conclude, "the 'great man' and the 'great slogan' theories do not work for city school systems."[20]

A variation on a merry-go-round of professional educators as superintendents has been to seek leadership from other quarters—retired generals, for example, in Seattle and Washington, D.C., and a former governor in Los Angeles—or, in an effort to change the political dynamics, having the mayor or state government assume control as in Boston, Chicago, Cleveland, and Detroit.

To date, none of these initiatives has been effective systemwide over a sustained period. These failures to stem the decline have widened the scope of possible solutions, with three dominating the current debate. The first argues that central city school systems will not, indeed cannot, change. They are too bureaucratic and too insulated. As long as they have a monopoly over public education within their jurisdictions, they will plod along, trying a reform here and a new leader there, but internal inertia and passive resistance will prevail. The only hope is to insert the forces of competition, using vouchers or charter schools "to rethink the way the U.S. public education system is organized."[21]

The second approach is to attack the underlying economic and racial segregation. If central cities remain the repositories for the least well off in metropolitan America and if school-district boundaries become a wall separating the inner city from the rest of the region, then it is folly to think that there will ever be sufficient resources or appropriate settings to educate students well. Schools can only be effective when their student bodies include substantial numbers of middle-class children.[22] To save the city schools, either the middle class must be attracted back to the urban core or district boundaries must be altered since it is questionnable that, even with able leadership and reasonable funding, schools consisting exclusively of lower-income pupils can succeed.[23]

The third recommendation states that the problems are more complex than anyone initially appreciated and that the city schools have been "the victims of what amounts to policy churn and educational quackery: quick-fix reforms that accomplish little, but leave the public more cynical about its schools after the good feeling accompanying their implementation has disappeared and nothing has changed."[24] There must be a comprehensive strategy and extensive involvement from and support by the community, including "a substantial widening of participation in schools and their politics" because "it takes broad mobilization of civic capacity to bring about a thoroughgoing effort at educational improvement."[25]

EDUCATIONAL EQUITY: FINANCES AND RACE

In a majority of metropolitan areas, central cities are the most glaring instance of economic and racial educational segregation but they are not the only such ones. Because each region has tens of school districts overlaying populations which tend to sort themselves out territorially by income and race and ethnicity, the necessary consequence is that, absent some outside intervention, school districts will range from very white to predominantly African American or Hispanic and from extremely wealthy to exceptionally poor.

This creates both efficiency and equity issues for metropolitan areas. As discussed earlier, regions need an educated work force and those poorly prepared will serve as a drag on economic growth and as a threat to social stability. So efficiency would argue for reallocating some resources from the better to the less well off—so that as many children as possible receive an adequate education. It would also suggest that, in order to succeed in a racially diverse society, classrooms should encompass all the variety existing in a metropolitan area. Keeping children racially apart during their formative years is a recipe for misunderstanding and miscommunication when they become adults, divisions which will hold regions back.[26]

The equity concerns are rooted in American tradition and reflected in the U.S. and state constitutions. From Thomas Jefferson forward, public education has been viewed as the best way to honor the Declaration of Independence's belief that all people are entitled to "the pursuit of happiness." Then and now it is difficult to prosper materially without a firm educational foundation. It is why every state guarantees, as a right of citizenship, a free public education. Although the U.S. Constitution says nothing about education, the Fourteenth Amendment does require that no state "deny to any person within its jurisdiction the equal protection of the laws." This clause, adopted in the aftermath of the Civil War, speaks directly to how states educate African Americans.

Finances

Local property taxes are a significant component of school district revenues everywhere except Hawaii. In the more urbanized states, it usually makes up two-fifths or more of the budget. The more property wealth a district has within its boundaries, the more it can spend. Take two inner-suburban districts in the St. Louis metropolitan area: Clayton and Normandy. Clayton has numerous office buildings and upscale residential neighborhoods, providing $247,137 in assessed valuation for each student. Normandy, with both middle- and lower-middle class housing and some scattered commercial structures, has just $38,655 per pupil. Even though Normandy's property tax rate ($5.19 per one hundred dollars assessed valuation) is over 50 percent higher than Clayton's ($3.41), the amount it spends per student ($6,486) is only 58 percent of Clayton's allocation ($11,239) per student.

These kinds of disparities led to a round of litigation in the early 1970s, starting in California and ultimately extending to forty-two other states.[27] The plaintiffs, residents of poorer districts, maintained that states were not living up to their constitutional pledges to support educational opportunity by permitting property valuation to have so much influence on public education spending and that this system also violated the Fourteenth Amendment's equal protection provision. In a Texas case,[28] the U.S. Supreme Court decided that the U.S. Constitution did not require equal spending but various state courts continued to rule that their constitutions would tolerate only so much discrepancy.

Although the judicial interpretations avoided mandating allocating the same amount for every student, many did specify that states are responsible for insuring that there is adequate support for every student. These rulings stimulated school finance reforms in most states, some court-ordered and others preempting judicial action.[29] The net effect of these laws has been to boost state education allocations to poorer districts while still allowing wealthy districts to reap the bounty within their boundaries.[30] Federal aid has also helped correct some of the imbalance since much of it is targeted toward poorer districts, where it subsidizes school lunches and supports remedial instruction.

Despite twenty-plus years of state educational finance reform and a modest national presence, metropolitan areas still feature substantial gaps in per pupil spending between wealthier and poorer districts. The affluent segments have been able to use political clout to insure their ability to spend as much of their local dollars as they wish on their children's public education even as they have been more willing to have added state dollars flow to the less well-off districts. But there is neither the political will nor the governmental mechanisms for metropolitan areas to redistribute dollars within regions to redress the imbalances. Instead the route to reallocation runs through state capitals.

Race

When the U.S. Supreme Court ruled in 1954 that public schools could not be racially separate and still be truly equal,[31] metropolitan area school districts had to confront what to do with the stark fact that most of their schools were racially segregated. In Southern and many border states, educational segregation was the law, mandated either by the state constitution or by statute. Even in states without such provisions, the combination of neighborhood-school attendance policies and segregated neighborhoods meant that there was little racial mixing. For the next fifteen-plus years, inaction prevailed, especially outside the South, and segregated schools remained the norm in most places. Even in the South, over ninety percent of blacks were in all-black schools in the mid-1960s.[32] Then, in a series of decisions between

1968 and 1973, the federal courts determined that desegregation should become meaningful and that school districts must act affirmatively, even if segregation had been caused by district practices rather than by state law.[33] During the same period, however, the Supreme Court ruled that suburban districts, even those which are predominantly white, could not be included in plans to desegregate central city schools unless it could be proven that those jurisdictions had historically helped create the racial separation.[34]

The impact of these decisions has been very uneven. Movement toward desegregation almost always came when someone filed a successful lawsuit, a process that usually extended over years. This occurred in some regions—Boston, Charlotte, and St. Louis for example—but many others have never implemented a desegregation plan and only a few, Seattle being a notable case, have done so voluntarily.[35]

Desegregation plans, most of which were implemented in the 1970s and 1980s, feature two ways to promote racial integration in the schools.[36] The first and most controversial is mandatorily reassigning students so that more schools have meaningful numbers of both African Americans and whites. Examples include Boston, Dallas, Dayton, and Louisville. This is a straightforward method, setting enrollment goals for each school building and then applying a busing plan to transfer children, typically more blacks than whites, to their new schools, often a considerable distance away from their homes.

The second and more politically palatable approach is allowing parents to choose where within a district their children could attend school and, if the building was beyond walking distance, paying for the transportation expenses. Among those taking this path are Buffalo, Houston, and Milwaukee. To entice white parents to switch, most plans established magnet programs, well-financed schools often specializing in fields like technology or the performing arts. The assumption, not always realized, was that enough parents would opt for enhanced opportunities for their children to balance the racial composition. At a minimum, not requiring white children to participate in desegregation would lower the chances that whites would flee the district, typically within the inner city, for the suburbs.

The research on desegregation's effects is mixed and inconclusive. Much of it has been commissioned to support one or another side in court cases, casting doubts about objectivity, and the settings and programs vary considerably from one district to the next, raising concerns about generalizability. Overall, African-American academic achievement usually increases modestly, as measured by test scores, graduation rates, and college attendance frequency.[37] At the same time, whites do not suffer educationally. Impact on race relations is murkier, with positive exposure among children often offset by increased tension in the community.[38]

Beginning in the 1990s, the federal courts became less aggressive about fighting segregation and more flexible about releasing districts from previous orders, finding that most jurisdictions had done all that could reasonably be expected and that, in legal terms, the districts are now "unified." Oklahoma City was the first to receive this designation[39] and many others—Buffalo, Denver, Houston, Kansas City, St. Louis—have also had their districts removed from federal judicial oversight.[40] To become unified, districts do not have to demonstrate that they eliminated or even significantly lessened segregation but only that they made a good faith effort to do so.

Although many desegregation programs remain in place, the dwindling number means fewer racially integrated classrooms. Although mandated segregation is part of an infamous past and can no longer cause single race schools, residential segregation persists in most metropolitan regions. If unified districts return to neighborhood attendance policies, as they most often do, then the pattern becomes resegregation.[41] The two-decade experiment with desegregation, essentially conducted under federal court orders, is coming to an end. Political support for integrating schools through state legislation is nonexistent. That raises two as yet unanswered questions for metropolitan areas: Can public schools be racially segregated and educationally comparable? What impact will educational segregation have on race relations?

POSTSECONDARY INSTITUTIONS

During the past fifty years, going to college has gone from being the exception to becoming the rule. Where once fewer than one in five matriculated, now a majority do. At present, more than 4 million Americans are attending two-year community colleges, over 8 million are pursuing baccalaureates in four-year institutions, and almost 3 million are seeking graduate or professional degrees.

The reasons for this explosion in college attendance are clear. Today's work place calls for a complex array of skills that require more than twelve years of formal education to acquire. Once largely finishing schools for the elites, places where gentlemen went to gain polish and earn their "C's" before returning to their father's business or profession, colleges and universities have become the gateway to success in the modern world.[42] No longer largely the preserve of upper-class white males, higher education is moving toward being a near-universal expectation, open to all classes, genders, and races.

The largest increase in the supply of postsecondary instruction to meet this enhanced demand has occurred within metropolitan areas with the establishment or expansion of community colleges and four-year public colleges and universities. Most state-supported universities had been located in small communities intentionally distant from the evil temptations of the big city by nineteenth century legislators. This meant that prospective students needing public subsidies to make college affordable had to move to these college towns, paying for transportation, room, and board. This geographic gap served as a barrier for many who were not able to pay all these expenses or whose family obligations kept them place bound.

Higher education in urban settings was typically private, making it financially inaccessible to many middle- and lower-income students. These institutions also had admission policies that often limited entry for those with spotty precollegiate records or unimpressive family backgrounds. Even the apparent exceptions, most notably the City University of New York, had selective academic requirements that restricted admission to only the most talented among the immigrant groups.

With higher education more important than ever to individuals and enterprises, metropolitan areas lobbied for state funds, the primary source for higher education support, to be invested within their regions rather than, for the most part, being spent in nonurban areas. Colleges and universities, they argued, should come to where the people are rather than making them relocate. With metropolitan areas having a growing share of state populations, and one-person, one-vote rulings giving them more clout in state legislatures, the politics worked and the states responded.

Community Colleges

There are now over one thousand community colleges in the United States, four times the number there were in 1950. Over 85 percent are public entities and most are found within metropolitan areas. Because they are inexpensive and nearby, they have done more to expand access to postsecondary education than any other educational development.[43] Over one out of three higher education students attends a community college and, during the past half century, their enrollments have increased fifteen-fold.

Community colleges play three roles within metropolitan areas. First, and most directly, they are the primary supplier for positions which require education

Miami-Dade Community College's Wolfson Campus

beyond high school but short of a baccalaureate degree. These are the rank-and-file technical and service jobs of the modern economy: engineering technicians, computer repair specialists, registered nurses, dental hygienists, food service managers, physical therapy assistants, day-care supervisors, and the like. These posts require a combination of liberal arts and sciences and job-related technical skills that, on a fulltime basis, can be completed in two years.

Second, they provide an inexpensive and convenient way to complete the first half of a baccalaureate program. Students can complete their general education requirements along with the initial foundation for the major. Community colleges feature a more hands-on teaching style and a less intimidating setting than do four-year institutions, as well as remedial instruction for those with weak high school backgrounds. By easing the transition between secondary school and a four-year university, they lower the college dropout rate.

Third, community colleges take their first name, "community," seriously. They are much more likely than four-year schools to take on assignments requested by local governments and businesses. An expanding industry requiring an on-site training program, a social service agency wanting assistance with a welfare-to-work initiative, or a local government needing computer training updates for its staff are all likely to have a receptive supplier in one or more of the local community colleges.[44]

Governance structures for community college vary considerably across the country. In some states, community colleges have their own elected boards and operate much like public school districts although a modest tuition and fee revenue stream is added to local property taxes and state aid. In other jurisdictions, there is a statewide system of community colleges, typically run by a governor-appointed board; in a few states, four-year universities have established two-year community college branches, and the university boards of trustees, also usually named by the governor, exercise control. Not surprisingly, the closer the governance to the metropolitan area, as is the case with local boards, the easier the connection between the region's overall policies and the community college's programs.

Metropolitan Public Universities

Although a few states placed one or more of their premier public universities within the largest region—Arizona State University in the Phoenix area, the University of Minnesota in Minneapolis, and the University of Washington in Seattle—the more common practice was to put it in the hinterlands: Amherst, Massachusetts, or Athens, Georgia, or Bloomington, Indiana.

As pressures grew for more higher education in the 1950s and 1960s, state legislatures responded by bringing both four-year and postgraduate university programs to metropolitan areas. In some places, such as Georgia State in Atlanta, Wayne State in Detroit, or Temple University in Philadelphia, the states transformed existing smaller entities into comprehensive institutions. In others, like the University of Massachusetts-Boston, the University of Missouri-St. Louis, or the University of Texas-San Antonio, states built them from scratch.[45] By the late 1960s, every 1-million-or-more major metropolitan area had its own.

In most instances, these schools are still working out their role with the region.[46] Staffed largely by administrators and faculty educated at more traditional institutions and being the newest entrants in the higher education arena, there is a self-imposed pressure to establish respect among their peers by conducting discipline-based research and teaching high-caliber students. This path leads them to become prestigious universities located in metropolitan areas but not necessarily to being part of their regions—although this perspective asserts that such an institution's first obligation to its community is to be a high-quality campus.

Another faction claims that metropolitan public universities should not mimic their small-town siblings. Instead they should promote problem-oriented and multidisciplinary investigations, aimed at issues confronting their areas. Regional priorities, not disciplinary trends, should set the research agendas. As for students, standards should remain high but admission requirements should be relaxed and class scheduling should be more flexible so that more can attend. Throughout the campus, there should be close connections between academic units and their community counterparts, between, for example, colleges of education and school systems, music departments and symphonies, medical schools and health clinics.

What has happened during their first few decades is a fusion, often tense, between both approaches. No campus has pursued either alternative single-mindedly and all have steered a course blending the two. But as one of the few institutions whose acknowledged service area matches the entire region's boundaries, metropolitan public universities are increasingly urged to link their destinies more closely with their communities.[47] Those with their own boards, such as the University of Cincinnati or the University of Louisville, find it structurally easier to bond with their region than those which are part of university systems, such as the University of California-Los Angeles or the University of Missouri-Kansas City, which are governed by statewide groups.

OUTSIDE THE SCHOOLHOUSE

Not all structured education can and does occur in the traditional K-12 and college settings. The cliché that learning is a lifelong enterprise has come much closer to becoming a reality in the past few decades. Where once parents waited until children were five or six to enroll them in some instructional program, now the preprimary years have become filled with learning options. Adult education courses have been available throughout America's history but enrollments are higher, subject coverage is broader, and links to the work world closer. Public libraries, also a metropolitan feature for a century or more, offer more diverse services to a wider clientele.

Early Childhood Education

In 1999, 70 percent of four-year-olds and 46 percent of three-year-olds were enrolled in preprimary education. These were up from the 1991 rates (62 percent and 43 percent, respectively) and continued the dramatic growth in giving these age cohorts structured learning, most of which has occurred during the past four decades.

What stimulated this growth? First came some striking research findings demonstrating how important the early years are for learning and how much could be accomplished.[48] Children are much readier to acquire knowledge than had earlier been thought and leaving it to parental happenstance was missing huge opportunities. Second, more households either had both parents working or a single parent in the labor force. Since more children were going to be in some type of day care, there might as well be a structured approach for educating them. Third, the federal government made early childhood education one of the elements of the War on Poverty. In 1965, the Head Start program began, an effort to help economically disadvantaged children to be ready for elementary school.

During the past decade, state governments have substantially expanded their efforts. Forty-three now have prekindergarten initiatives for 3- and 4-year-olds and thirty-one work with infants and toddlers. Collective spending by the states on these efforts exceeded $2 billion in 2000, up 24 percent over just two years earlier.[49] Universal coverage of preprimary education has not yet arrived, either by jurisdiction or by individual, but the trend is in that direction.

Despite these growing efforts, problems remain. Many different businesses, nonprofit agencies and governmental entities supply early childhood education, and there is little transition planning to ease the way between these organizations and the elementary schools.[50] Although there are positive results for some programs, there is also considerable slippage for many other youngsters once they enter the elementary schools.[51] As Vinovskis concludes, "we still do not know which practices and programs are particularly effective. . . ."[52]

Adult Education

Despite America's commitment to universal public education, everyone does not acquire the needed skills as youth. Many drop out and others forget. Moreover, as a nation of immigrants, the United States has to ease the transition to a new culture and a different language. So educational opportunities for adults have been available from the country's earliest days.[53]

In order to qualify for today's jobs, workers also need more knowledge. A recent study states that "the new basic skills" include reading and calculating at the ninth grade level or higher, solving semistructured problems, being able to work in diverse groups, communicating clearly both orally and in writing, and using personal computers.[54] So even those who may have been adequately educated by earlier standards find themselves falling short of current requirements.

Since the 1960s, the federal government has pumped funds into work-force training programs, first with the Manpower Development and Training Act (1962), then the Comprehensive Employment and Training Act (1975), then the Jobs Training Partnership Act (1982), and, most recently, the Workforce Investment Act (1998). The three earlier initiatives have been criticized for being passive, uncoordinated, and unimaginative[55] and the latest version is both more active and more flexible than its predecessors, establishing "one-stop service centers" throughout the United States.[56] It allows states and metropolitan areas to tailor the programs to fit their distinctive labor markets rather than applying a single template across the country. At the same time, nonprofit organizations involved in preparing adults for jobs have also stepped up their networking.[57]

The need for adult education is demonstrable. The 1992 National Adult Literacy Survey, the most recent systematic analysis, found that one in five adults read at the fifth-grade level or lower.[58] About one-quarter of this group are immigrants and the remainder native born. The link between skills and income was strong, with almost half of this group being below the poverty level. The survey also assessed quantitative skills with similar results.

Libraries

Spurred by Andrew Carnegie's philanthropy at the turn of the last century,[59] almost all metropolitan residents have access to one or more of the approximately 16,000 public libraries in the United States. Availability leads to usage since about two-thirds of the nation's households report using a library at least once during the previous year and slightly more than two-fifths had done so within the last month.

For most patrons, libraries are where you go for pleasure reading or to check out a compact disk for at-home listening. But for low-income households and small

New York Public Library's Central Branch

businesses, they are often the only source for individual job searches and expensive data bases. For them, it is their only portal to the Internet. In many ways, information is indeed power. The more affluent can afford to purchase it but having public libraries helps level the information playing field.

About two-thirds of libraries are units within municipalities or counties and the remainder take several governance forms: special districts, cooperative ventures between two or more jurisdictions, or nonprofit agencies or school districts contracting with local governments. Public libraries often have a dedicated tax, typically a property levy. Along with their popularity across the socioeconomic spectrum—leisure options for the better off, sole information source for the less well off—this helps insulate libraries from changes in political fortunes and generates stable funding.[60]

EDUCATION: RHETORIC AND REALITY

The widespread rhetorical recognition that education, broadly defined, is central for a metropolitan area's future would apparently lead to a consensus to develop comprehensive learning plans for the region and invest more resources in executing them. But the talk about doing more is rarely followed by the walk that makes it happen.

Why? First, there is no agreement about education's ultimate goal. Should it prepare people for the work force, empower them as citizens, boost them on the Maslovian self-actualization hierarchy, make them feel good about themselves, or some combination of these? Second, as the discussion on reforms showed, even those who might agree on ends frequently disagree on means. Third, within any metropolitan area, there are hundreds of organizations competing within the educational arena: school districts, colleges and universities, for-profit day-care centers and career education agencies, nonprofit entities, and more. Not only is there minimal coordination among and between these units, there is even less connection between educational organizations, taken collectively, and the economic sector. Fourth, educational improvement, when it does happen, is a long-term phenomenon. Spending more on 3-year-olds today by enriching their preprimary education will not pay dividends for the economy for another two decades, even if the program is highly effective. In a world where elected leaders and appointed officials must respond to short-term pressures—accomplishments that will help win a forthcoming election or earn the next promotion—twenty years can be too long to wait.

NOTES

1. James E. Rauch, "Productivity Gains from Geographic Concentrations of Human Capital: Evidence from the Cities," *Journal of Urban Economics*, 34, no. 3 (November 1993), pp. 380–400; and Vijay K. Mathur, "Human Capital-Based Strategy for Regional Economic Development," *Economic Development Quarterly*, 13, no. 3 (August 1999), pp. 203–16. The seminal work is Gary S. Becker, *Human Capital: A Theoretical and Empirical Analysis, with Special Reference to Education*, 3rd ed. (Chicago: University of Chicago Press, 1993).
2. Robert Putnam, *Bowling Alone: The Collapse and Revival of American Community* (New York: Simon and Schuster, 2000).

3.   Unless otherwise noted, all statistics in this chapter are from the National Center for Education Statistics.

4.   *Survey on Education 1999* (Washington: National Public Radio/Kaiser Family Foundation/ Kennedy School of Government, 1999), Tables C-7, C-8, C-9.

5.   *A Nation at Risk* (Washington: National Commission on Excellence in Education, 1983).

6.   Joseph Blase and Gary L. Anderson, *The Micropolitics of Educational Leadership: From Control to Empowerment* (New York: Teachers College Press, 1995); Richard F. Elmore, "Getting to Scale with Good Educational Practice," *Harvard Educational Review*, 66, no. 1 (Spring 1996), pp. 1–26; John I. Goodlad, *Educational Renewal: Better Teachers, Better Schools* (San Francisco: Jossey-Bass, 1994); and Andy Hargreaves and Michael Fullan, *What's Worth Fighting For Out There?* (New York: Teachers College Press, 1998).

7.   Helen F. Ladd, ed., *Holding Schools Accountable: Performance-Based Reform in Education* (Washington: Brookings Institution, 1996).

8.   John E. Chubb and Terry M. Moe, *Politics, Markets, and America's Schools* (Washington: Brookings Institution, 1990); Bruce Fuller and Richard F. Elmore, *Who Chooses? Who Loses? Culture, Institutions, and the Unequal Effects of School Choice* (New York: Teachers College Press, 1996); Chester E. Finn, Jr., Bruno V. Manno, and Gregg Vanourek, *Charter Schools in Action: Renewing Public Education* (Princeton, NJ: Princeton University Press, 2000); Jeffrey R. Henig, *Rethinking School Choice* (Princeton, NJ: Princeton University Press, 1994); and Richard D. Kahlenberg, *All Together Now: Creating Middle Class Schools through Public School Choice* (Washington: Brookings Institution Press, 2001).

9.   Sandra Waddock, *Not By Schools Alone: Sharing Responsibility for America's Educational Reform* (Westport, Connecticut: Praeger, 1995); and Clarence Stone, "Civic Capacity and Urban School Reform," in *Changing Urban Education*, ed. Clarence Stone (Lawrence: University Press of Kansas, 1998), pp. 250–73.

10. Theodore R. Sizer, *Horace's School: Redesigning the American High School* (Boston: Houghton Mifflin, 1991); Bruce L. Wilson and Gretchen B. Rossman, *Mandating Academic Excellence: High School Responses to State Curriculum Reform* (New York: Teachers College Press, 1993): and Ronald D. Anderson, *Studies of Education Reform: Study of Curriculum Reform* (Washington: U.S. Department of Education, 1996).

11. David B. Tyack and Larry Cuban, *Tinkering Toward Utopia: A Century of Public School Reform* (Cambridge, Massachusetts: Harvard University Press, 1995); also see Jeanne S. Chall, *The Academic Achievement Challenge: What Works Best in the Classroom?* (New York: Guilford Press, 2000) and Dianne Ravitch, *Left Back: A Century of Failed School Reforms* (New York: Simon and Schuster, 2000).

12. Frederick M. Hess, *Spinning Wheels: The Politics of Urban School Reform* (Washington: Brookings Institution Press, 1999), pg. 5.

13. *The Changing Landscape of Education Governance* (Denver: Education Commission of the States, 1999).

14. Lowell C. Rose and Alec M. Gallup, "The 31st Annual Phi Delta Kappa/Gallup Poll of the Public's Attitude toward the Public Schools," *Phi Delta Kappan*, 81, no. 1 (September 1999), pp. 41–56. Also see Jeffrey Henig and others, *The Color of School Reform: Race, Politics, and the Challenge of Urban Education* (Princeton, NJ: Princeton University Press, 1999), pg. 11.

15. John Portz, Lana Stein, and Robin R. Jones, *City Schools and City Politics: Institutions and Leadership in Pittsburgh, Boston, and St. Louis* (Lawrence: University Press of Kansas, 1999), pp. 4–7.

16. *Violence and Discipline Problems in U.S. Public Schools, 1996–97* (Washington: U.S. Department of Education, 1998), pp. 6–10.

17. James P. Comer, "Creating Successful Urban Schools," in *Brookings Papers in Education Policy 1999*, ed. Diane Ravitch (Washington: Brookings Institution Press, 1999), pg. 327.

18. Clarence M. Stone, "Introduction: Urban Education in Political Context," in *Changing Urban Education*, ed. Stone, pg. 5.

19. Hess, *Spinning Wheels*, pg. 13.

20. Paul T. Hill and Mary Beth Celio, *Fixing Urban Schools* (Washington: Brookings Institution Press, 1998), pg. 4.

21. Paul E. Peterson, "Top Ten Questions Asked About School Choice," in *Brookings Papers on Education Policy 1999*, ed. Ravitch, pg. 404; and Terry M. Moe, *Schools, Vouchers, and the American Public* (Washington: Brookings Institution Press, 2000).

22. Michael N. Danielson and Jennifer Hochschild, "Changing Urban Education: Lessons, Cautions, Prospects," in *Changing Urban Education*, ed. Stone, pg. 281.

23. Henig and others, *The Color of School Reform*, Chapter 8; and Richard D. Kahlenberg, *All Together Now: The Case for Economic Integration of the Public Schools* (Washington: Brookings Institution Press, 2000).

24. Paul Hill, Christine Campbell, and James Harvey, *It Takes a City: Getting Serious about Urban School Reform* (Washington: Brookings Institution Press, 2000), pg. 25.
25. Stone, "Civic Capacity and Urban School Reform," pg. 254.
26. Jennifer L. Hochschild, *The New American Dilemma: Liberal Democracy and School Desegregation* (New Haven, CT: Yale University Press, 1984), pp. 44–45.
27. The original case was *Serrano v. Priest*, 96 California Reporter 601 (1971).
28. *San Antonio Independent School District v. Rodriguez*, 411 U.S. 1 (1973).
29. Dan A. Lewis and Shadd Maruna, "The Politics of Education," in *Politics in the American States: A Comparative Analysis*, 7th ed., ed. Virginia Gray, Russell L. Hanson, and Herbert Jacob (Washington: CQ Press, 1999), pp. 410–15.
30. William N. Evans, Sheila E. Murray, and Robert N. Schwab, "Schoolhouses, Courthouses, and Statehouses after *Serrano*," *Journal of Policy Analysis and Management*, 16, no. 1 (1997), pp. 10–31.
31. *Brown v. Board of Education of Topeka*, 347 U.S. 483 (1954). It overruled an earlier decision—*Plessy v. Ferguson*, 163 U.S. 537 (1896)—that separate but equal schools were constitutionally permissible.
32. Christine H. Rossell, *The Carrot or the Stick for School Desegregation Policy: Magnet Schools or Forced Busing* (Philadelphia: Temple University Press, 1990), pg. 5.
33. The key decisions included *Green v. County School Board of New Kent County*, 391 U.S. 430 (1968); *Swann v. Charlotte-Mecklenburg Board of Education*, 402 U.S. 1 (1971); and *Keyes v. School District No. 1, Denver, Colorado*, 413 U.S. 189 (1973).
34. *Milliken v. Bradley*, 418 U.S. 717 (1974).
35. Jennifer Hochschild, "Is School Desegregation Still a Viable Policy Option?" *PS: Political Science and Politics*, 30, no. 3 (September 1997), pg. 458.
36. Rossell, *The Carrot or the Stick for School Desegregation Policy*, pp. 42–51.
37. Janet Ward Scholfield, "Review of Research on School Desegregation's Impact on Elementary and Secondary School Students," in *Handbook of Research on Multicultural Education*, ed. James A. Banks (New York: Macmillan, 1995), pp. 597–616.
38. Susan Olzak, Suzanne Shanahan, and Elizabeth West, "School Desegregation, Interracial Exposure, and Antibusing Activity in Urban America," *American Journal of Sociology*, 100, no. 1 (July 1994), pp. 196–241.
39. *Board of Education of Oklahoma v. Dowell*, 498 U.S. 237 (1991).
40. *Missouri v. Jenkins*, 115 S. Ct. 2038 (1995).
41. Gary Orfield, "Segregated Housing and School Resegregation," in *Dismantling Desegregation*, ed. Gary Orfield and Susan E. Eaton (New York: The New Press, 1996), pp. 291–330.
42. "More Education: Higher Earnings, Lower Unemployment," *Occupational Outlook Quarterly*, 43, no. 3 (Fall 1999), pg. 40.
43. Kevin J. Dougherty, *The Contradictory College: The Conflicting Origins, Impacts, and Futures of the Community College* (Albany: State University of New York Press, 1994), pp. 50–52.
44. G. Jeremiah Ryan, ed., *Partners in Economic Development: Community College Strategies for Collaboration* (Washington: American Association of Community Colleges, 1993).
45. Arnold B. Grobman, *Urban State Universities: An Unfinished National Agenda* (New York: Praeger, 1988), pp. 13–22.
46. Daniel M. Johnson and David A. Bell, eds., *Metropolitan Universities: An Emerging Model in American Higher Education* (Denton: University of North Texas Press, 1995).
47. Michael I. Luger and Harvey A. Goldstein, "What Is the Role of Public Universities in Regional Economic Development," in *Dilemmas in Urban Economic Development*, ed. Richard D. Bingham and Robert Mier (Thousand Oaks, California: Sage Publications, 1997), pp. 104–34.
48. Benjamin S. Bloom, *Stability and Change in Human Characteristics* (New York: John Wiley, 1964) and J. McVicker Hunt, *Intelligence and Experience* (New York: Ronald, 1961). For a more recent statement, see Rima Shore, *Rethinking the Brain: New Insights into Early Development* (New York: Families and Work Institute, 1997).
49. Nancy K. Cauthen, Jane Kritzer, and Carol H. Ripple, *Map and Track: State Initiatives for Young Children and Families* (New York: National Center for Children in Poverty, 2000), pp. 7–9.
50. Cauthen, Kritzer, and Ripple, *Map and Track*, pg. 13.
51. W. Stephen Barnett and Sarano Spence Boocock, eds., *Early Care and Education for Children in Poverty: Promises, Programs, and Long-Term Results* (Albany: State University of New York Press, 1998).
52. Maris A. Vinovskis, "Do Federal Compensatory Education Programs Really Work? A Brief Historical Analysis of Title I and Head Start," *American Journal of Education*, 107, #3 (May 1999), pg. 199.
53. Harold W. Stubblefield and Patrick Keane, *Adult Education in the American Experience: From the Colonial Period to the Present* (San Francisco: Jossey-Bass, 1994).
54. Richard Murnane and Frank Levy, *Teaching the New Basic Skills* (New York: The Free Press, 1996), pg. 3.

55. Don Nuckols, "Private/Public Partnerships as Implementing Strategy: The Job Training Partnerships Act," *Journal of Economic Issues,* 24, no. 2 (June 1990), pp. 645–51.
56. Cynthia Pantazis, "The New Workforce Investment Act," *Training and Development,* 53, no. 8 (August 1999), pp. 48–50.
57. Bennett Harrison and Marcus Weiss, *Workforce Development Network: Community-Based Organizations and Regional Alliances* (Thousand Oaks, California: Sage Publications, 1998).
58. *From the Margins to the Mainstream: An Action Agenda for Literacy* (Washington: National Institute for Literacy, 2000).
59. George Bobinski, *Carnegie Libraries: Their History and Impact on American Public Library Development* (Chicago: American Library Association, 1969).
60. Edwin Beckerman, *Politics and the American Public Library: Creating Political Support for Library Goals* (Lanham, Maryland: Scarecrow Press, 1996).

SUGGESTED READINGS

CHUBB, JOHN E., and TERRY M. MOE. *Politics, Markets, and America's Schools.* Washington: Brookings Institution, 1990. The intellectual rationale for greater choice in public education, laying the theoretical groundwork for initiatives like vouchers and charter schools.

ORFIELD, GARY, and SUSAN E. EATON, eds. *Dismantling Desegregation.* New York: The New Press, 1996. Ever since the publication of *Must We Bus? Segregated Schools and National Policy* (Washington: Brookings Institution, 1978), Orfield has been the leading scholarly advocate for integrated education.

RAVITCH, DIANE. *Left Back: A Century of Failed School Reforms.* New York: Simon and Schuster, 2000. One of the nation's leading specialists on public education critiques reform proposals.

STONE, CLARENCE, ed. *Changing Urban Education.* Lawrence: University Press of Kansas, 1998. The leading analysis of central-city public education, featuring both detailed case studies and interpretive essays.

DOING IT

Select one of the nation's urban school systems. For a handy list, check out the Council of Great City Schools web site: *www.cgcs.org.* Using library resources, the district's own web site, and the electronic archives for the principal newspaper in that metropolitan area, examine the following questions:

1. How many superintendents has the district had since 1990? What rationales were given when each former superintendent was fired or resigned? What expectations were expressed when each new superintendent was hired?
2. What have been the major reforms implemented by the district since 1990? What rationale was given at the time each reform was proposed? What problem(s) was it supposed to solve and why was it best suited for solving that problem? What updates, if any, were given about whether each reform was achieving its objective(s)?
3. What has been the relationship between the state government education agency and the district since 1990? What sticks and carrots has the state employed to improve education in the central-city district?

CHAPTER 9

Arts, Entertainment, and Tourism

THE SETTING

Once having a dominating basic industry was enough to make a metropolitan area a powerhouse. Good examples were Chicago and meatpacking, Detroit and automobiles, Milwaukee and beer, Pittsburgh and steel, St. Louis and shoes. Those sectors generated thousands of well-paying blue-collar jobs. The work was hard, the hours were long, but the pay was good. There was not much leisure time, either after the day was over or during the brief vacations. Having a beer, taking a nap, playing with the kids, going fishing in a nearby lake were about it. Only the wealthy traveled frequently to other parts of the country and the world. As long as the region could supply steady employment, it could attract and retain residents and achieve stature among the nation's metropolitan areas.

No more. Intercity travel is now part of everyday experience. During 1999, each American—both adult and child—took an average of four trips within the United States.[1] About two-thirds of these journeys were for pleasure, one-fifth for business, and the remaining one-seventh for personal events like weddings and funerals. When one adds international visitors to the mix, tourism in the United States is fast approaching a trillion-dollar industry, excluding the money spent on getting to and from the destination.

That's money worth fighting over. Metropolitan areas want to reap more than their share from the tourism trade. Although it is impossible to keep all the locals at home while attracting hundreds of thousands of visitors, any region wants more folks coming in than going out. Each tourist represents almost a pure economic gain. Apart from modest promotional expenses touting the pluses of visiting a

Chicago's McCormick Place Convention Center

metropolitan area, it costs little to get them and, once there, everything they spend stays within the region. For a few areas—most notably Las Vegas and Orlando—tourism is one of the top sectors but it plays an important and expanding role within almost every region.[2] Metropolitan areas, then, no longer just compete by producing goods to export to other regions. They also seek to become "centers of consumption," offering enticing opportunities for both residents and visitors to spend dollars.[3]

Aside from its gross dollar contribution to economic well-being, the hospitality sector—hotels, restaurants, entertainment venues—fills an important employment niche. It provides thousands of entry-level positions—reservation clerks, servers, janitors—which enable less well-educated individuals to gain a foothold. It is also an attractive taxation object: most regions now impose 10 percent or higher rates on hotel and motel rooms as well as rental cars, extracting still more dollars from tourist pockets.

Within tourism, conventions and business meetings are prime targets. Although pleasure travel constitutes the majority of trips, convention delegates and corporate employees spend more per visit. There are almost 12,000 conventions annually with an average attendance of approximately 1,000.[4] There are about a million corporate meetings each year with an average of fifty participants.[5] At a minimum, these sessions require appealing meeting spaces, convention centers for the larger sessions and hotel conference rooms for the smaller gatherings. Regions respond with a range of options, from giant exhibit halls like McCormick Place in Chicago and the Jacob Javits Center in New York for the major conventions to upscale hotels such as Four Seasons or Ritz-Carlton for the high-level corporate powwows.

In addition to meeting sites for conventioneers and businesspeople, metropolitan areas have been rushing to add other features which appeal both to that contingent as well as to pleasure travelers. As Susan Fainstein and Dennis Judd comment, "cities must be consciously molded to create a physical landscape that tourists wish to inhabit [and] no city can afford to stand still for a moment."[6]

What are metropolitan areas doing to make themselves tourist magnets? Quite a bit including revitalizing downtowns, rediscovering their histories, designing public spaces, creating festival malls and amusement venues, introducing gaming, expanding sports franchises and stadia, investing in zoos and museums, and expanding the performing arts. Along with tourist product comes market promotion, spreading the word near and far that their region is a spiffy place to come play. This is done by some entity, most commonly called a convention and visitors bureau. Some regions have just one serving the entire area while others have several, each speaking for one or more cities or counties within the region.

Attracting tourists and their dollars is not the only reason metropolitan areas are doing all this. Competing successfully in the new economy means recruiting and retaining "knowledge workers," those trained to use their brains in high technology endeavors. Although interesting and challenging jobs rank first for luring them, having a wide range of amenities also counts significantly, especially for those in their twenties and thirties.[7]

Stature is a final factor fueling the arts and entertainment chase. Every region wants to be "world class" and "major league," both because that makes the residents feel better about themselves and because, it is thought, many businesses and individuals will be more attracted to regions which merit those labels. Having an outstanding symphony or a National Football League franchise or an exceptional theater district can be a glittering jewel, making the region stand out among others.

DOWNTOWNS

A 1960's tune sung by Petula Clark and written by Tony Hatch captures it well:

Just listen to the music of the traffic in the city
Linger on the sidewalks where the neon signs are pretty
How can you lose
The lights are much brighter there
You can forget all your troubles, forget all your cares and go

DOWNTOWN
Things'll be great when you're
DOWNTOWN
Everything's waiting for you
DOWNTOWN, DOWNTOWN

By the time this tune topped the charts in the mid-1960s, that type of downtown was a fading memory. During the first three decades following World War II, the central-city downtowns in most metropolitan areas became 8 AM to 5 PM operations. Suburbanites commuted to their jobs, grabbed a quick bite at lunch and ran a few errands, then exited quickly at quitting time. By 7 PM, the streets were deserted and there was little to entice visitors to play or suburbanites to return.[8]

Residents who had once journeyed downtown to shop in the major department stores or see a film at one of the movie palaces now found they could do these things in suburban shopping malls. The process fed on itself. The more that people stayed away from downtowns, the more stores and theaters either moved to the suburbs or went out of business. The fewer reasons there were to go downtown, the less people did so. By the late 1960s, "the shells of . . . cities were getting to look like black-and-white newsreels of the Great Depression."[9]

Revitalizing downtown had three sets of advocates. First, central city elected officials needed tax revenues. As the inner-core residential neighborhoods became less affluent, they required more services at the same time their property values were declining. Downtown was one of the few assets left to tap.[10] Second, the corporations and professional firms officed downtown had sunk costs. Although moving to the suburbs was an option, it would mean abandoning years of investment. Better, at least as a first option, to work for a turnaround. Third, civic leaders and tourism officials fretted about image. Most convention centers and large hotels were located downtown. If convention delegates saw only deserted streets and abandoned retail outlets during the evening hours, their impressions of the entire region would dip and the likelihood of their association's returning would decline.

Downtown redevelopment strategies in the 1960s and 1970s focused on producing destinations, magnets which would attract more people to come to work, shop, and play. Since jobs are so critical to the daytime population, central cities granted tax subsidies and eased building restrictions to keep corporations from fleeing to campuslike settings in the suburbs. During the 1960s alone, 20 percent of the new office square footage arose in the downtowns of the nation's thirty largest metropolitan areas.[11]

Next came convention centers. Between the mid-1960s and the mid-1980s, convention space tripled, going from about 6 million square feet to 18 million.[12] Chicago's McCormick Place alone, after its expansion more than a decade ago, contains 2.6 million square feet, the equivalent of fifty-five football fields. The centers are usually public facilities which intentionally do not recover all their capital and operating costs from exhibitor and meeting rental fees, instead assuming that all the other dollars spent by people attending these events will more than make up the difference.

Out-of-towners conducting business in the office towers and delegates attending conventions needed places to stay, sparking a boom in downtown hotel construction. After all the attention received by John Portman's atrium design, introduced by his Hyatt Regency Hotel in Atlanta in 1967, cities vied for having dazzling lodging, either by reconditioning a grand old hotel that had become a bit seedy or by building their own variation of Portman's model. Often with some assistance from federal funding, especially Urban Development Action Grants, "the thirty-eight largest urban areas built 319 downtown hotels with 110,000 rooms between 1960 and 1982".[13]

To counter the loss of retail dollars to the suburban shopping malls, downtowns developed their own versions. Some imitate their peripheral rivals, featuring one or more major department stores with speciality shops and a food court, all contained in an enclosed setting. Examples include the Gallery in Philadelphia and Watertower Place in Chicago. Others take several blocks along one thoroughfare—16th Street in Denver or Nicollet in Minneapolis, for instance—and restrict it either to pedestrians only or to shoppers and buses, recreating a "Main Street" ambiance in the midst of downtown.

Sports stadia became another destination site.[14] In the 1960s, for example, Cincinnati, Pittsburgh, and St. Louis replaced their baseball parks (Crosley, Forbes, and Sportsmen's, respectively) located in urban neighborhoods with downtown stadiums (Riverfront, Three Rivers, and Busch), which could handle both baseball and football. New Orleans mounted the Superdome on the edge of its downtown and several cities added indoor arenas for basketball, hockey, concerts, and ice shows.

Making downtown a more popular place for the region's suburbanites created its own dilemma: where to park the automobiles.[15] In a few regions—New York and Chicago, for example—most could arrive by mass transit. But for the rest, driving was the sole or most popular option. That put downtowns at a disadvantage compared to sites outside the central city, locations where parking was plentiful and usually free. They have coped by building public garages, often with discounts for those who shop in nearby stores, and in some of the larger metropolitan areas—Atlanta, Dallas, San Diego, and St. Louis, for example—having rapid rail transit lines running into the downtown.

Even when it succeeded, the destination approach had one significant shortcoming. It transformed downtowns into a set of fortresses with almost all the activity occurring inside structures and little happening outside them.[16] As Kent Robertson concludes, "downtowns without pedestrians look lifeless and boring, whatever the quality of the built environment."[17] The dream that the streets would be as lively as Paris's had not been yet realized, despite all the towers, centers, hotels, malls, and stadiums.

That has led to a second wave of strategies, all designed to make downtowns more friendly for pedestrians. One initial and somewhat flawed tactic was skywalks, self-contained tubes above street level connecting various downtown buildings. Atlanta, Cincinnati, and Minneapolis led the way but the results have been mixed. Although foot traffic is high, it does nothing for street life, still leaving the sidewalks vacant and first-floor retail stores without walk-in trade.[18]

More promising practices include developing linear parks within downtown, especially along waterways. San Antonio's River Walk, a meandering two-and-a-half-mile paved path about fifteen feet below street level, is the classic example, but other cities such as Chattanooga and New Orleans have also rediscovered their streams. They also incorporate widening sidewalks, encouraging street vendors and entertainers, enhanced lighting, and removing freeway barriers either by eliminating the highway (Embarcadero in San Francisco) or putting it underground (Boston).

HISTORY, SPACE, AND TOURIST BUBBLES

Just as homeowners often redecorate before placing their residences on the market in order to make them more attractive to potential buyers, metropolitan areas have spruced up their surroundings to appeal to various tourist preferences. For the history buffs, regions have researched their past and inventoried their structures to find those with the most significance and charm. For the aesthetics, they have formed public spaces that excite the senses. For the fantasizers, they have developed "tourist bubbles"—"specialized areas . . . established as virtual tourist reservations."[19]

Historic Preservation

Cities have histories, interesting stories to tell about their past. In many instances, structures linked with these narratives still remain. In Robert Archibald's phrase, each can be positioned as "a place to remember,"[20] evoking memories linking today with yesterday. As Americans seek to learn more about their individual and collective heritage, metropolitan areas want some of the quest to occur within their boundaries.

Some regions find it easy to connect themselves with key periods in U.S. history: Boston and the American Revolution, Philadelphia and the Constitutional Convention, St. Louis and Westward Expansion. Others have a legendary site in their past: Baltimore and the Star Spangled Banner at Fort McHenry or San Antonio and the battle at the Alamo. A few have entire sections which have become historic districts: Old Alexandria in the Washington, D.C., area, Ybor City in Tampa, and the French Quarter in New Orleans. Each of these, and others, have taken this historic advantage and developed an integrated set of tourist attractions to make the experience more meaningful—and more lucrative.

But the historic imagination can and does range much wider. Some of the more creative efforts are New York's Lower East Side Tenement Museum, which features the millions of immigrants occupying that neighborhood in the late nineteenth and early twentieth centuries and Chicago's promotion of its oldest El line, the Ravenswood route, reminding riders that only there can they "see the Chicago that once was, a Chicago of steeples and rooftops and laundry lines," all for only a $1.50 fare.

Two changes in federal policy encouraged metropolitan areas to expand their history initiatives. First, the National Historic Preservation Act of 1966 elevated the importance of the past in making decisions about buildings. It armed those eager to

Ybor City in Tampa

protect aging structures with a process to accomplish just that, culminating in being placed on a national register of historic places. Second, this legislation and a series of amendments to the federal income tax code passed in the late 1970s and early 1980s made history financially attractive. Generous tax credits were granted for re-development projects which protected historic structures and, soon after the tax code had been amended, the cumulative subsidies totaled well into the billions of dollars.[21] Many states also passed laws adding their own incentives.

Whether to retain historic buildings or replace them with modern structures often generates controversy. The preservationists assert that the past is well worth protecting both because it is important for understanding where the community has been and because it retains an economic value. Developers often chafe at others defending something just because it is old, contending that change is inevitable and that those who obstruct it are holding back progress.

Public Spaces and Cityscapes

Just as a picture is worth a thousand words, a visual experience can create lifelong memories. It might be a sweeping scene such as the Mall in Washington viewed from the steps of the U.S. Capitol, or it could be an intimate setting like Bleecker Street

Seattle's Pike Place Market

in New York's Greenwich Village.[22] Europe's great cities have perennially nurtured these images: the Champs-Elysees and the Eiffel Tower in Paris, Oxford Street and Trafalgar Square in London, the Spanish Steps and the Trevi Fountain in Rome. America's metropolitan areas are now doing their best to erect their own such public spaces and cityscape perspectives.

There are many ways to make space striking and memorable. Some are indoors, such as Grand Central Station in New York or Union Station in Washington. Each contrasts vaulting ceilings, inspiring reflection, with busy crowds, generating energy. Many regions have redone their public markets which, obviously, add smell to the aesthetic appeal.[23] These include Seattle's Pike Place Market, featuring the Northwest's fish and produce, and the Eastern Market on Capitol Hill in Washington, offering an array of food.

Others are outside. There are the signature monuments, like the Space Needle in Seattle or the Gateway Arch in St. Louis, reaching to the sky, offering tourists a birds-eye perspective from the top and a stunning visual from below. There are public squares. Some date back decades, like Union Square in San Francisco. Others were done more recently, such as Pershing Square in Los Angeles and Pioneer Courthouse Square in Portland. The latter features two amphitheaters, several sculptures, and a performing weather machine. Some regions have emphasized fountains within their squares, most notably Kansas City's Country Club Plaza.

More difficult to categorize is public art, the remaining three-dimensional objects intended to catch the eye and stimulate the imagination. These range from the conventional statues of dead heroes, to lifelike mannequins, to abstract renderings. The latest fad is having several hundred pieces simultaneously appear throughout a region, each reflecting an artist's interpretation of a single theme. It started with cows in Zurich in 1998, came to North America with mooses in Toronto, then cows again in Chicago and New York, followed by buffalos in, of course, Buffalo, flamingos in Miami, cod in Boston, lizards in Orlando, fish in Baltimore, and people in St. Louis.

Art is inherently controversial. There is no consensus about what is beautiful. But public art is especially contentious. Often tax dollars pay for all or part of the project, making those finding the object ugly especially upset since they helped pay for it and, by definition, it is in public view, forcing those who find it distasteful to look at it regularly. Whose values receive what prominence is also an issue—witness the ongoing debates on who deserves what place on the Mall in Washington. As a result, elected officials usually place some elite selection commission between the basic policy to sponsor it and the specific decision about which objects to choose.

Tourist Bubbles

Cities have long set aside special places to play. The introduction of electricity at the turn of the twentieth century turned dangerous nights into glamorous evenings, enabling "great white ways," vaudeville houses, and amusement parks.[24] But many of the same forces that caused downtown decline undermined these venues and, by the 1960s, even venerable facilities like Bay Shore Park in Baltimore and Euclid Beach Park in Cleveland had closed.

In their stead rose a new kind of fantasy land, places specially designed for tourists. Unlike a Coney Island, which mixed all economic, racial, and ethnic groups in a honky-tonk atmosphere, the tourist bubbles have a "well-defined perimeter [which] separates the tourist space from the rest of the city, . . . leaving visitors shielded from and unaware of the private places where people live and work."[25] Once inside the bubble, you have escaped from mundane life and are transported to a dream world.

Walt Disney's theme parks are the clearest illustration. Whether in Disneyland, opened in Anaheim in 1955, or in Disney World, unveiled in 1971 in Orlando, you are in places like "Frontierland" or "Tomorrowland." Nothing is authentic, everything is recreated. It "inscribes utopia on the terrain of the familiar and vice versa, . . . just like the real thing, only better."[26] This process has become known as "Disneyfication," applied to settings as diverse as Times Square in New York to Williams Island in Miami.[27] It has also spawned a set of imitative and competitive facilities such as Sea World and Six Flags.

Festival malls offer similar insulation from the outside environment. James Rouse, an East Coast developer, started this movement in 1976 with the Faneuil Hall Marketplace in Boston, followed by Harborplace in Baltimore (1980), and Union Station in St. Louis (1986). Variations include Crown Center (Kansas City), Ghiradelli Square (San Francisco), Horton Plaza (San Diego), and South Street Seaport (New York).[28]

Baltimore's Harbor Place

These marketplaces feature speciality stores, cart vendors, upscale restaurants, and food courts, all in an upbeat setting. It is shopping as entertainment where looking is always fun and, as the tourist mood becomes more carefree, leads to impulsive spending on items from chocolate chip cookies to garish tee shirts. There are no bargains, few sales, just glitz. As their novelty has somewhat worn off, many malls have struggled financially.[29] That has made other metropolitan areas more cautious and, as a consequence, additional ones have not emerged during the past decade.

Beyond theme parks and festival malls, there are also smaller complexes which serve as modern arcades. They include "an increasingly standard array of components: . . . one or more themed restaurants (Hard Rock Cafe, Planet Hollywood, Rainforest Cafe), a megaplex cinema, an IMAX theater, record (HMV, Virgin, Tower) and book (Barnes & Noble, Borders) megastores, and some form of interactive, high-tech arcade complete with virtual reality games and ride simulators."[30] Just as McDonalds homogenized the fast food industry, so these brands seek to pattern urban entertainment.

CASINO GAMING

For more than forty-five years, from the early 1930s to the late 1970s, Las Vegas and Reno were the only towns in casino gaming. Many metropolitan areas have thoroughbred and harness racing and a few others greyhound tracks, all featuring parimutuel wagering, but Nevada was the only state where it was legal to gamble on the traditional casino games like blackjack and roulette.

Casinos have done much for Las Vegas, one of the most rapidly growing regions in the United States. The population increases have been even stronger after the area threw off its gangster-dominated reputation, passing the 1 million mark in the mid 1990s. About 30 percent of its work force is in the hospitality sector, it is has some of the world's largest hotels, and it hosts mega-conventions, some attended by over 100,000 delegates.[31]

In 1978, Atlantic City, New Jersey, became the first non-Nevada site for casinos and, within a decade, it was home to several facilities, most catering to day trippers from the New York and Philadelphia metropolitan areas. Other regions considering gambling as part of their entertainment strategy were thwarted by state legislatures. Although many states had instituted lotteries, usually with the profits earmarked for popular programs like education, casinos retained an aura of organized crime and political corruption.

Then American Indians and a nostalgic historical reinterpretation each provided a breach in the barrier. A 1987 Supreme Court decision determined Indians were not subject to state gaming laws.[32] In order to bring some order to the chaos that might have created, the next year Congress passed the Indian Gaming Regulatory Act. Seeing casinos both as revenue generators and employment sources, many tribes went into the casino business. Many are located in rural areas, such as in Connecticut and Wisconsin, but others are within metropolitan areas like Albuquerque and Phoenix.

A largely rural state, Iowa, seeking to recall the days of riverboat gambling along the Mississippi River, provided the next breakthrough. After Iowa permitted some boats along its banks in the early 1990s, neighboring states feared their residents and their discretionary dollars would succumb to the temptation to cross over the state line. Within two years, both Illinois and Missouri also authorized riverboat casinos, with several opening in the Chicago, Kansas City, and St. Louis metropolitan areas. Within another year, Louisiana, never a state to shy away from letting the good times roll, approved casinos in Baton Rouge and New Orleans. With cruising rivers both expensive for the owners and dangerous for barge traffic, all these quickly became permanently docked establishments, popularly called "boats in moats." The latest sizeable metropolitan area entering the casino sweepstakes, all with land-based units, has been Detroit which has had three open between 1998 and 2000, excluding the Casino Windsor immediately across the Detroit River in Canada, whose 1994 entry into the market spurred Michigan voters to authorize its outlets.

The experience with casinos as tourist attractions across many regions is limited, but the early assessments suggest that Las Vegas is distinctive. It is the only large metropolitan area with casinos where most of the gambling is done by visitors and therefore the only region which benefits from it as an economic development strategy. In the remaining sites, the overwhelming share of the wagers are made by residents, meaning that gaming is only shifting dollars and jobs from one activity to another inside the area's boundaries with minimal net gain for the region.[33] The only significant outside money comes with the construction and, after that, it is mainly a local show. But even if the balance sheet is not impressive, it adds still another slice of glitter to the metropolitan scene.

PROFESSIONAL SPORTS

No entity has benefitted more from the metropolitan chase than have professional sport franchises. As competition among regions has intensified, it has become increasingly important to be seen as a "big league" place. In a society where sports is a preoccupation for a great many, especially men, one shorthand way to achieve this label is to host teams in one or more of the four high status sports: baseball, basketball, football, and hockey. Gaining one reaps instant recognition while losing one blemishes the civic face.

Even with significant expansion over the past few decades, there are still only 120 franchises: 30 in Major League Baseball (MLB), 29 in the National Basketball Association (NBA), 31 in the National Football League (NFL), and 30 in the National Hockey League (NHL). Moreover, upwards of ten of these are in Canadian locales, leaving even fewer for U.S. metropolitan areas to fight over. For expanding metropolitan areas, those entering the million-or-more ranks, attracting at least one of these affirms their arrival in the "big time". Recent winners include Columbus (NHL Blue Jackets), Jacksonville (NFL Jaguars), and Memphis (NBA Grizzlies). Others in this group such as Las Vegas and Louisville are still looking.

For those further up the rung, it is important to have both MLB and NFL franchises and either an NBA or NHL entrant. This means teams in the two most prestigious sports—baseball and football—and at least one in the next tier. It also provides year-round coverage, with baseball from April to October, football from September to January, and hockey or basketball from October to May. So, for example, when St. Louis lost its NFL Cardinals to Phoenix in 1988, it went on an expensive wooing spree until finally landing the Los Angeles Rams in 1995; similarly, after the Colts left for Indianapolis, Baltimore worked vigorously for a replacement, finally succeeding by attracting the Cleveland Browns (reborn as the Ravens) in 1996.

The MLB, NFL, NBA, and NHL have made the most of this metropolitan yearning for athletic fame and glory. These leagues are monopolies and, better yet for them, their control is legally protected.[34] Attempts to form new leagues—the American Basketball Association or the World Hockey League—have not succeeded so these top four can restrict supply, keeping it limited while demand increases. If individual owners become the least bit unhappy with their existing locations, they can hint about moving, thus setting up a bidding war between the host region and eager suitors from other metropolitan areas. Occasionally, the leagues expand, typically selling two additional franchises for tens of millions apiece and then sharing the proceeds among themselves.

In recent years, the venues—baseball parks, football stadiums, basketball and hockey arenas—have become the principal chips in the contest for teams. In order to wring the most revenue out of a fixed number of games, teams want facilities designed with tens of luxury boxes and thousands of upscale club seats. Before the professional sports franchise competition escalated, the franchises themselves almost always built their own facilities, often naming it after the owner like Chicago's Comiskey Park and Wrigley Field. Now that regions are so eager to have them, the teams now ask for public assistance to help them maintain a competitive edge on the field, court, or ice.

The largest metropolitan areas—Los Angeles and New York, for example—have largely been able to resist these entreaties. Their regional status is quite secure and their very size dictates that the leagues will have a presence, although Los Angeles still has not seriously sought an NFL team to replace the departed Rams, even though it does have two teams each in the MLB, NBA, and NHL. But most of the remaining regions have entered the fray. Since 1990, more than forty venues have been built, almost all with some taxpayer contribution and most with majority public support.[35] The decisions to have local governments fund these ventures is usually controversial, raising objections about subsidizing already wealthy owners and indulging overpaid athletes, but in the end the teams almost always receive tax support.

Does investing public funds in sports venues pay off? If you use strict dollars and cents to answer that question, a classic cost-benefit analysis, the answer is *no*. There is no evidence that professional sports contributes anything significant to metropolitan economies, either in higher personal incomes or more jobs.[36] Most of the spectators come from within the metropolitan region, especially for the fall and winter sports, so there is little tourism generated. A majority of the revenues go to the players, many of whom spend the off-season outside the community, or to the owners who spend much of their millions elsewhere.

Cleveland's Jacobs Field

A few more recent projects have used urban revitalization as a reason for central cities to contribute. Examples include Jacobs Field in Cleveland, Coors Field in Denver, Comerica Park in Detroit, and the proposed new ballparks in San Diego and St. Louis. It is too early to determine whether sports venues can serve as a catalyst for turning around an area near or in downtown but Denver's "LoDo" warehouse near Coors Field provides one positive example.[37]

Finally, there is a less tangible factor: regional spirit. Professional sports teams are among the very few institutions within a metropolitan area emotionally connected to everyone inside the boundaries. Urbanites, suburbanites, and exurbanites alike all consider it to be their "home" squad. With so much dividing the regions, it is a rare shared bond, one of the few topics beyond the weather that can be easily addressed by strangers.[38]

AQUARIUMS, ZOOS, AND MUSEUMS

Sports contests may get the newspaper headlines and the television audiences, but aquariums, zoos, and museums win the foot traffic battle. Annual attendance at zoos and aquariums is approaching 150 million while museums draw about 500 million each year.[39] They call it "cultural tourism" and it has become big business for metropolitan areas. Whether it is a panda, a Monet exhibit, or an orchid display, it attracts visitors from near and far. On average, these cultural tourists are more upscale, spending more per day,[40] and these facilities appeal more to the new economy's work force.

Aquariums and Zoos

Some aquariums and zoos are tourist magnets. The National Aquarium in Baltimore, the New England Aquarium in Boston, and the San Diego Zoo—to take three leading examples—promote themselves intensively and draw large crowds. The San Diego Zoo alone has over 3 million guests each year. For metropolitan areas willing to invest in such a signature facility, it can become the primary reason people vacation there. Even if they do not recover all their costs from admission fees and concession sales, the spending outside the facility for meals and lodging more than compensates.[41]

But even regions outside the top tier are increasingly investing in zoos and, in a fewer cases, in aquariums. Responding to the competition from the innovative facilities, they are transforming their exhibits from iron-fenced concrete boxes to moat-enclosed natural settings. Not only does this have more visitor appeal, but

The San Diego Zoo Entrance

it also projects a favorable image about the region, one that says it cares about its animals and, by implication, its human residents. As conservation rises within the American value hierarchy, having an up-to-date zoo or aquarium demonstrates that a metropolitan area shares that belief. The facilities foster this environmental status even further by conducting extensive educational programs for both teachers and students.

To fund these revamped or brand new ventures, zoos and aquariums are increasingly using earned revenues and donations and relying less on public support, and on average, less than one-quarter of the budget comes from taxes. Public ownership typically remains but often a nonprofit organization handles day-to-day operations, giving them more management flexibility and added political insulation. They can then also attract civic leaders to these high-profile nonprofit boards, giving them enhanced access to philanthropic sources.

Museums

Museums are a growth enterprise in the United States. Excluding zoos and aquariums, there are more than 8,000 different establishments conducting operations at about 15,000 sites. Most are located within metropolitan areas and 40 percent started after 1970.[42] Some are familiar bastions: the Metropolitan Museum in New York, the Smithsonian Institution in Washington, the Field Museum in Chicago, the Getty Museum in Los Angeles. They attract visitors from throughout the world. Most are less well known, drawing their attendance from their immediate region.

The two most common museum types, accounting for more than half the total, feature history and art. The larger metropolitan areas also typically have a botanical garden, a natural history and anthropology facility, and a science center. Rarer are specialized children's museums and planetariums. About half are government-owned and half nonprofit organizations. Few of the public facilities rely solely on taxes and, as a group, more than half their revenues now come from fees and gifts.

Earlier museums had a passive approach. They were stark environments where people came to improve themselves and the exhibits themselves did little to entice interest. In today's more competitive environment, museums need patronage. The more people who come through their doors, the greater revenues from admission fees and concession sales and the higher the political support. They now provide experiences, interactive displays and integrated exhibitions, which both entertain and educate. They actively market their wares and vigorously promote their missions, reaching out for general audiences and community backing.[43]

The more aggressive metropolitan areas, especially those ranking below the top twenty in size, are also using museums to improve their images. One way to position a region as a scientific and technological comer is to build a snazzy center. Recent examples include the Center of Science of Industry in Columbus and Science City in Kansas City. Each required a nine-figure capital investment, a pricey tab for advertising that their community is on the cutting edge.

PERFORMING ARTS

Professional sports teams have a broad appeal extending across all socioeconomic classes and educational levels. They are everyone's home team. But they are plebeian, the *vin ordinaire* of a region's entertainment menu. So, too, are most of today's museums. They also seek a wider audience and, for many, it is difficult to distinguish some of their exhibits from Disneyland displays.

To add luster and to appeal directly to persons who see themselves as the most sophisticated, metropolitan areas want high culture, that which demonstrates human creativity at its best. Art museums meet part of this need but most of it is supplied by the performing arts—symphony orchestras, opera companies, dance ensembles, and theater groups. For a region to reach the pinnacle, for it to be truly world class, requires offering an exciting array of these performances.

For the nation's three largest regions—Chicago, New York, and Los Angeles—it is one of the ways, beyond absolute size, in which they demonstrate their superiority. They vie to offer the best in each of these genres, the top artists for every category. New York has traditionally finished on top, from Broadway theater to the Joffrey Ballet to the Metropolitan Opera, but the other two come close. The next tier often seek excellence in one of these to demonstrate their refinement: Minneapolis with the Guthrie Theater or Cleveland and St. Louis with their symphony orchestras.

Patrons for high culture are a minority. Among the nation's metropolitan residents, less than one in six attend a symphony performance or a nonmusical play annually and the rates for opera and ballet are about one in twenty.[44] But these shares double or even triple for households with six-figure annual incomes and persons with postgraduate degrees. Regions covet these individuals and, for one-third to one-half of this segment, high culture is a magnet.

Despite being popular among those most able to afford it, most performing arts organizations struggle financially. Quality demands they hire highly talented artists, both on stage and behind the scenes, who, as a scarce commodity, command relatively high salaries. The venues must be exceptional, with appeal to the eye and clarity for the ear. Even with lofty prices, box office receipts typically cover only one-half to two-thirds of expenses.[45]

These groups have usually relied on private donations, including endowments, to cover the difference and, starting in the 1960s, some national funds became available through the National Endowment for the Arts. More recently, just as sports teams have leveraged their status within the metropolitan chase to seek subsidies from local and state governments, so too have arts organizations made a similar plea. Some have tapped into taxes dedicated to tourism, such as lodging and rental car fees, while others have received subsidies for new or renovated performance venues.

The arts have also provided a unifying theme to redevelop deteriorating portions of central cities. New York's Lincoln Center, conceived in the 1950s and born in the 1960s, is the role model.[46] Now housing twelve resident arts companies, it has made its portion of the Upper West Side a top destination. Others have imitated this, all on a smaller scale, but none has matched Lincoln Center's success. More

The New Jersey Performing Arts Center in Newark

recent initiatives include the New Jersey Performing Arts Center in Newark,[47] the Kentucky Center for the Arts in Louisville,[48] the transformation of Boston's Combat Zone into a theater district,[49] and Pittsburgh's cultural district.[50]

CONCERNS

As they compete for visitors, some express concern that this race will distort metropolitan priorities.[51] Public capital is scarce. Funds reserved to pay back bonds for a stadium or an arena cannot be used to repave neighborhood streets or replace fire equipment. Most states limit the amount of debt any local government can incur and bonding agencies require reserved revenue streams. The risk is that a region's central cities will have play palaces for middle-class visitors and suburbanites and decaying facilities for its own lower-class residents.

There is also a tendency to separate physically not just tourist bubbles but sports venues and theater districts from everyday life. The goal is to make them seem safer by isolating them from the less esthetically attractive features of urban life, be they homeless beggars or boarded-up structures. This adds further to intrametropolitan divisions, not only keeping residents segregated by class but also walling off visitors from most of the locals.

Finally there is worry that the contest might not be worth the prize, that much of the expensive pursuit of the tourist dollar, particularly the hundreds of millions spent building and operating facilities, ultimately does not pay off economically. Would the funds have generated a better return if they had been invested in more basic functions, such as those discussed in early chapters—transportation or education—or in key essential services like safety and health described in the next segment? What is apparent is that the issue itself—how much attention to devote to arts, entertainment, and tourism—has risen to the upper rung of the metropolitan agenda and, in the foreseeable future, it will remain a matter of substantial debate.

NOTES

1. All travel statistics are from *Tourism Works for America, 2000* (Washington: Travel Industry Association of America, 2001). A trip is defined as traveling at least fifty miles away from home or staying overnight or both.
2. David Gladstone, "Tourism Urbanization in the United States," *Urban Affairs Review*, 34, no. 1 (September 1998), pp. 3–27; and "NLC Report Focuses on Importance of Tourism and Entertainment to Local Economic Development," *Nation's Cities Weekly*, 23, no. 46 (November 20, 2000), pg. 5. For the Orlando case, see Richard E. Foglesong, *Married to the Mouse: Walt Disney World and Orlando* (New Haven, CT: Yale University Press, 2001).
3. Edward L. Glaeser, Jed Kolko, and Albert Saiz, *Consumer City* (Cambridge, MA: National Bureau of Economic Research, 2000), pg. 2.
4. Cheryl-Anne Starken, "Association Meetings," *Meetings and Conventions*, 35, no. 9 (August 2000), pp. 18–23.
5. Sarah J.F. Brady, "Market Overview," *Meetings and Conventions*, 35, no. 9 (August 2000), pp. 1–3.
6. Susan S. Fainstein and Dennis R. Judd, "Global Forces, Local Strategies, and Urban Tourism," in *The Tourist City*, ed. Fainstein and Judd (New Haven, CT: Yale University Press, 1999), pg. 5. Also see Stephen Page, *Urban Tourism* (New York: Routledge, 1995).
7. Richard Florida, *Competing in the Age of Talent: Environment, Amenities, and the New Economy* (Pittsburgh, PA: R.K. Mellon Foundation, Heinz Endowments, and Sustainable Pittsburgh, 2000). Also see Paul D. Gottlieb, "Amenities as an Economic Development Tool: Is There Enough Evidence?" *Economic Development Quarterly*, 8, no. 3 (August 1994), pp. 270–85.
8. Partners for Livable Communities, "The New Downtown: City as Living Room, Playground, Nightclub," in *The Livable City: Revitalizing Urban Communities* (New York: McGraw Hill, 2000), pp. 116–18.
9. Bernard J. Frieden and Lynne B. Sagalyn, *Downtown, Inc.: How America Rebuilds Cities* (Cambridge, MA: The MIT Press, 1989), pg. 13. Also see Jon C. Teaford, *The Rough Road to Renaissance: Urban Revitalization in America, 1940–1985* (Baltimore, Maryland: Johns Hopkins University Press, 1990).
10. Sometimes neighborhood activists resented their elected officials' preoccupation with downtown. See Stephen J. McGovern, *The Politics of Downtown Development: Dynamic Political Cultures in San Francisco and Washington, D.C.* (Lexington: The University Press of Kentucky, 1998).
11. Frieden and Sagalyn, *Downtown, Inc.*, pg. 57.
12. Heywood T. Sanders, "Building the Convention City: Politics, Finance, and Public Investment in Urban America," *Journal of Urban Affairs*, 14, no. 2 (1992), pg. 136.
13. Frieden and Sagalyn, *Downtown, Inc.*, pg. 268.
14. Mark S. Rosentraub and others, "Sport and Downtown Development Strategy," *Journal of Urban Affairs*, 16, no. 3 (1994), pp. 221–39.
15. Richard Vorth, "The Downtown Parking Syndrome: Does Curing the Illness Kill the Patient?" *Business Review: Federal Reserve Bank of Philadelphia* (January/February 1998), pp. 3–14. Also see William Fulton, "The Garage: Wonder Where All That Downtown Redevelopment Money Went?" *Governing*, 11, no. 11 (August 1998), pp. 25–27.
16. The roots on this concern lie in ideas expressed by Jane Jacobs, *The Death and Life of Great American Cities* (New York: Vintage Books, 1961) and echoed in works like Roberta Brandes Gratz, *Cities Back from the Edge: New Life for Downtown* (New York: John Wiley, 1998). For empirical support, see Brian

J. Lorch and Mark J. Smith, "Pedestrian Movement and the Downtown Enclosed Shopping Center," *Journal of the American Planning Association,* 59, no. 1 (Winter 1993), pp. 75–86.

17. Kent A. Robertson, "Downtown Redevelopment Strategies in the United States," *Journal of the American Planning Association,* 61, no. 1 (Autumn 1995), pg. 431.

18. Barry Maitland, "Hidden Cities: The Irrestible Rise of the North American Interior City," *Cities,* 9 (August 1992), pp. 162–69. Also see Kent A. Robertson, "Pedestrianization Strategies for Downtown Planners: Skywalks Versus Pedestrian Malls," *Journal of the American Planning Association,* 59, no. 3 (Summer 1993), pp. 361–70; and Trever Boddy, "Underground and Overhead: Building the Analogous City," in *Variations on a Theme Park: The New American City and the End of Public Space,* ed. Michael Sorkin (New York: Hill and Wang, 1992), pp. 123–53.

19. Dennis R. Judd, "Constructing the Tourist Bubble," in *The Tourist City,* ed. Fainstein and Judd, pg. 36.

20. Robert R. Archibald, *A Place to Remember: Using History to Build Community* (Walnut Creek, CA: Alta Mira Press, 1999). Also see M. Christine Boyer, *The City of Collective Memory: Its Historical Imagery and Architectural Entertainments* (Cambridge, MA: The MIT Press, 1994).

21. Alexander J. Reichl, "Historic Preservation and Progrowth Politics in U.S. Cities," *Urban Affairs Review,* 32, no. 4 (March 1997), pp. 513–35; and Harvey K. Newman, "Historic Preservation Policy and Regime Politics in Atlanta," *Journal of Urban Affairs,* 23, no. 1 (2001), pp. 71–86.

22. Tony Hiss, *The Experience of Place* (New York: Knopf, 1990); and William H. Whyte, *The Social Life of Small Urban Spaces* (Washington: Conservation Foundation, 1980).

23. *Public Markets and Community Revitalization* (Washington: Project for Public Spaces and the Urban Land Institute, 1995).

24. David Nasaw, *Going Out: The Rise and Fall of Public Amusements* (New York: Basic Books, 1993), pp. 6–9.

25. Judd, "Constructing the Tourist Bubble," pg. 36.

26. Michael Sorkin, "See You in Disneyland," in *Variations on a Theme Park,* ed. Sorkin, pg. 226.

27. Ada Louise Huxtable, *The Unreal America: Architecture and Illusion* (New York: The New Press, 1997).

28. Alexander Garvin, *The American City: What Works, What Doesn't* (New York: McGraw Hill, 1996), pp. 102–20.

29. Robert Guskind and Neal R. Peirce, "Faltering Festivals," *National Journal,* 20, no. 38 (September 17, 1988), pp. 2307–10.

30. John Hannigan, *Fantasy City: Pleasure and Profit in the Postmodern Metropolis* (New York: Routledge, 1998), pg. 4.

31. William R. Eadington, "Casino Gaming: Origins, Trends, and Impacts," in *Casino Gambling in America: Origins, Trends, and Impacts,* ed. Klaus Meyer-Arendt and Rudi Hartmann (New York: Cognizant Communication, 1998), pp. 8–9.

32. *California v. Cabazon Band of Mission Indians,* 408 U.S. 202 (1987).

33. See William R. Eadington, "Contributions of Casino-Style Gambling to Local Economies," *The Annals of the American Academy of Political and Social Science,* 556 (March 1998), pp. 53–65; Daniel Felsenstein, Laura Littlepage, and Drew Klacik, "Casino Gambling as Local Growth Generation: Playing the Economic Development Game in Reverse?" *Journal of Urban Affairs,* 21, no. 4 (1999), pp. 409–21; Robert Goodman, *The Luck Business: The Devastating Consequences and Broken Promises of America's Gambling Explosion* (New York: The Free Press, 1995); and Meir Gross, "Legal Gambling as a Strategy for Economic Development," *Economic Development Quarterly,* 12, no. 3 (August 1998), pp. 203–13.

34. Kenneth L. Shropshire, *The Sports Franchise Game: Cities in Pursuit of Sports Franchises, Events, Stadiums, and Arenas* (Philadelphia: University of Pennsylvania Press, 1995), pp. 1–2.

35. Tens of smaller metropolitan areas like Birmingham, Des Moines, El Paso, and Syracuse have mimicked this trend by building new parks for minor league baseball teams. See David C. Petersen, *Sports, Convention, and Entertainment Facilities* (Washington: Urban Land Institute, 1996), pg. 16.

36. Dennis Coates and Brad R. Humphreys, "The Growth Effects of Sport Franchises, Stadia, and Arenas," *Journal of Policy Analysis and Management,* 18, no. 4 (1999), pp. 601–24; Ian Hudson, "Bright Lights, Big City: Do Professional Sports Teams Increase Employment?" *Journal of Urban Affairs,* 21, no. 4 (1999), pp. 397–408; Roger G. Noll and Andrew Zimbalist, eds., *Sports, Jobs, and Taxes* (Washington: Brookings Institution Press, 1997); Mark S. Rosentraub, *Major League Losers: The Real Cost of Sports and Who's Paying For It* (New York: Basic Books, 1999); and David Swindell and Mark S. Rosentraub, "Who Benefits from the Presence of Professional Sports Teams? The Implications for Public Funding of Stadiums and Arenas," *Public Administration Review,* 58, no. 1 (January-February 1998), pp. 11–20.

37. William Fulton, "The Neighborhood Ballpark," *Governing*, 12, no. 8 (June 1999), pg. 57.
38. Michael N. Danielson, *Home Team: Professional Sports and the American Metropolis* (Princeton, NJ: Princeton University Press, 1997).
39. *The Collective Impact of America's Zoos and Aquariums* (Washington: American Zoo and Aquarium Association, 1999); *Cultural Tourism* (Washington: National Endowment for the Humanities, 1995); and *Promotion of Cultural Tourism by Zoos and Aquariums* (Washington: American Zoo and Aquarium Association, 1998).
40. Julie Miller, "Cultural Tourism Worthy of Note," *Hotel and Motel Management*, 212, no. 15 (September 1, 1997), pg. 7.
41. The public share of the San Diego Zoo budget is less than 5 percent. See Tom Arrandale, "The Zoo Biz," *Governing*, 8, no. 9 (July 1995), pg. 39.
42. *Museums Count* (Washington: The American Association of Museums, 1994).
43. Neil Kotler and Philip Kotler, *Museum Strategy and Marketing: Designing Missions, Building Audiences, Generating Revenue and Resources* (San Francisco: Jossey-Bass, 1998); and Fiona McLean, *Marketing the Museum* (London: Routledge, 1997).
44. The statistics come from the 1997 Survey of Public Participation in the Arts conducted for the National Endowment for the Arts.
45. Philip Kotler and Joanne Scheff, *Standing Room Only: Strategies for Marketing the Performing Arts* (Boston: Harvard Business School Press, 1997), pp. 227–37.
46. Sharon Zukin, *The Cultures of Cities* (Cambridge, MA: Blackwell Publishers, 1995), pp. 118–21.
47. Elizabeth Strom, "Let's Put on a Show! Performing Arts and Urban Revitalization in Newark, New Jersey," *Journal of Urban Affairs*, 21, no. 4 (1999), pp. 423–35.
48. J. Allen Whitt, "The Role of the Performing Arts in Urban Competition and Growth," in *Business Elites and Urban Development: Case Studies and Critical Perspectives,* ed. Scott Cummings (Albany: State University of New York Press, 1988), pp. 49–70.
49. Marilyn Stasio, "Miracle on Tremont Street: A Down-On-Its-Luck Boston Theatre District Gets a Nonprofit Boost," *American Theatre*, 15, no. 9 (November 1998), pp. 40–45.
50. David Ebony, "Pittsburgh's Cultural District Takes Shape," *Art in America*, 88, no. 3 (March 2000), pg. 39.
51. Peter Eisinger, "The Politics of Bread and Circuses: Building the City for the Visitor Class," *Urban Affairs Review*, 35, no. 9 (January 2000), pp. 316–33.

SUGGESTED READINGS

FRIEDEN, BERNARD J., and LYNNE B. SAGALYN. *Downtown, Inc.: How America Rebuilds Cities.* Cambridge, MA: The MIT Press, 1989). This remains the best chronicle of central-city downtowns in the twentieth century, especially the revitalization initiatives between the 1960s and the 1980s.

JUDD, DENNIS R., and SUSAN S. FAINSTEIN, eds. *The Tourist City.* New Haven, CT: Yale University Press, 1999. Excellent analysis of how tourism affects metropolitan regions both in the United States and elsewhere.

NOLL, ROGER G., and ANDREW ZIMBALIST, eds. *Sports, Jobs, and Taxes.* Washington: Brookings Institution Press, 1997. The most definitive and thorough analysis of the linkages between professional sports and economic development.

SORKIN, MICHAEL, ed. *Variations on a Theme Park: The New American City and the End of Public Space.* New York: Hill and Wang, 1992. A series of imaginative and insightful essays on topics ranging from shopping centers to festival malls.

DOING IT

What has your favorite metropolitan area been doing to make itself a premier tourist destination? What sports and cultural venues have been built or expanded during the past two decades? Who paid for them? Is there a new or revamped convention center? A festival mall? One or more tourist bubbles? What changes has the zoo made? What have the museums (art, history, natural history, science) and botanical gardens done to enhance their appeal? Has the metropolitan area pursued one or more new sports franchises or has it lost any? What attempts were made to attract or retain these teams? How does the region market itself to tourists? What attractions does it feature? What unifying theme does it use? What images does it project?

To address these questions, consult the convention and tourism unit(s), write for their brochures, and review the leading newspaper of record. Also use the Internet to visit the web sites for the major tourist attractions within the region, seeing what appeals each makes. Other possible sources of information are the chamber of commerce web site and the state tourism department.

PART III

THE INTERNAL CHASE
COMPETITION WITHIN METROS

The external chase emphasizes economic competition. What development strategies, infrastructure facilities, human abilities, and entertainment venues are needed to stay abreast—and preferably ahead—of other metropolitan areas? Although the contest among regions has a local dimension as governmental units and functional sectors *within* the metropolis vie to benefit the most from economic prosperity and to pay the least for the costs of generating it, the focus is *outward,* always looking for ways to gain an edge.

Economic life, however, is not all that matters. People want to be safe and secure, they seek good health, they require adequate shelter, they desire pleasant settings. These are the basics, and individuals expect someone, most often one or more local governments, to supply them. Those areas within the region that do the best job in making these available become the most attractive places to live. Those which fall short suffer.

The most fundamental need is safety. It begins with personal security, the feeling that one will not be violently assaulted. It then extends to property, minimizing the chances that cars will be stolen, homes burglarized, or buildings burned down. People also want order in their immediate surroundings: no graffiti, no loitering, no loud noise, no stray animals. With disorder comes neighborhood decline.

Almost equally central is health. This starts with a robust environment: clean air and drinkable water. It requires sewer systems for handling human wastes, effective procedures for identifying and eliminating past pollutants, mechanisms for collecting and getting rid of trash. At a more individual level, people want quality health care which is affordable and accessible.

This, in turn, requires hospitals, clinics, and health care professionals. In crises, they demand emergency medical services which can respond swiftly and effectively.

Then there is shelter, not only just a place to call "home," but one which contains enough space, fits a person's or family's lifestyle, has an agreeable setting, is affordable, is conveniently located, and, if one needs to move on, can be readily sold for more than the purchase price. In metropolitan areas, houses come in groups—neighborhoods and subdivisions—so it is important not only that one's own home meets these needs but that the surrounding units are compatible and attractive.

After the primary needs have been addressed, Americans want some amenities. Even though most live in metropolitan areas and rural roots are often more than a century old, land and space still count. Even those who, by choice, reside in high-density neighborhoods—the Near North Side in Chicago or the Upper West Side in New York—want space nearby, a Lincoln Park or a Central Park. They want sports fields, cycling paths, hiking trails, swimming pools, and skating rinks for play and fun. As metropolitan areas expand, they retain concern that enough land be preserved for both passive pleasure and active experience.

When the services and facilities for conducting either the external or internal metropolitan chase are provided by the private sector, it is usually clear who pays the bill: the one using it. But when they are provided collectively, by one or more governments, then it becomes more complex. Sometimes it is closely analogous to business, like an admission fee to a municipal swimming pool, but more often there is no one-to-one connection between paying and consuming. The police services or educational programs or sewer plants are funded from taxes which may or may not be collected only from those who directly benefit from them. Part of the metropolitan contest is to shift as many of these public costs onto someone else. If the public lunch cannot be free, at least let it be at a discounted price, with the subsidy transferred to someone else.

Just as the external chase had its local dimension, so also the internal contest matters for competition among regions. If major parts of a metropolitan area gain a reputation for being unsafe, if it becomes the poster region for smog, if it does not offer an appealing array of housing options, if collectively it has minimal open space, if its taxes are too high, then it will fall behind. Regions cannot be so absorbed in the economic contest that they fail to pay attention to the basics.

CHAPTER 10

Protecting People and Property

In the competition for jobs and shoppers and especially in the contest for residents within any metropolitan area, being labeled as a dangerous place is extraordinarily damaging. Whether based on reality—actual crime statistics—or based on perception—the place looks and feels unsafe—once a neighborhood gains a reputation as being risky, it is difficult for it to recover. More people want to leave and fewer seek to enter. In recent years, many central cities have developed such an image and they have paid a hefty price for it. According to one recent analysis of 127 such jurisdictions, a 10 percent increase in the crime rate translates into a 1 percent decrease in residents.[1]

Because security is so central to success, jurisdictions devote significant parts of their budgets seeking it. Expenditures on police and firefighting services as well as on prosecutors, courts, and jails rank at or near the top, rivaled only by public education. Spending on police alone is over $60 billion annually, over $200 a year for each resident. There is a recurring debate about how best to achieve a safe environment with strategies ranging from preventive patrols to active problem solving.

The media intensify the competition for safety because they devote a disproportionate share of coverage to crime stories. Easy to cover and filled with human drama, these incidents dominate local television news and are a steady item in daily newspapers.[2] The more exotic incidents—a brutal murder or a daylight carjacking—are most apt to gain attention. As a consequence, public perceptions about which crimes are committed where by whom can and do become distorted.[3]

CRIME INCIDENCE

Violent personal crime—homicide, rape, robbery, and aggravated assault—hovered between 40 and 50 incidents for every 1000 persons ages 12 and over between the 1970s and the early 1990s.[4] Since then it has declined sharply and steadily, with the rates falling by more than one-third so that, by 1999, the national rate was about 34 per 1000. The decrease occurred in all categories.

Metropolitan area residents experience more personal crime than do rural Americans and it does not occur uniformly within regions. In 1999, the rate was about 42 per 1000 in central cities and approximately 34 per 1000 in suburbs. Rural areas, by contrast, had a rate of 25 per 1000. Comparing central cities with the suburbs, in the central cities one's chances of being raped are 43 percent greater, of being robbed 139 percent higher, and being the victim of aggravated assault 29 percent more likely.

As Figure 10–1 shows, people ages 12 to 24 are much more likely to be the target of violent crime with the 1999 rate being greater than 70 per 1000. Those

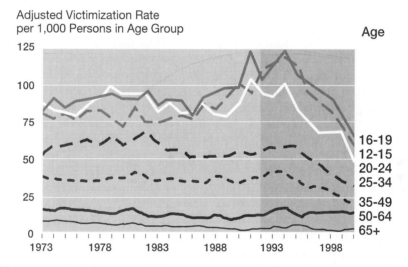

Note: Violent crimes included are homicide, rape, robbery, and both simple and aggravated assault. The National Crime Victimization Survey redesign was implemented in 1993; the area with the lighter shading is before the redesign and the darker area after the redesign. The data before 1993 are adjusted to make them comparable with data collected since the redesign. The adjustment methods are described in *Criminal Victimization 1973–95*. Estimates for 1993 and beyond are based on collection year while earlier estimates are based on data year. For additional information about the methods used, see *Criminal Victimization 2000*.

FIGURE 10–1   Violent Crime Rates by Age of Victim
Sources: Rape, robbery, and assault data are from the **National Crime Victimization Survey** (NCVS). Ongoing since 1972, this survey of households interviews about 80,000 persons age 12 and older in 43,000 households twice each year about their victimizations from crime. The homicide data are collected by the **FBI's Uniform Crime Reports** (UCR) from reports from law enforcement agencies.

50 and over, conversely, average about 10 incidents per 1000. African Americans are 31 percent more likely to be a personal crime victim than are whites and the rate is 28 percent higher among men than it is among women. The racial gap is much higher for homicides, especially among 18-to-24-year olds: blacks in this range are over eight times more likely to be murdered than are whites.

Why do central cities have higher crime rates, especially for violent offenses like robberies? Why do the largest among them—Los Angeles and New York—have rates much higher than other metropolitan areas? Two reasons, both rather obvious, stand out: attractive targets of opportunity are more concentrated in cities, creating easier access to those seeking illegal gains, and it is easier to fade into the masses in cities, lowering the chances of being arrested.[5]

Property crime—burglaries and thefts—have declined steadily since 1980. Twenty years ago, about half the households in the United States experienced such an incident. By 1999, it was about one in five. The central-city rate is 41 percent greater than the suburban proportion and African-American households are 32 percent more likely to have something stolen than are white units. On the other hand, there is little variation by household income: the poor, middle class, and rich are all about equally likely to be property crime victims.

There has been a lag between crime actually falling and people thinking that it has. Even by 1997, four years after the decline had started, 70 percent of Americans reported that crime in the United States was either higher or about the same as it was the year before.[6] Although the proportion dropped to 54 percent in 2000, still more thought crime had increased (47 percent) than had declined (41 percent), indicating the power that persistent media crime coverage has on public perceptions.

What accounts for the decline in crime, especially violent offenses? Have the past seven years just been part of a longer cycle, a flowing and ebbing possibly connected to economic conditions or demographic trends? If jobs are more plentiful and young people fewer, does that alone account for the change? Or can all or some of it be attributed to intentional policies like higher incarceration rates, tighter handgun controls, or improved police tactics?[7] Whatever the answer, and the analyses to date are preliminary, the contest within metropolitan areas for which is the safest area of all persists. Even with lower overall crime incidence, no segment wants to be among the least secure.

POLICE

Even though there is no substantial evidence that, short of giving every resident their own 24-hour body guard, police can actually prevent crime, citizens expect their law enforcement departments to be the front line for making their communities safe.[8] If crime is up, they ask the agency to do something about it. If a neighborhood appears unsafe, they demand that the police intervene. As the metropolitan age dawned in the early twentieth century, the more urbanized jurisdictions went from about 1.3 to 2.0 police officers for every thousand residents.[9] How have law enforcement units organized to address this demand, who staffs them and how do they define their roles, and what political issues arise about police behavior?

Structure and Governance

Police and sheriff's departments are quasi-military organizations, complete with uniforms, insignia, ranks, and firearms. Especially in central-city units, this helps sustain a warlike atmosphere with the good guys, the cops, daily battling the forces of evil. It is a hierarchical command-and-control structure, with a chief or sheriff at the top, patrol officers at the bottom, and ranked officials in between. During the past few decades, especially among the larger departments, all the elements of modern bureaucracy—detailed rules and procedures, heightened centralization, specialized roles for different functions like vice or drugs—now characterize how the organizations operate.

These units are close to home. Three out of every four public law enforcement officers in the United States works for a local government. Almost every municipality and county has its own police agency, independent of any other. Although there is growing cooperation among adjoining jurisdictions for specialized facilities like training academies and forensic laboratories, maintaining autonomy carries a high value. A multicounty or statewide law agency might be seen more as an occupying force than as a security source. Having one's own police department means that enforcement styles can adapt to individual circumstances and that, as the officers go about their duties, they can treat residents differently than visitors.

They are technology-driven. Three devices—the telephone, two-way radio, and the automobile—shape how much of modern policing is conducted. A citizen dials a centralized calling system ("911") asking for assistance, the dispatcher radios a patrol car, and it responds.[10] This has transformed policing from its more personal past: neighborhood-based foot patrols and close community interactions, the cop with the twirling baton in one hand and the half-eaten apple in the other.

Despite technology, the patrol officer, the everyday policeman, retains significant discretion about when and how to enforce the law. They are "streetcorner politicians" and "street-level bureaucrats."[11] In each shift, they make tens of yes-no decisions: who to stop for speeding, who to cite for vandalism, who to tell they should move on, and so forth. Although some of these judgments can be reviewed by supervisors, most cannot so that much of law enforcement policy is made at the bottom of the police hierarchy.

Although most officers are hired and promoted through a civil service system, those on top are accountable to the electorate. In most central-city units, the mayor either directly appoints the chief or a commission appointed by the mayor makes the choice. For those cities with a council manager form, urban or suburban, the city manager typically decides. In all these situations, the chief usually serves at the pleasure of the appointing authority. In exurban counties, the top law enforcement official, most often titled sheriff, is elected directly by the people for a fixed term.

For those who want more security than government can or will provide, the businesses have developed a large array of services. By the mid-1980s in the United States, the private sector passed the public segment in spending on protection.[12] Individual homeowners purchase alarm systems, gated neighborhoods hire their own watch guards, and shopping malls have their exclusive security forces. Sometimes off-duty public police officers staff these ventures but, for the most part, these security workers are fully private. This, in turn, raises issues both about the legitimacy of allowing force to be used by nongovernmental personnel and the training and capability of private police.[13]

Staffs and Styles

Policing is largely a young man's enterprise, especially among the patrol officer component. Nine out of ten are male and, giving the job's physical demands and burnout stress, most are under 40. The racial and ethnic mix—78 percent white, 12 percent black, 8 percent Hispanic, and 2 percent other—more closely resembles the national distribution. Only a handful of agencies require anything beyond a high school degree but the average officer has 600 hours of classroom and field training and, in the larger units, often more than twice that amount. With modest starting salaries, the average in 1999 was about $30,000, rotating shifts, and work that mixes monotonous routines with moments of terror, filling police ranks is becoming more difficult.[14]

Not all police departments interpret their task the same way.[15] There are four different approaches to policing, each with a particular focus. Although every style might be found at some point within any unit, usually one of them prevails. Whether by community tradition or by leadership edict, that is the way policing then gets done in that jurisdiction.

The first is the police department as *crime fighter*. Personified by Sergeant Joe Friday from the Dragnet TV show, the job is to find the perpetrators and put them behind bars. The emphasis is on those who have committed major felonies—murders, rapes, assaults—or, for property offenses, professional burglars or car thieves. Detectives are the stars, gathering the evidence and building open-and-shut cases. Success is measured by clearance rates, that is, the number of crimes solved.

Second is the police department as *law enforcer*. These units take the municipal code very seriously. Speed limits, parking meters, building codes, loitering regulations, and the like reflect what the community wants: 30-miles-an-hour means just that and exceeding it violates the norms. The key players are the patrol officers, applying the rules 24 hours a day, 7 days a week. Performance is evaluated by the number of tickets and other citations issued.

Third is the police department as the *maintainer of order*. The unit is expected to keep the lid on, "to ignore the 'little stuff' but to 'be tough' where it is important."[16] How much order depends on community expectations—New Orleans might have more tolerance for boisterous behavior than, say, Minneapolis—but wherever the majority want the standard set, it is the department's job, most of which falls upon the beat officers, to keep it there. Determining adequacy for this approach is more ambiguous since some laws and regulations can and should be overlooked under certain circumstances.

Fourth is the police department as *service provider*. The officers are there to help the citizens, checking in on the elderly widows, directing traffic at busy inter-sections, giving businesses advice on security procedures, aiding motorists who have locked their keys in the car. They are social workers in uniform, smiling "Officer Friendlies," poised and ready to lend a hand. Achievement is most often scored through citizen satisfaction surveys, asking a sample of residents how well the department executes these tasks.

Suburban municipalities, especially the smaller ones, are most likely to have a service provider style. Crime fighting is most prevalent in central cities as is main-tainer of order. The law enforcer can be found in all types of locations but is most common when there is some perceived threat to well-being, either from outsiders ("we need to stop those speeders") or a subset of residents ("we must make certain everyone keeps up their property").

Political Issues

It is called "DWB," an acronym for "driving while black," and it refers to the propen-sity for some police departments to stop members of a group who, statistically, are more likely to be violating some law. A poll conducted in March and April 2001 by The Washington Post, the Henry J. Kaiser Foundation, and Harvard University shows that this practice, more formally known as racial profiling, is real: 37 percent of African Americans but only 4 percent of whites reported that they had been "unfairly stopped by police" at some point in their lives. For black males, the share rose to 52 percent.[17]

Currently, this is the most visible example of an enduring concern about police. Who polices *them* or, as the Romans put it, who guards the guards? Once society assigns legal authority, including the ability to arrest and, in threatening circumstances, to kill citizens, how can it ensure that the police exercise it equi-tably and judiciously? Can departments be counted upon to have adequate discipli-nary boards within their organizations or should there be some external civilian review board? As of now, most jurisdictions retain the right to discipline their own although a few cities such as Houston and Detroit have allowed outsiders to play a role.[18]

Actual and potential criticism from the community combined with the sharp hierarchial distinction between police commanders and the rank-and-file patrol force has led to the unionization of more than half the police in the United States, including most of those in large central-city departments. Given the policing's em-phasis on supporting one another and the solidarity created by a military culture, these unions or association have more solidarity than most labor groups.[19] This allows them not only to influence police department procedures but also makes them a factor in local mayoral and council elections.

PROSECUTORS

The police's deciding whom to arrest for what offense is a critical decision point in the criminal justice process. Unless they apprehend someone, no other action can be taken. But the police cannot decide whether to press charges—that's the job of the prosecutors—or determine innocence or guilt—that's for the courts—or administer the sentence—that's for corrections to handle. All acting together constitute the criminal justice system.

Within metropolitan areas, each county typically has its own elected prosecutor. The names vary—county prosecutor, district attorney, prosecuting attorney, state's attorney—but the role is the same. In almost all the states, they are elected, usually for four-year terms. They are responsible for prosecuting almost all state felonies and most county misdemeanors.[20] Violations of federal statutes are prosecuted by U.S. Attorneys, appointed to one of the ninety-four divisions across the nation by the president, with the advice and consent of the Senate, and a few state matters are handled by its elected attorney general. Municipalities, especially mid-sized and smaller, hire an attorney part-time to prosecute ordinance violations. The overlap among the national, state, and local prosecutors can sometimes generate competition within a region when, for example, decisions must be made as to which jurisdiction will handle an organized crime case that is alleged to breach both federal and state laws.

Almost alone among American elected officials, county prosecutors are largely exempt from the checks and balances principle.[21] In a metropolitan area with, say, seven counties, those seven prosecutors, each acting on their own, make both micro- and macro-judgments which, collectively, set the rules for what safety means. Although the rules—what constitutes a crime and what are the penalties for committing it—are determined by the legislative process, it is the prosecutors who daily decide which ones will be enforced.

First, they and their staffs choose whether or not to file charges against each arrested person. Beyond each call having immediate importance for the individuals involved, the pattern of these decisions over time significantly influences the community. High profile crimes like murder will always be prosecuted but on many other offenses—child abuse, domestic violence, driving while intoxicated, petty theft, and so forth—there is a range all the way from strict enforcement to benign neglect.[22] This discretion extends to how thoroughly charges will be investigated— should there be staff specialists to check out arson-for-profit schemes—and what support services will be provided—should there be rape victim counselors both to help cope with the trauma but also to encourage better testimony.

Second, for those cases where charges are brought, prosecutors have the most say over what penalties will be implemented. The court system only has enough capacity to try a fraction of the cases. If everyone went to trial, complete with judge and jury, the whole process would bog down. Prosecutors handle this quandary by negotiating with defendants and their attorneys. The process is called "plea bargaining," lowering the charge (e.g., from aggravated assault to battery) or the recommended sentence (e.g., from ten years to seven years) in exchange for pleading guilty.[23] Which deals get made on what crimes is still another way prosecutors define the norms of behavior for their jurisdictions.

Third, prosecutors can initiate as well as react. In addition to managing the arrests police bring to them, they can also set out on crusades. For many, prosecutor is an early rung on a career ladder leading to higher office, and such ventures can help advance their political future. It might be an effort to shut down massage parlors, or curb underage drinking, or root out police corruption. Whatever the target, putting it in their prosecutorial sights makes it then a priority for that county.

COURTS AND CORRECTIONS

From a metropolitan area's perspective, courts are largely a state function organized by county or groups of counties. Although there are one or more federal courts in almost every region, they serve to adjudicate disputes and crimes under national laws and their jurisdictions extend beyond the metropolis's boundaries. Everyday justice, especially for felonies, is mostly dispensed in the state venues. Municipal courts with part-time judges, who usually are moonlighting attorneys supplementing their daytime incomes, handle matters like speeding charges and building code violations.

How judges are chosen varies considerably. The three most common mechanisms are nonpartisan elections, partisan elections, and merit selection. The last of these, also known as the Missouri Plan because it originated in that state, has become the most prevalent. Commissions screen applicants and send a short list, usually three names, to the governor who then selects one. These individuals are then subject to periodic retention elections although, as a practical matter, voters seldom remove any from office.

Judges are more referees than they are decision makers. Although they make rulings from the bench on matters ranging from bail to admissibility of evidence to instructions to juries, they depend on others for much of the information. They preside over "courtroom workgroups," confirming plea bargain negotiations made between prosecutors and defense counsel, reviewing sentencing recommendations from prosecutors and probation officers, and—above all else—keeping the docket moving.[24]

States also have the primary responsibility for corrections. They build and maintain prisons to house felons and operate the probation and parole system. Even though hundreds of new prisons have been built in the past two decades to handle the substantial growth, few facilities are located within metropolitan areas. Economically stagnant small towns have seen them as job creators, land there is less expensive, and the more urbanized communities have been more than content to keep them away from their boundaries.

County and municipal jails, however, have had to contend with the expanding entrants in the criminal justice system. Although originally intended to accommodate misdemeanor violators, they have increasingly been the place for those awaiting felony trials who either cannot afford bail or who have been denied it.[25] To meet this

Los Angeles County Patrol

demand and to avoid federal suits about prisoner overcrowding, many jurisdictions within metropolitan areas have had to expand their facilities or construct new ones.

FIGHTING CRIME

The traditional approach to crime prevention—police cars patrolling the streets and responding rapidly to radio calls for assistance—has been largely discredited as an effective strategy. Increasing or decreasing patrolling frequencies in neighborhoods, short of having a car permanently located on every block, has no discernible impact on the amount of crime.[26] Most calls for offenses like burglaries or car thefts occur after the criminal has left the scene so it matters little whether the police take five minutes or fifty minutes to arrive. Nevertheless, many continue to measure their performance based on how quickly they respond.[27]

Both because of organizational inertia and public expectations, departments continue to spend significant resources on patrolling and most still respond swiftly in many nonemergency situations. But other strategies have been added to the mix. The most clear cut has occurred primarily at the state and federal levels: incarcerating more criminals for longer periods. Since 1980, the number of state and federal prisoners has quadrupled and the number in local jails tripled with the combined total in custody now almost 2 million. Putting the bad folks away for a lengthy time has made a difference but it has come at a hefty price: the annual corrections tab nationally is now moving toward $50 billion.

The other strategies are more local, although they have sometimes been boosted by federal grants. Community policing has been the most pervasive and is used by units throughout the metropolitan area. Next most common is zero tolerance policing, cracking down on disorders like vandalism and loitering, stopping them before they evolve into more serious problems. The remaining approaches, either less widespread or more targeted, include redesigning space to make it safer, focusing on juveniles, and concentrating on drug trafficking.

Community Policing

This approach began in the late 1960s and early 1970s as a means to reconnect the police with the communities they serve. Remembering with some nostalgia the times when police walked a beat, knew who lived where and what they were up to, had trusting relationships with local leaders and neighborhood businesses, relying on them for assistance in preventing crime, they sought to recreate this strategy in a modern setting. Although getting officers to trade their patrol cars for sturdy shoes was largely unrealistic, could not the basic principles be reinstituted?

Since this sentiment is so popular, the term "community policing" is now used almost universally. Title I ("Public Safety Partnership and Community Policing Act") of the 1994 Crime Act put the federal government squarely behind the initiative, authorizing $9 billion over six years to encourage local units to implement it. Although not every department interprets community policing the same way, two components—problem solving and community involvement—characterize most applications.[28]

Instead of reacting to isolated incidents, answering calls as if there were no connection among them, police are now more active, grouping them to identify underlying causes.[29] Extensive data bases about violations and calls for assistance, analyzed with sophisticated geographic information software, makes such investigations speedier and more effective.[30] If tens or even hundreds of calls are coming from a single abandoned building, maybe the answer is to have the city crack down on the landlord.[31] If senior citizen robberies peak on the day social security checks come in the mail, perhaps encouraging them to have their payments directly deposited will solve matters.

The police involve the community, neighborhood by neighborhood, in detecting crime problems, identifying approaches, and implementing solutions. They also include other governmental and nonprofit agencies in these efforts. If citizens report too much speeding along a certain block, the answer might not be stationing a patrol car there several hours a day to give traffic tickets but instead working with the city's street department to install speed bumps. If a liquor store is presenting a constant nuisance, perhaps it is best to let the state's alcohol licensing bureau apply some pressure.

Deciding whether community policing lessens crime systematically is difficult to determine.[32] It assumes different forms across separate jurisdictions, it has not been applied long enough to reach definitive conclusions, and its implementation is often diffuse. Some contend that it is more form than substance, more a public relations ploy than a meaningful change, and that, beneath the rhetoric, it is largely policing as usual.[33] Others claim that community policing represents a different and healthier relationship between a community and its law enforcement operations and that, over time, it will have a broad and positive impact, producing more effective, equitable, and efficient results.[34]

Zero Tolerance

This strategy's popular label is "broken windows," based on a 1982 *Atlantic Monthly* article by James Q. Wilson and George L. Kelling.[35] The premise is that the quality of the surroundings significantly influence behavior. Even a little vandalism, a single broken window, will encourage some to break a few more. Just a scattering of loiterers will deter law-abiding citizens from using neighborhood shops and encourage other lawbreakers to congregate nearby. According to this approach, just as big oaks from little acorns grow, so too from minor misdemeanors do major crimes arise.[36]

The answer, then, is to crack down early. Instead of ignoring trivial violations or reacting with a warning, the police and the courts should have zero tolerance for any infraction. This is especially so in areas on the brink of deterioration. Prosperous neighborhoods can tolerate a little disorder and blighted ones are past saving. It is the ones in between where vigilantly combating disorder makes the most sense by law enforcement alone, if necessary, but involving the community, if possible.

New York City's adopting this approach in the early 1990s, from eliminating graffiti on the subways to abolishing urination on the side streets, has given it the most positive visibility. Not only were its streetscapes and subway lines transformed, but serious crimes like murder, robberies, and assaults all dropped substantially.[37] Other success stories come from Baltimore, San Francisco, and Seattle.[38]

Strictly enforcing minor offenses brings its own set of concerns. Does it encourage police officers to exercise too much discretionary power and, if so, what additional guidelines should be established?[39] Will civil liberties be violated and minorities disproportionately affected?[40] Does this approach promote too much of an us-them atmosphere, separating law abiding citizens from despicable hooligans, invoking too much blame and too little praise?[41]

Defensible Space

How one structures space—sight lines, lighting, ease of entry—can make it more or less dangerous.[42] The fewer people who can see a spot, the darker it is, and the more ways to exit from it, the more attractive it is for a criminal. That is one of the reasons why high-rise apartments, especially those constructed in the earlier days of public housing, experienced such exorbitant crime rates. Commenting on St. Louis's

Pruitt-Igoe, the now-destroyed exemplar of this housing mode, Oscar Newman notes that "because all the grounds were common and disassociated from the units, residents could not identify with them" and "it was impossible to feel or exert proprietary feelings, impossible to tell resident from intruder."[43]

Instead residences should be structured so that their occupants have a sense of ownership not only over the front, back, and side yards but also over the adjoining sidewalk and street. Each will then feel a responsibility for guarding their respective territory, challenging those unknown to them. Public lighting should not be placed mindlessly, such as a lamppost every one hundred feet, but should be focused on those areas most likely to be sought out by potential burglars and robbers. More grid-patterned streets should be transformed into a series of cul de sacs, making it more difficult for someone to escape after committing an offense.

At its most extreme, especially for upper-income households, defensible space now means gated communities.[44] Throughout metropolitan areas, in urban as well as suburban settings, more residential developments are surrounded by high fences and, among the more affluent, entrance is only through gates staffed by security guards. In these situations, more security is purchased by having increased separation.

A Gated Community in the Los Angeles Area

Focusing on Juveniles

Not only are young people, as mentioned earlier, much more likely to be crime victims, they are also more prone to be offenders. Juveniles, defined as those under 18, accounted for 17 percent of all felony arrests in 1999.[45] Not only does this share alone make concentrating on juvenile crime an appropriate strategy; there are also the longer-term consequences. Several studies have shown that violent behavior does not begin after reaching adulthood.[46] It starts young and thus, to keep it from spreading, early intervention is crucial.

Law enforcement agencies, working with other governmental units as well as nonprofit groups and often funded by federal grants, have mounted a wide range of juvenile programs aimed at preventing crime. These range from recreational efforts, such as "midnight basketball" to provide healthy outlets for teenage energy, to youth development programs, such as boys and girls clubs, to anger management workshops to teach peaceful ways for handling disputes. School-based initiatives, although politically popular, have been less effective since, despite the occasional sensational killings at schools which generate enormous publicity, relatively little violent crime happens at most educational sites.[47]

When prevention has not worked, communities then have to decide how to handle the first-time juvenile offender. This creates controversial alternatives. Should more be incarcerated, transferring the murderers and serial rapists to the adult system?[48] This removes them from the community for decades but eliminates any short-term rehabilitation. Should more juvenile retention facilities be constructed, giving youngsters a shock treatment about life behind bars and scaring them into changing their behavior? According to one study, this approach "might appeal to the emotional frustration many Americans feel over youth violence but it is unlikely to relieve the problem."[49] Or can some blend of community-based programming and justice system probation oversight stem the tide, avoiding imprisonment but still protecting the public?

Targeting Drug Trafficking

Crime and drugs are closely linked both in practice and policy. Repeated studies sponsored by the U.S. Drug Enforcement Agency and conducted regularly in over thirty of the nation's largest cities reveal that two out of every three people arrested test positive for an illicit substance. For some, the drugs have accentuated mental instability, making them more likely to commit an offense. Others are addicted and turn to crime for the resources to maintain their habit. Drug usage is down from its peak in the early 1980s but, according to a recent estimate, about 15 million Americans have used an illicit drug at least once during the past month.[50] That level of demand creates suppliers willing to risk imprisonment to achieve high profits and the battles among drug marketers for territory accounts for still more violence.

Led by the national government and spurred by the emergence of crack cocaine in the early 1980s, the criminal justice system at all levels decided that, by getting tougher on drugs, offenses could be lessened.[51] Both the state and federal governments increased penalties both for drug possession and for drug trafficking, the Reagan Administration established the Office of National Drug Control Policy whose head became quickly known as the "drug czar," and law enforcement agencies beefed up their antidrug units. Accompanying this was an extensive informational campaign such as the youth-directed Drug Abuse Resistance Education (DARE) program.

The consequences were significant but expensive. Hundreds of thousands of drug users and traffickers were imprisoned. In federal prisons alone, the number of drug offenders doubled in just three years between 1988 and 1991. All this came at a hefty price to taxpayers for more correctional facilities and, in addition, questions were increasingly raised about a policy approach that was all stick and no carrot.

That led in the late 1980s and early 1990s to forming special drug courts which blend legal sanctions with therapeutic treatment and there are now more than 600 throughout the United States.[52] Instead of automatically sending those guilty of drug usage to prison, judges are able to recommend alterative programs to help individuals overcome their substance dependency. Jail still remains an option for those who do not diligently follow the assigned therapy and the courts closely monitor their case loads, but many who would otherwise have been incarcerated now remain free.

FIRES AND NATURAL DISASTERS

Fires no longer devastate huge portions of cities as did the Chicago Fire of 1871 or the Boston Fire of 1872 but they still are an ongoing threat. In 1999, there were an estimated 1,823,000 fires either in structures (523,000), vehicles (368,500), or outside properties (931,500).[53] Collectively, they caused over $10 billion in property damage, killed about 3,570 persons, and injured another 21,875. Another 112 fire persons died fighting these blazes.

In central cities and inner suburbs, the greatest hazards for major catastrophes are high-rise office buildings and apartments. Even a modest conflagration in one of these units can trap tens or even hundreds of occupants. In the outer suburbs, grassland and forest fires can spread rapidly, imperiling entire subdivisions. Throughout regions, nursing home fires are still another threat. The quality of fire service within each part of a metropolitan area affects how much property owners pay for their residential or building insurance. All other things being equal, the better equipped the fire department, the lower the premium.[54]

Municipal departments provide fire protection services to most of the urbanized areas within metropolitan areas. They are largely staffed by professional firefighters and funded through general revenues. Some less dense and smaller suburbs use fire protection districts, a special purpose government also largely staffed by full-time employees, which then levies a property tax throughout its jurisdiction. At the periphery, however, trained volunteers often constitute most of the labor. The local government pays for buildings and equipment and a few managerial employees but, when the alarm is sounded, the part-time volunteer firefighters respond.

A Washington, D.C., Fire Truck

Fire departments work closely with other governmental agencies as well as with each other. They usually share a central dispatching unit, most commonly a "911" operation, with police and emergency medical services either throughout a county or, in some instances, across all or most of the metropolitan region. Because few departments can afford staffing and equipment for very large blazes, there are mutual aid agreements among adjoining departments, often extending over a several hundred square mile area.[55]

Disasters happen. For the past two decades, the national government has declared an average of thirty-four each year. Some have close links with certain metropolitan areas: hurricanes and Miami or earthquakes and San Francisco. Others, by-products of modern technology, can occur anywhere: a hazardous waste spill or widespread radioactive emissions. The lessons learned from past disasters is that preparation matters. Knowing in advance who will respond to what situations, having written plans in place, can substantially lower human casualties and physical damage. The national government centralized its disaster operations in 1979, forming the Federal Emergency Management Agency. It, in turn, has encouraged states, counties, and municipalities to have their own plans. As New York City's valiant response to the September 11, 2001, airplane crashes into the World Trade Center Towers demonstrated, being prepared can save thousands of lives even for unanticipated disasters caused by terrorist attacks.

CONCLUDING COMMENTS

Protecting people and property is stressful. Police, prosecutors, judges, and corrections officials spend most of their working hours dealing with the more distasteful aspects of metropolitan life: unruly youth, drunken vagrants, abusive spouses, incorrigible criminals. Firefighters intersperse hours of boredom-inducing chores with spurts of adrenaline-pumped excitement, going from washing the fire truck to entering a burning building's roof in a matter of minutes. For those on the front lines—the patrolling police officer and the responding firefighter—it is a young person's enterprise: more than four out of five are under 50 and a clear majority under 40 years old.

There is an ambivalent relationship between metropolitan communities and these individuals. For their part, citizens are grateful that someone else is handling the dirty work and that they are spared the physical danger and psychic grief. In the aftermath of a disaster, such as September 11, 2001, their gratitude temporarily soars. This appreciation, however, is often accompanied by avoidance. Maintaining order is the professionals' job, and the rest of the citizenry can largely abdicate their responsibility.

The protectors take pride in what they contribute. They experience the dark side every shift and realize more than others just how thin the line can be between civility and disorder. But with the community's distancing themselves, the protectors can come to feel alone in the struggle, spending both their work and leisure time mostly with other public-safety staff and removing themselves further from the civilian world, creating an uneasy divide between the guarded and the guards.

NOTES

1. Julie Berry Cullen and Steven D. Levitt, "Crime, Urban Flight, and the Consequences for Cities," *The Review of Economics and Statistics,* 81, no. 2 (May 1999), pp. 159–69. Also see Mark H. Moore, "Security and Community Development," in *Urban Problems and Community Development,* ed. Ronald F. Ferguson and William T. Dickens (Washington: Brookings Institution Press, 1999), pp. 293–337; and Christopher R. Bollinger and Keith R. Ihlanfeldt, *Intrametropolitan Locational Patterns of People and Jobs: Which Government Interventions Make a Difference?* (Cambridge, MA: Lincoln Institute of Land Policy, 2000).
2. Paul Klite, R.A. Bardwell, and James Salzman, "Local TV News: Getting Away with Murder," *Harvard International Journal of Press/Politics,* 2, no. 2 (Spring 1997), pp. 102–20.
3. Franklin D. Gilliam, Jr. and Shanto Iyengar, "Prime Suspects: The Influence of Local Television News on the Viewing Public," *American Journal of Political Science,* 44, no. 3 (July 2000), pp. 560–73.
4. Unless otherwise noted, the criminal justice data are from the National Crime Victimization Surveys conducted by the U.S. Department of Justice and reported through its Bureau of Justice Statistics. The surveys have been conducted annually since 1973. The other major source for crime incidence are the yearly *Uniform Crime Reports,* assembled by the Federal Bureau of Investigation. The latter have two deficiencies: (1) they are not necessarily uniform since there is no assurance that each reporting law enforcement agency applies precisely the same standards and procedures; and (2) they only count crimes reported to the police and thus omit events which do not come to the attention of the criminal justice system. Despite these methodological differences, the two generally trend in the same direction. For more information about these crime data sets, see A.D. Biderman and J.P. Lynch, *Understanding Crime Incidence Statistics: Why the UCR Diverges from the NCS* (New York: Springer-Verlag, 1991).
5. Edward L. Glaeser and Bruce Sacerdote, "Why Is There More Crime in Cities?" *Journal of Political Economy,* 107, no. 6 (December 1999), pp. S225–S258. For an ethnographic perspective, see

Richard T. Wright and Scott H. Decker, *Armed Robbers in Action: Stickups and Street Culture* (Boston, MA: Northeastern University Press, 1997).

6. The public opinion data are drawn from Gallup Polls as reported in the online edition of the *Sourcebook of Criminal Justice Statistics*, Table 2.39.

7. For a preliminary assessment, see Alfred Blumstein and Joel Wallman, eds., *The Crime Drop in America* (Cambridge, England: Cambridge University Press, 2000). What is clear is that most of the victimization decline occurred among youth. See Jeffrey A. Butts, *Youth Crime Drop* (Washington: Urban Institute, 2000).

8. David H. Bayley, *Police for the Future* (New York: Oxford University Press, 1999), pp. 1–12.

9. Eric H. Monkkonen, "History of Urban Police," in *Modern Policing*, ed. Michael Tonry and Norval Morris (Chicago: University of Chicago Press, 1992), pg. 554.

10. Peter K. Manning, "Information Technologies and the Police," in *Modern Policing*, ed. Tonry and Morris, pp. 349–98.

11. William Ker Muir, Jr., *Police: Streetcorner Politicians* (Chicago: University of Chicago Press, 1977); and Michael Lipsky, *Street-Level Bureaucracy: Dilemmas of the Individual in Public Service* (New York: Russell Sage Foundation, 1980).

12. Clifford D. Shearing and Philip C. Stenning, eds., *Private Policing* (Newbury Park, CA: Sage Publications, 1987).

13. Brian Forst and Peter K. Manning, *The Privatization of Policing: Two Views* (Washington: Georgetown University Press, 1999).

14. Christopher Swope, "The Short Blue Line," *Governing*, 13, no. 2 (November 1999), pp. 32–34.

15. James Q. Wilson was one of the first to call attention to this difference. See his *Varieties of Police Behavior: The Management of Law and Order in Eight Communities* (Cambridge, MA: Harvard University Press, 1968).

16. Wilson, *Varieties of Police Behavior*, pg. 145.

17. Richard Morin and Michael H. Cottman, "Discrimination's Lingering Sting: Minorities Tell of Profiling, Other Bias," *Washington Post*, June 22, 2001, pg. A01.

18. Samuel Walker and Vic W. Bumpus, *Civilian Review of the Police: A National Survey of the 50 Largest Cities* (Omaha: University of Nebraska-Omaha Department of Criminal Justice, 1991).

19. Dorothy Guyot, *Policing as though People Matter* (Philadelphia: Temple University Press, 1991), pp. 210–11.

20. The length of the maximum sentence distinguishes felonies (one year or more) from misdemeanors (less than one year).

21. Joan E. Jacoby, *The American Prosecutor: A Search for Identity* (Lexington, Massachusetts: Lexington Books, 1980).

22. For more examples, see Roy Flemming, Peter Nardulli, and James Eisenstein, *The Craft of Justice: Politics and Work in Criminal Court Communities* (Philadelphia: University of Pennsylvania Press, 1992).

23. Milton Heumann, *Plea Bargaining: The Experiences of Prosecutors, Judges, and Defense Attorneys* (Chicago: University of Chicago Press, 1977).

24. The "courthouse workgroup" interpretation is from James Eisenstein and Herbert Jacob, *Felony Justice* (Boston: Little, Brown, 1977). Also see Martin A. Levin, *Urban Politics and the Criminal Courts* (Chicago: University of Chicago Press, 1977) and Paul B. Wice, *Chaos in the Courthouse: The Inner Workings of the Urban Criminal Courts* (New York: Praeger, 1985).

25. Richard S. Frase, "Jails," in *The Handbook of Crime and Punishment*, ed. Michael Torny (New York: Oxford University Press, 1998), pp. 474–506.

26. George L. Kelling and others, *The Kansas City Preventive Patrol Experiment: A Summary Report* (Washington: Police Foundation, 1974). Also see John E. Eck and William Spelman, "Who Ya Gonna Call? The Police as Problem-Busters?" *Crime and Delinquency*, 33, no. 1 (January 1987), pp. 31–52.

27. David N. Ammons, *Municipal Benchmarks: Assessing Local Performance and Establishing Community Standards* (Thousand Oaks, California: Sage Publications, 1996), pp. 197–99.

28. Dennis P. Rosenbaum, "The Changing Role of the Police: Assessing the Current Transition to Community Policing," in *How To Recognize Good Policing: Problems and Issues*, ed. Jean-Paul Brodeur (Thousand Oaks, CA: Sage Publications, 1998), pp. 3–29.

29. Herman Goldstein, *Problem-Oriented Policing* (Philadelphia: Temple University Press, 1990).

30. Diana R. Gordon, *The Justice Juggernaut: Fighting Street Crime, Controlling Citizens* (New Brunswick, NJ: Rutgers University Press, 1990), pp. 50–91; and Christopher Swope, "The Comstat Craze," *Governing*, 12, no. 12 (September 1999), pp. 40–43.

31. Wesley G. Skogan and Susan M. Hartnett, *Community Policing, Chicago Style* (New York: Oxford University Press, 1997), pp. 3–4. Also see Wesley G. Skogan and others, *On the Beat: Police and Community Problem Solving* (Boulder, CO: Westview Press, 1999).

32. Lawrence W. Sherman, "Conclusions: The Effectiveness of Local Crime Prevention Funding," in *Preventing Crime: What Works, What Doesn't, What's Promising* (Washington: U.S. Department of Justice, 1997), pp. 10–14. Also see Jeffrey A. Roth and others, *National Evaluation of the COPS Program: Title I of the 1994 Crime Act* (Washington: U.S. Department of Justice, 2000), pp. 234–38.

33. Ralph H. Saunders, "The Politics and Practice of Community Policing in Boston," *Urban Geography*, 20, no. 5 (1999), pp. 461–82; also see William DeLeon-Granados, *Travels through Crime and Place: Community Building as Crime Control* (Boston: Northeastern University Press, 1999).

34. John E. Eck and Dennis P. Rosenbaum, "The New Police Order: Effectiveness, Equity, and Efficiency in Community Policing," in *The Challenges of Community Policing: Testing the Promises,* ed. Dennis P. Rosenbaum (Thousand Oaks, CA: Sage Publications, 1994), pp. 3–26.

35. James Q. Wilson and George L. Kelling, "Broken Windows: The Police and Neighborhood Safety," *The Atlantic Monthly,* 248, no. 3 (March 1982), pp. 29–38. Also see James Q. Wilson, *Thinking About Crime,* rev. ed. (New York: Vintage Books, 1983), pp. 75–89.

36. For supporting evidence see Wesley G. Skogan, *Disorder and Decline: Crime and the Spiral of Decay in American Neighborhoods* (New York: Free Press, 1990); and Robert G. Bursik, Jr. and Harold G. Grasmick, *Neighborhoods and Crime: The Dimensions of Effective Community Control* (New York: Lexington Books, 1993).

37. George L. Kelling and Catherine M. Coles, *Fixing Broken Windows: Restoring Order and Reducing Crime in the Communities* (New York: Free Press, 1996), pp. 151–56.

38. Kelling and Coles, *Fixing Broken Windows,* pp. 194–235.

39. George L. Kelling, *"Broken Windows" and Police Discretion* (Washington: U.S. Department of Justice, 1999).

40. Gary Stewart, "Black Codes and Broken Windows: The Legacy of Racial Hegemony in Anti-Gang Civil Injunctures," *Yale Law Journal,* 107, no. 7 (May 1998), pp. 2249–79.

41. Bernard E. Harcourt, "Reflecting on the Subject: A Critique of the Social Influence Conception of Deterrence, the Broken Windows Theory, and Order-Maintenance Policing New York Style," *Michigan Law Review,* 97, no. 3 (November 1998), pp. 291–389.

42. Oscar Newman has been the leader in promoting this approach. See his *Defensible Space* (New York: Macmillan, 1972); *Community of Interest* (Garden City, New York: Anchor Press, 1980); and *Creating Defensible Space* (Washington: U.S. Department of Housing and Urban Development, 1996).

43. Newman, *Creating Defensible Space,* pp. 10–12.

44. Edward J. Blakely and Mary Gail Snyder, *Fortress America: Gated Communities in the United States* (Washington: Brookings Institution Press and Lincoln Institute of Land Policy, 1997).

45. Butts, *Youth Crime Drops,* pg. 3.

46. Paul H. Hahn, *Emerging Criminal Justice: Three Pillars for a Proactive Justice System* (Thousand Oaks, CA: Sage Publications, 1998), pg. 39.

47. Lawrence H. Sherman, "The Safe and Drug-Free Schools Program," in *Brookings Papers in Education Policy 2000,* ed. Diane Ravitch (Washington: Brookings Institution Press, 2001), pp. 125–71.

48. Jeffrey Fagan and Franklin E. Zimring, *The Changing Borders of Juvenile Justice: Transfer of Adolescents to the Criminal Court* (Chicago: University of Chicago Press, 2000).

49. *The Real War on Crime: The Report of the National Criminal Justice Commission* (New York: HarperCollins, 1996), pg. 135. Also see Barry C. Feld, "Juvenile (In)Justice and the Criminal Court Alternative," *Crime and Delinquency,* 39, no. 4 (October 1993), pp. 403–24.

50. *The National Household Survey on Drug Abuse: 1999* (Washington: U.S. Substance Abuse and Mental Health Services Administration, 2000).

51. Adele Harrell, "Drug Abuse," in *Reality and Research: Social Science and U.S. Urban Policy Since 1960,* ed. George Galster (Washington: Urban Institute Press, 1996), pp. 169–73.

52. Shane Harris, "Dragged into Drug Court," *Governing,* 14, no. 11 (August 2001), pp. 62–64; James L. Nolan, Jr., *Reinventing Justice: The American Drug Court Movement* (Princeton, NJ: Princeton University Press, 2001); Elizabeth A. Peyton and Robert Gossweiler, *Treatment Services in Adult Drug Courts: Report on the 1999 National Drug Treatment Survey* (Washington: U.S. Department of Justice, 2001).

53. All the fire statistics are from Michael J. Karter, Jr., *Fire Loss in the United States During 1999* (Quincy, MA: National Fire Protection Association, 2000).

54. Ammons, *Municipal Benchmarks,* pp. 109–11.

55. Ronald J. Oakerson, *Governing Local Public Economies: Creating the Civic Metropolis* (Oakland, CA: Institute for Contemporary Studies, 1999), pg. 72; and Pamela Werntz, *Public Safety Services: Alternative Service Delivery* (Washington: International City/County Management Association, 1999), pp. 15–22.

SUGGESTED READINGS

BLUMSTEIN, ALFRED, and JOEL WALLMAN, eds. *The Crime Drop in America.* Cambridge, England: Cambridge University Press, 2000. A thorough and sophisticated analysis of how demographic factors and law enforcement strategies have contributed to the decline in crime.

KELLING, GEORGE L., and CATHERINE M. COLES. *Fixing Broken Windows: Restoring Order and Reducing Crime in Our Communities.* New York: Free Press, 1996. Explains the zero tolerance strategy and describes how it has been applied in Baltimore, New York City, San Francisco, and Seattle.

SKOGAN, WESLEY G., and SUSAN M. HARTNETT. *Community Policing, Chicago Style.* New York: Oxford University Press, 1997. A comprehensive account of applying community policing in Chicago.

TONRY, MICHAEL, ed. *The Handbook of Crime and Punishment.* New York: Oxford University Press, 1998. Twenty-seven chapters, each written by leading specialists, on each aspect of the criminal justice system.

WILSON, JAMES Q. *Varieties of Police Behavior: The Management of Law and Order in Eight Communities.* Cambridge, MA: Harvard University Press, 1968. A classic study by one of the leading thinkers on criminal justice policy.

DOING IT

Almost every police department now employs "community policing" but it can and does have very different meanings from place to place. For two law enforcement agencies in a metropolitan area, one central city and one suburban, find out how they are using community policing. How do they define their community policing initiatives? In what neighborhoods are they applying it? What changes have they made in their police organization, including training new officers and retraining the existing force? What techniques have they used to involve the community? What impact has it had on crime reduction, public attitudes, and community support?

Sources can include newspaper accounts, federal and state grants submitted by the departments, evaluations conducted by outside agencies, and interviews with both police and community leaders.

CHAPTER 11

Health and the Environment

Americans are living longer—and they want that trend to continue. In just one century, from 1900 to 2000, the life expectancy for the average American increased by thirty years, going from 47 to 77.[1] A majority have achieved the good life economically, and they want to stay around as long as possible to enjoy their prosperity. Along with increased longevity, they desire a more robust existence, free from disease and bursting with vitality.

They back up this priority with dollars, spending more on health than on any other item. In 1998, the total tab was over a trillion dollars, slightly more than $1 out of every $8 expended, or about $4000 for each person.[2] Over the past twenty years, health's slice of the consumption pie has increased over 50 percent, going from 8.9 percent in 1980 to 13.5 percent in 1998. Most of this goes for personal care, with hospital fees, physician services, and prescription drugs being the largest three items.

This preoccupation with health and its growing share of the gross national product has generated an ongoing debate about how best to meet the demand.[3] Is health care a consumer product, like automobiles or hamburgers, one which the market will provide for those willing and able to purchase it? Or is it a basic right, something which governments should guarantee? Should the market decide how much health care professionals, hospitals, and drug companies can charge for their services and products or should government regulate costs?

As of now, the answers are mixed. Some health care is a right for some people, especially seniors, some of the time but protection is far from universal. About one out of six Americans has no health insurance and no coverage under a government program. Nevertheless, almost half the expenditures for health ultimately come from governmental funds, up considerably from a generation ago.[4] Costs are more regulated, both by national and state governments and by managed care and insurance operations, but they continue to rise higher than the overall inflation rate.

Paralleling the rising importance of health has been a growing concern about environmental quality. Part of this arose from a heightened awareness about the threats dirty air, polluted streams, and toxic substances posed for individual well-being, vividly described by Rachel Carson's *Silent Spring* in 1962.[5] Part was more aethestically driven. With material needs largely met, many sought additional pleasure from their surroundings.[6] In the 1960s, a full-fledged environmental movement arose, spawning a new federal entity, the Environmental Protection Agency, and major national legislation starting in the 1970s.

As health and the environment rose on the national agenda, local governments within metropolitan areas have had minimal control over federal policies but they, along with the nonprofit and private sectors, must deal with their consequences. An uninsured person with a medical crisis does not go to Washington for help but instead shows up at a community clinic or a hospital emergency room. Federal regulations might determine that a region's air is too polluted—but the metropolitan area, working with state authorities, must implement a plan to clean it. Citizens expect someone within regions to respond to their health needs and to safeguard the environment.

Thus both the internal and external chases within metropolitan areas have health and environment dimensions. Those parts of the region with limited health-care access or exposure to disease or hazardous sites will suffer not just with lower property values but, ultimately, shorter lives. Metropolises that have mediocre medical facilities, or prevailing smog, or polluted rivers will not compete effectively with those offering superior hospitals, clean air, and sparkling streams.

HEALTH CARE: TREATMENT

When illness strikes, especially a life-threatening episode, people want skilled assistance, instantly available and effectively applied. This includes primary care and speciality physicians, trained technicians, accessible clinics and well-equipped hospitals, and responsive emergency medical services. Although, in a crisis situation, price is no object to the threatened individual and is sometimes overlooked by the provider, ultimately financial affordability has much to say about who receives how much medical attention.

Physicians

Attracting adequate numbers of physicians is not a problem for most metropolitan areas. Overall, there is about one medical doctor for every 400 persons in the United States but a majority of regions exceed that mark and a few—Boston, New York, Washington-Baltimore—have physician-resident ratios under one to 300.[7] In addition to all the other factors that draw residents to urbanized space, physicians desire advanced medical technology and each other's professional company. Neither are available in rural America.

But physicians and other health professionals are not evenly distributed within regions. Like other enterprises in capitalist societies, they follow their customer market. As affluent households have concentrated in the suburbs, medical doctors and dentists, now increasingly practicing in groups rather than as individuals, have followed, creating surpluses there and shortages in the inner city while retaining a modest undersupply in the exurban areas.[8] This has direct consequences for health quality. The more distant a medical professional, all other factors being equal, the less likely one will seek immediate treatment when symptoms arise. Poverty and allied causes already make staying healthy a greater challenge in the central city and having too few physicians makes things worse.[9] Central cities and inner suburbs make some effort to compensate for this shortage with community clinics—but they do not close the gap.

Both within underserved areas and for regions as a whole, there is also a growing imbalance between specialists and primary-care practitioners.[10] Restricting practices to specific illnesses, for instance, oncologists for cancer, or parts of the anatomy, cardiologists for hearts, carries more prestige within the medical community and commands higher compensation. The traditional family doctors, be they pediatricians or internists or gynecologists, have less status and lower incomes. As a consequence, even though there are enough physicians overall, many metropolitan areas struggle to attract and retain primary-care doctors.

Hospitals

Between the 1950s and the 1970s, the hospital was "the pinnacle of the U.S. health care system."[11] The number of community hospital beds almost doubled, peaking at just over 1 million in 1985.[12] Rare was the metropolitan area that did not have more than enough space for those requiring hospitalization. But hospitals are expensive enterprises and, since the 1980s, bed capacity has declined by almost one-fifth.

Overnight usage has declined even more rapidly. In 1980, on average, one out of six Americans spent at least one night in a hospital with an average stay of seven days. By 1998, it was down to one out of ten for a five-day hospitalization. What has increased is ambulatory care, especially emergency visits.[13] In 1998, they passed the 100 million mark, more than one for every three Americans.

This shift to using the hospital for outpatient care has made proximity more important, especially for emergency cases. Like physicians, a large number of hospitals moved during the 1970s and 1980s from central cities to suburbs, especially to the more affluent parts, leaving many city and inner-suburban neighborhoods more distant for crisis situations.[14] When minutes mean the difference between life and death, having a state-of-the-art trauma center within a few miles becomes crucial.

As interests within metropolitan areas seek to influence where hospitals locate as well as what services they dispense, they are confronting a more centralized and distant structure. The stand-alone community hospital, operated by a nonprofit organization with a board dominated by natives, is a vanishing species. Although nonprofit groups still are the prevailing sector for running hospitals with 70 percent of the beds, they now typically belong to much larger conglomerates, often head-quartered outside the region. Nonfederal public hospitals have declined by one-third between 1975 and 1998, now having a 17 percent share, while during the same period for-profit chains have increased their slice from 8 percent to 13 percent. This also means that local concerns play a smaller role in hospitals' decision making.[15]

Metropolitan areas compete for having cutting-edge medical care, the top sites for advanced procedures like open heart surgery or organ transplants. Not only are these a plus for residents needing such operations, but they add luster to the region's image and, for those coming from elsewhere for care, a modest boost to the local economy. Those faring best in this contest are usually hospitals affiliated with the premier medical schools, such as Johns Hopkins Hospital (Baltimore), Massachusetts General Hospital and the Harvard Medical School (Boston), and Barnes-Jewish and Washington University Medical School (St. Louis).[16]

Emergency Medical Services

Although local governments have little control over the distance to the nearest hospital, they have gained command over how fast they can get someone there in an emergency, as well as over the quality of the care they receive en route. Prior to the 1960s, the private sector managed most of the ambulance calls and hospitals also had a noticeable presence. Since then, emergency response has become a public function, with most of it being conducted through fire departments.[17]

The past three decades have witnessed the rapid expansion of a new group of health professionals, emergency medical service technicians, and the development of EMS vehicles which are miniature emergency rooms on wheels, all linked into the 911 dispatching systems.[18] They, in turn, have lowered death and disability rates especially from automobile accidents and heart attacks.

This has raised public expectations about EMS performance, especially response times, and jurisdictions now compete for target response times of 8 minutes or less.[19] Although many fire departments initially resisted adding an EMS component, they all now see it as their political salvation. EMS calls now account for more than half of their workload and, unlike fire responses, most can be billed either to the individual or to an insurance company, thereby generating another revenue stream.

Affordability and Access

What happens to the approximately 30 million metropolitan-area residents without health insurance, most of whom also cannot afford to make any significant payments from their own resources? What can they do in a medical emergency? Where can they go to treat a chronic illness?

It depends on their location.[20] If a hospitalization is necessary, some urban counties and a few cities still have public hospitals, although the number continues to fall. These can provide the basics—emergency room intervention, obstetrics, general surgery—but less often can offer more specialized procedures. In most

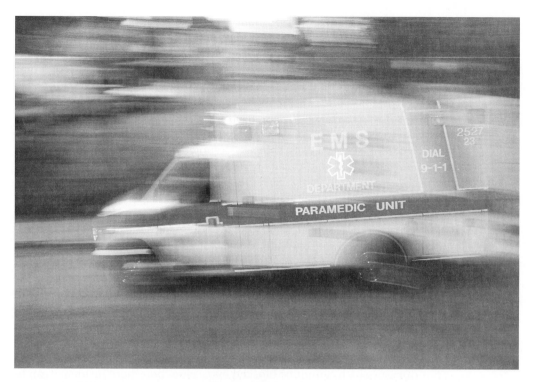

An EMS Ambulance Heading for the Hospital

jurisdictions, the medically indigent must rely on charitable care from a nonprofit or for-profit facility which, more often than not, will not be reimbursed by any government. If that is not available, then the injury or illness goes untreated—often with grave consequences.

If physician care is required, a majority of urban counties and many larger cities operate community clinics. The support staff are usually full-time public employees while the physicians are typically part-time contract workers, either hired individually or through medical schools. These facilities face special challenges, especially providing continuity of care. Seeing a different doctor each visit, even with a coordinated patient-information system (itself a rarity), is a recipe for misdiagnosis and contradictory treatment.

HEALTH CARE: PREVENTION

"An ounce of prevention is worth a pound of cure" is a cliché rooted in reality. As health costs escalated starting in the 1960s, the national government, as well as state and local units, began investigating how educational campaigns and other initiatives might lower the incidence of illnesses and injuries.[21] Quickly joining this effort were philanthropic foundations and nonprofit agencies and, by the 1990s, words like "wellness" and phrases such as "healthy communities" became commonplace.

Local health departments, largely organized at the county level, have been at the center of this movement. Historically involved in preventive services like immunization and prenatal care, they have also added promoting positive health behavior to their repertoire, often working closely with state units. At the same time, the federal government has taken the lead on protective measures like seat-belt usage and occupational safety. This has culminated in a national competition for which community is the healthiest of them all, complete with its own web site (*www.communityhealth.hrsa.gov*) featuring county-based data on an array of factors.

Preventive Services

Scientific breakthroughs throughout the late nineteenth and twentieth centuries identified the biological causes of numerous infectious diseases, leading the way to successful searches for vaccines to prevent them. From widespread phenomena like diphtheria (1921), measles (1941), and mumps (1968), to less prevalent but more deadly diseases like tetanus (1923) and polio (1952), the march toward invincibility through immunization progressed. Universal application, however, remains elusive. Although state laws require proof of immunization for five-year-olds before enrolling in schools, the ideal is to have the shots during infancy, a goal local health departments are still working to achieve.

For diseases which cannot be blocked by vaccines but whose incidence can be lowered by isolating and treated those already infected, public-health units act as investigators to identify cases. For some maladies, such as tuberculosis, this is more straightforward and, over the twentieth century, it has gone from being the leading cause of death to a minor statistical blip.

For other infections, most notably sexually transmitted diseases, social embarrassment limits cooperation. People are less willing to admit having an infection and even less cooperative in identifying sexual partners.

During the past two decades, this has been an extraordinary trial for detecting those carrying the Human Immunodeficiency Virus (HIV), the precursor of the mostly fatal Acquired Immunodeficiency Syndrome (AIDS). Over three-quarters of AIDS cases occur among drug users, contaminated by tainted needles, and gays, infected through anal intercourse. The one behavior is illegal and the other socially controversial and, as a result, the disease continues to spread, presenting a crisis that the health care system has yet to check.[22]

Because a child's health is so affected by the mother's conduct during pregnancy and by the quantity and quality of the infant's care during the first year of life, public-health departments place special emphasis on maternal services, particularly for low-income and teenage women. These include free screenings, nutritional assistance, and child-rearing training. To a great extent these initiatives are funded through the federal government's Maternal and Child Health Block Grant.[23]

Health Promotion

Preventive services, the core activity for public health efforts for most of the twentieth century, remain close to traditional medical practice, procedures such as shots or screenings administered in a clinical setting. Promotion moves beyond that, encouraging behavior that research shows contributes to good health. Some of these efforts are noncontroversial—championing regular exercise ("do your daily dozen") or fostering adequate nutrition ("strive for five").

Others are more contentious. Preaching against cigarette smoking or discouraging binge drinking certainly advances health. But carried too far they can antagonize those who produce and sell the products and create debates, especially with alcohol, about whether abstinence or moderation is the preferred approach. Sex education is even more volatile. Should public health units assume that some teenagers will be sexually active and encourage them to use condoms? Or should the community maintain that abstaining from sex is the only morally acceptable position and that promoting the use of contraceptives undermines this stance?

Most health promotion began as advertising campaigns conveyed through the mass media, educational kits, and printed brochures. Although there has been

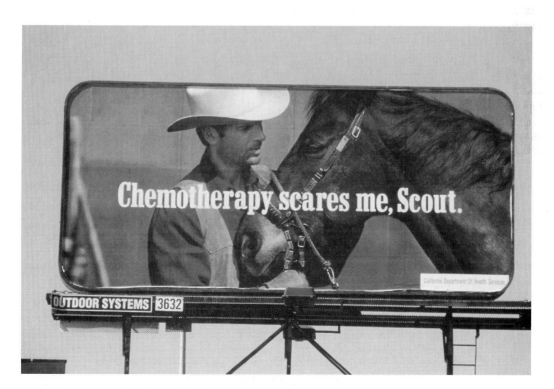

An Anti-Smoking Billboard

some success—tobacco and alcohol usage have both declined over the past twenty years—the impact has been less than optimal.[24] This is especially so in neighborhoods with the highest incidences of illnesses connected with unhealthy lifestyles. Recent initiatives have been less top down—the health professionals telling people what they are supposed to do—and more bottom up—partnering with selected communities to improve outcomes.[25]

Health Protection

Once accidents were seen as uncontrollable events that just happened. If there was anyone at fault, then it was probably the individuals who had been harmed. Now many accidents are viewed as either preventable or, if they do occur, causing less injury. The national government has led the way but state and local governments and nonprofit agencies such as safety councils have become partners in this effort.

The most well-known examples are the state and federal seat-belt and motor-cycle/bicycle-helmet laws which are then publicized by the nonprofit groups ("buckle up") and enforced by local law-enforcement agencies. Analogous programs exist for water safety, protection against falls in the home, fireworks accident prevention, and occupational hazards ranging from use of helmets on construction sites to ways of minimizing carpal tunnel syndrome for computer users.

MENTAL HEALTH

Mental illnesses are often less visible than physical ailments but they are no less real. In any year, about 20 percent of a metropolitan area's population has one or more mental disorders. Some are permanent, like mental retardation, others are chronic, such as schizophrenia, and still others are episodic, like depression.[26] Although modern society has moved from the fallacy that most mental illness was a character flaw or a family failing and now generally recognizes that most are biologically based and all can be treated, the transition in thinking is not complete and some stigma remains. That hampers initiatives to treat mental illness and deters many from seeking help.

Until the 1950s, the prevailing public policy for those suffering from mental illness, especially the more severe cases, was to lock them up in state-run psychiatric hospitals and about half a million were housed there. As more effective treatments were discovered, many based on psychotropic drugs, a "deinstitutionalization" movement began to medicate the mentally ill as outpatients and to integrate them into the general population so that now fewer than 100,000 are found in inpatient facilities.[27] To help coordinate this approach, states established community mental-health centers, often using grant funds provided under federal legislation passed in 1964.[28]

Because the states had historically taken responsibility for the mentally ill, their mental-health agencies have typically maintained control over these community units and local governments have at best had a marginal role. Mental health, however, has not fared well in the competition for state allocations, losing out to more popular initiatives like building more prisons to fight crime and increasing state funding for elementary and secondary education. Many private insurance programs also have less support for mental-health treatment, further undercutting financial support.

Part of this service gap is being filled by a growing number of nonprofit social service agencies. Relying partially on federal and state payments for services and covering the remaining costs with private donations, they initially tended to focus on a specific illness for a defined population, say, substance abuse among teenagers or schizophrenia among the homeless. This method had two shortcomings: some niches went unfilled and there were no bridges linking programs for people who needed a follow-upon continuing program after they had completed an initial program. More recently, both states and United Ways have encouraged these organizations to develop a continuum of care, and many metropolitan areas now either have one or more comprehensive mental-health nonprofit organizations or, if that is not feasible, an active collaboration and shared information systems among smaller groups.

PERSONS WITH DISABILITIES

About one out of every seven metropolitan-area residents has a disability which, using the legal definition, limits them from performing some essential daily activity.[29] Most physical disabilities are quite apparent: the almost 2 million who use wheelchairs or the 1½ million who are blind. Other are less visible and overlap with mental illness: mental retardation or learning deficiencies. Although disability is no stranger to any age group, it is especially prevalent among the elderly.

Until the 1970s, the public policy response to persons with disabilities was either to handle them as charity, the typical method for those with physical handicaps, or to ignore them, the prevailing reaction to those with mental challenges. Then three federal laws—the Rehabilitation Act (1973), the Education for All Handicapped Children Act (1975), and the most dramatic of them all, the Americans with Disabilities Act (1990)—brought disability "out of the closet."[30] What once were unfortunate circumstances has become a political movement with bipartisan support.

Instead of being a burden on their communities, persons with disabilities seek ways to allow them to live independently and participate economically. With both a stick—federal mandates that both public and private entities make "reasonable accommodations"[31]—and a carrot—if communities promoted inclusiveness for persons with disabilities they could lower their long-term subsidies and improve economic productivity—governments, businesses, and nonprofit organizations within metropolitan areas have spent the past twenty-five years, especially the last decade, transforming both their physical settings and their social practices.

For those with physical disabilities, sidewalks now have cuts rather than curbs at street intersections, buildings have ramp entrances, traffic lights use sound as

Curb Cuts Make Sidewalks Accessible

well as light so that the blind can cross safely, bathrooms have stalls which can handle wheelchairs, and telephones and other communication devices can be readily
used by those with hearing and speech impairments. This conversion is not yet complete, but those communities within metropolitan areas which have moved the
fastest have the edge in attracting persons with disabilities—as residents, shoppers,
and workers.

For those with developmental disabilities and learning handicaps, there are
more early-childhood screenings and more coordinated services both in special
educational facilities and within mainstream schooling.[32] Instead of giving up on
those for whom learning is a trial, intensive efforts are made to enable them to be
productive adults. At that stage, instead of warehousing so many in large public institutions, nonprofit agencies with some tax support are sponsoring smaller group
homes for groups of six to fourteen and supported living for even smaller numbers.[33]

Mixing the developmentally disabled into either public schools as children or
residential neighborhoods as adults has sparked controversy in many neighborhoods. Within education, there are concerns that teachers in classrooms with just a
few special education students intermingled with others will be so distracted that
they will neglect those without learning disabilities.[34] Within communities, fear
exists that group homes will lower property values.[35]

WATER

Metropolitan areas need water both for the obvious—human survival—and the not so obvious—economic productivity. The cities which serve as the starting core for today's regions almost all began beside lakes or astride streams and, from their earliest days, had to develop systems for obtaining water for household and industrial purposes and then ways for disposing of the wastewater.

Follow a drop of water: it must come from a stream, lake, or aquifer, go through a cleansing process to remove contaminants, and be piped to a building. After being used—for a drink, to launder clothes, to flush a toilet, to cleanse a silicon wafer—it must find another way out of the building, be transmitted to a treatment facility, and then returned to a stream or lake. It is an essential commodity and part of both the internal and external metropolitan competition is to provide quality water and sewer services at reasonable costs.

Water Supply

Demand for water is high. The average household uses over 125,000 gallons a year, enough to fill ten medium-sized swimming pools. Many industrial processes require millions of gallons daily. Some regions have an abundant supply—St. Louis at the confluence of the Mississippi and Missouri Rivers, Cincinnati and Louisville on the Ohio River, Chicago beside Lake Michigan—but others struggle. Los Angeles's growth was dependent on shipping water from Northern California, and regions like Las Vegas and Phoenix fight over flows from the Colorado River watershed. Expansion in South Florida—Miami-Fort Lauderdale and West Palm Beach—is threatened by reductions from nearby lakes and aquifers. Water-deficient regions must often institute rationing, limiting when and how often lawns can be watered or mandating conservation fixtures for toilets and showers, creating a crimp in the quality of life for freedom-minded Americans.

For personal consumption, water must be safe and, more subjectively, tasty. The more contaminants water has when taken from a source, the more a jurisdiction must spend cleaning it. With the discovery that chlorine would free water from typhoid and cholera, deaths from those diseases have plummeted from the thousands to a statistical rarity. High chlorine levels, however, can make the water less palatable.

About half the jurisdictions rely on surface water (streams or lake) from one of the nation's 2,000 or so watersheds while the others obtain their supply from underground. For the former, it is far better to be at the head of the stream or the top of the lake than at the middle or the bottom. The farther water is from its source—underground springs or mountain snow packs—the more likely it is to have picked up contaminants, either from agricultural run-off or from communities higher up in the watershed.

But, by definition, most are not at the source and everyone below is dependent upon the behavior of those upstream. Working one's way up the Mississippi River, New Orleans depends on Memphis which relies on St. Louis which counts on Minneapolis-St. Paul. That, along with the rise of environmentalism and the fact that watersheds do not follow neatly local or state governmental boundaries, caused the federal government to become the water-quality enforcer, passing a string of legislation between 1965 and 1977, most notably the Water Pollution Control Act and the Clean Water Act, and establishing the Environmental Protection Agency to develop, implement, and monitor standards. Also aiding this crackdown was the increasingly visible pollution in urban waterways, making them unsafe for swimming and fishing.[36]

Wastewater

Flush and it goes away. That seems simple but it requires sewer systems routing human and other wastes from each building, from small pipes entering each residence to trunk sewers underneath many major streets, and ultimately to treatment plants. There the water and solids are separated and disinfectants added; the water is then released to a river or lake. When the system operates well, it is largely invisible. When it fails, odors abound, health is threatened, and waterways are polluted.

Sewer systems are an urban phenomenon. Once people started to cluster together, natural processes—absorption in the ground or in a nearby stream—could no longer handle the volume of waste. Today, over 99 percent of the residences in metropolitan buildings have indoor plumbing. In central cities, more than 98 percent are connected to sewer systems, while in suburban areas septic tanks still account for 23 percent of wastewater disposal.[37]

These systems must also handle storm water. Urbanization means paving much of the land. Much of the rain can no longer be soaked up in the ground but instead must be routed into the sewers, preferably in pipes separated from wastewater. If capacity is inadequate, most often the case at a region's urbanizing edge, then local flooding causes property damage. If the stormwater and wastewater pipes are combined and overflow happens, then raw sewage becomes exposed in creeks and streams.[38]

Structure and Issues

Most water and wastewater systems are public, operated typically by either municipalities or special districts. They are funded by a mixture of general revenues and user fees, with the latter usually contributing most of the income. Calculating who should pay how much is often both difficult and politically charged. Because determining precisely each unit's monthly discharges is essentially impossible, low-volume users often pay more than they should while high-volume entities receive a price break. Proposing that stormwater prices be based on the amount of impervious space rankles anyone with large parking lots, such as shopping centers, apartment complexes, or religious facilities.

The federal government's regulations create ongoing tensions between it and local units. The relationships were smoother in the early days following the 1970s legislation because the national government paid billions to help localities improve their water and sewer systems. Those funds are severely diminished so now the municipalities and special districts are under mandates that can only be funded by increasing taxes or raising fees, neither a politically popular option. In the inner portions of many of the older regions, much of the infrastructure is more than a century old so improvements can be very costly.

Within metropolitan areas, the outer-suburban and central-city/inner-suburban segments are frequently at odds. Sewers are an example. At some point, increasing density requires the outer suburbs to move from septic tanks or a small community system to a larger network. If it seeks to join an existing wastewater system operated by the inner suburbs or the central city, how should the costs be allocated, not only for the new connections but also for future improvements in the older segments?

AIR

Air Quality

Dirty air became commonplace in American metropolitan areas during the 1950s. As populations expanded after World War II, power plants burned more high sulphur coal, automobiles emitted more hydrocarbons, and factories spewed out more

A Smoggy Day in Los Angeles

particulates. "Smoke" and "fog" joined to form a new word—*smog*—and it became part of metropolitan areas' everyday vocabulary.

The polluted air was not only a nuisance, soiling both structures and clothes, it was also unhealthy. Anyone with lung ailments, most notably asthmatics, is immediately affected and breathing disorders contribute to other health problems, especially those related to the heart. Research indicates that, even with progress in cleaning the air between the 1960s and 1990s, atmospheric pollution causes between 50,000 and 100,000 deaths annually.[39]

As with water pollution, the bulk of the public policy reaction occurred at the national level.[40] Congress passed the Clean Air Act in 1963, the Motor Vehicle Air Pollution Control Act in 1965, and the Air Quality Act in 1967. By the early 1970s, the newly formed Environmental Protection Agency, sometimes acting unilaterally and other times through its state counterparts, was establishing standards, setting up monitoring stations, and enforcing regulations.

Today the national government maintains a daily "Air Quality Index" for every metropolitan area, and it encourages local media to publicize it, using six color categories ranging from brown (the worst) to green (the best) to display conditions, both to raise policy awareness and influence individual behavior. Although the index has several components, the principal culprit is ozone, smog's main ingredient, formed when sunlight interacts with hydrocarbons such as those emitted by automobiles.

Issues

No metropolitan area would choose to have dirty air. It creates health hazards and is aesthetically displeasing. But keeping the air clean costs money and the politics happen over who should pay the bill.[41] Based primarily on ozone level, the national government has warned several metropolitan areas that they are in "nonattainment" of the standards. As of January, 2001, Los Angeles had an "extreme" nonattainment rating while Baltimore, Chicago, Houston, Milwaukee, New York, Philadelphia, and Sacramento had a "severe" mark.

How to lower these scores, how to reach attainment, is where the battle is joined. Should the state and local units tell the national government to make automobile manufacturers produce cars with lower emissions or, more radically, vehicles which do not require fossil fuel? That would pass the costs along initially to the auto companies and ultimately to their customers. Should national and state governments crack down on power plants, requiring them to improve smokestack cleaning and use lower sulphur fuel? That would mean higher prices for electricity.

Should the federal government threaten the states with the loss of hundreds of millions in transportation funding, as it now has the power to do? That passes the buck to the states, forcing them to decide whose ox to gore. One common response is tougher emission control inspections conducted by state agencies, an almost certain recipe for angering motorists and creating voter backlash. Can taking political heat be avoided by getting metropolitan residents to lessen automobile trips through car pools, mass transit, bicycling, and walking? That assumes that many residents are willing to change their behavior, in itself a dubious proposition.

Currently all these strategies are being discussed and some aspect of each is being tried. The challenge is that, even though every citizen agrees that cleaner air is an admirable goal and no one disagrees that it would be wonderful to have, most are hoping that *someone else* will pick up the tab and that they can get for free.

TRASH

Every day the average metropolitan household generates about four and one-half pounds of trash.[42] Paper is by far the most common item but other significant categories include yard waste, plastics, metals, wood, food waste, and glass. The competition occurs over what should be done with it. The disposal options are clear—transport trash to a landfill, incinerate it, recycle, or produce less—but there is considerable controversy over which options should be chosen.

Landfills remain the place where a majority of the trash ends up, although their share has dropped steadily from 83 percent in 1985 to 54 percent in 2000. It is convenient: just put the stuff in a can or a dumpster and let someone come and take it away. It also remains the least expensive alternative.

But it is not without its problems, both political and environmental. Because few communities relish having a landfill, they are increasingly in rural areas. New York City, which once had tens of dumps within its boundaries, closed its last landfill on Staten Island in 2001; all its trash is shipped outside the region, some as far away as Virginia. This solves the internal competition for who is going to store the trash but it raises the price of disposal.

Federal and state environmental regulations have also required landfills to transform themselves from open air facilities, emitting foul odors into the air and leaking nasty liquids into ground water systems, into plastic-lined containers, complete with complex mechanisms for venting the millions of cubic feet of methane gas produced each day by decomposing waste. This, also, has raised costs for the landfill option.

The final concern about landfills is that they are finite. Only so much land is available for this usage, much of it inconveniently located. Once their capacity is reached, then landfills must be either abandoned or, at considerable cost, reconverted for other uses such as golf courses or parks. Each time the limits are approached, increasingly common in many metropolitan areas, it initiates a debate about what to do next: find one more landfill within the region, ship the trash even further away, or begin using another means.

Why not burn the trash? When America was less densely settled, that was how many households took care of their own refuse. Given fire dangers and air pollution, most metropolitan jurisdictions now ban individuals from burning rubbish, even the perennial autumn leaves. Waste-to-energy incinerators are the modern equivalent, with the added benefit of producing electricity to help recover some or all of the costs, and they handle about one-sixth of the trash.

Incinerators also have their challenges. Unlike landfills, they must be sited somewhere within the region. To be efficient, they must be able to consume well

Landfills Contain a Majority of Metropolitan Trash

over 100 tons of trash daily. Few neighborhoods are excited about having a smoke-belching facility fed by hundreds of trucks arriving from dawn to dusk. These plants must also screen the incoming trash to eliminate items such as mercury, which would pollute the air.[43]

Landfills' and incinerators' political and environmental disadvantages, along with rising environmental awareness, have sparked the recycling option. During the last decade, the share of recycled trash has doubled, going from 15 percent to 30 percent. Separate containers for paper, yard waste, and cans are now common in many municipalities and even more have recycling stations where householders can take such items. Even though this imposes an inconvenience on individuals, most residents cooperate, getting psychic satisfaction from doing their part to help the environment.[44]

The hurdle confronting further recycling is finding customers. Most of the marketable items—aluminum cans, corrugated boxes, newspapers—are already represented in the current totals and, even for them, there are occasionally cheaper options—as when falling lumber prices make purchasing new fiber less expensive than buying recycled paper. The remaining components in the trash stream will be a harder sell.

The most obvious way to reduce the solid-waste disposal problem is to produce less of it and, partially through such initiatives, amounts are leveling off in many regions. Some of the initiatives used to accomplish this are encouraging households to have their own compost piles, supplied by their yard and food wastes; container deposit programs, giving an incentive to return them to retailers; and junk mail restrictions, reducing the amount of throwaway paper items.

HAZARDOUS WASTE SITES

Metropolitan areas spent much of the twentieth century polluting their environment. Oil refineries and chemical plants spread dangerous substances on their sites, builders used lead paint and asbestos insulation, arms productions left radioactive wastes, metal producers deposited abandoned tailings, and contractors employed dioxin-laded materials. As a consequence, by late in the century, every region had a significant residue of hazardous wastes.

For the most part, the polluters knew not what they did. They were either getting rid of stuff as easily and inexpensively as possible or employing what were then considered acceptable practices. Only the hindsight given by modern science enables communities to realize the amount of toxicity that has accumulated over decades of ignorance. Even limiting the count to those sites which qualify for the Environmental Protection Agency's Superfund National Priorities List, the total is over 1,000, with each major metropolitan area having several.[45]

These and other hazardous waste sites, including those which are still being determined, are not randomly distributed throughout the metropolitan areas. Several studies have shown that they are disproportionately located in poor and minority neighborhoods.[46] This is both because property values have declined in these areas, partially because of their environmental danger, but also because, in the competition for where undesirable things go, these parts of the region are at a political disadvantage.[47] This inequity, in turn, has spawned its own countervailing force, the environmental justice movement.[48]

One policy response has been to attempt to make economic lemonade out of these environmental lemons, especially in central cities and inner suburbs. Their leadership is persistently lobbying the federal government to focus remediation funds on sites, popularly known as "brownfields," which have the potential to attract new businesses.[49] These jurisdictions have identified thousands of sites where, in their judgment, brownfields can produce economic returns.

SUSTAINABILITY

For those especially concerned about environmental quality, the mantra has become "sustainable development," a term promoted by the World Commission on Environment and Development in its 1987 report, defined as activity which enables people "to meet the needs of the present without compromising the ability of future generations to meet their own needs."[50]

This perspective argues that metropolitan areas can be both financially and environmentally green, that it is not necessary to incur pollution and toxicity in order to achieve economic prosperity. Balancing development, sustaining it over time, requires appreciating that regions are complex ecologies and understanding how each part affects the other.[51] Humans and their metropolitan activities are not outside the biological setting but embedded within it, part of the intricate regional web.

Seattle has done the most to apply this perspective. Under the leadership of Sustainable Seattle, an organization formed in the early 1990s, it regularly examines indicators ranging from the number of wild salmon returning to the region's streams, to fuel and water consumption efficiency, to youth involvement in the community. The effort, mirrored in several other regions, is to find the right blend among economic viability, environmental quality, and social responsibility.

NOTES

1. The life expectancy data are from the U.S. National Center for Health Statistics.
2. Katharine Levit and others, "Health Spending in 1998: Signals of Change," *Health Affairs*, 19, no. 1 (January-February 2000), pp. 124–32.
3. Sherry Glied, *Chronic Condition: Why Health Care Reform Fails* (Cambridge, MA: Harvard University Press, 1997); Theodore R. Marmor, *Understanding Health Care Reform* (New Haven, CT: Yale University Press, 1994); and James A. Morone and Gary S. Belkin, eds., *The Politics of Health Care Reform: Lessons from the Past, Proposals for the Future* (Durham, NC: Duke University Press, 1994).
4. Expenditure data are from the U.S. Health Care Financing Administration.
5. Rachel Carson, *Silent Spring* (Boston, MA: Houghton Mifflin, 1962).
6. Samuel P. Hays, *A History of Environmental Politics Since 1945* (Pittsburgh, PA: University of Pittsburgh Press, 2000), pp. 22–51.
7. The physician data were collected by the American Medical Association and are reported in the *State and Metropolitan Data Book 1997–1998* (Washington: U.S. Bureau of the Census, 1998), Table B-4.
8. Thomas Bodenheimer, "The American Health Care System: Physicians and the Changing Medical Marketplace," *The New England Journal of Medicine*, 340, no. 7 (February 18, 1999), pp. 584–88.
9. Arline T. Geronimus, "To Mitigate, Resist, or Undo: Addressing Structural Influences on the Health of Urban Populations," *American Journal of Public Health*, 90, no. 6 (June 2000), pp. 867–72. The consequences for children are especially grim. See *Health Disparities: Bridging the Gap* (Washington: National Institute of Child Health and Human Development, 2000).
10. Marc L. Rivo and David A. Kindig, "A Report Card on the Physician Work Force in the United States," *The New England Journal of Medicine*, 334, no. 14 (April 4, 1996), pp. 892–96. Nationally there are about two specialists for every one primary-care physician.
11. Eli Ginzberg, *Tomorrow's Hospital: A Look to the Twenty-First Century* (New Haven, CT: Yale University Press, 1996), pg. 8.
12. The hospital statistics are from the National Center of Health Statistics.
13. Kevin W. Barr and Charles L. Breindel, "Ambulatory Care," in *Health Care Administration*, 2nd ed., ed. Lawrence F. Wolper (Gaithersburg, MD: Aspen Publishers, 1995), pp. 547–73.
14. Ginzberg, *Tomorrow's Hospital*, pg. 14. Also see Eli Ginzberg, Howard S. Berliner, and Miriam Ostow, eds., *Changing U.S. Health Care: A Study of Four Metropolitan Areas* (Boulder, CO: Westview Press, 1993).
15. J. Rogers Hollingsworth and Ellen Jane Hollingsworth, *Controversy about American Hospitals: Funding, Ownership, and Performance* (Washington: American Enterprise for Public Policy Research, 1987).
16. "Best Hospitals 2000," *U.S. News and World Report*, 129, no. 3 (July 17, 2000), pg. 72.
17. James O. Page, "Emergency Medical Services," in *Fire Protection Handbook*, 17th ed., eds. Arthur E. Cote and Jim L. Linville (Quincy, Massachusetts: National Fire Protection Association, 1991), pg. 9–115; and Carl J. Post, *Omaha Orange: A Popular History of EMS in America* (Boston, MA: Jones and Bartlett Publishing, 1992). The National Research Council's *Accidental Death and Disability:*

The Neglected Disease of Modern Society (Washington: National Academy Press, 1966) stimulated this change and it was further assisted by funding from the Emergency Medical Services System Act of 1973.

18. *Emergency Medical Services: Agenda for the Future* (Washington: U.S. Department of Transportation and U.S. Department of Health and Human Services, 1996), pp. 61–4.

19. David N. Ammons, *Municipal Benchmarks: Assessing Local Performance and Establishing Community Standards* (Thousand Oaks, CA: Sage Publications, 1996), pp. 71–73.

20. Bernard J. Turnock, *Public Health: What It Is and How It Works* (Gaithersburg, MD: Aspen Publishers, 1997), pp. 157–62.

21. Marguerite A. Guinta and John P. Allegrante, "The President's Committee on Health Education: A Twenty Year Retrospective on Its Politics and Policy Impact," *American Journal of Public Health*, 82, no. 7 (July 1992), pp. 1033–41; and Ross C. Brownson, Elizabeth A. Baker, and Lloyd F. Novick, *Community-Based Prevention: Programs That Work* (Gaithersburg, MD: Aspen Publishers, 1999).

22. Leonard S. Robins and Charles Backstrom, "The Politics of AIDS," in *Health Politics and Policy*, 3rd ed., eds. Theodor J. Litman and Leonard S. Robins (Albany, NY: Delmar Publishers, 1997), pp. 419–38.

23. Trude Bennett and Alan Cross, "Maternal and Child Health," in *Principles of Public Health Practice*, eds. F. Douglas Scutchfield and C. William Keck (Albany, NY: Delmar Publishers, 1997), pp. 327–36.

24. Max Heirich, *Rethinking Health Care: Innovation and Change in America* (Boulder, CO: Westview Press, 1998), pp. 239–44.

25. Thomas A. Bruce and Steven Uranga McKane, *Community-Based Public Health: A Partnership Model* (Washington: American Public Health Association, 2000).

26. Susan L. Ettner, "Mental Health Services and Policy Issues," in *Changing the U.S. Health Care System: Key Issues in Health Services, Policy, and Management*, eds. Ronald M. Andersen, Thomas H. Rice, and Gerald F. Kominski (San Francisco: Jossey-Bass, 2001), pp. 291–319.

27. David Mechanic and David A. Rocheport, "Deinstitutionalization: An Appraisal of Reform," *Annual Review of Sociology*, 16 (1990), pp. 301–27.

28. The law was the Mental Retardation Facilities and Community Mental Health Construction Act of 1964.

29. John T. Pardeck, "An Update on the Americans with Disabilities Act: Implications for Health and Human Services Delivery," *Journal of Health and Social Policy*, 13, no. 4 (2001), pp. 1–15.

30. Susan Allen, "Introduction: Converging Trends," in *Living in the Community with Disability: Service Needs, Use, and Systems*, eds. Allen and Vincent Mor (New York: Springer Publishing Company, 1998), pg. 1.

31. The term "reasonable accommodation" is from the Americans with Disabilities Act: Public Law 101–336, 42 U.S.C. 12101.

32. Marsha Mailick Seltzer, "Service Use and Delivery for Persons with Mental Retardation and Other Developmental Disabilities," in *Living in the Community with Disability*, eds. Allen and Mor, pp. 219–40.

33. David Braddock and others, *The State of the States in Developmental Disabilities*, 4th ed. (Washington: American Association on Mental Retardation, 1995).

34. Nancy Mamlin, "Despite Best Intentions: When Inclusion Fails," *Journal of Special Education*, 33, no. 1 (Spring 1999), pp. 36–53.

35. Raymond F. Currie and others, "Maybe on My Street: The Politics of Community Placement of the Mentally Disabled," *Urban Affairs Quarterly*, 25, no. 2 (December 1989), pp. 298–321; and Robert Wilton, "Grounding Hierarchies of Acceptance: The Social Construction of Disability in NIMBY Conflicts," *Urban Geography*, 21, no. 7 (October 2000), pp. 586–608.

36. Hays, *A History of Environmental Politics*, pp. 62–63.

37. The statistics are from the *1999 Annual Housing Survey*.

38. G.V. Loganathan, D.F. Kibler, and T.J. Grizzard, "Urban Stormwater Management," in *Water Resources Handbook*, ed. Larry W. Mays (New York: McGraw-Hill, 1996), Chapter 26.

39. Douglas W. Dockery and C. Arden Pope III, "Acute Respiratory Effects of Particulate Air Pollution," *Annual Review of Public Health*, 15 (1994), pp. 107–32.

40. Charles O. Jones, *Clean Air: The Policies and Politics of Pollution Control* (Pittsburgh, PA: University of Pittsburgh Press, 1975).

41. Daniel J. Fiorino, *Making Environmental Policy* (Berkeley: University of California Press, 1995); and Gary C. Bryner, *Blue Skies, Green Politics: The Clean Air Act of 1990 and Its Implementation*, 2nd ed. (Washington: CQ Press, 1995). For a business perspective, see *What Price Clean Air? A Market Approach to Energy and Environmental Policy* (New York: Committee for Economic Development, 1993).

42. The solid waste statistics are from the *Municipal Solid Waste Fact Book* (Washington: U.S. Environmental Protection Agency, 2001).

43. Tom Arrandale, "The Big Burnout," *Governing*, 11, no. 11 (August 1998), pp. 34–35.

44. Everett Carll Ladd and Karlyn H. Bowman, *Attitudes toward the Environment* (Washington: American Enteprise Institute for Public Policy Research, 1995).

45. Michael E. Kraft and Norman J. Vig, "Environmental Policy from the 1970s to 2000: An Overview," in *Environmental Policy: New Directions for the Twenty-First Century*, 4th ed., eds. Vig and Kraft (Washington: CQ Press, 2000), pg. 22. The Comprehensive Environmental Response, Compensation, and Liability Act (1980), commonly called the Superfund, was established to clean up these sites.

46. Andrew Szasz and Michael Meuser, "Environmental Inequalities: Literature Review and Proposals for New Directions in Research and Theory," *Current Sociology*, 45, no. 3 (July 1997), pp. 99–120; Raymond J. Burby and Denise E. Strong, "Coping with Chemicals: Blacks, Whites, Planners, and Industrial Pollution," *Journal of the American Planning Association*, 63, no. 4 (Autumn 1997), pp. 469–80; and Andrew Hurley, *Environmental Inequalities: Class, Race, and Industrial Pollution in Gary, Indiana* (Chapel Hill: University of North Carolina Press, 1995).

47. Manuel Pastor, Jr., Jim Sadd, and John Hipp, "Which Came First? Toxic Facilities, Minority Move-In, and Environmental Justice," *Journal of Urban Affairs*, 23, no. 1 (2001), pp. 1–21.

48. Daniel Faber, ed., *The Struggle for Ecological Democracy: Environmental Justice Movements in the United States* (New York: Guilford Press, 1998).

49. *Recycling America's Land: A National Report on Brownfields Redevelopment* (Washington: U.S. Conference of Mayors, 2000).

50. World Commission on Environment and Development, *Our Common Future* (New York: Oxford University Press, 1987), pg. 1; and Adam S. Weinberg, David N. Pellow, and Allan Schnaiberg, *Urban Recycling and the Search for Sustainable Community Development* (Princeton, NJ: Princeton University Press, 2000), pp. 4–7.

51. Judith E. Innes and David E. Booher, "Metropolitan Development as a Complex System: A New Approach to Sustainability," *Economic Development Quarterly*, 13, no. 2 (May 1999), pp. 141–56. Also see *Cities and Counties: Thinking Globally, Acting Locally* (Washington: Public Technology, Inc., 1996) for case studies on sustainability initiatives in selected regions.

SUGGESTED READINGS

ANDERSON, RONALD M., THOMAS H. RICE, and GERALD F. KOMINSKI, editors. *Changing the U.S. Health Care System: Key Issues in Health Services, Policy, and Management.* 2nd edition. San Francisco, CA: Jossey-Bass, 2001. Twenty essays on various aspects of the health care system.

BROWNSON, ROSS C., ELIZABETH A. BAKER, and LLOYD F. NOVICK, editors. *Community-Based Prevention: Programs that Work.* Gaithersburg, MD: Aspen Publishers, 1999. Describes a wide range of prevention efforts including immunization, promotion, and regulation.

HAYS, SAMUEL P. *A History of Environmental Politics since 1945.* Pittsburgh, PA: University of Pittsburgh Press, 2000. Excellent analysis of the environmental movement's roots, strategies, and accomplishments.

VIG, NORMAN J., and MICHAEL E. KRAFT, editors. *Environmental Policy: New Directions for the Twenty-First Century.* 4th edition. Washington: CQ Press, 2000. Discusses environmental policy at all stages, agenda setting through implementation, and at all governmental levels.

DOING IT

The federal government has established web sites so that citizens can check how their areas are doing on key health and environmental indicators. Numerous health statistics, aggregated to the county level, can be found at *www.communityhealth.hrsa.gov.* Take the counties in a metropolitan region (Appendix B lists them for those having 1 million or more residents) and see how it is doing. To help with comparisons, the web site gives "peer counties" from elsewhere in the United States so that, for example, suburban counties can be compared with similar jurisdictions.

The U.S. Environmental Agency has considerable air quality information, most of it reported by metropolitan area. Its home web site is *www.epa.gov* and you can follow the links to the air-quality section. One segment, *www.epa.gov/airnow,* provides information about current conditions. Again, take a metropolitan region and assess its performance. If it is a "nonattainment" area, what is its plan for achieving adequate air quality? The answer to this item can often be found at the region's metropolitan planning organization web site. For a listing of these for the major regions see Appendix B.

CHAPTER 12

Housing

Attracting and retaining desirable residents is at the heart of the contest within metropolitan areas. Jobs and shoppers are not enough to make a community whole. People must also *live* there. So exurban subdivisions, inner-suburban municipalities, and central-city neighborhoods all vie for being the place where people want to dwell.

The competition never stops. Tens of thousands enter the metropolitan area each year, creating potential demand. Similar numbers die or leave, generating housing supply. Within the region, others think about relocating and, as some actually do, they simultaneously create houses to sell and apartments to lease—and potential purchasers and renters.

The American value system and national policies fuel this.[1] For most, owning a home is an expectation, not an aspiration. At the end of World War II, less than half of U.S. adults owned a home. Now two out of three do and, among those 45 years and older, the proportion approaches 80 percent.[2] The ownership shares are slightly lower in metropolitan areas, especially within central cities, but the upward trend extends across all jurisdictions.

The federal government spurs home owning in both word and deed. The Housing Act of 1949 states boldly that "a decent home for every American family" is a national goal. The home mortgage interest deduction on personal income taxes amount to a $100 billion-plus annual subsidy for purchasing residences. To make mortgages more plentiful, the federal government insures their repayment through the Federal Housing Administration (FHA) and supports a secondary market through the Federal National Mortgage Association (Fannie Mae) and the Federal Home Loan Mortgage Corporation (Freddie Mac). Together, these affect over a million mortgages a year.[3]

Within a metropolitan area's overall housing market, the competitors seek appealing niches. No community can offer all residential alternatives and each, strategically, plays to its strengths, attempting to position itself for some of the attractive segments. Downtowns might stress excitement, inner-suburbs convenience, outer-suburbs schools, exurbs space. The housing choice is not just the structure itself but a package, complete with its immediate setting, public goods and services, and other factors.

Areas with older housing stock must work to keep their inventory in good shape. Since much of the central-city and inner-suburban housing was built prior to World War II and some extends back to the nineteenth century, these jurisdictions are regularly devising and implementing programs to revitalize neighborhoods, either restoring them to their original status or repositioning them for a new niche.

Housing also is part of the external chase among metropolitan areas. Internally, each community wants the prime residents: economically affluent, socially respectable, civically minded. Few seek out the working poor or the impoverished. But regional economies need people willing and able to take minimum wage jobs and, as a social collectivity, they are responsible for finding shelter for those unable to do so themselves. So the competitive region must have an array of affordable housing.

Equity is also an issue. Should affordable housing be concentrated in just a few parts of the region or should each community assume a share of the burden? Should economic and racial residential segregation be discouraged, both because it exacerbates regional divisions and because it is morally suspect, or should governments allow individual tendencies to reside near others of similar backgrounds be the determinant of who lives where?

THE HOUSING MARKET

Metropolitan housing markets have the standard economic components: supply (dwelling units), demand (households), and price (purchase or rental). The interactions among them—which types of households seek what sort of housing at what levels of price—determine the residential scape for the region. Several factors, however, make "housing a special kind of commodity."[4]

On the supply side, each dwelling is physically anchored, accounting for the real estate cliché that housing is all about "location, location, location." The unit's value is affected not just by what it contains but by its surroundings: who the neighbors are, what the schools are like, and so forth. Two 2001 Ford Tauruses have about the same price no matter where they are. Not so two with identical houses.

Almost all housing is used. Each year sees less than 2 percent added to the available stock. Most units are built to last indefinitely and, over their lengthy existence, will be occupied by several households. More disposable commodities can respond to market changes by substituting a new line for the old: out with large cell phones, in with smaller ones. Not so with housing. Any alteration must be largely made on the existing stock.

"And it's only a stone's throw from the local school."

Housing = Location, Location, Location
Source: John Morris/Cartoon stock

Housing comes in all shapes and sizes. Other products also vary but few vary as much as dwelling units. Number of stories, room square footage, lot acreage, floor plan, construction materials, aesthetic features—the list is almost endless, especially given all the possible combinations. Moreover, within some limitations, several of these features can be modified both structurally, say adding a deck, or cosmetically, like repainting from white to brown.

For most, especially the two-thirds who own their dwelling, the housing decision is by far the most important purchasing judgment they make. It is far more than just another consumption item, quite different from a vacation or a set of golf clubs and even an automobile. For most, it is the largest investment in their personal portfolio—the leading asset (the unit's value) and the greatest liability (the unpaid mortgage). It is also the place they call "home," a term infused with memories and feelings. Decisions to change residences are not taken lightly since they carry high financial costs for moving and refinancing and substantial psychological disruption, abandoning the familiar for the unknown.

A household's demographic characteristics significantly influence their residential preferences. The typical person with reasonable means journeys through several stages between early adulthood and senior citizenry.[5] Starting by living with one's parents, next comes a rental apartment, then marriage and a two-or-three bedroom starter home, next children and a larger residence where school quality is a key consideration, then an empty-nester home with a yard, through one's 50s to 70s, ending with a condominium or apartment where others can look after maintenance and repairs.

To be competitive, metropolitan areas must have housing which addresses each of these stages, as well as housing for the growing number of exceptions to this normal cycle, such as divorced individuals or gay couples. Within the region, communities must decide which parts of this demographic spectrum to seek. For those with existing housing, adjusting to market changes is more difficult although some modifications can be made, by encouraging additions to smaller units, for example. For jurisdictions with vacant land, responding to preferential shifts is easier, a factor which favors those at the periphery.

Three demographic trends significantly influence current and future metropolitan housing markets.[6] First, the baby boom bulge, formed by the almost 80 million born between 1946 and 1964, is gradually working its way through the life cycle. During the 1980s and 1990s, these "boomers" were in their childbearing years, driving up demand for family units. Looking ahead, adults will be more evenly spread across age categories and the average household size, already having dropped from 3.6 in 1970 to 2.6 in 1999, will be lower, meaning more diversity in housing needs, especially among whites.

Second, minority and immigrant households are growing. By 2020, they will constitute more than one-third of the U.S. metropolitan residents. Both groups are more likely to have extended families occupying the same dwelling. They also are younger and more than half these families will have children under 18. These patterns will create demand for housing structures which accommodate households with more than one nuclear family and a broader age range.

Third, within every age cohort and each family composition, suburbia wins out over central cities. The only segment near parity is nonfamily households, ages 25 to 44. The builders continue to respond to this locational preference. A study of new housing construction in the thirty-nine largest areas for three years (1986, 1991, 1998) found that more than four-fifths occurred in the suburbs.[7] In 1999, five households moved to the suburbs for every three who entered the cities.[8]

Americans spend more on housing than on any other single commodity, devoting about one-fifth of their income to mortgage or rental payments alone.[9] For the increasing number of homeowners, it has been a good buy. Since 1985, in constant dollars, the value of a home has risen 23 percent while, thanks to lowering interest rates, the average monthly payment has slipped 8 percent to $920 before taxes. The typical monthly rental during this period has remained relatively constant, now standing at $528.

The mean sales price for a owner-occupied home is now $141,160 for the nation as a whole—but there is considerable variation by metropolitan area. Topping the list are San Francisco ($393,391), San Diego ($240,881), New York ($233,742), and Los Angeles ($214,082) while, among the million-plus regions, the least expensive include Buffalo ($90,367), Louisville ($100,890), Houston ($103,098), San Antonio ($91,175), and Tampa ($107.069).

For about one out of every eight, however, the market price is difficult to handle and, as a consequence, they spend over half their income on housing.[10] Using the federal standard of paying no more than 30 percent of income for housing, there is no metropolitan area where a minimum-wage job could cover the rent on a modest two bedroom apartment. Elderly persons on fixed incomes also confront serious barriers. Absent adequate subsidies, insufficient affordable housing leads to substandard units and, in the extreme case, homelessness.

HOUSING NICHES

Although new construction each year only adds a modest amount to the existing stock—40,000 to 60,000 units in growth areas like Atlanta or Phoenix and 10,000 to 20,000 in static regions like Cleveland or St. Louis—what type of housing is built and where it is located significantly affects future residential patterns. Over one or two decades, the cumulative consequences of these decisions can dramatically alter where people choose to live and determine the relative prosperity among communities within a metropolitan region.

For the past several decades, the newer suburbs have been winning most of this contest and their subdivision approach remains popular. As a result, most suburbs are sticking with it. In recent years, exurbs have often featured planned communities, most recently what is called the "new urbanism," and central cities have been countering with downtown living, such as converting industrial space into loft units.

The competition engages both the private sector and local governments. The former are the hundreds of builders within any region who design, construct, and sell the structures and the latter are the jurisdictions which zone the land and issue the permits. Both are essential and every housing project is, at root, a public-private partnership. If municipalities do not want a certain type of housing, say townhouses, they can write their zoning code to exclude it, such as by requiring a minimum lot size. If entrepreneurs do not think they can make money on a housing venture, it will not be done no matter how much a local government wishes it were so.

Suburban Subdivisions

Since World War II, the winning entry in the housing sweepstakes has been the suburban subdivision. Featuring single-family dwellings, each centered on its own lot, they have become the "McMansion" of metropolitan residences.[11] As builders learned to take advantage of the economies of scale, leveling tens of acres and constructing hundreds of homes in a single continuous process, they have given middle- and upper-middle-income households considerable value at an affordable price.

The subdivision has become the prevailing metropolitan neighborhood. With limited entrances, usually just one or two onto a single major road, it has curving streets and multiple cul de sacs, discouraging entry from anyone who does not live there. Capturing the desire to have a bit of the country while still being near the city, it hinders anything but homes from being within its boundaries. With the exception of an occasional recreational facility or an elementary school, all other commercial enterprises are banned, sent to do their business along the arterial roads, usually in strip malls.

As the nation has become more affluent, the suburban subdivisions have become more upscale.[12] In the 1950s, the norm was a one-story home with two or three bedrooms, one bathroom, a single-car garage, and about 1,000 square feet. By the 1990s, the standard had become a two-story structure with three to five bedrooms, two or three bathrooms, a two-car garage, and more than 2,000 square feet. In the interim, the 1950's subdivisions have become working-class suburbs, usually located near the central city, while the newer ones are located further out from the urban core.

At the upper end of the spectrum, the new subdivisions are gated communities, explicitly denying access to all but the residents and their guests.[13] They are most often found in Sun Belt metropolitan areas like Los Angeles or Miami, but examples exist within each region. These enclaves signal prestige for their residents while simultaneously walling them off from the less prosperous.

Planned Communities and the New Urbanism

Despite their market success, suburban subdivisions have their critics. For some, they lack a sense of community, a place where relationships are formed and sustained.[14] For others, they are too homogeneous—cookie-cutter houses all attracting residents with the same lifestyles. For many, they cater too much to the automobile, forcing residents to use the car for even minor errands.

The first large counter reaction were a few large-scale planned communities, often called "new towns," starting in the 1960s.[15] The leading examples are Reston, Virginia, and Columbia, Maryland, both within the Baltimore-Washington metropolitan area, as well as Irvine in the Los Angeles region and Woodlands in the Houston area. Each of these initiatives required thousands of acres, space only available in the exurban segments. They have been followed in the 1990s by smaller but similar initiatives, now labeled new urbanism, such as Laguna West in the Sacramento area and Kentlands in suburban Washington.

These efforts seek to recapture a small town atmosphere, complete with a civic center easily reached on foot or by bicycle.[16] They stress functional and human diversity. Instead of just dwellings, they also offer retail enterprises, professional offices, and, in some, larger businesses. They do not restrict themselves to single-family homes on separate lots but add townhouses and apartments into the mix, thereby seeking to attract people at different points in their life cycle and with varying incomes.

The new urbanists' vision for a region is a series of villages, each able to meet most daily needs, but connected to each other by highways and public transit lines. In addition to new ventures at the periphery, they aim to retrofit inner suburbs and central-city neighborhoods so they also encourage walkability and diversity. The effort has become a movement, complete with its own organization, the Congress for the New Urbanism, and a charter of principles.[17]

A Kentlands Streetscape

Downtowns

Central cities and inner suburbs have little open land so, for the most part, they must compete in the housing market by keeping their neighborhoods attractive and, where that has failed, revitalizing them—issues which will be described in the next segment. Although a handful of central cities, most notably New York and San Francisco, have stressed downtown living for decades, many have just rediscovered it in the 1990s.

During that decade, a majority of downtowns had population increases.[18] While the absolute numbers are modest, usually a few thousand, the percentage gains are much higher, over one-third, in Chicago, Denver, Houston, Seattle, and Portland. Even central cities with overall population declines—Baltimore, Cleveland, Detroit, Milwaukee, Philadelphia—have had their downtown populations increase.

With encouragement from central-city governments, developers are purchasing underutilized or vacant office buildings and warehouses and transforming them into apartments and condominiums, often with open loft-style designs. In Denver, for example, numerous three- and four-story brick warehouses in the lower downtown ("LoDo") have been redeveloped into housing.[19]

With their urbanity and ready access to entertainment and shopping, downtown housing has been attracting both young professionals and 50-and-60-something empty nesters. Both segments are growing; without children at home neither group cares about the public schools, each has money to spend on the attractions, and many find forgoing lawn maintenance a blessing.[20] A considerable number also work nearby, making the commute a walk instead of a drive.

NEIGHBORHOOD REVITALIZATION

Jurisdictions with older housing—central cities and inner suburbs—face special challenges in competing for residents within the metropolitan area. For those in the Northeast and Midwest, over half the units were constructed prior to World War II and even several West Coast cities—Portland, San Francisco, and Seattle—have more than one-third of their stock built before 1939. Some of the inner-suburban housing is also of this vintage with most of the rest erected between 1946 and 1965.

Age is not necessarily a plus in the metropolitan housing market or, more broadly, within the American value system. Older units have higher maintenance costs, demanding more attention from their owners, and often lack modern features like spacious garages, requiring residents to park on the streets instead. Then there is location, perhaps fears about personal safety and concerns about public school quality.

As a result of these factors and more, absent any countering attempts, market forces will create a trickle-down effect where, relative to suburban units, the dwelling's value steadily declines. Each time a resident leaves for, literally, greener pastures in the suburbs or a resident dies, the home's competitive standing slips. The lower price can only attract someone of a lower socioeconomic status who, financially, is less able to maintain the property, which contributes to further deterioration and, after several cycles, potential abandonment.[21]

Although, in the United States, most housing will physically survive for up to a century, cities and inner suburbs wish to avoid a premature demise for their stock. Infill housing is an option for the occasional vacant lot, but even it will likely only succeed if the rest of the block is doing well.[22] At the neighborhood level, these jurisdictions confront a triage situation: ignore those neighborhoods with buildings so dilapidated that immediate recovery is unlikely, applaud those which will make it on their own because they possess some appealing attribute like architecturally distinctive stock, and focus on those where some public-private intervention can make a difference. To revitalize these target neighborhoods, there must a strategy which attracts both capital investment, entrepreneurial engagement, and residential interest.

Capital Investment

Sustaining neighborhoods requires ongoing capital, and rebuilding them demands even more infusions. As many inner-city neighborhoods began declining during the late 1960s and early 1970s, as both their own property owners and outside entities began to disinvest in the areas, they struggled to find both local and national investment funds to reverse the trend. Lacking much economic clout, central city forces mobilized politically to change national policy.

The initial trial was getting local financial institutions to invest in their neighborhoods. Many had "redlined" inner-city housing, a term referring to drawing a red line around certain areas where banks and savings and loans refused to make loans. In reaction, Congress passed the Home Mortgage Disclosure Act in 1975 and the Community Reinvestment Act in 1977.[23] The former mandates that the financial institutions make their mortgage acceptance and denial information by census tract publicly available, making any discriminatory behavior easier to detect. The latter requires them to state how they are meeting their community's credit needs with the primary enforcement being that this can be taken into account in federal regulatory reviews, especially when banks wish to merge.

During the same period, the federal government combined several categorical housing-related grant programs into a single block grant, passing the Community Development Block Grant (CDBG) Act in 1974. This formula-based program began allocating tens of millions annually to central cities and urban counties. Although there were some conditions attached, most notably requiring that the funds be targeted to low- and moderate-income households, these dollars give the local jurisdictions considerable leeway in how they can be targeted, both geographically and programmatically.[24]

To encourage more nonprofit participation, Congress chartered the Neighborhood Reinvestment Corporation in 1978. Along with the Neighborhood Housing Services of America and networked through NeighborWorks to more than two hundred organizations with most major metropolitan areas having at least one, it provides a secondary mortgage market which encourages and protects private investments.[25]

Along with these policies, there are provisions in the federal income tax code and many state tax statutes which grant deductions for investing in neighborhood revitalization. Some foundations, most notably Ford, have also championed this cause. Combined, they have made the climate more favorable for private firms and individuals to invest their dollars and, for the latter, their own time, most frequently called "sweat equity."

Entrepreneurial Engagement

Beyond the presence of capital, neighborhood revitalization requires economic, political, and social entrepreneurs who can transform it into results. All housing initiatives within the metropolitan region are private-public partnerships but neighborhood revitalization also involves nonprofit organizations. It takes skilled performance by all three sectors to make housing competitive.[26]

Most homebuilders make money where it is easiest to do so and, for the past five decades, that has been in the suburbs. The process there is relatively straightforward: obtain a conventional loan, buy vacant land, get it rezoned, bulldoze it, and then up goes the subdivision, tens or hundreds of similar homes which can be sold with conventional marketing schemes. In central cities and inner suburbs, the project might be placing a few townhouses on an abandoned lot or industrial site, rehabbing historic units, or transforming single-family units into duplexes. All this requires learning new financing programs, understanding past architectural processes, and adopting distinctive selling strategies.

Political skill is required to assemble the funding commitments and the governmental approvals. Which federal program, administered by what agency, with which conditions, applies best? How can it be leveraged to attract state or local public dollars? Which elected and appointed officials must be lobbied, how best can each be approached, and who will receive what credit? What can be done so that the current residents see the revitalization effort as a blessing and not an invasion?

Within the neighborhood itself, there must be an ongoing presence which links the residents with the economic and political actors and reassures everyone that there is an anchoring institution. Often this is a community development corporation, described in Chapter 4, but it can also be a religious congregation, an adjoining institution like a hospital or a university, or an indigenous neighborhood association.

Residential Interest

Ultimately, of course, adequate capital and talented entrepreneurs will not be enough if too few people want to live in the neighborhood. For the central cities and inner suburbs to survive in the intraregional housing competition, they must attract middle- and upper-income households. Otherwise, their populations will decline and those remaining will be disproportionately poor.

For neighborhoods which might be in the early stages of decline, with just a few deteriorating structures and a trickle of movers, the focus is frequently on retaining the middle-class residents. This might be accomplished by attracting capital for home improvement loans, aiding owners with finding capable rehabbers, replacing the small number of substandard units with new townhouses compatible with the existing architecture, all aimed at restoring confidence and stabilizing property values. Once that stage has been reached, then there can be an effort to attract equally or slightly more prosperous residents, gradually upgrading the area.[27]

For areas that have slipped further, where for example formerly attractive single-family dwellings have either become single-room occupancy rooming houses or been abandoned altogether, the strategy might be a full-fledged turnaround, "islands of renewal in a sea of decay."[28] With schools still remaining a barrier to drawing households with children, the appeal has been to those for whom children's education is less a factor. Using an urban pioneer theme, this has sometimes been young professionals and older empty nesters. Gays and lesbians have also been a key component in many cases.[29]

Gentrification

Neighborhood revitalization success can have negative effects.[30] If the neighborhood changes character, like the Mission District in San Francisco, or Lafayette Square in St. Louis, or Capitol Hill in Washington, an outcome known as

Gentrified Neighborhood Near Downtown San Francisco

"gentrification" where middle- and upper-class residents replace poorer inhabitants, then it is no longer a welcome place for those who have recently been there. The message to them is clear: get out and stay out. The tone can become racial when it is predominately white newcomers uprooting African Americans.

But where do the displaced residents go and, once they depart, what happens to the small retail businesses they patronized? For the most part, cities have not anticipated this chain of events. As rents escalate, people are forced to leave when their leases expire, thrown into a market where there may not be viable alternatives. Businesses which cater to the poor are left without customers and they also must pull up stakes. If there is little forward planning for these transitions, then some of gentrification's positives are counterbalanced by these negatives.

AFFORDABLE HOUSING

A well-accepted federal standard holds that no household should spend more than 30 percent of its income on housing if it is to have enough money for its other basic needs. Three out of ten American households exceed this mark, meaning that in order to have adequate housing they must sacrifice other essentials. One out of eight use more than half their income for shelter.[31]   These households are disproportionately metropolitan, and regions with high housing costs like Boston and San Francisco have acute shortages. Although a majority of those affected are the poor and the elderly, about one in four are working families.[32]

Contributing to the large numbers of households unable to afford market rate housing has been the gradual reduction in units with moderate rents, that is, those available for less than thirty percent of the median wages in a metropolitan area. Between 1991 and 1997, it dropped 5 percent, almost 700,000 apartments, even as the overall stock was rising.[33] Another 200,000 were lost between 1997 and 1999.[34]

Federal Policy

National involvement in providing housing for those unable to pay for it began in the 1930s. The initial approach was for the federal government to build public housing, picking up the capital costs, and then assign local public housing authorities the responsibility for operating them. Conducted until the early 1980s, more than 1 million units remain, mostly either within the stereotypical concrete high rises or two- and three-story sterile brick buildings, usually located near the urban core.[35]

Even though these are the least desirable subsidized units, demand for them still exceeds supply. In 1999, applicants still were waiting about eleven months to obtain them.[36] The local operating authorities must cover much of the operating expenses with tenant rents, capped at 30 percent of their incomes. This creates a perverse incentive. If the poorest are chosen, rents decline and there are insufficient revenues to maintain the property. If the better off among the lower-income groups are selected so that cash flows are healthy, then those at the bottom suffer.[37]

In 1974, the federal government started shifting its emphasis from building public housing itself and instead moved toward encouraging the private sector to step forward. To stimulate supply, the policy paid developers to build new units or rehabilitate deteriorated structures by guaranteeing loans and up to forty years of rental payments. This added almost 1½ million units between the mid-1970s and the early 1980s, many of which are nearing the end of their contract period.[38] To spur demand, it gave qualified households a voucher which would make up the difference between 30 percent of their income and an area's "fair market rent."

The latter initiative, most commonly known as "Section 8," dominates the current national effort, with the government supporting over 1½ million vouchers. As project-based certificates from the 1970s and 1980s expire, many are being transformed into supply vouchers.[39] It enables low-income families to choose from a wider array of units, thereby enabling them to escape high-poverty areas.[40] Limiting this, however, is the provision that the local housing authorities administer the program. Since, typically, each metropolitan area has several such agencies, each responsible for the vouchers within its jurisdiction, this hampers flexibility in handling vouchers on a metropolitan-wide basis.[41]

Local Policy

Starting with the Reagan Administration in the 1980s, the federal government has pared its commitments to affordable housing. Having already stopped paying directly for its construction, it has also lowered the rate of increase for production subsidies and held the lid on growth in Section 8 vouchers.[42] Although it remains the largest subsidizing factor, the message to metropolitan areas was clear: start assuming more of the burden.[43]

One tool a minority of local governments had been using was rent control. Most popular in older and more expensive areas like New York City, they limit what landlords can charge, intending to keep more units accessible to low- and moderate-income households. The real estate industry has traditionally opposed them, arguing that they artificially interfere with market processes and deter new construction. Their arguments have been widely heard: more than half the state governments prohibit local jurisdictions from using them and, while about 100 remain on the books, few cities have adopted them in the past two decades.[44]

Housing trust funds have become the leading state and local response to providing support for affordable housing.[45] More than two-thirds of the states have adopted them as well as more than 100 cities and counties. Most frequently these programs tax real estate transactions, using the proceeds primarily to underwrite either new construction or extensive rehabilitation. The underlying principle is that those benefitting from the normal housing market should have some of their activity taxed to assist those not able to do so.

Instead of establishing public-housing production entities to build and administer affordable housing, state and local governments operate primarily through nonprofit organizations. Entrepreneurial agencies are entering the field to address the need, community development corporations have tapped these new sources, and more traditional nonprofits like religious congregations have added housing to their social portfolio.[46]

Elderly

The number of older persons, those 65 and up, is high and growing. As the baby boom generation ages, with the leading edge reaching age 65 in 2011, the rate will increase, peaking at about 70 million seniors in 2030. By then, one in five Americans will be in this category. People are also living longer: today one out of every seven seniors is 85 or older but, over the next five decades, that share will rise to one out of four.[47]

Most of the elderly, upwards of three out of four, handle their housing needs through the regular market. For them, affordability is not an issue. Those with low incomes can participate in conventional public-housing programs, either the owned-and-operated units or vouchers, but there are also special units for them. The largest is Section 202, part of the National Housing Act of 1959, which now accommodates more than 300,000 seniors. These units are in high demand. Each time a vacancy occurs, there are nine applicants waiting to fill it.[48]

Even older people with adequate incomes confront a housing challenge when they require some ongoing assistance with daily living because of physical limitations or mental deterioration. What once was affordable—their own home or apartment—no longer is enough. They either must receive some help within their own residence, such as hot meal delivery, or move to an assisted living facility which can provide a continuum of care. That then raises the per-unit price considerably, placing this option out of reach for more seniors unless it is subsidized either through Medicare, some other governmental program, or charity.[49]

Homeless

When all else fails, people have no permanent shelter. Their very status—having no single place to call home and often fearing any overt effort to contact them—makes it difficult to estimate their numbers but reasonably careful censuses indicate that large metropolitan areas like Philadelphia or St. Louis, on any given night, have a few thousand. City-by-city trend comparisons suggest that there are more homeless now than two decades ago.[50]

About two-thirds of the homeless are adult men, most of whom are either mentally ill or substance abusers or both.[51] The footloose hobo, riding the rails voluntarily, has vanished. About a quarter are women, roughly evenly divided between the mentally ill ("bag ladies") and the economically desperate single mothers. The remaining tenth are runaway children. The adults are relatively young, typically in their 30s, come from a background of poverty, and have become disconnected from their family and friends.

Metropolitan areas have responded by increasing the number of emergency housing shelters, most of which cater to one of the segments within the homeless population, such as single males or women with children. Nonprofits usually operate the shelters, relying both on governmental grants and private donations. Many regions have developed a sophisticated network for seeking out the homeless each evening and transporting them to whichever shelter has beds for that night.

Although shelters are a stopgap solution, responding to the symptom by supplying a safe place to sleep but not addressing any of the underlying causes for the condition, they can become the starting point for additional care and treatment. A bed and hot meal become attractive incentives for letting a suspicious homeless person allow social service professionals to develop and implement a plan for getting the individual back into the mainstream.[52]

EQUITY

The competition within metropolitan areas to attract the most socially and economically desirable residents would, in and of itself, lead to some separation by class. Once an area started to do well, that alone would cause still others to move there. Conversely, having a disproportionate number of lower-class residents would deter middle- and upper-income householders from settling, meaning that only the poor would locate in such areas. If the latter were also African American, the perceived impact on property values could be greater.[53]

These class differences then become reflected in local government policies. Elected officials in central cities with high poverty populations, seeking to attract votes from that segment, might adopt redistributive policies to assist them.[54] Suburban municipal councils, wanting to protect their residents' property values, might zone the remaining vacant land so that only individuals with similarly high incomes could afford to build on it.[55]

Combining these consequences of the competition for residents with past and present racial discrimination has contributed significantly to the economic and racial housing segregation described in Chapter 1. Those harmed by these inequities and those who sympathize with their plight have and continue to wage a public-policy war to remove the injustices within metropolitan housing markets, arguing they are inherently unfair and that, ultimately, they work against regions' common good.[56] This movement has taken three tacks: eliminating discriminatory lending and real estate practices, dispersing low-income housing throughout regions, and outlawing exclusionary zoning.

Fair Housing

The Fair Housing Act of 1968 put the federal government on record that all housing market transactions should be color-blind. The initial legislation, however, had weak enforcement provisions, placing most of the burden for correcting alleged discrimination on those experiencing it. Someone denied a mortgage or an apartment on racial grounds had to file their own complaint and, even if successfully upheld after months or even years of hearings, no fines were imposed on the discriminators. They were just told to grant the loan or lease the unit.

It was not until the 1980s and early 1990s that additional legislation provided the potential for effective enforcement.[57] Federal agencies can now bring actions on their own, state and local fair housing units could be included in these cases, fines can be levied, and damages awarded. Perhaps most importantly the national government now supports "open housing" nonprofit agencies in most metropolitan areas. These groups have been increasingly aggressive in investigating real estate steering and initiating class action suits.[58]

Dispersing Low-Income Housing

A tension exists between developing more affordable housing and making it available in each part of a metropolitan area. The least political opposition—and often some encouragement—comes from already poor neighborhoods which are seeking more assistance. But placing it there only adds to economic and racial segregation. The most uproar occurs when efforts are made to have subsidized units in middle-class areas, generating anguish that the existing homeowners' investment will be threatened.

In most regions, production has won out over dispersal despite some efforts to distribute low-income housing more widely. There are a few exceptions. Montgomery County (Maryland), one of Washington's largest suburban jurisdictions, has since 1975 required developers to build what it calls "moderately priced dwelling units" in every new subdivision, a provision which has created 10,000 residences in its first twenty-five years.[59] Also during the 1970s both the Dayton and the Minneapolis-St. Paul metropolitan areas implemented "regional fair-share plans," asking each local jurisdiction to take a portion of the federally subsidized allocation.[60]

Exclusionary Zoning

Although legal attacks on municipalities using their zoning power to limit minorities from entering their communities have sometimes succeeded in the federal courts,[61] they have continued to rule that local governments have a right to zone their land in ways that exclude low-income households.[62] The burden of proof to demonstrate an overt intent to discriminate is high, and simply having a negative impact on minorities is not enough.

At the state level, however, the New Jersey Supreme Court in 1975 said that the New Jersey Constitution did prohibit municipalities from keeping the poor away. It expanded that ruling in 1983 to give builders of low-income housing the right to sue jurisdictions who excluded them. Together, both cases have led New Jersey to take an activist approach. In 1985, the state legislature passed fair housing legislation that allocates state funds for affordable housing in areas having shortages. To date, however, no other state has followed this direction, either in the courts or through the legislature.

NOTES

1. Irving Welfeld, *Where We Live: A Social History of American Housing* (New York: Simon and Schuster, 1988), pp. 45–60.
2. *Housing at the Millennium: Facts, Figures, and Trends* (Washington: National Association of Home Builders, 2000), pg. 19.
3. *Financing America's Housing* (Washington: Federal Home Loan Mortgage Corporation, 1996).
4. Jerome Rothenberg and others, *The Maze of Urban Housing Markets: Theory, Evidence, and Policy* (Chicago: University of Chicago Press, 1991), pg. 2. The market's characteristics are drawn from this discussion.
5. Hal L. Kendig, "A Life Course Perspective on Housing Attainment," in *Housing Demography: Linking Demographic Structure and Housing Markets,* ed. Dowell Myers (Madison: University of Wisconsin Press, 1990, pp. 133–56.
6. Martha Farnsworth Riche, *The Implications of Changing U.S. Demographics for Housing Choice and Location in U.S. Cities* (Washington: Brookings Institution Center on Urban and Metropolitan Policy, 2001), pp. 4–21.
7. Alexander von Hoffman, *Housing Heats Up: Home Building Patterns in Metropolitan Areas* (Washington: Brookings Institution Center on Urban and Metropolitan Policy, 1999).
8. *The State of the Nation's Housing: 2001* (Cambridge, MA: Harvard University Joint Center for Housing Studies, 2001), pg. 7.
9. All the financial statistics are for 2000 and come from *The State of the Nation's Housing: 2001,* Appendix A.
10. Ibid., pp. 22–23.

11. Andres Duany, Elizabeth Plater-Zyberk, and Jeff Speck, *Suburban Nation: The Rise of Sprawl and the Decline of the American Dream* (New York: North Point Press, 2000), pg. 41.
12. *Housing at the Millenium*, pg. 2.
13. Edward J. Blakely and Mary Gail Snyder, *Fortress America: Gated Communities in the United States* (Washington: Brookings Institution Press and Lincoln Institute of Land Policy, 1999), pp. 74–95.
14. Alan Ehrenhalt, *The Lost City: The Forgotten Virtues of Community in America* (New York: Basic Books, 1995); and Ray Suarez, *The Old Neighborhood: What We Lost in the Great Suburban Migration, 1966–1999* (New York: Free Press, 1999).
15. Nicholas Dagen Bloom, *Suburban Alchemy: 1960s New Towns and the Transformation of the American Dream* (Columbus: Ohio State University Press, 2001).
16. Peter Katz, *The New Urbanism: Toward an Architecture of Community* (New York: McGraw-Hill, 1994); and Philip Langdon, *A Better Place to Live: Reshaping the American Suburb* (Amherst: University of Massachusetts Press, 1994).
17. Michael Leccesse and Kathleen McCormick, eds., *Charter of the New Urbanism* (New York: McGraw-Hill, 2000).
18. Rebecca R. Sohmer and Robert E. Lang, *Downtown Rebound* (Washington: Fannie Mae Foundation and the Brookings Institution Center on Urban and Metropolitan Policy, 2001).
19. Jennifer T. Moulton, *Ten Steps to a Living Downtown* (Washington: Brookings Institution Center on Urban and Metropolitan Policy, 1999).
20. Robert Lang, "Targeting the Suburban Urbanites: Marketing Central City Housing," *Housing Policy Debate*, 8, no. 2 (1997), pp. 437–70; Alice Murray, "Will Dallas Move Downtown?" *Urban Land*, 57, no. 9 (September 1998), pp. 78–82; and Rebecca Sohmer and others, "Downtown Housing as an Urban Redevelopment Tool: Hype or Hope?" *Housing Policy Debate*, 10, no. 2 (1999), pp. 477–505.
21. William C. Baer, "Aging of the Housing Stock and Components of Inventory Change," in *Housing Demography*, ed. Myers, pp. 249–73; and Rothenberg and others, *The Maze of Urban Housing Markets*, pp. 249–90.
22. Richard M. Haughey, *Urban Infill Housing: Myth and Fact* (Washington: Urban Land Institute, 2001); and Diane R. Suchman, *Developing Infill Housing in Inner-City Neighborhoods: Opportunities and Strategies* (Washington: Urban Land Institute, 1998).
23. Gregory D. Squires, ed., *From Redlining to Reinvestment: Community Responses to Urban Disinvestment* (Philadelphia, PA: Temple University Press, 1992).
24. Timothy Conlan, *From New Federalism to Devolution: Twenty-Five Years of Intergovernmental Reform* (Washington: Brookings Institution Press, 1998), pp. 44–63; and R. Allen Hays, *The Federal Government and Urban Housing: Ideology and Change in Public Policy* (Albany: State University of New York Press, 1995), pp. 187–232.
25. Edward G. Goetz, "The Community-Based Housing Movement and Progressive Local Politics," in *Revitalizing Urban Neighborhoods*, eds. W. Dennis Keating, Norman Krumholz, and Philip Star (Lawrence: University Press of Kansas, 1996), pp. 157–58.
26. For nine cases studies describing how these sectors interact in cities ranging from Cleveland to Chicago to Los Angeles, see W. Dennis Keating and Norman Krumholz, eds., *Rebuilding Urban Neighborhoods: Achievements, Opportunities, and Limits* (Thousand Oaks, CA: Sage Publications, 1999). For examples from six cities, see Elise M. Bright, *Reviving America's Forgotten Neighborhoods: An Investigation of Inner City Revitalization Efforts* (New York: Garland Publishing, 2000).
27. Sean Zielenbach, *The Art of Revitalization: Improving Conditions in Distressed Inner-City Neighborhoods* (New York: Garland Publishing, 2000), pg. 29.
28. Brian J. L. Berry, "Islands of Renewal in Seas of Decay," in *The New Urban Reality*, ed. Paul E. Peterson (Washington: The Brookings Institution, 1985), pp. 69–96.
29. Simon LeVay and Elizabeth Nonas, *City of Friends: A Portrait of the Gay and Lesbian Community in America* (Cambridge, Massachusetts: MIT Press, 1995); and Mitchell L. Moss, "Reinventing the Central City as a Place to Live and Work," *Housing Policy Debate*, 8, no. 2 (1997), pp. 471–90.
30. Maureen Kennedy and Paul Leonard, *Dealing with Neighborhood Change: A Primer on Gentrification and Policy Choices* (Washington: Brookings Institution Center on Urban and Metropolitan Policy, 2001).
31. *The State of the Nation's Housing: 2001*, pg. 22. Also see Jennifer Twombly and others, *Out of Reach: The Growing Gap Between Housing Costs and Income of Poor People in the United States* (Washington: National Low Income Housing Coalition, 2000).
32. Michael A. Stegman, Roberto G. Quercia, and George McCarthy, *Housing America's Working Families* (Washington: The Center for Housing Policy, 2001); and Suzanne Davies Withers, "Demographic Polarization of Housing Affordability in Six Major United States Metropolitan Areas," *Urban Geography*, 18, no. 4 (1997), pp. 296–323.

33. *Rental Housing Assistance: The Worsening Crisis* (Washington: United States Department of Housing and Urban Development, 2000), pg. 22.

34. *The State of the Nation's Housing: 2001*, pg. 24.

35. Alexander von Hoffman, "High Ambitions: The Past and Future of American Low-Income Housing Policy," in *New Directions in Urban Housing Policy*, eds. David P. Varady, Wolfgang F.E. Preiser, and Francis P. Russell (New Brunswick, NJ: Center for Urban Policy Research, 1998, pp. 3–22; and Roger Biles, "Public Housing and the Postwar Urban Renaissance," in *From Tenements to the Taylor Homes: In Search of an Urban Housing Policy in Twentieth Century America*, eds. John F. Bauman, Roger Biles, and Kristin M. Szylvian (University Park: The Pennsylvania State University Press, 2000), pp. 143–62.

36. *Waiting in Vain: An Update on America's Rental Crisis* (Washington: United States Department of Housing and Urban Development, 1999), pg. 1.

37. John M. Quigley, "A Decent Home: Housing Policy in Perspective," in *Brookings-Wharton Papers in Urban Affairs 2000*, eds. William G. Gale and Janet Rothenberg Pack (Washington: Brookings Institution Press, 2000), pg. 57.

38. Low-income housing tax credits, enacted in 1986 and still available, have generated an estimated 700,000 units.

39. Heather I. MacDonald, "Renegotiating the Public-Private Partnership: Efforts to Reform Section 8 Assisted Housing," *Journal of Urban Affairs*, 22, no. 3 (2000), pp. 279–99.

40. Sandra J. Newman and Ann B. Schnare, " . . . And a Suitable Living Environment: The Failure of Housing Programs to Deliver on Neighborhood Quality," *Housing Policy Debate*, 8, no. 4 (1997), pp. 703–41.

41. Bruce Katz and Margery Austin Turner, *Who Should Run the Housing Voucher Program? A Reform Proposal* (Washington: Brookings Institution Center on Urban and Metropolitan Policy, 2000).

42. Hays, *The Federal Government and Urban Housing*, pp. 233–44.

43. Edward G. Goetz, *Shelter Burden: Local Politics and Progressive Housing Policy* (Philadelphia, PA: Temple University Press, 1993), pp. 19–44.

44. Christopher Swope, "Rent Control: Invincible No More," *Governing*, 11, no. 4 (January 1998), pp. 28–29.

45. John J. Ammann, "Affordable Housing: New Opportunities and Challenges for Housing Trust Funds," *Journal of Affordable Housing and Community Development Law*, 8, no. 3 (Spring 1999), pp. 198–205; and Mary E. Brooks, "Housing Trust Funds: A New Approach to Funding Affordable Housing," in *Affordable Housing and Urban Redevelopment in the United States*, ed. William Van Vliet (Thousand Oaks, CA: Sage Publications, 1997), pp. 229–45.

46. Goetz, *Shelter Burden*, pg. 39.

47. Robert Schafer and others, *Housing America's Seniors* (Cambridge, MA: Harvard University Joint Center for Housing Studies, 2000), pp. 5–7.

48. Leonard F. Heumann, Karen Winter-Nelson, and James Anderson, *The 1999 National Survey of Section 202 Elderly Housing* (Washington: American Association of Retired Persons, 2001). Also see Stephen M. Golant, *Housing America's Elderly: Many Possibilities/Few Options* (Newbury Park, CA: Sage Publications, 1992), pp. 116–47.

49. Benjamin Schwarz and Ruth Brent, editors, *Aging, Autonomy, and Architecture: Advances in Assisted Living* (Baltimore, MD: Johns Hopkins University Press, 1999).

50. *A Status Report on Hunger and Homelessness in America's Cities 2000: A 25–City Survey* (Washington: U.S. Conference of Mayors, 2000).

51. These estimates are based on numerous studies summarized in James D. Wright, Beth A. Rubin, and Joel A. Devine, *Beside the Golden Door: Policy, Politics, and the Homeless* (New York: Aldine de Gruyter, 1998), pp. 14–19.

52. Christopher Swope, "Beyond Shelter," *Governing*, 13, no. 3 (December 1999), pp. 26–30.

53. David R. Harris, " 'Property Values Drop When Blacks Move in, Because . . . ': Racial and Socio-economic Determinants of Neighborhood Desirability," *American Sociological Review*, 64, no. 3 (June 1999), pp. 461–79.

54. Edward L. Glaeser, Matthew E. Kahn, and Jordan Rappaport, *Why Do the Poor Live in Cities?* (Cambridge, MA: Harvard Institute of Economic Research, 2000), pg. 4.

55. Henry O. Pollakowski and Susan M. Wachter, "The Effects of Land-Use Constraints on Housing Prices," *Land Economics*, 66, no. 3 (August 1990), pp. 315–24.

56. Anthony Downs, *Opening Up the Suburbs: An Urban Strategy for America* (New Haven, Connecticut: Yale University Press, 1973).

57. Michael H. Schill and Samantha Friedman, "The Fair Housing Amendments of 1988: The First Decade," *Cityscape: A Journal of Policy Development and Research*, 4, no. 3 (1999), pp. 57–78.

58. William R. Tisdale, "Fair Housing Strategies for the Future: A Balanced Approach," *Cityscape: A Journal of Policy Development and Research*, 4, no. 3 (1999), pp. 147–60.

59.   David Rusk, *Inside Game/Outside Game: Winning Strategies for Saving Urban America* (New York: The Century Foundation, 1999), pp. 178–200; and Christopher Swope, "Little House in the Suburbs," *Governing*, 13, no. 7 (April 2000), pp. 18–21.

60.   W. Dennis Keating, *The Suburban Racial Dilemma: Housing and Neighborhoods* (Philadelphia, Pennsylvania: Temple University Press, 1994), pp. 40–44. In the 1970s, the U.S. Supreme Court upheld a lower court ruling imposing a similar plan on the Chicago metropolitan area as part of a lawsuit initiated by minority residents in Chicago's public housing. See *Hills v. Gautreaux et al.*, 425 U.S. 284 (1974).

61.   See, for example, *United States v. City of Black Jack, Missouri*, 442 U.S. 1042 (1975).

62.   The cases are known as the Mount Laurel decisions (I and II). For a thorough analysis, including a discussion of subsequent unsuccessful challenges, see Charles M. Haar, *Suburbs under Siege: Race, Space, and Audacious Judges* (Princeton, NJ: Princeton University Press, 1996).

SUGGESTED READINGS

HAYS, R. ALLEN. *The Federal Government and Urban Housing: Ideology and Change in Public Policy.* 2nd edition. Albany: State University of New York Press, 1995. A thorough account of federal housing policy from the 1930s to the 1990s.

KEATING, W. DENNIS, NORMAN KRUMHOLZ, and PHILIP STAR, editors. *Revitalizing Urban Neighborhoods.* Lawrence: University Press of Kansas, 1996. Fifteen essays on various aspects of the neighborhood revitalization process, drawing on successes and failures from throughout the United States.

ROTHENBERG, JEROME and others. *The Maze of Urban Housing Markets: Theory, Evidence, and Policy.* Chicago: University of Chicago Press, 1991. A solid microeconomic analysis of how metropolitan housing markets operate.

WELFELD, IRVING. *Where We Live: A Social History of American Housing.* New York: Simon and Schuster, 1988. An entertaining exploration of housing in America, past and present.

DOING IT

1.   Get the real estate classifieds from a recent Sunday edition of the leading newspaper in a metropolitan area. For the single family homes segment, probably organized by geography within the region, how do various new and existing housing units for sale position themselves? What adjectives are used to attract households to purchase in a particular neighborhood, subdivision, or municipality? What demographic segments are they attempting to lure?

2.   Most central-city downtowns now have a written residential housing strategy. For a metropolitan area near you, obtain a copy of their plan. What types of units are being developed? Who is being sought as buyers and renters? To what extent is the plan succeeding? Major newspapers tend to cover downtown housing so those articles can be another helpful source.

3.   Identify a new urbanism project in a metropolitan area. You can search by type and region on the Congress for the New Urbanism web site (*www.cnu.org*). Where, within the region, is the project located? What is it trying to accomplish? You can supplement your description with newspaper articles.

4.   Contact the principal fair housing nonprofit agency in your metropolitan area. You can locate it on the National Fair Housing Advocate web site (*www.fairhousing.com*). Through interviews with agency officials, review of agency documents, and related newspaper articles, what actions have they taken during the past few years to make the housing market in their region more equitable?

CHAPTER 13

Open Space, Parks, and Recreation

Even as Americans have converged upon metropolitan areas, exchanging rural pastoralism for urban dynamism, they have not abandoned their affection for open space. What was sung more than fifty years ago, "Give me land, lots of land, under starry skies above—don't fence me in," still resonates today. Building outward trumps building up; people generally want shorter structures spread over wider expanses rather than higher edifices with denser populations.

Two forces are at work, one private and individual and the other public and collective. For most residents, the desired option is single-family homes on spacious lots. Almost all the land ripe for development is on the region's periphery, so the combined impact of these millions of personal decisions is pressure to expand the boundaries, to increase the land devoted to urban use, to transform agricultural and forested territory into houses, followed quickly with stores for retail shopping, and often later by offices and plants for jobs. This has generated the metropolitan expansion—urban sprawl to its critics and economic growth for its supporters—summarized in Chapter 1 and described more extensively in the next section.

At the same time that these market forces, all propelled by individual preferences, are pushing regions outward, the same people express an urgency to preserve some collective open space, to avoid an exclusively urbanized land use. They not only want their individual backyards—they also desire larger places, either left in their natural state or transformed into outdoor playing fields. Somewhat ironically, they urge public action to ameliorate the problems they themselves have helped create.

To accomplish this societal goal, citizens are increasingly turning to the political process, especially initiatives and referenda, to approve measures which set aside more land for the community as a whole.[1] In 2000, for example, the Fort

Lauderdale region's largest county (Broward) passed a $400 million bond issue for buying undeveloped land and improving parks, five counties in the St. Louis region simultaneously approved a 0.1 percent sales tax to fund a new metropolitan parks and recreation district, and Seattle adopted a higher property-tax levy for parks and land acquisition. Not all such measures pass, but more than two-thirds have been approved in the last two general elections.

ACCELERATING EXPANSION

For most metropolitan areas, urbanized land use is expanding much more rapidly than population growth, with some estimates placing the ratio at three-to-one over the past four decades.[2] Between 1982 and 1997, the urbanized acres rose 47 percent, from 51 million to 76 million, well over twice the rate of population increase.[3] A *USA Today* study found that 83 percent of the nation's 271 largest metropolitan areas added more urbanized land than they did people between 1990 and 1999.[4]

Using the Department of Agriculture's definition,[5] one which relies primarily on the number of structures per acre, the five *least dense* metropolitan areas among the million-plus segment are Atlanta, Austin, Charlotte, Greensboro, and Nashville.[6] Using the Census Bureau standard, which is the share of acres having 1,000 or more residents, the five *most expansive* within this same cohort are similar but not identical: Charlotte, Greensboro, Nashville, Raleigh-Durham, and Rochester.[7]

The lists change somewhat when measuring the rate of recent dispersion. Using the structural definition, the greatest spreading between 1982 and 1997 has occurred in Boston, Louisville, Minneapolis-St. Paul, Nashville, and Pittsburgh. By the population measure, the top five between 1990 and 1999 are Atlanta, Austin, Charlotte, Memphis, and Nashville.

Atlanta has become the poster region for rapid expansion. Its explosive population growth between 1982 and 1997, up 60.8 percent, has been outpaced by the increase in urbanized land, up 81.5 percent. The consequences are real: 68 hours delayed in traffic for the average driver in 1997, up from 16 in 1982; 40 unhealthy air days in 1998, one of the highest incidences in the nation; and a growing distance gap between entry-level job and low-income household locations.[8]

What has caused this rapid expansion? Again, it is essentially produced by Americans' residential preferences but abetting that basic thrust are three other factors: there are more Americans, so more are available to move to the periphery; the average household income has risen, so it is more affordable to act upon this desire; and the cost of commuting has dropped, making it less crucial to live near one's employment.[9] Reinforcing these trends has been the wider dispersion of jobs throughout a metropolitan area. Within the one hundred largest regions, less than one in four of the labor force now works within three miles of the traditional central business district.[10]

Not all regions are losing density at the same rate. For some, geographic settings limit dispersion. Being bordered on the west by the Pacific Ocean and on the east by mountains and deserts limits Los Angeles's ability to spread.[11] Phoenix

Atlanta: An Expanding Metro

and Atlanta have had similar population growth during the past two decades as have Las Vegas and Charlotte, but the need to remain close to scarce water sources has kept the two Southwestern regions considerably more dense than their South-eastern counterparts.[12] Less populous and demographically younger regions are also expanding more rapidly than are larger and more "elderly" metropolitan areas.

GROWTH OR SPRAWL? POLITICS AND VALUES

How to react to rapid expansion has become a central issue in most metropolitan areas. "Sprawl is now a bread-and-butter community issue, like crime," said Jan Schaffer, Pew Center for Civic Journalism Executive Director, based on a January 2000 national survey, supplemented with metropolitan samples in Denver, Philadelphia, San Francisco, and Tampa.[13] More generally, as Paul Peterson notes, "urban politics is above all the politics of land use . . . [since] land is the factor of production over which cities exercise the greater control."[14] Land control is largely the prerogative of the states and they, in turn, have delegated much of the authority to local jurisdictions who, in turn, have been allowed by the courts to exercise it broadly.[15]

Within regions, the geographic divide is between central cities and inner sub-urbs, on one side, and outer suburbs and exurbs, on the other. The former typically suffer from the expansion process. Even if there are enough people moving into the region to fuel growth at both the center and the periphery, the core is getting a lower share of it. More often, it is a net loser. This is especially so in a static region where, essentially, movement is a zero-sum game.

Those with political and economic stakes in the older areas—central-city mayors, downtown businesses, neighborhood organizations—have formed alliances with their inner-suburban counterparts in an effort, usually directed at state legislatures, to change the rules of the game. Using tools which will be described in the next section, they either want to raise the costs for developments at the edge or subsidize them for redevelopment at or near the center. In Minneapolis-St. Paul, for example, these groups have aligned to secure changes in state legislation on tax-base sharing and housing policies.[16] The political leader of this movement, Minnesota State Representative Myron Orfield, has been active in advocating similar efforts in Chicago, Philadelphia, and St. Louis.[17]

Also working to have limits set on land use growth are environmentalists.[18] Lobbying at all levels of government, they stress expansion's negative effects on traffic congestion, air and water pollution, and loss of open space, especially forests and wetlands. Joining with them are professional planners who are worried about disorderly development. Their national organization, the American Planning Association, has its own initiative devoted to countering sprawl.[19]

Below the regional level, operating within a more contained context, are exurban areas which are changing rapidly. Examples would include Loudoun County (Virginia) within the Washington region and Marin County in the San Francisco metropolitan area. Those who have moved to these jurisdictions for their spacious and gracious surroundings quickly become worried that too many are following in their footsteps. To stop the flow, they impose strict controls on further expansion.[20]

During the past decade, as this issue has risen on the public agenda, these groups have strengthened their relationships with one another. Alliances have been formed at the metropolitan, state, and national level. Since labeling a movement as "antigrowth" would be politically suspect within the American value system, symbolically placing it against progress, these efforts now usually call themselves "smart growth." The largest coalition is the Smart Growth Network, whose members include agricultural (American Farmland Trust), governmental (International City/County Managers Association), and environmental (Scenic America) organizations.

On the other side of the contest is the growth machine, the set of interests described in Chapter 4. They are the ones who benefit from new construction: homebuilders, financial institutions, materials providers, construction trades, and many others. They find it easier to ply their trade on the periphery, where land is plentiful and local governments more compliant, than near the core, where sites are more scattered and jurisdictions more bureaucratized.

The growth machine has four allies. First are the local governments benefitting from strengthened tax bases. Although keeping up with growth can be hectic and falling behind temporarily is commonplace, the rising revenues soon enable these jurisdictions to provide enhanced services. Second are those people wanting to move into the new housing. They are both voting with their pocketbooks, purchasing the homes, and with their heads, supporting policies which allow them to move freely.

Third is the prevailing political ideology. Choice and individualism are prized, control and collectivism decried. As Peter Gordon and Harry W. Richardson comment, "the principle of consumer sovereignty has played a powerful role in the increase in America's wealth and in the welfare of its citizens . . . [and] it is a giant step backward to interfere with this effective process unless the benefits of intervention substantially exceed its costs."[21] Fourth is inertia. Almost all current policies and practices promote expansion and these societal trends, once set in motion, will continue unless a significant counter force is applied.

MANAGING GROWTH

Those seeking to manage growth so that expansion is more orderly employ many strategies. Some efforts aim at the national level, altering federal practices which aid expansion and adopting those which will assist the core. Others target the states, urging them to assume a more active role in regulating land use. A smaller number address cities and counties within regions, encouraging them to spend more funds on land acquisition, and those on the periphery, urging them to be tougher on developers. Cutting across all three governmental levels are nonprofit advocacy and philanthropic organizations, lobbying for policy change and contributing financially to conservation acquisitions.

Federal

Federally funded highways, particularly interstates, are seen as influencing decentralization by shortening commuting times between the periphery and the core, making residential development at the edge more viable. Although the causal direction can be confusing—(Do limited access highways attract residential growth or do they simply track ongoing development trends?)—at a minimum the roads accelerate the change.[22]

Those wishing to control growth see highways as the enemy and fight to limit their present and future role. They advocate shifts in funding from roads to mass transit, support the ISTEA and TEA-21 provisions described in Chapter 7 which give metropolitan planning organizations more discretion in making such reallocations, and recommend subsidizing "transit-oriented development" near heavy and light rail stations.

Federal funding for conservation efforts is primarily targeted at nonmetropolitan land but there is a small program, the Urban Park and Recreation Recovery Act (1978), to assist with open space purchases. More subtly, the federal government leases significant amounts of office space in almost every metropolitan area. Various executive orders have instructed the General Services Administration to favor central-city locations and, according to a 1999 General Accounting Office report, 91 percent are now located in the core community.[23]

States

For the most part, the states are the premier governmental level for regulating land use. Although the national government can and does declare some areas to be national parks and recreation areas, relatively few are within metropolitan regions. The rest of zoning authority resides with the states. They have assigned it largely to counties and municipalities but, under Dillon's rule, they retain the ability to modify or even reverse this delegation of authority.

The starkest state involvement is Oregon's. In 1973, it passed legislation mandating that Portland and other municipalities establish "urban growth boundaries" and, by the late 1970s, this line (see Figure13–1) was in place. Inside it, development can occur although local zoning still applies. Outside the boundary, natural use, including agriculture, prevails and residential subdivisions are effectively prohibited. The boundary can be adjusted periodically to accommodate a twenty-year supply of land for future expansion but, in the short run, it is essentially fixed.[24]

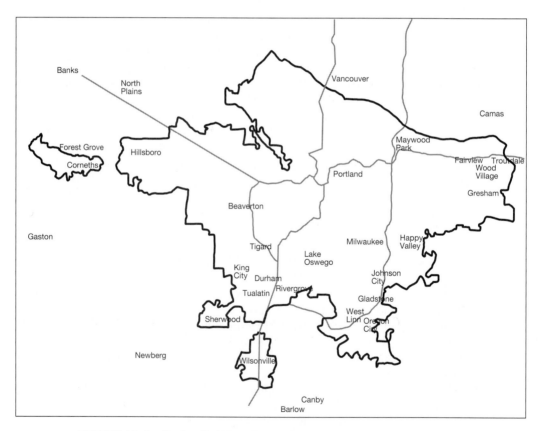

FIGURE 13–1   Portland's Urban Growth Boundary Map
Source: Portland Metro Council *www.metro-region.org*

Florida followed with its own Growth Management Act in 1985. In addition to demanding more cooperation among local and regional entities in making land use decisions, it introduced a new element, a "concurrency" requirement. So that residential development would not outpace accompanying infrastructure like public school buildings, roads, and sewers, it commands that all these be underway at least simultaneously with the residential construction.[25]

Since then, seven other states—Georgia, Maine, Maryland, New Jersey, Rhode Island, Vermont, and Washington—have implemented some type of growth management policy.[26] Washington's law, passed in 1990, combines Oregon's urban growth boundary and Florida's concurrency feature but substitutes a regional hearing body for a state agency as the overseeing entity. Its primary application has been in the Seattle region.[27]

The latest variant is Maryland's Smart Growth Program, enacted in 1997. With considerable local input, but ultimately with state control, it divides the state into two categories: "priority funding areas," which include all existing urbanized entities plus selected development targets, and everything else.[28] The state will only fund infrastructure improvements like school buildings and roads in the priority segment. The legislation also provides state assistance for land conservation.

States have been encouraged to establish regional bodies which would exercise more control over land-use zoning for their metropolitan areas.[29] These entities would still allow individual municipalities and counties considerable leeway but would have the authority to coordinate zoning across the entire region. This process exists to some extent in Florida and Oregon, and the Georgia Regional Transportation Authority, primarily focused on Atlanta, moves in this direction.

Economists worry that urban growth boundaries, by artificially restricting the supply of land available for development, will "lead to an inappropriate escalation of housing costs."[30] As Portland and Seattle add jobs and residents, for example, those seeking space for offices and homes are more limited in their choices than their counterparts in other metropolitan areas. They either must build within the boundary or forget about expanding or relocating there. That, ultimately, might slow the rate of economic growth for those metropolitan areas. The initial studies indicate that, separated from other factors, growth boundaries do not have a significant independent effect on increasing housing prices.[31]

Local

When housing subdivisions are built, ultimately infrastructure must follow. The homes will need water, sewers, and roads. If the capital costs for new water lines or expanded treatment plants or additional arterial streets are spread over a broad territory—an entire water or sewer special district or, for roads, the whole county—then other taxpayers are subsidizing those purchasing in these growth areas. This then lessens the actual price for the new residences, making them a better buy and giving them another edge in the metropolitan housing market.

To achieve greater equity by making those creating the added costs pay for them, eighteen states now allow local jurisdictions to impose "impact fees" on those purchasing these new units.[32] These are either paid by the developers, who might attempt to pass them on to the ultimate buyer through a higher price, or directly by the owners. Although their chief purposes are to make infrastructure payments fairer and to provide jurisdictions in growth areas with badly needed revenues, they can slow the pace of development by making these properties more expensive than they would be without the fees.

Calculating the impact fees is complex and can be controversial. State courts have determined that the fees cannot be simply what people are willing to pay and, instead, must be justified by some reasoned cost estimate.[33] The prevailing practice is to estimate the incremental capital costs, per housing unit, for the next five years and then assign this amount, making certain that the owner does not pay twice for any item, once through the impact fee and then again from property taxes.[34]

Individual counties or municipalities in the path of rapid growth sometimes use their zoning powers to manage its pace, most often after an antigrowth coalition has gained control of the local jurisdiction, ending a previous alliance between the growth-machine interests and the elected officials. Their tactics include zoning large segments as off-limits for development, insisting on larger lot sizes, restricting builders to high-density developments like the new urbanism projects described in Chapter 12, thereby preserving more open space, and using extensive bureaucratic approval procedures to discourage developers.

As mentioned earlier, many local governments are also passing bond issues for land conservation. Their popularity is increasing and the 2000 list alone includes units from numerous metropolitan areas ranging from several cities in the Los Angeles region (Costa Mesa, Huntington Beach, Malibu), to a major county (Alameda) within the San Francisco metropolitan area, to special districts on Denver's western edge, and on to Atlanta (City of Atlanta) in the south, Chicago (Lake County) in the Midwest, and several municipalities in New York's Westchester County.

Unilateral actions by some units within a metropolitan area to limit growth, however, do not have much impact on slowing the overall region's pace and, indeed, might accelerate it. If an outer suburban jurisdiction becomes antigrowth, the best alternative for developers is often to leapfrog over it to an area even further away from the core. As Anthony Downs concludes, local growth controls "merely shifts the region's growth to other communities less hostile to growth, often farther into the countryside [and] hence efforts by local governments to halt sprawl actually tend to aggravate it."[35]

PARKS, GREENWAYS, TRAILS, AND TREES

Metropolitan residents want open space throughout the region: spacious parks in the central city, playing fields in the suburbs, and semiwilderness areas at the periphery. Joining these are narrow greenways, often bordering creeks or streams, and, more recently, networks of trails used both for walking and cycling. As urbanization proceeds, parks are the amenity which borders on a necessity. New York

City, the epitome of high-rise density in the United States, devotes 52,938 acres, about one-quarter of its total territory, to parkland.[36]

Parks

Assigning a high priority to parks is not a recent happening. Beginning in the mid-nineteenth century, the nation's principal cities began developing expansive parks. Frederic Law Olmsted, who was the force initially behind New York City's Central Park, is the godfather of this movement and, either by imitation or Olmsted's own involvement, the older parks in metropolitan areas reflect his designing approach.[37] Instead of being the near-exclusive refuge for the noble class, as was the case in Europe, he wanted America's urban parks open to all.[38]

These urban parks have become part of the American fabric. Everyone in the region, not just the central-city residents, identifies with them: Balboa Park in San Diego, the Commons in Boston, Fairmount Park in Philadelphia, Forest Park in St. Louis, Golden Gate Park in San Francisco, Griffith Park in Los Angeles, Swope Park in Kansas City, and many more. Not unlike the professional sports franchises, they are a unifying symbol for their regions, a place shared by people from diverse economic and social backgrounds. They are a common ground, a place to escape from urban chaos, a space for relaxation and play.

New York's Central Park

They are also financially challenged. Most are owned and operated by central-city governments which, as discussed in Chapter 2, have confronted increasing social-service demands with shrinking tax bases during the past few decades. Park maintenance was an easy item to postpone. Between 1963 and 1998, for example, the New York City Parks and Recreation Department went from 6,071 to 1,156 full-time employees.[39]

One frequent response to this deterioration has been the formation of partnerships between the urban park and a nonprofit organization. In St. Louis, for example, a support group called Forest Park Forever joined forces with the city government on a master plan for redeveloping its landscape, redesigning the roads and revamping the waterways.[40] Together they have raised almost $90 million for this venture, about half from an earmarked sales tax and the remainder from private gifts.

While central-city parks' first objective is to provide refuge, green oases in concrete deserts, suburban facilities are primarily playgrounds. Catering to families, most municipalities feature a community park with athletic fields for baseball, soccer, and softball as well as courts for basketball and tennis. All this is interspersed with playgrounds and picnic sites. If these cities are to be attractive residential sites for middle- and upper-middle-income households, especially thirty-and-forty-somethings with children, having such a complex, preferably lighted at night, is essential.

Scattered throughout the central city and suburbs are neighborhood parks, small areas with less than fifteen acres. Their function is to serve the immediate surrounding area, residences within walking distance. Usually owned and operated either by the municipality or the residential association, they are sites for informal recreation, a game of catch or flying a kite, walking the dog, or taking a stroll. Again, especially for family-oriented areas, the expectation is that there will be a neighborhood park within a half-mile of every residence.

At the fringe are more rustic parks, usually operated either by state government or one of the region's counties. Aside from a few picnic sites and walker-friendly trails, their aim is to provide a semiwilderness experience within easy driving distance, often accompanied by the opportunity to observe wildlife. Since these sites can be part of the state system, metropolitan areas often lobby to have the state expand its parks at the region's edge, arguing that greater urbanized use is both more equitable—the metropolitan residents pay taxes also—and politically astute—city and suburban voters will be more likely to support state expenditures on parks.

Public demand for more parks continues unabated but it confronts two constraints: lack of available land and a shortage of funds. The recent spate of bond issues has helped with the finances but even those infusions are often inadequate for cities and counties within the region to maintain a competitive position inside their metropolitan area. Filling the gap has been a relatively new type of philanthropic nonprofit organization, the land trust. The most prominent is the Trust for Public Land. Established in 1972, it started a metropolitan initiative in 1994 and, since then, has been involved in over 250 projects. Regions have also become more creative in finding locations, converting former landfills and abandoned military bases into parks.[42]

Greenways

Unlike the prototypical urban park with its rectangular shape, greenways are linear spaces following some corridor, most often a river or stream but sometimes an abandoned railroad right-of-way or a former canal. Washington, for example, features a pair: Rock Creek Park, which winds along that stream from the Mall to the District of Columbia line and the Chesapeake and Ohio Canal, starting in the Georgetown area and heading westward along the Potomac River.[43]

Several jurisdictions have turned to greenways after one or more devastating floods along one of their waterways. In the 1970s, Denver developed a ten-mile-long version along the South Platte River. Two decades later, Kansas City has been applying a similar approach to a shorter stretch of Brush Creek. As part of its revitalization, Chattanooga has implemented a twenty-two-mile greenway along the Tennessee River and the Minneapolis-St. Paul region is laced with an intricate network dotted with numerous lakes.

Greenways offer three advantages. They use land that cannot be otherwise developed, either because it is in floodplain or, as an abandoned narrow corridor like a rail route or a canal, there is no economically viable application. Such property is less expensive to acquire. They also appeal to walkers, joggers, and bicyclists—activities increasing in popularity. For regionalists, they have a distinctive appeal since they are physical connections across a broad swath of the metropolitan area, linking otherwise diverse segments.

Their linear form, however, creates two obstacles. First, they touch hundreds and sometimes thousands of private properties. For many residences, they literally border the "back yard" in the "not-in-my-back-yard" syndrome. Fearing having a public space adjacent to their private home, many residents oppose a greenway initiative and, since their potential numbers are quite high, that can be a formidable political hurdle. Second, they frequently go through several municipalities and even counties, meaning that multiple jurisdictions need to cooperate in order to make them a reality.

Trails

As metropolitan residents become more physically active—walking, jogging, rollerblading, and cycling—their governments have responded by building more trails. The added flexibility in spending federal transportation funds, contained in the ISTEA and TEA-21 legislation described in Chapter 7, has enabled local jurisdictions to expand their efforts. In the 2000–2001 fiscal year, for example, almost a $1/4 billion in these allocations went for bicycle or pedestrian projects.[44]

Many of these trails wind through urban parks or thread along waterways. Others, such as the 47-mile Pinellas Trail stretching from St. Petersburg to Dunedin in the Tampa region, have improved an abandoned rail line with additional overpasses and expanded right-of-ways. Still other paths use existing sidewalks to link historical sites, such as the Freedom Trail in Boston or the Heritage Trail in Alexandria, Virginia. As new light rail lines are built, many are accompanied by an accompanying paved trail.

Recreation was originally the prime impetus for trail development and it still remains by far the principal reason that people use them. More recently it has been joined by the goal to reduce automobile trips, either for commuting or retail purchases, by having more walking and, especially, bicycling.[45] The number of bike trips has doubled in the past twenty years, leading not only to additional trails but also to dedicated lanes on many streets, public bicycle parking, and front-mounted bike racks on buses.[46]

Until now, each new trail tended to have its own individual story, taking advantage of some distinct opportunity, such as a railroad's ending service, to transform a corridor into a trail. As the number of trails has grown during the past decades and as public and private funding for them has increased, many metropolitan areas are now moving toward a network of trails, consciously planning to have as many as possible connect with one another. In the St. Louis region, for example, the Confluence Greenway project envisions linking all parts of the metropolitan area.

Trees

Urbanization means transforming vegetation into built structures. This both alters the landscape and affects the metropolitan ecosystem. Ogden Nash once wrote that "I think that I will never see a billboard lovely as a tree," and people simultaneously want skyscrapers and forests. Beyond adding beauty, trees conserve energy as their shade cools the air, furnish a home for birds and other wildlife, lower air pollution, and soak up water, preventing storm runoff.

American Forests, a leading study group, recommends that 40 percent of a region's land be covered by trees' canopy, 15 to 25 percent in the central city and 50 percent in the remainder, with a slightly lower mark, 30 percent, for arid regions. Their 1997 study of five metropolitan areas found that all of them fell short of that standard: Austin was best with 34 percent, followed by Baltimore at 31 percent, Atlanta with 27 percent, Milwaukee at 18 percent, and Miami with 10 percent.[47]

Only about 10 percent of a region's trees are on public property, so it requires a serious effort to have governmental action affect the overall totals.[48] Local governments not only plant and maintain trees at obvious sites like parks, but they also do so along streets and sidewalks. They can and do utilize their zoning authority. Where once developers were allowed to remove all or most of the trees when building residential subdivisions or office complexes, now they are often required to protect most of them, even if that raises the construction costs. Prince George's County (Maryland), in the Washington metropolitan area, requires housing projects to retain at least half the trees while Fulton County in the Atlanta region mandates a minimum of fifteen trees per acre.[49]

RECREATION

To compete forcefully for middle- and upper-middle-income residents, local jurisdictions must now offer an enticing array of recreational facilities and programs. Recreation addresses multiple needs: promoting healthy lifestyles, encouraging family togetherness, enjoying leisure time, and preventing juvenile delinquency. Although the most affluent Americans can and do purchase their recreation from private sources, primarily country clubs where they can control who plays alongside them, most find it more efficient to buy it collectively through public providers. As a result, all but the most exclusive suburbs are now engaged in an intensifying recreation contest.

Facilities

The recreational arms race is most apparent in leisure facilities. Take playgrounds, for example. Once adequate standard fare was a sandbox, a set of chair swings, and a seesaw. This is no longer seen as sufficient to challenge childrens' needs.[50] Now the thoroughly modern playground must include all or most of the following: landscaping to accommodate different social groupings, equipment which is imaginatively designed, and activities for children of every age between 2 and 12.

Swimming pools are another illustration. The pre-1990s conventional version had deep and shallow water segments and, perhaps, a diving board. Today's state-of-the art model includes separate pools for lap swimming and diving competitions as well as two or more water slides, one targeted for younger children and the other for older ones. What was once the local pool has now become a water park.

Golf courses are still another competitive feature. Most middle-income golfers cannot afford private club memberships and playing on for-profit courses open to all usually means long waiting lines. That makes a municipal course giving preference to residents a real plus. Local governments, wise enough to have reserved land for them years ago, are now benefitting from that decision. Those who did not sometimes try acquiring a private club which has fallen on hard times.

The latest battleground is the mammoth recreation complex.[51] Most jurisdictions had a modest community center with meeting rooms and, in some cases, a small gymnasium. That is increasingly being supplanted by multimillion complexes featuring a dizzying assortment. In metropolitan Detroit, for example, Dearborn's new center, which cost over $40 million, features two theaters, an indoor rock-climbing wall, and a five-thousand-square-foot fitness center. Its counterpart in Jefferson County, one of Denver's western suburbs, "will offer a coffee bistro, a Jumbotron TV and four sets of locker rooms—including one for families to use together."[52] Still others have ice skating rinks, bowling lanes, electronic games, and day-care centers.

Ford Community and Performing Arts Center, Dearborn, Michigan

Programs

County and municipal recreation departments offer programming for all ages and almost every interest. For ages 3 to 5, there are storytelling classes and tap dancing; for those 6 to 12, arts and crafts and children's theater; for teenagers, babysitter training and athletic competition. For twenty-somethings, sand volleyball and Taekwondo. For 30-to-50 year olds, parenting classes and dog obedience courses, and for older adults, ballroom dancing and fitness programs.

In central cities and inner suburbs, recreation programs have become part of the juvenile justice strategy.[53] Children left unsupervised in the after-school hours are prime prospects for illegal actions. Giving them appealing activities like arts and athletics delivered by trained professionals not only removes temptation but also delivers positive lessons about cooperation and conflict resolution.

Governance, Management, and Financing

Recreation departments have become major operations in most local governments, complete with their own higher education degree programs and management manuals.[54] Counties and municipalities often remove them partially from politics by inserting a parks and recreation citizens' commission with responsibility for approving programming plans, thus keeping the elected council away from these decisions.

More than any other local component, these units operate in an entrepreneurial environment. Their elected and appointed leaders expect them to help their jurisdictions keep ahead of the competition, especially the nearby suburban units. But they rarely assign these units enough general revenues to pay even one-third of the overall operating costs.[55] An earmarked tax or a bond issue might have generated the capital funds, but fees are expected to cover the day-to-day expenses.

So parks and recreation managers scramble to squeeze every possible revenue dollar from their enterprises, making them strategic players in the metropolitan area's leisure sector, competing not only with their public counterparts but also with private entities. Keeping one eye on what the competition is charging, say for a private fitness club membership, and the other eye on what the citizens want enough to be willing to pay for it, they adjust their programming to adapt to the latest fad, lease their facilities to outside groups for special events, sell advertising space on scoreboards, and hawk beverage and food concessions.

NOTES

1. Phyllis Myers, *Livability at the Ballot Box: State and Local Referenda on Parks, Conservation, and Smarter Growth, Election Day 1998* (Washington: Brookings Institution Center on Urban and Metropolitan Policy, 1999); Phyllis Myers and Robert Puentes, *Growth at the Ballot Box: Electing the Shape of Communities in November 2000* (Washington: Brookings Institution Center on Urban and Metropolitan Policy, 2001); and Alan Greenblatt, "Thumbs Up on Land for Leisure," *Governing*, 14, no. 5 (February 2001), pg. 110.

2. David Rusk, "Growth Management: The Core Regional Issue," in *Reflections on Regionalism*, ed. Bruce Katz (Washington: Brookings Institution Press, 2000), pg. 78.

3. William Fulton and others, *Who Sprawls the Most? How Growth Patterns Differ Across the U.S.* (Washington: Brookings Institution Center on Urban and Metropolitan Policy, 2001), pg. 1.

4. Haya El Nasser and Paul Overberg, "What You Don't Know About Sprawl?" *USA Today* (February 22, 2001), pg. 1.

5. *National Resources Inventory: 1997 State of the Land Update* (Washington: U.S. Department of Agriculture, 1999). This analysis is conducted every five years.

6. Fulton and others, *Who Sprawls the Most?* Appendix B.

7. The Census-based numbers come from the *USA Today* analysis and are found on its web site: *www.sprawlusatoday.com.*

8. *Moving Beyond Sprawl: The Challenge for Metropolitan Atlanta* (Washington: Brookings Institution Center on Urban and Metropolitan Policy, 2000), pp. 24–29.

9. Jan K. Bruecker, "Urban Sprawl: Lessons from Urban Economics," in *Brookings-Wharton Papers on Urban Affairs 2001*, eds. William G. Gale and Janet Rothenberg Park (Washington: Brookings Institution Press, 2001), pp. 67–71.

10. Edward L. Glaeser, Matthew Kahn, and Chenghuan Chu, *Job Sprawl: Employment Location in U.S. Metropolitan Areas* (Washington: Brookings Institution Center on Urban and Metropolitan Policy, 2001); and Robert E. Lang, *Office Sprawl: The Evolving Geography of Business* (Washington: Brookings Institution Center on Urban and Metropolitan Policy, 2000).

11. *Sprawl Hits the Wall: Confronting the Realities of Metropolitan Los Angeles* (Los Angeles: The Southern California Studies Center and the Brookings Institution Center on Urban and Metropolitan Policy, 2001).

12. Fulton and others, *Who Sprawls the Most?* pg. 15.

13. "Sprawl Now Joins Crime as Top Concern," Pew Center for Civic Journalism, February 15, 2000, press release.

14. Paul E. Peterson, *City Limits* (Chicago: University of Chicago Press, 1981), pg. 25.
15. The landmark case, decided by the U.S. Supreme Court in 1926, is *Village of Euclid v. Ambler Realty Co.*, 272 U.S. 365.
16. Myron Orfield, *Metropolitics: A Regional Agenda for Community and Stability* (Washington: Brookings Institution Press and the Lincoln Land Institute of Land Policy, 1997), pp. 74–155.
17. Rusk, "Growth Management: The Core Regional Issue," pg. 93–98.
18. See, for example, *Sprawl: The Dark Side of the American Dream* (Washington: Sierra Club, 1998).
19. *Legislative Guidebook for Growing Smart* (Chicago: American Planning Association, 1998).
20. Christopher Swope, "Rendezvous with Density," *Governing*, 14, no. 6 (March 2001), pp. 32–38.
21. Peter Gordon and Harry W. Richardson, "Prove It: The Costs and Benefits of Sprawl," *Brookings Review*, 16, no. 4 (Fall 1998), pg. 26.
22. Marlon G. Boarnett and Andrew F. Haughwont, *Do Highways Matter? Evidence and Policy Implications of Highways' Influence on Metropolitan Development* (Washington: Brookings Institution Center on Urban and Metropolitan Policy, 2000).
23. *Community Development: Extent of Federal Influence on "Urban Sprawl" Is Unclear* (Washington: U.S. General Accounting Office, 1999), pp. 14–15.
24. Peter Calthorpe and William Fulton, *The Regional City: Planning for the End of Sprawl* (Washington: Island Press, 2001), pp. 107–8; and Alexander C. Marshall, *How Can Cities Work: Suburbs, Sprawl, and the Roads Not Taken* (Austin: University of Texas Press, 2000), pp. 157–86. For a thorough account of the legislation's passage, see John M. DeGrove, *Land, Growth, and Politics* (Washington: American Planning Association, 1984).
25. Efraim Ben-Zadok and Dennis E. Gale, "Innovation and Reform, Intentional Inaction, and Tactical Breakdown: The Implementation Record of the Florida Concurrency Policy," *Urban Affairs Review*, 36, no. 6 (July 2001), pp. 836–71.
26. Hawaii also has a state-wide growth management but it has a long tradition of centralized decision making. Also see John DeGrove, *The New Frontier for Land Policy: Planning and Growth Management in the States* (Cambridge, MA: Lincoln Institute of Land Policy, 1992); and Dennis E. Gale, "Eight State-Sponsored Growth Management Programs: A Comparative Analysis," *Journal of the American Planning Association*, 58, no. 4 (Fall 1992), pp. 425–39.
27. William Fulton, "Ring Around the Region," *Planning*, 65, no. 3 (March 1999), pp. 18–21.
28. Rob Gurwitt, "The State vs. Sprawl," *Governing*, 12, no. 4 (January 1999), pp. 18–23.
29. Anthony Downs, "What Does 'Smart Growth' Really Mean?" *Planning*, 67, no. 4 (April 2001), pp. 20–25.
30. Brueckner, "Urban Sprawl: Lessons from Urban Economics," pp. 81–86.
31. Arthur C. Nelson and others, *The Link Between Growth Management and Housing Affordability: The Academic Evidence* (Washington: Brookings Institution Center on Urban and Metropolitan Policy, 2002). Also see Justin Phillips and Eban Goodstein, "Growth Management and Housing Prices: The Case of Portland, Oregon," *Contemporary Economic Policy*, 18, no. 3 (July 2000), pp. 334–44.
32. Joni L. Leithe and Matthew Montavon, *Impact Fee Programs: A Survey of Design and Administrative Issues* (Washington: Government Finance Officers Association, 1990).
33. Alan A. Altshuler and Jose A. Gomez-Ibanez, *Regulation for Revenue: The Political Economy of Land Use Exactions* (Washington: Brookings Institution, 1993).
34. Arthur C. Nelson, ed., *Development Impact Fees: Policy Rationale, Practice, Theory, and Issues* (Chicago: American Planning Association, 1988).
35. Downs, "What Does 'Smart Growth' Really Mean?" pg. 23.
36. Peter Harnik, *Inside City Parks* (Washington: Urban Land Institute, 2000), pg. 121.
37. Charles E. Beveridge and Paul Rocheleau, *Frederic Law Olmsted: Designing the American Landscape* (New York: Rizzoli, 1995).
38. Spiro Kostof, *America by Design* (New York: Oxford University Press, 1987), pp. 216–27.
39. Alexander Garvin, *Parks, Recreation, and Open Space: A Twenty-First Century Agenda* (Washington: American Planning Association, 2000), pg. 28.
40. Harnik, *Inside City Parks*, pp. 101–6.
41. Martin J. Rosen, "Partnerships: The Key to the Future for America's Urban Parks," in *Urban Parks and Open Space*, eds. Alexander Garvin and Gayle Berens (Washington: Urban Land Institute, 1997), pp. 205–17.
42. Heather Hepler, "Treez in the 'Hood: A Look at City Parks," *American City and County*, 110, no. 2 (February 1995), pp. 20–27.
43. Charles A. Flink and Robert M. Searns, *Greenways: A Guide to Planning, Design, and Development* (Washington: Island Press, 1993); and Charles Little, *Greenways for America* (Baltimore, MD: Johns Hopkins University Press, 1990).

44. *Transportation Enhancement: Final Report* (Washington: National Transportation Enhancement Clearinghouse, 2001), pg. 20.

45. Rodney Toller, ed., *The Greening of Urban Transport: Planning for Walking and Cycling in Western Cities* (New York: John Wiley, 1997).

46. Robin T. Peterson and others, "Adoption of the Bicycle as an Urban Commuter Vehicle," *Journal of Nonprofit and Public Sector Marketing,* 3, no. 3–4 (1995), pp. 25–36; and John Pucher, Charles Komanoff, and Paul Schimek, "Bicycling Renaissance in North America? Recent Trends and Alternative Policies to Promote Bicycling," *Transportation Research Part A—Policy and Practice,* 33, no. 7–8 (September-November 1999), pp. 625–54.

47. Gary Moll, "America's Urban Forests: Growing Concerns," *American Forests,* 103, no. 3 (Autumn 1997), pp. 14–18.

48. Gary Moll and Cheryl Kollin, "A New Way to See Our City Forests," *American Forests,* 99, no. 9–10 (September-October 1993), pp. 29–32.

49. Robert W. Miller, *Urban Forestry: Planning and Managing Urban Greenspaces,* 2nd ed. (Upper Saddle River, NJ: Prentice Hall, 1997), pg. 200.

50. Susan D. Hudson and Donna Thompson, "Are Playgrounds Still Viable in the 21st Century?" *Parks and Recreation,* 36, no. 4 (April 2001), pp. 54–62.

51. Charles Mahtesian, "Edifice Rec," *Governing,* 13, no. 10 (July 2000), pp. 34–36.

52. Ibid., pg. 36.

53. Ernest W. Burkeen, Jr. and Martha Arnold Alston, "Using Recreation to Prevent Violence and Drug Abuse," *Parks and Recreation,* 36, no. 3 (March 2001), pp. 80–85.

54. See, for example, Betty van der Smissen and others, eds., *Management of Park and Recreation Agencies* (Ashburn, Virginia: National Park and Recreation Association, 1999).

55. Charles Mahtesian, "Reinventing the Rec Department," *Governing,* 9, no. 3 (November 1996), pp. 34–37.

SUGGESTED READINGS

CALTHORPE, PETER, and WILLIAM FULTON. *The Regional City: Planning for the End of Sprawl.* Washington: Island Press, 2001. Examines land uses from several perspectives: architectural, ecological, economic, governmental, and social.

GARVIN, ALEXANDER, and GAYLE BERENS, editors. *Urban Parks and Open Space.* Washington: Urban Land Institute, 1997. Describes fifteen innovative projects in metropolitan areas throughout the United States, along with essays on the public sector's responsibility and partnership strategies.

HARNIK, PETER. *Inside City Parks.* Washington: Urban Land Institute, 2000. Pictures, descriptions, and statistics about city parks in twenty-five of the nation's largest metropolitan areas.

ORFIELD, MYRON. *Metropolitics: A Regional Agenda for Community and Stability.* Washington: Brookings Institution Press, 1997. An intriguing blend of social science advocacy and political strategy, all drawn from the Minneapolis-St. Paul debates about space and regionalism.

DOING IT

Every metropolitan area has its controversies about land use. With the growth machine on one side and open space advocates on the other, the sparks fly regularly and, in recent years, the mass media have given the issue much attention. Take a region which interests you and, using a newspaper index such as Lexis-Nexis, identify one or two situations where, how, and whether land should be developed became the focal point. It might have been a proposal to develop some property, widen or build an expressway, change a zoning code, or construct a bridge. Try "smart growth," "sprawl," and "growth management" as possible search terms.

For each issue, address the following questions: What started the conflict? Who wanted to do what? What arguments were used by those wishing to develop the property or support the project or back the zoning change? Who were the interests putting forth these assertions? What arguments were employed by those opposing the initiative? Which interests did they represent? Who, if anyone, tried to negotiate the conflict? What tactics did they use? What was the ultimate outcome?

CHAPTER 14

Paying the Bill

Economists often say there are no free lunches. But although it is true that someone must pay the bill that does not keep people from trying to have others pick up the tab for all or part of what they consume. It is difficult to shift the burden elsewhere when operating in the private marketplace but relatively easy to do so within the public arena. If someone wants a hamburger, for example, it is almost impossible to have some stranger pay for it. One pays the stated price and then obtains the desired product.

Exchanges are cloudier for governmental goods and services where there is seldom a one-to-one connection between what one pays and what one receives. People are not charged a specific price for, say, police protection. Instead, national and state and local governments collect taxes in numerous ways, process them through their respective budgetary routines, and then allocate them across many expenditure categories. The police officer's car may have been purchased with federal grant funds, her training might have been delivered by a state academy, and her salary paid from local property and sales taxes. Even when people pay fees for governmental services, like admission to a municipal swimming pool, the charges may be more or less than the actual cost, meaning that they are either providing subsidies to or receiving them from other taxpayers.

Efforts to pass the buck occur at all levels. For each county and municipality and special district, households seek to have their neighbors pay more than they do. Within metropolitan areas, the local jurisdictions vie to extract funds from those living elsewhere in the region by, for example, taxing shoppers or employers. Across the nation, metropolises compete for federal funds, either by having programs designed so that they favor their demographics, such as a senior citizen housing initiative supported by regions having an above average share of 65-and-older residents, or by attracting funds for capital projects like airports or bridges.

There is considerable money at stake. In 1996–1997, the most recent complete census of governmental spending, local governments throughout the United States collected over $800 billion, slightly more than $3,000 per person.[1] Since public services are generally more extensive in metropolitan areas, their average is somewhat higher. General purpose governments—counties and municipalities— account for about 55 percent of the $800 billion, public school districts for approximately 35 percent, and special districts for the remaining 10 percent.

Local jurisdictions raise about three-fifths of the $800 billion from within their boundaries and obtain the other two-fifths through intergovernmental transfers from the state and national level. For the dollars gathered internally, about three-fifths come from taxes and two-fifths from fees and charges. Property levies are the dominant taxation mode for all types of local governments. General and specific sales taxes are a distant second, raising only about $1 for every $4 collected through property taxes. Together property and sales levies account for approximately 90 percent of the local tax collections.

Deciding whom to tax or to charge fees, when and how to obtain funds from the national and state governments, and whether to incur debt are ongoing questions for local jurisdictions as they compete in both the internal and external metropolitan chase. All this occurs within an antitax mood where Americans, more than the citizens in other counties, resent governmental intrusions into their pocketbooks.

PROPERTY TAXES

Scope and Role

Within the American federal system, all levels of government impose multiple taxes but each layer has its primary source: incomes and wages (what people earn) for the national government, sales (what people buy) for most state governments, and property (what people own) for almost all local governments. For school districts, the property tax is essentially the only local source. For counties and municipalities, property tax leads the way although many also have sales and income taxes. For special districts, property tax is a stabilizing anchor to counter the ebb and flow of fees and charges.

Taxes on real estate, both the land itself as well any buildings upon it, are applied in every metropolitan area. A smaller number of states, well under half, also allow taxing either personal property such as vehicles, or intangible property like stocks and bonds, or both.[2] Property levies are expressed as a rate (e.g., $1.58) per unit of value (e.g., $100). In this example, the owner of property assessed at $100,000 would pay $1,580 annually. Depending on state law, the assessments, typically administered by county governments, can be based on market value (how much the property would be worth if it were sold), cost (how much the current

REAL ESTATE TAXES COLLECTOR OF REVENUE, ST. LOUIS COUNTY, MISSOURI Q00770430						BREAKDOWN OF YOUR TAX DOLLARS		

LOCATOR NUMBER	SCHOOL CODE	SUB CODE	AMOUNT DUE	PIN	TAX YEAR
18J510110	131	R	$6,598.60	3987	2001

DESCRIPTION	RATE Per $100	AMOUNT
ST. OF MISSOURI	.03	2461
COUNTY GENERAL	.19	15584
CO. PARK MAINT.	.035	2871
COUNTY BOND RETIRE	.085	6973
ROAD & BRIDGE	.105	8613
COUNTY HEALTH FUND	.165	13535
ST L COMM COLL	.23	18867
SPEC SCH DIST	.835	68495
METRO ZOO	.222	18211
SHELTERED WORKSHOP	.085	6973
SCH-UNIVERSITY CTY	4.99	409330
CTY-UNIVERSITY CTY	.949	77846
METRO SEWER DIST	.069	5660
MISS RIV ANTI POLL	.02	1641

<<< TAXING LOCATION >>>

BLK 10   LOT 20

0110/0050 X 0128/0129

Illustrations (barcode)

0888   0000000000   RESIDENTIAL

SEWER LATERAL   2800

35491 REV. 8/01 FMT6

RETAIN THIS PORTION OF THE BILL FOR YOUR RECORDS

PLEASE PAY EARLY

Missouri Law mandates the assessment of a late penalty and interest for taxes that remain unpaid by 12 midnight, on December 31st of the tax year. The interest charged is 2% per month, or any part thereof, not to exceed 18% per year, plus a 2% penalty.

Compliance with this law (139.100 & 140.100 R.S. Mo. 1994) for payments made by mail requires a United States Post Office postmark on or before December 31st.

Real Estate tax payments may be made on-line by accessing St. Louis County's web site at WWW.STLOUISCO.COM and authorizing a direct debit to your checking or savings account.

You may pay Personal Property and Real Estate Taxes with one check. Please use either enclosed envelope or mail to the Collector of Revenue, 41 South Central Ave., St. Louis, Missouri 63105.

"Make checks payable to Collector of Revenue"

TEAR HERE AND RETURN LOWER PORTION WITH PAYMENT

A Property Tax Bill from St. Louis County, Missouri

owner paid for it), or, for business or rental property, its income potential (how much it can earn).

Most households are subject to property taxes from several different jurisdictions: the municipality, the county, the school district, and perhaps a few special districts. Many pay real estate taxes as part of their mortgage payment with all these separate levies combined into a single item, making it confusing to determine how much goes to each entity. Merging the bills for these levies makes the total property tax loom large among the household's obligations.

This lump sum payment practice combined with complaints about assessment inequities—many often think that the government assigns a higher value to their property than is merited—has made the property tax increasingly unpopular. The annual surveys conducted by the Advisory Council on Intergovernmental Relations between the 1970s and the 1990s usually found that it competed with the federal income tax for being the "worst" and "least fair" tax.[3] As a result, its share is gradually declining, especially for those municipalities and counties which have other tax options.[4]

Incidence

Taxing property to pay for local services seems equitable. There is a rough parity between how much property someone occupies and how many local governmental goods they consume. For items like police and fire protection and street maintenance, the connection is quite close. For other services, such as public education, the direct correlation is lower since not every household has school age children but, in a general way, everyone's property value benefits from having a strong school system.

To the extent, however, that middle- and lower-income families spend a greater share of their income on housing than do upper-income households, then the property tax is regressive, taking proportionally more from the lower end of the economic spectrum than it does from the higher segments. A family earning $50,000 a year might easily spend $12,500, or 25 percent, of their earnings on their residential property. That, on average, would be a *higher fraction* than, say, a household bringing in $500,000 a year which would probably spend no more than $50,000, or 10 percent, of their income on housing.[5]

Assessing different property classifications at separate rates also affects who pays how much. In several states—examples include Arizona, Kansas, Missouri, and Tennessee—commercial and industrial sites have higher levies than do residential units, thereby placing more of the burden on them and, if they are able to pass it through, on their customers. In even more states, agricultural land has the lowest rates of all. In the exurban portions of metropolitan areas, this provides still another incentive for local governments to rezone farming property to residential or commercial since, even without additional development, the classification change alone will generate more revenue.

Issues

The concern that the property tax hits hardest on poorer households, especially on senior citizens living on fixed incomes, has led most states to implement "homestead exemptions" and more than thirty states to establish "circuit breakers." The former require local units to exempt the first "x" thousand of assessed value of residences from taxation, a benefit that means relatively more for families with modest homes. The latter provide a credit against the state income tax either for persons over a certain age, usually 60 or 65, or for those below some income threshold. For homestead exemptions, the state is mandating that the local units receive less revenue but, for circuit breakers, the governments still receive the property tax payments, which are then offset by the state lowering the income tax.

For those counties using market value to determine how much property tax households and businesses pay, there are ongoing disputes about disparities between them. The exurban units often have elected assessors responsible for this task while their urban and suburban counterparts have appointed officials applying a professional process, usually a predictive equation based on sales of comparable property. Since those elected have a political incentive to keep rates down, this can mean lower charges at the periphery than in the core.

This, in turn, becomes part of a larger property tax competition among a region's local governments. On the one hand, they want relatively high property tax revenues to provide quality services which will attract and retain residents and enterprises. But if the rates become too onerous, then a municipality or a school district can become overpriced compared to its neighbors, making it less attractive as a place to live or do business.[6]

SALES TAXES

Scope and Role

Taxing consumption is common in most industrialized countries but it is usually accomplished through a "value-added" tax, initially applied to businesses at each stage in the production and distribution process and then captured in the overall price at the time of purchase. When one buys a sweater in France, the tax is contained within the price tag on the item and, to some extent, is hidden. In the United States, on the other hand, a sales tax—some percent of the retail tab—is added when the transaction is completed.

The first sales tax was established in 1932 and now all but five states impose a general sales tax, one which applies to all or most retail transactions. Fewer, however, share this mechanism with their local governments: about three-fifths of the states allow counties and about half allow municipalities to enact separate levies. Even these states want to retain the bulk of the revenues for their own purposes. As a consequence, the local jurisdictions are limited to a minor slice, typically a rate between 0.5 percent and 2.0 percent. In a few states, selected special districts are also allowed to apply a modest sales tax.[7]

In addition to general sales taxes, many states allow levies on specific items. The most common are those imposed on visitors through taxes on lodging, restaurant meals, and rental cars—an effort to squeeze even more revenues from nonresidents. Other frequent targets are public utility (cable television, electricity, natural gas, telephone, water) charges, motor fuel, amusement venues, and tobacco products.

Even though the average household pays upwards of two thousand dollars a year in state and local sales taxes, they are less unpopular than either property or income taxes. In large part, this is because people pay them in small increments, a few cents here and, even on larger items, a modest amount of dollars there. This lower resistance, in turn, has made them an increasingly attractive taxation target.

The fact that businesses rather than government do the actual collection adds to their popularity.

Incidence

The higher a household's income, the less it spends on items subject to the sales tax. That means that the less well off pay proportionally more in sales taxes.[8] To help counter some of this regressivity, most states exempt certain necessities. Almost all exclude prescription drugs and over half also eliminate food. These prohibitions usually apply to both the state and local components of the sales tax.

Municipalities and counties with major retail centers are especially fond of general sales taxes since many of the shoppers come from outside their jurisdictions. Although it costs them a bit to provide services to these nonresidents, most notably police protection, the taxes they pay considerably outweigh the costs, allowing these units either to lower taxes for their own residents or furnish additional services to them.

The principal drawback, for local units, is that sales-tax revenues are less reliable than property-tax receipts. The latter are based on property valuation, which rises incrementally every year and almost never declines. What sales taxes produce, conversely, varies with the amount people buy. In economic downturns, discretionary spending drops, especially for pricier items like vehicles and appliances with greater sales tax potential. That then causes dips in municipal and county revenues.

Issues

What sales should be taxed is an ongoing debate. Beyond the food and drug exemptions, many other businesses seek to find reasons why their products should be exempt. In many states, for example, newspapers have won a dispensation by successfully arguing that they are essential to an informed electorate. In a few states, department stores have been able to add clothing to the food-and-drug essential list.

The largest discrepancy is between goods and services, with the former largely taxed and the latter typically excluded. As the service economy has grown over the past several decades, state and local governments have been tempted to extend the sales taxes to that sector, covering activities like advertising, legal charges, and real estate broker fees. Florida broke this barrier in 1987, applying its tax to many of these items, but the political backlash caused a speedy retreat and, within two years, it was abolished.[9] Since then, no other government has dared try.

Worse yet for state and local governments, the share of goods sold through traditional retail outlets has been steadily declining. First, mail order catalog sales started to cut into local markets and, more recently, electronic commerce through the Internet has gained.[10] Although state and local governments can tax catalog items used within their boundaries, the U.S. Supreme Court has ruled that they cannot require out-of-state retailers to collect them, making administration and enforcement difficult.[11] Those selling over the Internet have persuaded the U.S.

Congress to ban sales taxes on electronic purchases in order to encourage their fledgling enterprises and avoid confusion over what is taxed at what rate in which jurisdiction.[12]

The competition for sales-tax revenues often generates a contest among municipalities for attracting large retail outlets like a Home Depot or Circuit City. These "big box" developments attract shoppers within a wide radius and, for a currently underserved market, are open to locating in any one of the suburban cities. This then ignites a bidding war among these jurisdictions, often using property tax incentives and infrastructure improvements to woo the store.

OTHER LOCAL REVENUE SOURCES

Income Taxes

Although the federal and state governments rely heavily on taxing personal and corporate income, it is a significant revenue source among local governments in only six states: Kentucky, Michigan, Missouri, New York, Ohio, and Pennsylvania. If applied to personal incomes, it is usually a flat rate. When imposed on businesses, it sometimes taxes payrolls (a percentage of the total wages) or jobs (a set fee per employee). In other cases, it applies to that part of a business's income which can be legitimately allocated to that jurisdiction.[12]

Central cities have been the primary wielder of income and business taxes. The deep corporate coffers and the highly paid managers, many of whom live in the suburbs, present opportunities to retrieve some revenues for expensive urban services, including those required by low-income residents and aging infrastructure. As businesses have become more mobile, with many no longer believing that a downtown site is required for their enterprise, avoiding both personal and corporate income taxes has been another incentive pushing them toward suburban settings. This, in turn, has prevented most jurisdictions from considering adding income levies and caused those currently using them to reconsider how they affect their intrametropolitan competitiveness.

User Charges

The closer a governmental service resembles a private good, the more likely that the municipality or county or special district will charge people a fee for using it rather than paying for it from general revenues. Relatively pure public goods like police protection apply to everyone. It would be difficult for each person to hire round-the-clock security guards. Playing golf on the municipal course, however, differs little from doing so at a private club and, consequently, there is almost always a fee for doing so. In addition to recreational facilities and programs, local governments apply user charges to bridge crossings, cultural institutions, health services, mass transit, parking, trash collection, and utilities.[13]

Beyond raising funds, user charges promote equity by requiring the consumer to pay for all or most of the service. Citizen satisfaction is often higher, both because residents see the direct connection between what they pay and what they receive and, for discretionary items like recreational programs, they can choose whether or not to purchase them. You must pay property taxes for police services but you are not required to buy a swimming pool pass.

Pricing services can be complex. Should the charge recover all the costs or should the general revenues subsidize some cases, such as free recreation programs for low-income children? What market factors must be considered? If mass-transit rates are set too high, will so many passengers shift to automobiles that overall revenues will decline? If the tennis-court fees go beyond a certain level, will players take their business to private facilities? To deal with these factors, local governments must blend both collective interests—what's best for the community—and market considerations—what will consumers tolerate—as they determine what to charge.

INTERGOVERNMENTAL TRANSFERS

Role and Scope

The United States federal system creates an enormous financial contest among local governments. The national and state governments gather upwards of $3 trillion in taxes annually. Although most of these funds are spent on things which either benefit everyone, such as aircraft carriers for national security, or on individual assistance, like social security payments for senior citizens, about half a trillion, roughly evenly divided between national and state grants, are returned annually to local jurisdictions. These funds, called intergovernmental transfers, become the prize in an intense competition both among and within metropolitan areas. While there have been occasional dips in the transfer funds, the overall trend for the last three decades has been upward.[14]

This half a trillion amount understates the dollars at stake in the metropolitan chase since they represent only those funds directly transferred to local governments. Also in play are infrastructure projects like airport expansions or new bridges, where the funds go straight from the higher government to private contractors. In these situations, regions compete on behalf of proposals from their areas. In addition, how individual assistance dollars are distributed can affect winners and losers within metropolitan areas. Central cities, home to a disproportionate number of low-income households, push for programs like the Earned Income Tax Credit since it provides billions in benefits for the working poor.[15]

Incidence

Local jurisdictions do not make good Robin Hoods. If they heavily tax the rich in order to help the less fortunate in their communities, then the affluent residents will simply choose another nearby locale in which to live while, at the same time, more poor will come to take advantage of the assistance.[16] The same logic applies to businesses: if they are hit too hard with levies, many will relocate and fewer will enter. Consequently, to remain competitive within their regions, municipalities generally avoid using their own tax system to redistribute resources across income categories.

Even states find it challenging to enact redistributive taxes for much the same reasons. For individuals, states' larger borders makes it more difficult for the wealthy to flee in order to avoid a hefty lug although, over time, more will bypass such a state for one which takes less from their pocketbook. It presents a more serious obstacle for economic development. States with very progressive taxes which draw disproportionately from upper-income persons and profitable enterprises are hampering their ability to compete. So, while states often do some modest redistribution, they rarely go beyond that.

That leaves the national government to achieve whatever significant redistribution is to occur. Relatively few will leave the country because of its tax policies. Since two of its primary revenue sources, the personal income tax and the corporate income tax, do take more proportionally and absolutely as earnings rise, even if it spreads those funds evenly across the income spectrum, the net effect is redistributive. If it devotes relatively more to programs like public housing or job training, then the impact is even higher. Somewhat ironically, tax dollars from a wealthy suburban enclave can ultimately end up in an impoverished neighborhood in that same region's central city, but only after it has gone to Washington and back.

Issues

The governments which are transferring the funds—national to state and local as well as state to local—want to maintain maximum control over how they are spent. Since they are taking the political heat for raising the taxes, they at least want to receive the credit for the benefits they may produce and, to do so, they typically insist on having certain conditions met. The receiving governments, on the other hand, want as much discretion as possible. They claim that, since they are closest to the people and best understand their needs, the sending governments should trust them to do the right thing.

As they dispense aid, however, national and state governments rarely have faith that the local units will end up doing what they are supposed to accomplish. They fear inefficiency and diversion. But since the higher-level governments are not directly spending the funds themselves, they must employ various implementation tactics to make the lower units conform to their wishes, such as by mandating expenditures (e.g., crime funds must go to hire police patrol officers) or insisting on outcomes (e.g., highway allocations will only be made if air quality is satisfactory).[17] Not unlike children chafing under their parents' orders, local governments frequently seek ways to evade these restrictions through creative redefinitions (e.g., a juvenile detective sometimes goes out on patrol) or one-time exceptions (e.g., give us another chance to meet the air quality standard).

With so many dollars up for grabs, local jurisdictions devote considerable political energy and staff capacity to seeking them. For categorical grants, allocations for specific projects, they hire grant writers to make the best possible case. They then use their state or national legislators to lobby executive departments on their behalf, reaffirming the principle that all politics is local. As they run for reelection, these officials often brag about how much they have been able to deliver for their metropolitan area.

The categorical struggle is fought project by project. Other allocations like federal community-development funds and state educational aid are based on formulas which are part of the statutory language. In these situations, the battle is waged in the legislative chambers with similar jurisdictions, acting both individually and through associations, pleading their cases. Older cities might urge that the proportion of housing built before 1939 be part of the federal community-development formula, good for a Cleveland or Pittsburgh but not so beneficial for a Las Vegas or Phoenix. Central-city school districts might push for including the number of poverty households in the education aid formula while suburban districts might desire more credit for population growth rates.[18]

CAPITAL AND DEBT

Like individuals borrowing for homes and businesses for buildings, so also local jurisdictions must incur debt, committing future years' resources in order to meet current needs. Many of the services within a metropolitan area are capital intensive: airport terminals, bridges and roads, mass-transit lines, school buildings, sewer-treatment plants, and more. If local governments had to finance these on a pay-as-you-go basis, they would rarely happen. Just as a young couple would not want to postpone having a nice residence until they could save the entire purchase price, so too communities would not wish to forgo critical facilities until they could accumulate adequate funds from taxes.

Equity also argues for using debt to underwrite long-term capital initiatives. A recreation complex or a high school will be used for several decades. Why should the present taxpayers foot the entire bill for future generations? Some will move away and others will die long before the facility becomes obsolete, thereby not receiving a full return on their investment. By handling such initiatives on the installment plan, especially if the payment period, say thirty years, closely matches the useful life of the project, then each round of participants contributes to its construction cost.

The amount of local governmental debt has risen steadily over the past decades. It is approaching $800 billion, about double what it was fifteen years ago, and grows by $30 to $50 billion annually. Although this is less than 20 percent of the federal debt, it is still a significant sum, reflecting the growing complexity of metropolitan regions. It is about half again as large as state debt, demonstrating that the local jurisdictions bear the brunt for paying for the capital costs of most public projects serving community needs.

Although states do not incur the bulk of the debt for local projects, they do impose significant constitutional or statutory limits on capital financing, especially for counties, municipalities, and school districts. These restrictions are usually expressed as a proportion of a unit's assessed property valuation so that, for example, it can only have indebtedness up to 10 percent of its total worth. They also confine debt for capital initiatives, forbidding local governments to borrow money to cover a shortfall in operating expenditures.

Local units and their allies have chafed under these constraints and, with considerable success, have developed alternative financing mechanisms. Often the state limits apply only to general obligation bonds, those backed by the "full faith and credit" of the issuing government where it must use any and all of its taxes and assets to repay the bondholders. Such debt still exists but it now is only about two-fifths of the overall total, a share decreasing over time.[19]

To avoid this ceiling, many projects now use revenue bonds, instruments backed by dollars generated by the initiative such as tolls from a bridge, entrance fees for a swimming pool, or residential charges for a sewer treatment facility. This makes the proposition riskier for the investors since they can no longer rely on the local government's entire fiscal capability. Instead, investors must determine whether the individual project is economically viable for, if it fails to produce an adequate return to cover the debt repayment, they will lose their investment.

Since the state limits also usually apply only to general purpose governments, another circumvention strategy for metropolitan areas has been to form and use the public authorities described in Chapter 2 as the debt issuers. For instance, when Atlanta won the 1996 Summer Olympics, it persuaded the State of Georgia to establish the Metropolitan Atlanta Olympic Games Authority. That vehicle could then raise debt for facilities which could ultimately be repaid by the subsequent visitors to the events.[20] The grandest example is the Port of New York Authority which has sponsored the bonds for much of that metropolitan area's infrastructure.[21]

When local governments decide they need more money for operating expenses, they can increase taxes or raise user fees. Those taxed or charged might not like paying more, but they have little choice other than exiting the jurisdiction or avoiding the service. When local units issue debt, however, they cannot require that anyone purchase the bonds. They must compete in a private market for investors, a market which includes both business and governmental competitors.

The price paid for debt is interest and a small change in rates can make an immense difference over a twenty- or thirty-year repayment period. Even a tenth of a percent difference, say 5.4 percent compared to 5.3 percent, can amount to paying millions more over the entire funding cycle on a $100,000,000 project. In the rivalry for investors, local governments have one edge over their private sector counterparts: interest on their debt does not count as income under the federal code, making it nontaxable.[22] This means that, on average, the price local governments must pay for borrowed money is less than the private sector's tab.

Among local governments, the interest rates they pay depends largely on their ratings by the three independent organizations which assess creditworthiness: Fitch Investors Service, Moody's Investor Service, and Standard & Poor's.[23] For revenue bond projects, the chances that they will generate enough business predominates. For general obligation bonds, the factors include expectations about the issuing government's future tax base, how much debt is already outstanding, and how

Tampa's Sunshine Skyway Bridge: A Revenue Bond Project

much power the unit has to increase revenues. Growing municipalities and counties with little existing debt and strong authority pay less interest than declining units with high debt and limited power.

Defaults on local government bonds are rare but it happens often enough to remind investors that the risk is real. New York City and Cleveland had temporary defaults in the 1970s but were ultimately able to cover their obligations. In the 1980s, on the other hand, the Washington Public Power Supply System, a public authority, declared bankruptcy, making $2 billion of their bonds worthless. Most recently,

Orange County, one of the Los Angeles metropolitan area's largest governments, went bankrupt although their high stakes investment practices were the primary cause.[24]

TAX LIMITATIONS

Former U.S. Supreme Court Justice Oliver Wendell Holmes once wrote that "taxes are the price we pay for civilization" but even that reminder about their ultimate purpose does not make people happy about paying them. The property tax, the primary revenue source for local governments, has been especially unpopular and, over time, that has led to restrictions on its use. Most have been instituted by state legislatures but, during the past few decades, others have been implemented through citizen initiatives. The latter include Proposition 13 in California (1978), the Hancock Amendment in Missouri (1980), and Proposition 2 1/2 in Massachusetts (1980).[25] Colorado and Florida passed their own constraints in 1992.[26]

All but four states place one or more limits on local governments' use of the property tax. A majority establish a maximum rate, either for all property or for some classifications. About half restrict how much units can gain from higher reassessments, keeping local governments from fully benefiting from increases in property value. If the revenue would exceed a set cap, the units must lower the tax rate so that the revenues are not greater than the limit. In Missouri, for example, the growth cannot exceed the consumer price index or 5 percent, whichever is lower.

Seven states, including California, Florida, and New York, limit how much a property's assessed value can rise in any given year. California's is among the strictest, inflation up to a maximum of 2 percent, and Florida's is almost as tight, inflation up to 3 percent. A few states limit overall revenues and expenditures and many require voter approval for tax and fee hikes, especially those required to fund bond issues.

These stipulations cause three effects. First, as intended, local governments spend less than they otherwise would, especially in states with the most stringent provisions.[28] Second, it has spurred local units to increase user fees and seek more intergovernmental assistance. Third, for states mandating voter referenda, it has shifted priorities to those programs and facilities more easily marketed in a public campaign.

TAX SUBSIDIES

Tax policies are an important instrument in the economic development competition among municipalities and counties within metropolitan areas. As local units contend for commercial, manufacturing, and retail projects, promising some type of tax break can enhance their appeal. Elected officials find it is politically more palatable to reduce a business's taxes than to allocate it some funds. Even though the effect is economically identical, the former can be labeled an incentive while the latter is apt to be called a handout.

Prior to the passage of the Tax Reform Act of 1986, industrial revenue bonds were the primary device. Since local governments' debt was exempt from federal income taxes, it could use its bonds to construct facilities for private businesses at a lower interest rate than the enterprises would incur if they had to borrow it themselves. These factories or warehouses were then leased to the companies with the payments covering the principal and interest obligations. When the bonds were retired, the businesses received title to the facilities.

At the local level, it was a win-win situation: the community gained a new business and the business secured a structure at a reduced price. The only loser was the national government which lost the tax revenues it would have reaped if the enterprise had used private funding where the bondholders paid income taxes on their interest earnings. The 1986 legislation essentially closed this loophole by requiring that local government revenue bonds could only be used for public purposes.[29]

Since then, another abatement mechanism—tax increment financing (TIF)—has become the principal tool, now employed in every state except Delaware and North Carolina.[30] As it is normally applied, a TIF "freezes the assessed valuation of all parcels in a designated area."[31] The additional property taxes raised from the development—a shopping mall or an office center, for example—are then dedicated to public improvements at or around it. These might include widening streets, building parking garages, expanding sewer lines, installing lighting, and so forth. Since these enhancements must be done before or simultaneously with the private development, the local government issues revenue bonds backed by the tax increment to fund them. Because the dollars are paying for public items, albeit ones boosting the private enterprise, they still qualify for federal tax exemption.

The widespread availability of TIFs has encouraged developers to play one municipality or county off against another in a contest to see which is willing to give the largest breaks and the best improvement package. Even the winning local government must forgo using the extra revenues produced by a new development across all its services for upwards of twenty years since, under the TIF, they are committed to paying off the bonds which financed the property enhancements.

School districts and other special purpose governments which share a property tax revenue base with municipalities and counties are often losers in the TIF wars. The general purpose governments usually possess the authority to make a TIF deal unilaterally. But since the arrangement keeps the assessed valuation from rising, it means the other districts will not receive the benefits from the development until the bonds have been retired. What might be a good deal for the municipality or county, limiting their property taxes in return for more jobs or greater sales, rarely helps the districts since jobs or sales do not translate into more revenues for them.

TAX SHARING

As separate jurisdictions within a metropolitan area compete for development, a big box retailer here and a manufacturing facility there, inevitably some win and others lose. Over time, as the presence of one facility attracts still more developments, certain units have robust tax bases, more than ample to meet their service needs. They can either lower their residents' taxes, letting the business revenues pay for existing services, or add more programs and facilities to the public offering. Should the victorious local governments be able to keep all the spoils, the full array of property and sales taxes generated by the project, or should they share some of them with others in the region?

Those who have successfully pursued investment typically claim that they should be able to retain their winnings. It is both an appropriate reward for their entrepreneurial skills and a justified payment for their willingness to mix businesses with their residences. The proponents for sharing some of the proceeds make three arguments. First, if everyone benefits from developments, jurisdictions will not be so generous with incentives like tax incremental financing, businesses will not be able to leverage local governments, and more money will be retained for public purposes. Second, neighboring jurisdictions often incur some additional costs from development, such as more traffic going through their borders to reach a shopping center or an office complex. Third, the metropolitan area is an integrated whole and spreading the wealth will ultimately make for a stronger region.[32]

For the most part, the keep-it-at-home perspective prevails. In all but a few metropolises, local government retains all the tax revenues. The most extensive exception is the Minneapolis-St. Paul region. In 1971, the Minnesota legislature passed the Fiscal Disparities Act which applies to all counties within the Twin Cities metropolitan area.[33] Two-fifths of all post-1971 assessed valuation increases on commercial and industrial sites goes into a common pool, a single property tax rate is applied, and it is then allocated based on a municipality's population and property values. The more people and the lower the assessed value, the higher the allotment, thereby redistributing revenue from the stronger to the weaker tax-base jurisdictions. By the mid-1990s, the pool contained $367 million, about one-fifth of the region's tax base.[34]

Montgomery County, the Dayton metropolitan area's largest jurisdiction and the one containing its central city, implemented an experimental tax-sharing program for economic development in the early 1990s.[35] The County commits $5 million annually and municipalities, singly or cooperatively, apply to use these funds for developments. In return, they agree to share some of the benefits with the other participating units. The net effect has been some lessening of the differences between the haves and the have-nots.[36]

A final variation of tax redistribution has been burden sharing. This approach takes institutions like zoos and museums which had been supported typically by the central city or the largest county and spreads the support over two or more counties. The City of St. Louis and St. Louis County, for example, formed a Zoo-Museum District in the early 1970s, and it now includes five entities, each supported by a property-tax levy.[37] In 1988, six counties in the Denver metropolitan area formed the Scientific and Cultural Facilities District and approved an earmarked sales tax to support it.[38]

NOTES

1. Unless noted, all governmental financial data are from the U.S. Bureau of the Census's Census of Governments conducted every fifth year in years ending in "2" and "7."

2. Ronald John Hy and William L. Waugh, Jr., *State and Local Tax Policies: A Comparative Handbook* (Westport, Connecticut: Greenwood Press, 1995), pg. 159.

3. In 1991, for example, it led the "worst" list with 30 percent. See *Changing Public Attitudes on Government and Taxes: 1991* (Washington: Advisory Commission on Intergovernmental Relations, 1991), pg. 4.

4. Chris Hoene, "History, Voters Not Kind to Property Tax," *Nation's Cities Weekly*, 24, no. 9 (May 14, 2001), pg. 3.

5. For a full airing of these issues, see Henry J. Aaron, *Who Pays the Property Tax?* (Washington: Brookings Institution, 1975); and Wallace E. Oates, editor, *Property Taxation and Local Government Finance* (Cambridge, MA: Lincoln Institute of Land Policy, 2001).

6. Dick Netzer, "Property Taxes: Their Past, Present, and Future Place in Government Finance," in *Readings in State and Local Public Finance*, eds. Netzer and Matthew P. Drennan (Cambridge, MA: Blackwell Publishers, 1997), pp. 174–97.

7. William F. Fox, "Importance of the Sales Tax in the 21st Century," in *The Sales Tax in the 21st Century*, eds. Matthew N. Murray and Fox (Westport, CT: Praeger, 1997), pp. 1–14; and Joseph A. Pechman, *Who Paid the Taxes, 1966–85?* (Washington: Brookings Institution, 1985).

8. Donald Phares, *Who Pays State and Local Taxes?* (Cambridge, MA: Oelgeschlager, Gunn and Horn, 1980); and Andrew Reschovsky, "The Progressivity of State Tax Systems," in *The Future of State Taxation*, ed. David Brunori (Washington: Urban Institute Press, 1998), pp. 161–89.

9. Walter Hellerstein, "Florida's Sales Tax on Services," *National Tax Journal*, 41, no. 1 (March 1988), pp. 2–18.

10. Thomas Bonnett, "Technological Change and Tax Policy: The Future of State and Local Tax Structures," *Government Finance Review*, 14, no. 6 (December 1998), pp. 45–47.

11. Hy and Waugh, *State and Local Tax Policies*, pp. 102–5.

12. *Critical Issues in State-Local Fiscal Policy: A Guide to Local Option Taxes* (Denver, CO: National Conference of State Legislatures, 1997), pp. 21–24.

13. John L. Mikesell, *Fiscal Administration: Analysis and Applications for the Public Sector*, 5th ed. (Orlando, FL: Harcourt Brace, 1999), pp. 436–45.

14. Timothy Conlan, *From New Federalism to Devolution: Twenty-Five Years of Intergovernmental Reform* (Washington: Brookings Institution Press, 1998); and David B. Walker, *The Rebirth of Federalism: Slouching Toward Washington* (Chatham, NJ: Chatham House, 1995).

15. *Rewarding Work: The Impact of the Earned Income Tax Credit* (Washington: Brookings Institution Center on Urban and Metropolitan Policy, 2001).

16. Paul E. Peterson, *The Price of Federalism* (Washington: Brookings Institution, 1995), pp. 27–33.

17. See, for example, Martha Derthick, *The Influence of Federal Grants* (Cambridge, MA: Harvard University Press, 1970); and Paul L. Posner, *The Politics of Unfunded Mandates: Whither Federalism?* (Washington: Georgetown University Press, 1998).

18. For more on state education aid formula debates, see Daniel DiLeo, "The State-Local Partnership in Education," in *Governing Partners*, ed. Russell L. Hanson (Boulder, CO: Westview Press, 1998), pp. 109–38; and Joseph F. Zimmerman, *State-Local Relations: A Partnership Approach*, 2nd ed. (Westport, CT: Praeger, 1995), pp. 71–75.

19. Mikesell, *Fiscal Administration*, pg. 542.

20. Alberta M. Sbragia, *Debt Wish: Entrepreneurial Cities, U.S. Federalism, and Economic Development* (Pittsburgh, PA: University of Pittsburgh Press, 1996), pg. 137.

21. Robert A. Caro, *The Power Broker: Robert Moses and the Fall of New York* (New York: Alfred A. Knopf, 1974).

22. A long-standing constitutional principle in the United States holds that the national government should not have the power to tax state governments or their subunits since, in the words of *McCulloch v. Maryland* (4 Wheaton 316), a landmark decision issued by the Supreme Court in 1819, "the power to tax is the power to destroy."

23. B.J. Reed and John W. Swain, *Public Finance Administration*, 2nd ed. (Thousand Oaks, CA: Sage Publications, 1997), pp. 254–55.

24. Mark Baldassare, *When Government Fails: The Orange County Bankruptcy* (Berkeley: University of California Press, 1998).

25. See, respectively, David O. Sears and Jack Citrin, *Tax Revolt: Something for Nothing in California* (Cambridge, MA: Harvard University Press, 1982); Donald Phares, "State and Local Revenue and

Expenditure Policies," in *Missouri Government and Politics,* eds. Richard J. Hardy, Richard R. Dohm, and David A. Leuthold (Columbia: University of Missouri Press, 1995), pp. 205–21; and Douglas M. Cutler and Douglas W. Elmendorf, "Restraining the Leviathan: Property Tax Limitation in Massachusetts," *Journal of Public Economics,* 71, no. 3 (March 1999), pp. 313–34.

26.   Steven D. Gold and Sarah Ritchie, "State Policies Affecting Cities and Counties in 1992," *Public Budgeting and Finance,* 13, no. 1 (Spring 1993), pp. 16–18.

27.   *Tax and Expenditure Limits on Local Government* (Washington: Advisory Commission on Intergovernmental Relations, 1995).

28.   Ronald J. Shadbegian, "The Effect of Tax and Expenditure Limitations on the Revenue Structure of Local Government, 1962–87," *National Tax Journal,* 52, no. 2 (June 1999), pp. 221–37.

29.   Robert L. Bland and Li-Khan Chen, "Taxable Municipal Bonds: State and Local Governments Confront the Tax-Exempt Limitation Movement," *Public Administration Review,* 50, no. 1 (January-February 1990), pp. 42–48.

30.   Richard F. Dye and Jeffrey O. Sundberg, "A Model of Tax Increment Financing Adoption Incentives," *Growth and Change,* 29, no. 1 (Winter 1998), pp. 90–110; Craig L. Johnson, "Tax Increment Debt Finance: An Analysis of the Mainstreaming of a Fringe Sector," *Public Budgeting and Finance,* 19, no. 1 (Spring 1999), pp. 47–67; and Daphne A. Kenyon and John Kincaid, editors, *Competition Among States and Local Governments: Efficiency and Equity in American Federalism* (Washington: Urban Institute Press, 1991).

31.   Joyce Y. Man and Mark S. Rosentraub, "Tax Increment Financing: Municipal Adoption and Effects on Property Value Growth," *Public Finance Review,* 26, no. 6 (November 1998), pg. 523.

32.   Andrew F. Haughwout, "Regional Fiscal Cooperation in Metropolitan Areas: An Exploration," *Journal of Policy Analysis and Management,* 18, no. 4 (1999), pp. 579–600; and Dick Netzer, "Metropolitan-Area Fiscal Issues," in *Intergovernmental Fiscal Relations,* ed. Ronald C. Fisher (Boston, MA: Kluwer Academic Publishers, 1997), pp. 199–240.

33.   Judith A. Martin, "Renegotiating Metropolitan Consciousness: The Twin Cities Faces Its Future," in *Metropolitan Governance Revisited: American/Canadian Intergovernmental Perspectives,* ed. Donald N. Rothblatt and Andrew Sancton (Berkeley: University of California-Berkeley Institute of Governmental Studies Press, 1998), pp. 237–72.

34.   Myron Orfield, *Metropolitics: A Regional Agenda for Community and Stability* (Washington: Brookings Institution Press, 1997), pg. 87.

35.   David Rusk, *Inside Game/Outside Game: Winning Strategies for Saving Urban America* (Washington: Brookings Institution Press, 1999), pp. 201–21.

36.   William J. Pammer, Jr. and Jack L. Duston, "Fostering Economic Development through County Tax Sharing," *State and Local Government Review,* 25, no. 1 (Winter 1993), pp. 57–71.

37.   E. Terrence Jones, *Fragmented by Design: Why St. Louis Has So Many Governments* (St. Louis, MO: Palmerston and Reed, 2000), pp. 115–23.

38.   David Hamilton, *Governing Metropolitan Areas: Response to Growth and Change* (New York: Garland Publishing, 1999), pp. 341–42.

SUGGESTED READING

CONLAN, TIMOTHY. *From New Federalism to Devolution: Twenty-Five Years of Intergovernmental Reform.* Washington: Brookings Institution Press, 1998. Thorough review of federal intergovernmental transfer programs including those targeted toward metropolitan areas.

HY, RONALD JOHN, and WILLIAM W. WAUGH, JR. *State and Local Tax Policies: A Comparative Handbook.* Westport, CT: Greenwood Press, 1995. A clear and succinct explanation of each type of taxation used by state and local governments.

MIKESELL, JOHN L. *Fiscal Administration: Analysis and Applications for the Public Sector.* 5th edition. Orlando, FL: Harcourt Brace, 1999. The leading reference work on governmental finances written by one of the topic's top scholars.

SBRAGIA, ALBERTA M. *Debt Wish: Entrepreneurial Cities, U.S. Federalism, and Economic Development.* Pittsburgh, PA: University of Pittsburgh Press, 1996. A politically informed account of how American cities have handled debt issues over the past 150 years.

DOING IT

1. Do a fiscal profile for four different types of jurisdictions in a metropolitan area: the central city, the largest county, the biggest school district, and a multicounty special district. Obtain copies of their most recent budgets or financial reports. For each, what are the principal revenue sources? What is the long-term debt and for what was it incurred? What state constitutional or statutory provisions apply to each one's revenue and debt capabilities and what limits apply?

2. Using Lexis-Nexis or another newspaper index, identify a recent tax increment financing deal in a metropolitan area. What were the critical features? Which taxes were abated for what period, what bonds were issued, what public improvements were made, and for what type of development? Who supported and who opposed the TIF proposal?

EPILOGUE

CHAPTER 15

Looking Ahead

We are at the beginning of the first full metropolitan century. One hundred years ago, the United States and the world were more sets of smaller communities and rural settlements than they were regional complexes. From an historical perspective, where a few decades is but a blink in time, metropolitan life is in its infancy. So it is not surprising that there are more questions than answers, greater uncertainty than comfort, more change than continuity.

In the immediate years ahead, four issues dominate the metropolitan agenda. First, looking at the external chase, how can each region compete economically? What developmental strategy, which infrastructure array, what educational investment, and which amenities will be most crucial? Without success in commerce, little else is possible. What will it take to win the contest—or at least avoid being a loser?

The second and third issues arise from the internal chase and are connected: How should regions structure their space and what should they do to promote equity? As outlined in Chapter 1 and further described in Chapter 13, metropolitan territories are steadily spreading, urbanizing land at a rapid pace. At the same time, economic and racial segregation persists and, many argue, geographic dispersal fosters greater divisions. What should metropolitan areas opt for spatially, and how will those decisions as well as other factors prevent an enlarged gulf between the haves and the have-nots?

The fourth issue spans the first three: How should metropolitan areas govern themselves? Is there a single approach which will work best for making regional decisions about the economy, land use, and equity as well as other matters? Or does each metropolis need to evolve a method which best fits its own needs? What implications does more regionalism have for leaders? Is a new cadre required? What

about citizens? How should they balance the obligations between their own immediate neighborhood or subdivision or municipality and those of the larger region?

Although these questions have just been emerging, there is no shortage of
recommendations. Especially during the past few years, numerous scholars and
practitioners have stepped forward with their advice. Some are comprehensive
platforms while others are more limited suggestions. Taken as a whole, they constitute a rich source for stimulating debate about what metropolitan areas should do
and how they should go about it.

EXTERNAL CHASE

More than anything else, the emergence of regional economies as the key component within the national and global marketplace has made metropolitan areas the
focal place for human settlement during the past half century. Economic activity
simultaneously moved in two directions: from the nation-state downward and from
the local jurisdiction upward, meeting at the natural juncture which has become the
metropolitan area. Interdependent economic activity determines a region's boundaries and, as residents become more aware of the interconnections, they drive its
sense of identity.[1]

What should a metropolitan area do to maintain and enhance its economic
competitiveness? What attributes will be most beneficial? Looking both at which
regions are presently faring best as well at what trends will have the greatest future
impact, eight characteristics surface. Each can be captured in a single word: smart,
global, nimble, digital, technological, capital, cooperative, and entertaining.[2]

Smart

At the turn of the last century, economic prowess could be achieved through one
leader, an Andrew Carnegie in Pittsburgh or a Henry Ford in Detroit. These vision-
aries could establish an entire industry, forging steel or assembling automobiles.
They needed only a modest number of educated staff. The bulk of the production
could be accomplished through repetitive effort, shoveling coal into the furnaces or
attaching a tire on the assembly line. Workers for these tasks were easily recruited
and, once trained, needed only perfunctory supervision. The only educational
requirement was the ability to learn and follow simple directions.

Vision is still crucial—but it is not sufficient. Bill Gates can sketch exciting
software concepts, providing the framework for Seattle's largest enterprise. But
Microsoft also requires tens of thousands of specialists, ranging from those who
devise algorithms to those who write the program code. The skills required go
well beyond reading, writing, and arithmetic. They encompass problem solving and
critical thinking. Moreover, the learning is ongoing. What a worker needed to know
last year becomes obsolete, and now the job demands different competencies.

All this has profound implications for the educational system. Most of the
workforce, not just a select few, must learn more as they proceed through the K-12

curriculum, additional numbers must attend community colleges and four-year institutions, and a greater portion of these must obtain postbaccalaureate degrees. Once formal education is completed, there must be more continuing education, both inside and outside the employing enterprise. Finally, there must be closer coordination between what schools and colleges teach and what the present and future jobs require.

Global

A worldwide marketplace means that the successful metropolitan area must sell its goods and services throughout the globe, not just in the immediate vicinity. It must also attract talent from other countries, sustaining a cosmopolitan atmosphere supportive for an internationally diverse workforce. Trade barriers among nations are falling, protectionism is on the wane, and therefore the competition includes all metropolitan areas, not just those in the United States.

Globalism comes easier for some regions—Los Angeles, New York, and San Francisco, for example—than for others, especially those in the country's interior. The larger coastal metropolises have a long tradition of looking outward and have immediate access to ocean ports. Those, say, in the Midwest must work harder to be more global, providing export assistance to medium and small firms, establishing nonstop international air service to Asia, Latin America, and Europe, and promoting a multicultural environment.

Nimble

Once major corporations seemed to persist indefinitely. They had an air of permanency, a sense of stability. A region with several Fortune 500 firms could look forward to a long and prosperous future. But corporations disappear or are bought out by others. Allied Can, American Smelting, Corn Products Refining, National Steel, Woolworth, all members of the Dow Jones Industrial Average's thirty corporations in 1956, now no more.

Change is both inevitable and accelerating. Firms are born, have a few decades of achievements, then falter and fade away. Their life cycles are shorter. That means that effective regions must have a "farm" system, encouraging hundreds of start-up businesses, counting on some to make the breakthrough to prosperity, if even for a short period. They must also contain flexible workers, able to survive the collapse of one company or industry, rapidly adapting to the proficiencies required by the next entrant.

Transportation flexibility is also important. As regions move from one economic speciality to another, they must have the appropriate modes to move raw materials and finished products. Those metropolitan areas which can transfer swiftly from water to rail, to road, to air will do best. Keeping such a multimodal system fully operational demands a willingness to devote significant public funds for their construction and maintenance.

Digital

Information drives much of the new economy—facts are needed to plan strategically, market effectively, produce efficiently, deliver rapidly. Metropolitan areas must be wired, literally and figuratively, so that their enterprises have speedy access to data bases from anywhere and everywhere. They must also possess the capacity to manipulate billions of items, arraying them to analyze problems and develop solutions.

In addition to the physical infrastructure to support information processing, they must also have people who know how to use the technology. This places a premium on computer proficiency, starting at the earliest education levels and extending into adulthood. It values regions where both companies and residences are connected, all linked to one another through the Internet. Such a network furthers productivity, making the region more competitive.[3]

Internet Hub with Linked Servers

Technological

American metropolitan areas cannot compete with their third world counterparts in low-technology manufacturing. Be it toys or shoes or shirts, countries with wage rates much beneath those in the United States will be the most efficient producers, even after adding transportation costs to and from those sites. Instead, U.S. regions must place much of their effort in high-technology enterprises, those where brains add considerable value to the product, be it software, or medical devices, or pharmaceuticals.

This, in turn, requires engineers and scientists, most preferably graduating from local universities to keep the labor supply plentiful and steady. These higher educational institutions must possess the state-of-the-art laboratories for ongoing research, both basic and applied. It also means that regions must select a niche within the technology spectrum, since it would be very difficult to compete across the entire range.[4]

Capital

Economic victories rarely happen without risk takers, those willing to support a vision with investment dollars. Venture capitalists, those prepared to back entrepreneurs with substantial sums, realizing that only a fraction of the enterprises will ever make a profit, are a critical element. More traditional lending sources, the commercial banks, are unwilling to speculate too much, lest they offend their depositors and stockholders. State and local governments also fear having political backlash from underwriting losers.

That leaves wealthy individuals, acting alone or through small venture operations, who are willing to dip into their deep pockets. Although, according to pure economic theory, these dollars should seek out the best opportunities, no matter where they are geographically located, psychologically people are more comfortable investing close to home, where they can monitor their stakes. Thus metropolitan areas which can generate much of their own venture capital internally have an edge.

Cooperative

Because many separate cities and counties within each metropolitan area pursue economic development, with each having its own unit responsible for developing and implementing a strategy, there can be more competition for businesses within the region rather than between it and others. Although, in the short run, one county might benefit by wooing an enterprise away from a neighboring unit, in the long run it makes economic development a zero-sum game for the region.

An intrametropolitan focus also wastes time and energy, taking those valuable elements away from either regionwide development, such as identifying and nurturing a promising cluster, or from attracting outside firms to the region. Unbridled competition within a region also allows businesses to maximize public subsidies as they benefit from the bidding war between two or more local governments.

Those regions which act cooperatively, banding together with a coordinated economic-development strategy, are more likely to have net gains. Doing so, however, is not easy and, with few exceptions, the immediate benefits for any single project will only be reaped by a portion of the region. It is only over time that sharing leads to a larger common good and, in the interim, jurisdictions which are told to wait for their day in the economic sun can grow impatient.

Entertaining

Boring is bad. Exciting is good. People, especially those most critical for complex enterprises, want to live in places where amenities abound. Without such attractions, native twenty-somethings will move away to more vibrant regions and few will relocate from elsewhere. Since leisure tastes vary, this means regions must have something for everyone—water for boating, trails for hiking, symphonies for listening, professional sports for spectating, and more.

Because tourism, be it trade conventions or family vacations, are a growing share of economic activity, having a stimulating metropolis is also key to being a net winner in this industry. To be a destination region, a place almost everyone wants to visit, dictates that there be lots happening, a modern version of the carnival midway. All these offerings, moreover, must compose a coherent whole, a New Orleans "Big Easy" or a Los Angeles "Tinsel Town."

INTERNAL CHASE

Structuring Space

The net population increase for the United States's metropolitan areas will be approximately 2 million annually for the next two decades. Where these additional residents live and work, what land they occupy, will alter each region's space. Recent experience indicates that the spatial impact will be disproportionately higher since "population increases are accompanied by much larger increases in land consumption and somewhat larger increases in residential dwellings and private vehicles."[5]

Even without these additional inhabitants, current forces are spreading the metropolis over a wider territory. Within regions, more people move outward from the central city and inner suburbs to the more distant suburbs and exurbs than flow in the reverse direction. Trailing this migration are retail outlets, office complexes, warehouse districts, and manufacturing plants. There is much debate about which term—growth, dispersal, sprawl—should describe this phenomenon—but there is not disagreement that it is happening and, absent any counter force, that it will continue to do so.

Dispersion has consequences for the entire region. It generates more and longer automobile trips, thereby consuming more energy, polluting more air, and congesting more roads and highways. It means that there is less open space nearby, depriving the entire metropolitan area of having it to enjoy. But the population increase also brings benefits for the region, most notably greater economic prosperity.[6]

Regions have broad options for how they respond to dispersal. The first viewpoint is they can do nothing collectively and, as individuals and firms, they accept its effects. This perspective believes the private market, the cumulative impact of everyone's separate decisions, is the preferred means for allocating space. It - respects everyone's freedom to locate where they choose. To the extent that governmental action is appropriate, it should be made by the smallest possible jurisdiction, allowing each one to have its own zoning code for the land within its boundaries.

At the other end of the ideological spectrum is the option of mandating who can locate where, designing a comprehensive and integrated land-use plan for an entire metropolitan area and then enforcing it vigilantly. This would require either direct intervention by state government, which under Dillon's rule possesses the authority to do so, or indirect intervention through some regional entity, empowered by the state.

Consensus is emerging that neither of these options is acceptable and that some middle path must be followed.[7] Having a minimalist regional approach to land use will only worsen problems like air pollution and traffic congestion and, for some, doing nothing keeps in place some policies, such as spending most transportation funds on new highways, which subsidizes expansion. On the other hand, massive governmental regulation threatens liberty and, for a sizeable majority, is politically unacceptable.

Most also recognize that no single policy makes economic, social, and political sense for every metropolitan area. Both the physical settings and the political cultures differ too much. Instead, each should develop its own package, drawing from the growth management proposals described in Chapter 13. A few regions are well advanced in their planning, especially those where state government has stepped forward. Most, however, have just begun these conversations during the past few years.

The public policy process moves through several stages.[8] The first is simply agreeing that something is a problem which commands public action, typically because market mechanisms cannot adequately handle it. For a majority of regions, that is where the growth management discussion now lies.[9] Before it moves to the next major step, approving some mix of public policies and private actions, much sorting out must occur. This initially includes framing the issue more precisely and deciding who is helped and hurt by present practices. Those advocating change must find one another, build coalitions, negotiate programs, and assemble support from elected officials.

All this takes years even under the simplest of circumstances and land-use policy is far from elementary. It has enormous economic implications, triggering attention from many interests. It involves core values like liberty preservation and environmental stewardship. It touches all governments, from the national (e.g., transportation policy) to the state (e.g., land-use authority) to the local (e.g., zoning regulations). Accordingly, how to structure space will be on every regional agenda for the foreseeable future.[10]

As these deliberations ensue, there are competing visions for what a region scape should be, even if it is publicly planned rather than privately determined.[11] One perspective takes Chicago as a model and continues to see the preferred pattern as a dense central city, containing the highest concentration of economic and cultural activity, surrounded by revitalized city and inner suburban neighborhoods, complete with in-fill housing on previously abandoned sites, then encompassed by outer suburbs reasonably adjacent to the core and connected to it by mass transit. The alternative viewpoint uses Los Angeles as its paradigm. Once satirized as "hundreds of suburbs in search of a downtown," it now can be portrayed as tens of activity-linked clusters, none central but each important. At a more ideal level, this approach envisions a metropolis with multiple pedestrian-friendly planned communities, each combining a wide range of residential types with commercial activity, interspersed among open space, connected by highways and mass transit.

Promoting Equity

Lessening disparities is a challenge for the nation as well for its metropolitan areas. Even after the economic good times through most of the 1990s, the gap between rich and poor widens and has been doing so for the past two decades.[12] The top quintile's share of overall income has risen the most, the bottom quintile has dropped the furthest. Within the three middle quintiles, the higher pair are up slightly and the lowest has had no change.

Metropolitan inhabitants are part of this trend but geography also enters the analysis. Within regions, not only have the rich become richer and the poor poorer, but they increasingly are more spatially segregated from one another. The gap between central-city and suburban household incomes grew between 1960 and 1990,[13] and beginning in the 1980s, suburbs experienced "greater polarization in income."[14] As described in Chapter 1, this pattern extends down to the neighborhood and census tract level.[15] During the past few years, as welfare reform has taken many off the rolls, those remaining are disproportionately in central cities, with "the 89 top urban counties . . . accounting for 58 percent of the nation's welfare cases, up 10 percentage points since 1994."[16]

While economic segregation has heightened, racial division declined modestly over the past decade although, in most regions, it remains quite high. An analysis of 291 metropolitan areas finds that all but 19 are more integrated in 2000 than they were in 1990.[17] Within the nation's 102 largest regions, the suburban components became more diverse, with racial and ethnic minorities rising from 19 percent to 27 percent of the population.[18] Nevertheless, as portrayed in Chapter 1, most neighborhoods are racially segregated.

Both economic and racial segregation threaten metropolitan areas. As jurisdictions slip too far below the norm, more who can afford to do so exit, few enter except those with no alternative, and those remaining are unable to support the existing infrastructure. Absent intervention to reverse these trends, the process feeds on itself and regions have more deteriorated pockets. This is obviously harmful for those living in these segments but it also affects those elsewhere. Too much inequity, in the intermediate and long run, harms everyone.

Although the rest of a metropolitan area's residents can seek to isolate themselves physically and psychologically, they cannot do so completely and the problems bred in ghettoes spill over into the rest of the metropolis. Concentrated poverty breeds crime and while most of the victims will be within the impoverished segments, some will occur in the more affluent parts of the region.[19] These neighborhoods also promote "risky health behaviors," adding to a region's AIDS infection rates, sexually transmitted diseases, and alcohol-related accidents.[20]

For those living in the bottom-rung communities, the consequences are dramatic and often disastrous. Inadequate tax bases translate into subpar public services. Children have less educational opportunity because the schools are not nearly as well funded as those in more prosperous areas. Adults find jobs further away, making commuting costs higher and unemployment more likely. As poverty becomes more concentrated, its effects multiply, each creating an additional burden on the residents and a higher obstacle to overcome.[21]

Then there are the lost opportunities, regions' failure to take advantage of all its residents' talents. Segregation means unequal chances, depriving qualified people from fulfilling their potential. In metropolitan areas with significant racial polarization, for example, the best among the minority youth will, as they reach adulthood, move to more congenial regions to establish their careers.

What to do? Much of the answer lies outside metropolitan areas, primarily at the national level but also among state governments. For reasons mentioned in Chapter 14, regions find it almost impossible to engage in widespread redistribution through taxation, transferring wealth within their own boundaries. That means if income gaps are to stop expanding and begin contracting, it will require some combination of federal actions: raising the minimum wage, expanding the earned income tax credit, and improving health care and day care.[22]

As the governments primarily responsible for K-12 education, states must do even more to assist districts with inadequate tax bases. It is not enough to *equalize* funding, since it costs more to educate a poverty neighborhood resident than one from an affluent suburb. The former also require social services and other assistance so that they can obtain in schools what is not available in their homes. It is difficult to break the cycle of poverty (staying poor from one generation to the next) without schools being the means to escape.

Within regions, the immediate need is more awareness, learning that extreme inequality is not just morally wrong but empirically harmful. How to compete economically has been on regional agendas for more than two decades. How to handle growth has been there for about ten years. What to do about inequity is on very few regions' radar screens. It will not get there solely by the poor advocating change, for their political clout is minimal. It will not make it only by having clergy preach sermons or social scientists parade statistics, for they are too easily ignored. It will only become an action item when the well off appreciate that they, too, are victims of economic and racial segregation.

GOVERNING

The New Regionalism: Governance

The national government, each of the fifty states, and all local jurisdictions have their own set of challenges and issues. But they have established procedures contained in constitutions, charters, statutes, and ordinances for dealing with them. In contrast, as metropolitan areas address economic competitiveness, land-use policies, and equity considerations, they have to debate both what to do and how to decide. It is a daunting task.

Chapter 5 discussed the alternatives for making regional decisions: metropolitan planning organizations; consolidated governments like those in Indianapolis, Jacksonville, and Nashville; special metropolitan councils such as Minneapolis-St. Paul and Portland; and a host of informal collaborations, some largely within governmental units and others involving the public, private, and nonprofit sectors.

As metropolitan areas talk more about acting collectively, as they attempt to do "regionalism on purpose,"[23] none are seriously proposing an overarching metropolitan government encompassing many functions. Even the two closest approximations to this approach, the Twin Cities Metropolitan Council and Portland Metro, fall short of a comprehensive authority. Whatever the path to greater regionalism, it will not be another layer of government—the "metropolitans"—inserted into the existing national-state-local triad.

Recently and for the foreseeable future, the prevailing method will be governance, not government. Instead of public entities exercising formal authority, governance assumes "that existing institutions can be harnessed in new ways, that cooperation can be carried out on a fluid and voluntary basis among localities, and that people can best regulate themselves through horizontally linked organizations."[24]

Governance is already prevalent in regional action for economic growth. For example, as Cleveland acted to recover from its downfall in the late 1970s, when the City of Cleveland flirted with bankruptcy, the Cuyahoga River's pollution set it afire, and the local economy struggled, improvement began with a partnership among the business organizations such as Cleveland Tomorrow and the Greater Cleveland Growth Association, nonprofits like the Citizens League and the Cleveland Foundation, and municipal, county, and state governments, which formed several collaborative governance entities, including the Work in Northeast Ohio Council (labor-management policy), Build Up Greater Cleveland (infrastructure policy), and the Cleveland Initiative for Education (education policy).[25]

More than land use and equity, economic development provides the most fruitful policy arena for regionwide action to begin.[26] It is a natural for businesses, central to their purpose and familiar to their thinking. It is an easier place for local governments to cooperate. Most recognize that enlarging the metropolis's economy means more sales and residents for everyone, even if a particular enterprise's property taxes go to just one of the many local governments. Nonprofits can help provide the common setting and the organizational staff both to develop and

Denver Leaders Sign Mile High Compact

to implement strategies. And when a crisis atmosphere prevails, such as in Cleveland, there is an added stimulus to collaborate.

Governance also includes cooperative agreements among local governments and, in a few instances, it is beginning to address how to structure the region's space. After lengthy deliberations facilitated through and staffed by the Denver Regional Council of Governments, the area's metropolitan planning organization, thirty-three jurisdiction representing about four-fifths of the region's residents have signed the Mile High Compact. In doing so, they have voluntarily agreed to conduct their zoning within an overall framework that promotes greater densities and more mixed uses.[27]

Through governance, regionalism becomes "a process, not a result."[28] Instead of a one-time movement to create metropolitan governmental institutions which, once established, would be presumed to act regionally indefinitely, incorporating those values in their elected and appointed officials, no identifiable and separate metropolitan layer exists. Instead, all existing public, private, and nonprofit units are expected to participate in regional deliberations when, in their judgment, circumstances call for it.

Reaching regional decisions through *governance* rather than *government* has both advantages and limitations. Fluidity is both a virtue and a vice. It allows for flexibility and inclusivity, bringing all interested and affected groups into the deliberations. It avoids fixed routines and set patterns, encouraging fresh perspectives and innovative actions. But it requires significant time both to build and to sustain the endeavor. Most governance coalitions are fragile and, like a tender plant, require constant cultivation. This consumes valuable civic time from all three sectors.

Most worrisome, governance often lacks legitimacy and accountability. Governmental participation can sometimes but not always furnish a public blessing, enabling the people's elected representatives to approve the policy direction. Once underway, however, holding someone responsible can be elusive. Unlike government, where the in's can be voted out, it is difficult to assign blame for any misdeeds.

Other Governments

States retain much potential to promote regionalism. Since they write the rules under which local governments operate, they can alter them either to mandate or, less overtly, encourage joint endeavors. Chapter 13 described the steps several states have taken to impose growth-management policies on one or more of their metropolitan areas and, as mentioned above, they have a crucial role to play in alleviating inequities. Each year witnesses more states reexamining their relationships with their metropolitan areas. A recent Wisconsin commission, for example, recommends incentives to reward local government cooperation, an effort to institutionalize governance practices.[29] State involvement is more challenging when regions are in two or more states, such as Chicago, New York, Philadelphia, and St. Louis. In such situations, each state's own priorities, rarely identical with the others, often override the metropolitan area's needs.

With the exception of transportation and environmental policies, the national government has been more a bystander than a participant in advancing regionalism. The ISTEA and TEA-21 legislation has given metropolitan planning organizations a greater role, thereby elevating much of the decision making on these issues from a local to a metropolitan level. But the federal government has avoided having a broader metropolitan policy that might, for example, encourage more regional cooperation, play a greater redistributive role, or gather more data on metropolitan matters. Although its policies definitely affect regions, the impact is more inadvertent than planned.[30]

More regionalism does not necessarily mean less localism. The evidence is ample that residents like having control over local services like policing and education.[31] When economically possible, they have chosen their particular general purpose government, a municipality or unincorporated county, both for the basket of public goods and services it provides as well for the style with which it delivers them. So, too, if they have school-age children, the school district has been selected to fit their preferences.

That is why the number of municipalities and special districts within a metropolitan area will either stay the same or increase moderately. They offer diverse choices about government goods and services as well as approachable and accessible elected representatives. Within regional discussions, these local units can serve as their surrogates in the metropolitan debates, their representatives in the governance process.

Leaders and Followers

A popular bumper sticker exhorts people to "think globally, act locally." It is a reminder that everyone shares a single planet but that, to honor that common globe, more than rhetoric is required. Each person must live out their commitment, in this case to the environment, by doing things like recycling daily to contribute to the larger cause. This appeal has raised ecological consciousness and contributed to the earth's physical well-being.

As metropolitan areas become more central for their residents' destinies, a similar challenge exists for them to "think regionally, act locally." Citizens and their leaders have understandably grown accustomed to focusing on their own immediate surroundings within the region. When they think about policies within the region, they are most apt to worry about their schools or their municipality, not about the overall metropolitan area. The region is more an abstract concept than a concrete reality.

As Kathryn Foster writes, "thinking like a region implies a measure of regional identity" and one of its components is "regional consciousness, . . . the internal sense of place felt by those living within the region."[32] For most metropolitan areas, there are relatively few regional icons: professional sports franchises, perhaps a monument like St. Louis's Gateway Arch, a park like Boston's Commons, or a song like "I Left My Heart in San Francisco"—but not much else.

Those advocating more regionalism understand this shortcoming and are implementing practices to champion regional perspectives. One approach is to sponsor visioning sessions, such as those in Chattanooga and St. Louis described in Chapter 5. Other examples include the Austin (Texas) 360 Summit, the Potomac Conference (Washington, D.C.), and the Silicon Valley (California) Civic Action Network. Most of these initiatives center on already established leaders but some also reach out to ordinary citizens. The premise is that fostering conversations about where the region should head will give it more prominence.

Regional benchmarking is another tactic. After conducting a strategic planning process in the late 1990s and establishing goals for the region, Chicago Metropolis 2020 is periodically issuing a report card charting progress toward each objective.[33] This approach appeals to Americans' competitive gamesmanship, keeping the score for regions much like the media reports the standings for football teams.

Since acting regionally, placing higher priority on the metropolitan area's needs than on the local community's, can be lonely for leaders within any single metropolis, national organizations have been started to bring these individuals together, both personally and through list serves, to boost their morale and to share success stories. Leading examples include the Alliance for Regional Stewardship and the Partnership for Regional Livability.[34]

Over the next decade, increasing regional thinking among both leaders and followers is the greatest challenge metropolitan areas face. At the moment, the

Preparing Metropolitan Chicago for the 21st Century

Chicago Metropolis 2020: A Regional Initiative

balance tilts much more toward the local. The internal chase's concerns about who gets what within a region usually trump the external chase's preoccupation with what is best for the entire metropolitan area. Acting for the overall benefit of the region will not happen regularly and effectively until more citizens appreciate its centrality to themselves and their families, and realize that it is indeed a metropolitan world.

NOTES

1. William R. Barnes and Larry C. Ledebur, *The New Regional Economics: The U.S. Common Market and the Global Economy* (Thousand Oaks, CA: Sage Publications, 1998).

2. These characteristics are drawn from several sources: Robert D. Atkinson and Paul D. Gotttlieb, *The Metropolitan New Economy Index: Benchmarking Economic Transformation in the Nation's Metropolitan Areas* (Washington: Progressive Policy Institute, 2001); Terry Clark and others, "Amenities Drive Urban Growth," paper presented at the American Political Science Association Annual Meeting, September, 2001); Anthony Downs, *New Visions for Metropolitan America* (Washington: Brookings Institution, 1994); Edward L. Glaeser, Jed Kolko, and Albert Saiz, *Consumer City* (Cambridge, MA: National Bureau of Economic Research, 2000); Joel Kotkin and Ross C. DeVol, *Knowledge-Value Cities in the Digital Age* (Santa Monica, CA: Milken Institute, 2001); Larry C. Ledebur and William R. Barnes, "Directions for Further Research on Regional Economics and Regional Economic Governance," paper presented at the Urban Affairs Association Annual Meeting, April 1999; and Linda McCarthy, *Competitive Regionalism: Beyond Individual Competition* (Washington: United States Economic Development Administration, 2000).

3. See, for example, Thomas Horan, *Digital Places: Building Our City of Bits* (Washington: Urban Land Institute, 2000); and Joel Kotkin, *The New Geography: How the Digital Revolution Is Reshaping the American Landscape* (New York: Random House, 2000).

4. Joseph Cortright and Heike Mayer, *High Tech Specialization: A Comparison of High Technology Centers* (Washington: Brookings Institution Center on Urban and Metropolitan Policy, 2001).

5. Joel Hirschhorn, *Growing Pains: Quality of Life in the New Economy* (Washington: National Governors Association, 2000), pg. 1.

6. Anthony Downs, "Some Realities about Sprawl and Urban Decline," *Housing Policy Debate*, 10, no. 4 (1999), pp. 955–74.

7. *The Smart Growth Tool Kit: Community Profiles and Case Studies to Advance Smart Growth Practices* (Washington: Urban Land Institute, 2000).

8. Charles O. Jones, *An Introduction to the Study of Public Policy*, 3rd ed. (Monterey, CA: Brooks/Cole Publishing, 1984).

9. Reports stimulating these discussions include *Sprawl Hits the Wall: Confronting the Realities of Metropolitan Los Angeles* (Los Angeles: Southern California Studies Center and the Brookings Institution Center on Urban and Metropolitan Policy, 2001); *Whither Eastward Ho! Strategies for Strengthening Regional Stewardship in Southeastern Florida* (Fort Lauderdale: Growth Management Institute and Florida Atlantic University/Florida International University Joint Center for Environmental and Urban Problems, 2001); and Elmer W. Johnson, *Chicago Metropolis 2020: The Chicago Plan for the Twenty-First Century* (Chicago: University of Chicago Press, 2001). Also see Bruce Katz and Amy Liu, "Moving Beyond Sprawl: Toward a Broader Metropolitan Agenda," *Brookings Review*, 18, no. 2 (Spring 2000), pp. 31–34.

10. Mark Baldassare, "Citizen Preferences for Local Growth Controls: Trends in U.S. Suburban Support for a New Political Culture Movement," in *The New Political Culture*, eds. Terry Nichols Clark and Vincent Hoffman-Martinot (Boulder, CO: Westview Press, 1998), pp. 261–76; Robert Fishman, *The American Metropolis at Century's End* (Washington: Fannie Mae Foundation, 1999); and David Rusk, "Growth Management: The Core Regional Issue," in *Reflections on Regionalism*, ed. Bruce Katz (Washington: Brookings Institution Press, 2000).

11. Peter Calthorpe and William Fulton, *The Regional City* (Washington: Island Press, 2001); Michael J. Dear, *From Chicago to L.A.: Making Sense of Urban Theory* (Thousand Oaks, CA: Sage Publications, 2001); and Edward Soja, *Postmetropolis: Critical Studies of Cities and Regions* (Oxford, England: Blackwell Publishers, 2000).

12. Lawrence R. Mishel, Jared Bernstein, and John Schmitt, *The State of Working America, 1998-99* (Ithaca, NY: ILS Press, 1999).

13. Alan Altshuler and others, *Governance and Opportunity in Metropolitan America* (Washington: National Academy Press, 1999), pp. 41–52; and Larry C. Ledebur and William R. Barnes, *City Distress, Metropolitan Disparities, and Metropolitan Growth* (Washington: National League of Cities, 1992).

14. William H. Lucy and David L. Phillips, *Confronting Suburban Decline: Strategic Planning for Metropolitan Renewal* (Washington: Island Press, 2000), pg. 181. Also see Gregory R. Weiher, *The Fractured Metropolis: Political Fragmentation and Metropolitan Segregation* (Albany: State University of New York Press, 1991).

15. Paul Jargowsky, *Poverty and Place: Ghettos, Barrios, and the American City* (New York: Russell Sage Foundation, 1996). For more detailed analyses of four large regions, see David L. Sjoquist, *The Atlanta Paradox* (New York: Russell Sage Foundation, 2000); Barry Bluestone and Mary Hoff Stevenson, *The Boston Renaissance: Race, Space, and Economic Change in an American Metropolis* (New York: Russell Sage Foundation, 2000); Reynolds Farley, Sheldon Danziger, and Harry J. Holzer, *Detroit Divided* (New York: Russell Sage Foundation, 2000); Lawrence D. Bobo and others, editors, *Prismatic Metropolis: Inequality in Los Angeles* (New York: Russell Sage Foundation, 2000); and Alice O'Connor, Chris Tilly, and Lawrence D. Bobo, *Urban Inequality: Evidence from Four Cities* (New York: Russell Sage Foundation, 2001).

16. Bruce Katz and Katherine Allen, "Cities Matter: Shifting the Focus of Welfare Reform," *Brookings Review*, 19, no. 3 (Summer 2001), pp. 30–33.

17. Edward L. Glaeser and Jacob L. Vigdor, *Racial Segregation in the 2000 Census: Promising News* (Washington: Brookings Institution Center on Urban and Metropolitan Policy, 2001).

18. William H. Frey, *Melting Pot Suburbs: A Census 2000 Study of Suburban Diversity* (Washington: Brookings Institution Center on Urban and Metropolitan Policy, 2001).

19. Carol W. Kohfeld and John Sprague, "Urban Unemployment Drives Urban Crime," *Urban Affairs Quarterly*, 24, no. 2 (December 1988), pp. 215–41.

20. Peter Dreier, John Mollenkopf, and Todd Swanstrom, *Place Matters: Metropolitics for the Twenty-First Century* (Lawrence: University Press of Kansas, 2001), pp. 66–74.

21. William Julius Wilson, *When Work Disappears: The World of the New Urban Poor* (New York: Alfred A. Knopf, 1996).

22. Dreier, Mollenkopf, and Swanstrom, *Place Matters*, pp. 219–22.

23. Kathryn A. Foster, *Regionalism on Purpose* (Cambridge, MA: Lincoln Institute of Land Policy, 2001).

24. H.V. Savitch and Ronald K. Vogel, "Paths to New Regionalism," *State and Local Government Review*, 32, no. 3 (Fall 2000), pg. 161.

25. Bruce Adams, "Cleveland: The Partnership City," in *Boundary Crossers: Case Studies of How Ten of America's Metropolitan Regions Work*, ed. Bruce Adams and John Parr (College Park, MD: James MacGregor Burns Academy of Leadership, 1997), pp. 57–78.

26. Gerald Benjamin and Richard P. Nathan, *Regionalism and Realism: A Study of Governments in the New York Metropolitan Area* (Washington: Brookings Institution Press, 2001), pg. 257.

27. John Parr, *Regional Innovation: Mile High Regional Governance* (Palo Alto, CA: Alliance for Regional Stewardship, 2001).

28. Benjamin and Nathan, *Regionalism and Realism*, pg. 267.

29. *Governor's Blue-Ribbon Commission on State-Local Partnerships for the 21st Century* (Madison: State of Wisconsin, 2001).

30. Drier, Mollenkopf, and Swanstrom, *Place Matters*, pp. 212–14.

31. Roger B. Parks and Ronald J. Oakerson, "Regionalism, Localism, and Metropolitan Governance: Suggestions from the Research Program on Local Public Economies," *State and Local Government Review*, 32, no. 5 (Fall 2000), pp. 169–79.

32. Kathryn A. Foster, "Being Like a Region," paper presented to the Roundtable on Regions, Regional Identity, and Regionalism in Greater Boston, December 1, 2000.

33. *Regional Realities: Measuring Progress Toward Shared Regional Goals* (Chicago: Chicago Metropolis 2020, 2001).

34. Peter Plastrik, *The Hope of Regions: An Assessment of the Partnership for Regional Livablity's Potential* (Benicia, CA: Partnership for Regional Livability, 1999); and *Regional Stewardship: A Commitment to Place* (Palo Alto, CA: Alliance for Regional Stewardship, 2000). These movements fit within the broader call for more civic participation. See Robert D. Putnam, *Bowling Alone: The Collapse and Revival of American Community* (New York: Simon and Schuster, 2000); and Carmen Sirianni and Lewis Friedland, *Civic Innovation in America: Community Empowerment, Public Policy, and the Movement for Civic Renewal* (Berkeley: University of California Press, 2001).

SUGGESTED READINGS

ADAMS, BRUCE, and JOHN PARR, editors. *Boundary Crossers: Case Studies of How Ten of America's Metropolitan Regions Work.* College Park, MD: James MacGregor Burns Academy of Leadership, 1997. Examples of governance in action from Atlanta, Charlotte, Chattanooga, Cleveland, Denver, Detroit, Kansas City, Portland, San Antonio, and San Diego.

DREIER, PETER, JOHN MOLLENKOPF, and TODD SWANSTROM. *Place Matters: Metropolitics for the Twenty-First Century.* Lawrence: University Press of Kansas, 2001. A powerful indictment of how past and present policies have created and sustained space, race, and class inequity and recommendations for how to reverse these trends.

FOSTER, KATHRYN A. *Regionalism on Purpose.* Cambridge, MA: Lincoln Institute of Land Policy, 2001. An insightful review of regionalism from one of the topic's leading scholars.

SIRIANI, CARMEN, and LEWIS FRIEDLAND. *Civic Innovation in America: Community Empowerment, Public Policy, and the Movement for Civic Renewal.* Berkeley: University of California Press, 2001. An extensive analysis of present civic renewal initiatives in the United States with examples from all sectors.

DOING IT

Time to look ahead for your favorite metropolitan area and plot a course for its future. The plan should address the following questions for its economy, land use, economic and racial/ethnic equity, and governance:

1. What are the region's strengths and weaknesses? What opportunities does it have and what threats does it confront?
2. Looking specifically at the eight characteristics for a competitive economy, how does it rate? What should it do to improve?
3. What are the key land-use issues? To what extent is urbanization of land exceeding population growth? What policies, if any, are state and local governmental units proposing? What approaches would you recommend?
4. What are the trends over the past two decades for economic and racial/ethnic segregation? Heightened? Same? Less? What are the principal inequities arising from these trends? What do you recommend to deal with them?
5. How well is regional governance working? What has been attempted lately at the metropolitan level? What suggestions do you have for advancing a regionalist approach?

APPENDIX A

Helpful Web Sites

Alliance for Regional Stewardship *www.regionalstewardship.org*

The Alliance for Regional Stewardship is a national peer-to-peer learning network of regional leaders. The leaders come from business, government, education, and community sectors to learn about best practices from other regions, communicate to state/federal leaders and the media about regional challenges and innovations, and develop new leaders for regional civic efforts. The site provides information on regional leadership forums, publications on regional best practices, and web resources on the topics of the new economy, livable community, social inclusion, and governance reform.

American Planning Association *www.planning.org*

The American Planning Association is a nonprofit public interest and research organization representing 30,000 practicing planners, officials, and citizens involved with urban and rural planning issues. There is information on the American Planning Association and American Association Institute of Certified Planners, legislative and policy issues, education and career opportunities, and consultant services as well as publications on planning research and planning advisor reports on specific issues.

Association for Research on Nonprofit Organizations and Voluntary Action
www.arnova.org

The Association for Research on Nonprofit Organizations and Voluntary Action (ARNOVA) is an international, interdisciplinary network of scholars and nonprofit leaders fostering the creation, application, and dissemination of research on voluntary action, nonprofit organizations, philanthropy, and civil society. The site contains information on the annual conference, publications, data, and electronic discussions.

Brookings Institution *www.brook.edu*

The Brookings Institution performs public-policy research to bring knowledge to the attention of decision makers and scholars. The site contains information on economic, government, foreign policy studies. Information such as reports, publications, and initiatives specifically concerned with urban and metropolitan areas can be found on the site at *www/brook.edu/es/urban*.

Center for Neighborhood Technology *www.cnt.org*

The Center for Neighborhood Technology has worked on the issue of sustainability for more than twenty years. The organization implements new tools and methods that create livable urban communities for everyone. Information is focused on transit-oriented development, smart growth, transportation and air quality, energy, efficiency/energy conservation, pollution prevention, information as empowerment, and community economic development/jobs creation. Information is also available on specific projects that promote sustainability and community development.

Center for Urban Policy Research *policy.rutgers.edu/cupr*

The Center for Urban Policy Research studies urban poverty and community development, housing, land use, economic development and forecasting, environmental policy, policy evaluation and modeling, survey research, and analyses of special-needs populations.

Citistates Group, LLC *www.citistates.com*

This is a network of journalists, speakers, and advisers "committed to competitive, equitable and sustainable 21st century metropolitan regions." The site provides information on publications about regionalism, Peirce reports on cities, and links to other web sites on regionalism.

Civic Practices Network *www.cpn.org*

Civic Practices Network (CPN) is a collaborative nonpartisan project bringing together a diverse array of organizations and perspectives within the new citizenship movement. This site includes case studies and essays on community, health, youth and education, work and empowerment, families, gender/children, community networking, religion, journalism, and environment. Information on models, techniques, manuals, syllabi, and training centers are also available, as well as essays and theories on civic renewal and movement building.

CivicSource *www.civicsource.org*

CivicSource is a project of the James MacGregor Burns Academy of Leadership at the University of Maryland College Park. It provides brief descriptions of and links to organizations working in the areas of children, youth, families, community development, environment, government and public policy, health, information technology, organizational development, social justice, and web resources.

Collaborative Economics *www.coecon.com*

Collaborative Economics is a firm that helps civic entrepreneurs build communities that collaborate to compete globally by assisting the leaders in the use of collaborative processes to design and implement initiatives for regional economic change. The site contains information and publications on regional innovation, collaboration, leadership and projects.

Council of the Great City Schools *www.cgcs.org*

> The Council of Great City Schools is an organization of the nation's largest urban public school systems, advocating K-12 education in inner-city schools, and governed by superintendents and board of education members from fifty-eight cities across the country. The site provides a database of information on management services, initiative and partnerships, council resources, reports, and other data.

Council of State Community Development Agencies *www.coscda.org*

> The Council of State Community Development Agencies is a national association that provides information, training and advocacy on housing, community development, local economic development and state-local relations. The site provides information on publications and issues related to the aforementioned areas, links to other agencies and resources, and information about their partnerships.

Council for Urban Economic Development *www.cued.org*

> The Council for Urban Economic Development works to create new public-private approaches to urban economic development by promoting discussion of federal, state, and local policy to help urban areas foster greater economic opportunity. The site provides information on research tools, technical assistance, publications, and hosts discussion forums.

Cyburbia *cyburbia.ap.buffalo.edu/pairc*

> Cyburbia is a web site specifically designed as a resource directory. The site contains a comprehensive directory of Internet resources on planning, architecture, and built environments. There are resource directories on community and economic development, education and career development, environment, government, history and preservation, land use, planning agencies and firms, publications and plans, technology, transportation, and urban design. Cyburbia also contains information about architecture and planning related mailing lists and Usenet newsgroups, and it hosts several interactive message areas.

Education Commission of the States *www.ecs.org*

> The Education Commission of the States is a national nonprofit organization that helps governors, legislators, state education officials, and others identify, develop, and implement policies to improve student learning at all levels. This site provides access to information on education issues ranging from accountability and class size to special education finance and vouchers. The site has links to the chief education public officials and executive administrative offices for each state.

Fannie Mae Foundation *www.fanniemaefoundation.org*

> The Fannie Mae Foundation works on affordable homeownership and housing opportunities through partnerships and initiatives with communities across the United States. The site includes home buyer information and a directory of home buying resources for twenty cities. Information is also available on housing research and grant-making programs that focus on supporting affordable homeownership, rental-housing opportunities, and community development.

Governing: The Magazine of States and Localities *www.governing.com*

> Governing is a monthly magazine whose primary audience is state and local government elected and appointed officials. The site includes highlights of current and archived issues of

the magazine, daily governance news from around the country, information about conferences, managers' concerns, links to Internet resources, studies, reports, and guidebooks.

Independent Sector *www.indepsec.org*

The Independent Sector is a coalition of leading nonprofits, foundations, and corporations and it provides information on leadership, public policy and research topics such as household giving, volunteering, and lobbying in the public interest.

International City/County Management Association *www.icma.org*

The International City/County Management Association is a professional and educational organization representing appointed managers and administrators in local governments throughout the world. The site provides information on local government management issues, news, conferences, workshops, publications, selected local government topics, and access to survey research results.

International Downtown Association *ida-downtown.org*

The International Downtown Association seeks to be the principal advocate for North America's urban and community centers by coalescing public, business, and nonprofit interests into civic partnerships. The site contains information on the organization's consulting services, legislative issues, publications, conferences, and links to other downtown associations.

Initiative for a Competitive Inner City *www.icic.org*

The Initiative for a Competitive Inner City is a national, nonprofit organization studying the business potential of inner cities. The site includes information on city studies, cluster studies, public-policy research, and the Inner City 100.

Jobs for the Future *www.jff.org*

The site provides information on programs to create opportunities for youth to succeed in postsecondary learning and high-skill careers, on opportunities for low-income individuals to move into family-supporting careers, and on how to meet the growing economic demand for knowledgeable and skilled workers. There is also information on publications and other resources.

Local Initiatives Support Corporation *www.liscnet.org*

Local Initiatives Support Commission (LISC) is the nation's largest community building organization. It provides grants, loans and equity investments to community development corporations for neighborhood redevelopment. The web site provides information on the LISC urban and rural programs around the nation. These programs include the Community Investment Collaborative for Kids, Organizational Development Initiative, Community Security Initiative, Jobs and Income, and LISC AmeriCorps.

Metropolitan Area Research Corporation *www.metroresearch.org*

The Metropolitan Area Research Corporation studies growing social and economic disparity and low-density outward growth in metropolitan areas, and it assists individuals and groups in fashioning local remedies. The site provides information developed from regional reports on seven general socioeconomic factors: poverty cores, schools, crime, infrastructure, land-use patterns, fiscal disparity, and jobs.

National Affordable Housing Training Institute *www.nahti.org*

> The National Affordable Housing Training Institute is a nonprofit organization composed of eight national public interest groups that provide technical assistance and training to their respective members in the area of affordable housing. The site provides links to the eight members as well as information on services provided and publications.

National Association of Counties *www.naco.org*

> The National Association of Counties acts as a liaison with other levels of government, works to improve public understanding of counties, and serves as a national advocate for counties. The site includes data about counties, legislative issues, and programs and projects on community and economic development, the environment, financial services, information technology, public affairs, workforce development, and social services.

National Association of Housing and Redevelopment Officials *www.nahro.org*

> The National Association of Housing and Redevelopment Officials (NAHRO) is a housing and community-development advocate for adequate and affordable housing and strong, viable communities, particularly for those with low and moderate incomes. The site provides information on affordable housing, community development, legislative affairs and regulations, public housing, rental assistance/ Section 8 and other special programs related to housing, as well as information on publications.

National Association of Regional Councils *www.narc.org*

> The National Association of Regional Councils is an alliance fostering regional cooperation and building regional communities. It represents the legislative and regulatory interests of regional councils and advocates at the national and state level for regional initiatives that improve the quality of life in communities. The site provides information on publications, economic development, and the Institute for Regional Community that was created to develop regional partnerships by the advancement of knowledge on collaboration and regionalism.

National Civic League *www.ncl.org*

> National Civic League (NCL) is an advocacy organization promoting the principles of collaborative problem-solving and consensus-based decision making in local community building.

National Community Building Network *www.ncbn.org*

> The National Community Building Network is an alliance of individuals and organizations that work to reduce poverty and create social and economic opportunity through comprehensive community-building strategies. The site provides information on the principles of community building and policy issues such as gentrification, equitable development, smart growth, education, housing, welfare reform, and crime.

National Congress for Community Economic Development *www.ncced.org*

> The National Congress for Community Economic Development (NCCED) is a trade association and advocate for community-based development industry. NCCED represents over 3,600 community-development corporations. It serves the community-development industry through public-policy research and education, special projects, newsletters, publications, training, conferences, and specialized technical assistance.

National Institute of Justice *www.ojp.usdoj.gov/nij/*

The National Institute of Justice is the research and development branch of the Department of Justice. The site provides information on National Community Policing Survey data and numerous federal programs. There is also information on publications, funding opportunities, and links to other sites useful to researchers.

The National Neighborhood Coalition *www.neighborhoodcoalition.org*

The National Neighborhood Coalition convenes people and organizations concerned about neighborhoods. It is also a conduit for information about programs and policies as well as an advocate for neighborhoods and community and neighborhood-based organizations. The site describes projects, opportunities for information exchange on current issues, legislation and program activities, workshops, conferences and trainings, and gives links to neighborhood and community web sites.

National Trust of Historic Preservation *www.nthp.org*

The National Trust of Historic Preservation works to help neighborhoods and communities through historic preservation. The site provides information on news, stories, action items, and resources for preservation. There is information for the historic homeowners, descriptions of National Trust Historic Site, historic preservation law and public policy, a calendar of preservation-related events, and publications that run the gamut from the economics of historic preservation to travel guides to historic places.

NeighborWorks Network *www.nw.org*

NeighborWorks is a national network of local nonprofit organizations working to revitalize declining neighborhoods by stabilizing home ownership and preserving affordable housing for low- and moderate-income families. The site has information on lending, homeowner insurance, asset management, capacity building, neighborhood reinvestment corporations, and neighborhood housing services.

Partners for Livable Communities *www.livable.com*

Partners for Livable Communities is a nonprofit organization that works with community-development organizations, foundations, and city governments to improve community well-being through economic development, social equity, amenity assets and quality of life. The site has information on organization work on social equity, economic development, leadership, finance, neighborhoods, regionalism, and the natural and built environments.

Partnership for Regional Livability *www.prlonline.org*

The Partnership for Regional Livability was started to help civic leaders in regions across the United States address large-scale problems such as air pollution, growth management, poverty, and unemployment. The Partnership delivers technical assistance to regions, drawing on a national network of experts. The site provides information on five projects to promote livable cities as well as publications and links to other resources on public policies, sustainable growth, and transportation.

Pew Partnership *www.pew-partnership.org*

The Pew Partnership is a civic research organization whose mission is to document and disseminate community solutions. The site provides information programs that demonstrate best practices in communities and civic entreprenueralism. There is also a library of information on civic research.

Piper Resources *www.piperinfo.com/index.cfm*

Piper Resources provides information on state and local government resources. The guide provides links to states' home pages, statewide offices including legislative, judicial, and executive offices as well as boards, commissions, and regional organizations. Additional links include counties, cities, and libraries.

Project for Public Spaces, Inc. *www.pps.org*

The Project for Public Spaces is a nonprofit organization that works to rebuild communities. The site provides information on the organization's technical assistance and education and training opportunities, as well as publications and information on national and regional community-rebuilding initiatives and projects.

Smart Growth Network *www.smartgrowth.org*

The Smart Growth Network provides a forum for facilitating smart growth in neighborhoods, communities, and regions across the United States including information to encourage development that serves the economic, environmental, and social needs of communities.

Smart Library on Urban Poverty *poverty.smartlibrary.org*

The Smart Library on Urban Poverty is a quick resource for research provided in four thematic areas on the topic of urban poverty: urban community, family, economy, and work and welfare. Specific research on trends, explanations, and effects of poverty on communities and poverty policies are identified.

Sprawl Watch Clearinghouse *www.sprawlwatch.org*

The Sprawl Watch Clearinghouse identifies, collects, compiles, and disseminates information on best practices in land use. Tools, techniques, and strategies developed to manage growth for use by citizens, grassroots organizations, environmentalists, public officials, planners, architects, the media and business leaders.

Sustainable Communities Network *www.sustainable.org*

This site has links to resources in six categories: creating community, smart growth, growing a sustainable economy, protecting natural resources, governing sustainably, and living sustainably.

The Urban Institute *www.urban.org*

The Urban Institute is a nonpartisan economic and social-policy research organization. It focuses on education policy, health policy, human resources policy, income and benefits policy, international activities, nonprofits and philanthropy, population studies, metropolitan housing and communities, and justice policy. The centers are located on the web site at *www.urban.org/centers/centers.html*. The web site also includes the National Neighborhood Indicators Partnership at *www.urban.org/nnip*. It provides information and tools to further the development and use of neighborhood information systems in local policy making and community building.

Urban Land Institute *www.uli.org*

The Urban Land Institute is a prominent institution in the field of nonpartisan research and education in urban planning, land use, and development. This site provides information on publications, educational workshops and conferences on finance, housing, retail, office development, transportation, smart growth, and urban revitalization.

The U.S. Conference of Mayors *www.usmayors.org*

The United States Conference of Mayors is the official nonpartisan organization of cities with populations of 30,000 or more. The site provides a connection to the U.S. Mayors' newspaper, information about the U.S. Conference of Mayors, links to cities and mayors in the United States, a database of best practices of city governments, and online publications. There are also legislative updates on arts and sports, community and economic development, civil and human rights, crime and drugs, education and workforce training, environment, health and human services, housing, international trade, taxes and budget, transportation infrastructure and telecommunications, and unfunded mandates.

U.S. Department of Education *www.ed.gov*

The web site provides information on education, student financial assistance, grants and funding opportunities, education research and statistics, publications, program services and links to other education web sites.

U.S. Department of Housing and Urban Development (HUD) *www.hud.gov*

HUD is the U.S. government department responsible for administering housing programs and other urban initiatives. These include fair housing, affordable housing and home ownership, homelessness, jobs and economic opportunity, and empowerment programs. The most helpful component is the HUD USER and Policy Development and Research's Information Service at *www.huduser.org*. HUD USER is the primary source for federal government reports and information on housing policy and programs, building technology, economic development, urban planning, and other housing-related topics. The site provides information on publications, data sets, ongoing research, and listservs related to housing and community development.

U.S. Department of Transportation *www.dot.gov*

The site provides information on transportation plans and performance, reports and publications, grant funding, transportation education opportunities, transportation laws and regulations, as well as links to other resources.

U.S. State and Local Gateway *www.statelocal.gov*

The site was developed to give state and local government officials and employees easy access to federal information. It has information on best practices, funding, tools, laws, news, technical assistance and training for twelve categories: administrative management, communities and commerce, disasters and emergencies, education, housing, environment and energy, money matters, families and children, public safety, transportation and infrastructure, workforce development, and presidential initiatives.

W.E. Upjohn Institute for Employment Research *www.upjohninst.org*

The W.E. Upjohn Institute is an independent, nonprofit research organization devoted to finding, evaluating, and promoting solutions to employment-related problems. The site provides information on the organization's research including current and recently completed projects and publications on the topics of disability and workers compensation, economic development and local labor markets, family labor issues, unemployment insurance, welfare-to-work, and grant opportunities.

Welfare Information Network *www.welfareinfo.org*

The Welfare Information Network is a national initiative to improve the effectiveness, efficiency, and equity of public- and private-sector financing for education, other children's services, and community building and development. This site provides information on program and management-related resources, best practices, federal legislation and guidance on welfare programs, state legislation, state plans, research reference and data resources, welfare-related web sites, welfare services and technical assistance, and grant and contracting opportunities.

World Trade Centers Association *iserve.wtca.org*

The World Trade Centers Association is an organization of over 300 World Trade Centers in more than 100 countries that are connected to expand global business. The site has a pay-as-you-go on-line database resource for business information such as international company profiles, trade opportunities, credit reports, trademarks, patents, market research, and industry news. There is a world trade library that categorizes links of international trade-related web sites on the Internet. Information on markets, tariffs, importers, and logistics for global business ventures is also available.

APPENDIX B

Metro Area Profiles
MILLION-PLUS REGIONS

(Population as of April 1, 2001 in 1,000s)

New York-Northern New Jersey-Long Island, NY-NJ-CT-PA-CMSA[1]

Population:	21,199	
Largest Cities[2]:	New York, NY	*home.nyc.gov/portal/index.jsp?pageID=nyc_home*
	Newark, NJ	*www.gonewark.com*
	Jersey City, NJ	*www.cityofjerseycity.com*
	Yonkers, NY	*www.cityofyonkers.com*
	Paterson, NJ	*www.state.nj.us/commercepaterson.htm*
Counties:	**Bergen-Passaic, NJ PMSA**	
	Bergen, NJ	*www.co.bergen.nj.us*
	Passaic, NJ	*www.injersey.com:80/Living/County/Passaic.html*
	Dutchess, NY PMSA	
	Dutchess, NY	*www.dutchessny.gov*
	Jersey City, NJ PMSA	
	Hudson, NJ	*www.hudsoncounty.org*
	Middlesex-Somerset-Hunterdon, NJ PMSA	
	Hunterdon, NJ	*www.co.hunterdon.nj.us*
	Middlesex, NJ	*co.middlesex.nj.us*
	Somerset, NJ	*www.co.somerset.nj.us*
	Monmouth-Ocean, NJ PMSA	
	Monmouth, NJ	*www.monmouth.com/cgi-bin/dbsearch/ db_search.cgi?setup_file=community.setup*
	Ocean, NJ	*www.oceancountygov.com*

Nassau-Suffolk, NY PMSA
Nassau, NY   *www.co.nassau.ny.us*
Suffolk, NY   *www.co.suffolk.ny.us*

New York, NY PMSA
Bronx, NY
Kings, NY
New York, NY   *home.nyc.gov/portal/index.jsp?pageID=nyc_home*
Putnam, NY   *www.putnamcountyny.com*
Queens, NY   *www.queens.nyc.ny.us*
Richmond, NY
Rockland, NY   *www.co.rockland.ny.us*
Westchester, NY   *www.co.westchester.ny.us*

Newark, NJ PMSA
Essex, NJ   *co.essex.nj.us/essex2.html*
Morris, NJ   *co.morris.nj.us*
Sussex, NJ
Union, NJ   *www.unioncountynj.org*
Warren, NJ   *www.injersey.com/Living/County/Warren.html*

Newburgh, NY-PA PMSA
Orange, NY   *www.co.orange.ny.us*
Pike, PA

Trenton, NJ PMSA
Mercer, NJ   *www.mercercounty.org*

Metropolitan Planning
    Organizations: New York
                              Metropolitan
                              Transportation
                              Council   *www.nymtc.org*
                           (Serves the counties of Nassau, Putnam, Suffolk, Rockland,
                           Westchester, and New York city, NY.)
                           North Jersey
                              Transportation
                              Planning
                              Authority   *www.njtpa.org*
                           (Serves the counties of Bergen, Essex, Hudson, Hunterdon, Middlesex,
                           Monmouth, Morris, Ocean, Passaic, Somerset, Sussex, Union, and
                           Warren, NJ.)

Largest Transit
    Agency: New Jersey Transit
                              (NJ Transit)   *www.njtransit.state.nj.us*

Largest Public
    School District: Community
                              School District 10 *www.nycenet.edu/csd10/district_site*
                           (Board of Education of the City of New York)

Metropolitan Public
    Universities: City University of
                              New York   *www.cuny.edu*

| State University of New York at Stony Brook | www.sunysb.edu |
| Rutgers University at Newark | www.rutgers.edu |

Los Angeles-Riverside-Orange County, CA CMSA

Population:	16,373	
Largest Cities:	Los Angeles	www.ci.la.ca.us
	Long Beach	www.ci.long-beach.ca.us
	Santa Ana	www.ci.santa-ana.ca.us
	Anaheim	www.anaheim.net
	Riverside	www.ci.riverside.ca.us

Counties:

Los Angeles-Long Beach, CA PMSA

| Los Angeles | www.co.la.ca.us |

Orange, CA PMSA

| Orange | www.oc.ca.gov |

Riverside-San Bernardino, CA PMSA

| Riverside | www.co.riverside.ca.us |
| San Bernardino | www.co.san-bernardino.ca.us |

Ventura, CA PMSA

| Ventura, CA | www.ventura.org/vencnty.htm |

| Metropolitan Planning Organization: | Southern California Association of Governments | www.scag.ca.gov |

(Serves the counties of Imperial, Los Angeles, Orange, Riverside, San Bernardino, and Ventura.)

Largest Transit Agency:	Los Angeles County Metropolitan Transportation Authority (Metro)	www.mta.net
Largest Public School District:	Los Angeles Unified School District	www.lausd.k12.ca.us
Metropolitan Public Universities:	University of California-Los Angeles	www.ucla.edu
	University of California-Riverside	www.ucr.edu

Chicago-Gary-Kenosha, IL-IN-WI CMSA

Population:	9,157	
Largest Cities:	Chicago, IL	www.ci.chi.il.us
	Gary, IN	www.gary.in.us

	Aurora, IL	www.aurora.il.us
	Naperville, IL	www.naperville.il.us
	Hammond, IN	www.ci.hammond.in.us
Counties:	**Chicago, IL PMSA**	
	Cook, IL	www.co.cook.il.us
	DeKalb, IL	www.dekalbcounty.org
	DuPage, IL	www.co.dupage.il.us
	Grundy, IL	
	Kane, IL	www.co.kane.il.us
	Kendall, IL	
	Lake, IL	www.co.lake.il.us
	McHenry, IL	www.co.mchenry.il.us
	Will, IL	www.willcountyillinois.com
	Gary, IN PMSA	
	Lake, IN	www.lakecountyin.com
	Porter, IN	www.porterco.org
	Kankakee, IL PMSA	
	Kankakee, IL	www.co.kankakee.il.us
	Kenosha, WI, PMSA	
	Kenosha , WI	www.co.kenosha.wi.us
Metropolitan Planning Organization:	Chicago Area Transportation Study	www.catsmpo.com

(Serves the counties of Cook, DuPage, Kane, Lake, McHenry, and Will, and a portion of Kendall, IL.)

Largest Transit Agency:	Chicago Transit Authority (cta)	www.transitchicago.com
Largest Public School District:	Chicago Public Schools	www.cps.k12.il.us
Metropolitan Public University:	University of Illinois-Chicago	www.uic.edu

Washington-Baltimore, DC-MD-VA-WV CMSA

Population:	7,608	
Largest Cities:	Baltimore, MD	www.ci.baltimore.md.us
	Washington, DC	www.washingtondc.gov
	Alexandria, VA	ci.alexandria.va.us
	Rockville, MD	www.ci.rockville.md.us
	Frederick, MD	www.cityoffrederick.com
Counties:	**Baltimore, MD PMSA**	
	Anne Arundel, MD	www.co.anne-arundel.md.us
	Baltimore, MD	www.co.ba.md.us
	Carroll, MD	ccgov.carr.org

Harford, MD	www.co.ha.md.us
Howard, MD	www.co.ho.md.us
Queen Anne's, MD	www.qac.org
Baltimore city, MD	www.ci.baltimore.md.us

Hagerstown, MD PMSA

Washington, MD	pilot.wash.lib.md.us/washco/index.html

Washington, DC-MD-VA-WV PMSA

District of Columbia, DC	www.dc.gov
Calvert, MD	www.co.cal.md.us
Charles, MD	www.govt.co.charles.md.us
Frederick, MD	www.co.frederick.md.us
Montgomery, MD	www.co.mo.md.us
Prince George's, MD	www.co.pg.md.us
Arlington, VA	www.co.arlington.va.us/scripts/default.asp
Clarke, VA	www.co.clarke.va.us
Culpeper, VA	www.co.culpeper.va.us
Fairfax, VA	www.co.fairfax.va.us
Fauquier, VA	co.fauquier.va.us
King George, VA	
Loudoun, VA	www.co.loudoun.va.us
Prince William, VA	www.co.prince-william.va.us
Spotsylvania, VA	www.spotsylvania.va.us
Stafford, VA	www.co.stafford.va.us
Warren, VA	
Alexandria city, VA	ci.alexandria.va.us
Fairfax city, VA	www.ci.fairfax.va.us
Falls Church city, VA	www.ci.falls-church.va.us
Fredericksburg city, VA	www.efredericksburg.net
Manassas city, VA	www.manassascity.org
Manassas Park city, VA	www.ci.manassas-park.va.us
Berkeley, WV	www.berkeleycountycomm.org
Jefferson, WV	www.intrepid.net/county

Metropolitan Planning
Organizations:

Baltimore
    Metropolitan Council   www.baltometro.org
    (Serves the counties of Anne Arundel, Baltimore, Carroll,
    Harford, Howard, and Baltimore city, MD.)
National Capital
    Region Transportation
    Planning Board at
    Metropolitan
    Washington Council
    of Governments   www.mwcog.org
    (Serves the counties of Loudoun and Prince William, VA, and
    Fairfax, Frederick, Montgomery, Prince George's, MD, and the
    District of Columbia, DC.)

Largest Transit Agency:	Washington Metropolitan Area Transit Authority (Metro)	www.wmata.com
Largest Public School Districts:	Fairfax County Public Schools	www.fcps.k12.va.us
	Prince George's County Public Schools	www.pgcps.pg.k12.md.us
	Montgomery County Public Schools	www.mcps.k12.md.us
	Baltimore City Public School System	www.bcps.k12.md.us
	Baltimore County Public Schools	www.bcps.org
	District of Columbia Public Schools	www.k12.dc.us
	Anne Arundel County Public Schools	www.aacps.org
	Prince William County Schools	www.pwcs.edu
Metropolitan Public Universities:	George Mason University	www.gmu.edu
	University of Maryland-Baltimore	www.umaryland.edu
	University of Maryland-College Park	www.umd.edu

San Francisco-Oakland-San Jose, CA CMSA

Population:	7,039	
Largest Cities:	San Jose	www.ci.san-jose.ca.us
	San Francisco	sfgov.org
	Oakland	www.oaklandnet.com
	Fremont	www.ci.fremont.ca.us
	Sunnyvale	www.ci.sunnyvale.ca.us
Counties:	**Oakland, CA PMSA**	
	Alameda	www.co.alameda.ca.us
	Contra Costa	www.co.contra-costa.ca.us
	San Francisco, CA PMSA	
	Marin	
	San Francisco	sfgov.org
	San Mateo	www.co.sanmateo.ca.us
	San Jose, CA PMSA	
	Santa Clara	claraweb.co.santa-clara.ca.us

Santa Cruz-Watsonville, CA PMSA

Santa Cruz   *www.co.santa-cruz.ca.us*

Santa Rosa, CA PMSA

Sonoma   *www.sonoma-county.org*

Vallejo-Fairfield-Napa CA PMSA

Napa   *www.co.napa.ca.us*

Solano   *www.co.solano.ca.us*

Metropolitan Planning Organization:	Metropolitan Transportation Commission *www.mtc.ca.gov* (Serves the counties of Alameda, Contra Costa, Marin, Napa, San Francisco, Santa Clara, San Mateo, Solano, Sonoma.)
Largest Transit Agency:	San Francisco Bay Area Rapid Transit District (BART) *www.bart.org*
Largest Public School Districts:	Oakland Unified School District *www.ousd.k12.ca.us* San Francisco Unified School District *www.sfusd.k12.ca.us*
Metropolitan Public Universities:	University of California-Berkeley *www.berkeley.edu* University of California-San Francisco *www.ucsf.edu* San Jose State University *www.sjsu.edu*

Philadelphia-Wilmington-Atlantic City, PA-NJ-DE-MD CMSA

Population: 6,188

Largest Cities:

Philadelphia, PA	*www.phila.gov*
Camden, NJ	*www.ci.camden.nj.us*
Wilmington, DE	*www.ci.wilmington.de.us*
Vineland, NJ	*www.ci.vineland.nj.us*
Chester, PA	*www.chestercity.com*

Counties:

Atlantic-Cape May, NJ PMSA

Atlantic, NJ	*www.aclink.org*
Cape May, NJ	*www.capemaycity.com*

Philadelphia, PA-NJ PMSA

Bucks, PA	*www.buckscounty.org*
Chester, PA	*www.chesco.org*
Delaware, PA	*www.co.delaware.pa.us*
Montgomery, PA	*www.montcopa.org*
Philadelphia, PA	*www.phila.gov*

	Burlington, NJ	*www.burlco.lib.nj.us*
	Camden, NJ	*www.co.camden.nj.us*
	Gloucester, NJ	*www.co.gloucester.nj.us*
	Salem, NJ	

Vineland-Millville-Bridgeton, NJ PMSA

Cumberland, NJ   *www.co.cumberland.nj.us*

Wilmington-Newark, DE-MD PMSA

New Castle, DE   *www.co.new-castle.de.us*

Cecil, MD   *www.ccgov.org*

Metropolitan Planning
   Organization:

Delaware Valley
   Regional Planning
   Commission   *www.dvrpc.org*
(Serves the counties of Burlington, Camden, Gloucester, and Mercer, NJ,
and Bucks, Chester, Delaware, Montgomery, and Philadelphia, PA.)

Largest Transit
   Agency:

Southeastern
   Pennsylvania
   Transportation
   Authority (SEPTA)   *www.septa.org*

Largest Public School
   District:

School District of
   Philadelphia   *www.philsch.k12.pa.us*

Metropolitan Public
   University: Temple University   *www.temple.edu*

Boston-Worcester-Lawrence-Lowell-Brockton, MA-NH NECMA

Population: 5,819

Largest Cities:
   Boston, MA   *www.ci.boston.ma.us*
   Worcester, MA   *www.ci.worcester.ma.us*
   Lowell, MA   *web.ci.lowell.ma.us*
   New Bedford, MA   *www.ci.new-bedford.ma.us*
   Manchester, NH   *ci.manchester.nh.us*

Counties:
   Bristol, MA
   Essex, MA
   Middlesex, MA
   Norfolk, MA
   Plymouth, MA
   Suffolk, MA
   Worcester, MA
   Hillsborough, NH
   Rockingham, NH   *co.rockingham.nh.us*
   Strafford, NH

Metropolitan Planning
   Organizations:

Boston Metropolitan
   Planning
   Organization   *www.ctps.org/bostonmpo*
(Serves 101 cities and towns in the Boston metropolitan area.)

	Central Massachusetts Regional Planning Commission	www.cmrpc.org

(Serves the southern two-thirds of Worcester county.)

Northern Middlesex
Council of
Governments   www.nmcog.org
(Serves the municipalities of Billerica, Chelmsford, Dracut, Dunstable, Lowell, Pepperell, Tewksbury, Tyngsborough, and Westford.)

Largest Transit
  Agency: Massachusetts Bay
                       Transportation
                       Authority (T)   www.mbta.com

Largest Public
  School District: Boston Public Schools   www.boston.k12.ma.us
Metropolitan Public
  University: University of
                       Massachusetts-
                       Boston   www.umb.edu

Detroit-Ann Arbor-Flint, MI CMSA
Population: 5,456
Largest Cities: Detroit   www.ci.detroit.mi.us
                       Warren   www.cityofwarren.org/index.htm
                       Flint   www.ci.flint.mi.us
                       Sterling Heights   www.ci.sterling-heights.mi.us
                       Ann Arbor   www.ci.ann-arbor.mi.us

Counties: **Ann Arbor, MI PMSA**
                       Lenawee
                       Livingston
                       Washtenaw   www.co.washtenaw.mi.us
                       Detroit, MI PMSA
                       Lapeer   lapeer.org/lasso.lasso?-database=
                                              Sponsors&-layout=Main&-response=
                                              MainPage.html
                       Macomb   www.co.macomb.mi.us/boardofcommissioners
                       Monroe   monroe.lib.mi.us/cwis/county.htm
                       Oakland   www.co.oakland.mi.us
                       St. Clair
                       Wayne   www.waynecounty.com
                       Flint, MI PMSA
                       Genessee   www.co.genesee.mi.us
Metropolitan Planning
  Organization: Genessee County
                         Metropolitan
                         Planning
                         Commission
                       Southeast Michigan

	Council of Governments	www.semcog.org

(Serves Livingston, Macomb, Monroe, Oakland, St. Clair, Washtenaw, and Wayne counties.)

Largest Transit Agency:	City of Detroit Department of Transportation (D-DOT)	www.ci.detroit.mi.us/DDOT
Largest Public School District:	Detroit Public Schools	www.detpub.k12.mi.us
Metropolitan Public University:	Wayne State University	www.wayne.edu

Dallas-Fort Worth, TX CMSA

Population:	5,221	
Largest Cities:	Dallas	www.ci.dallas.tx.us
	Fort Worth	ci.fort-worth.tx.us
	Arlington	www.ci.arlington.tx.us
	Garland	www.ci.garland.tx.us
	Irving	www.ci.irving.tx.us
Counties:	**Dallas, TX PMSA**	
	Collin	www.co.collin.tx.us
	Dallas	www.dallascounty.org
	Denton	dentoncounty.com/default1001.htm
	Ellis	
	Henderson	
	Hunt	
	Kaufman	
	Rockwall	
	Fort Worth-Arlington, TX PMSA	
	Hood	
	Johnson	
	Parker	
	Tarrant	www.tarrantcounty.com
Metropolitan Planning Organization:	North Central Texas Council of Governments	www.nctcog.dst.tx.us

(Serves Collin, Dallas, Denton, Ellis, Erath, Hood, Hunt, Johnson, Kaufman, Navarro, Palo Alto, Parker, Rockwall, Somervell, Tarrant, and Wise counties.)

Largest Transit Agency:	Dallas Area Rapid Transit Authority (DART)	www.dart.org/home.htm
Largest Public School Districts:	Dallas Independent School District	www.dallasisd.org

	Fort Worth Independent School District	www.ftworth.isd.tenet.edu
Metropolitan Public Universities:	University of Texas-Dallas	www.utdallas.edu
	University of Texas-Arlington	www.uta.edu
	University of North Texas	www.unt.edu

Houston-Galveston-Brazoria, TX CMSA

Population:	4,669	
Largest Cities:	Houston	www.cityofhouston.gov
	Pasadena	www.ci.pasadena.tx.us
	Baytown	www.baytown.org
	Galveston	www.cityofgalveston.org
	Texas City	www.texas-city-tx.org
Counties:	**Brazoria, TX PMSA**	
	Brazoria	
	Galveston-Texas City, TX PMSA	
	Galveston	www.phoenix.net/~cntyjdge/homepage.htm
	Houston, TX PMSA	
	Chambers	co.chambers.tx.us
	Fort Bend	www.co.fort-bend.tx.us
	Harris	www.co.harris.tx.us
	Liberty	
	Montgomery	www.montgomerycounty.com
	Waller	wallercounty.org/index.htm
Metropolitan Planning Organization:	Houston-Galveston Area Council	www.hgac.cog.tx.us
	(Serves Austin, Brazoria, Chambers, Colorado, Fort Bend, Galveston, Harris, Liberty, Matagorda, Montgomery, Walker, Waller, and Wharton counties.)	
Largest Transit Agency:	Metropolitan Transit Authority of Harris County (METRO)	www.ridemetro.org
Largest Public School Districts:	Aldine Independent School District	www.aldine.k12.tx.us
	Cypress-Fairbanks Independent School District	www.cfisd.net
	Houston Independent School District	www.houston.isd.tenet.edu
Metropolitan Public University:	University of Houston	www.uh.edu

Atlanta, GA MSA

Population:	4,112	
Largest Cities:	Atlanta	*www.ci.atlanta.ga.us*
	Roswell	*ci.roswell.ga.us*
	Marietta	*www.city.marietta.ga.us*
	East Point	*www.eastpointcity.org*
	Smyrna	*www.ci.smyrna.ga.us*
Counties:	Barrow	
	Bartow	
	Carroll	*carrollcountyga.com*
	Cherokee	
	Clayton	*www.co.clayton.ga.us*
	Cobb	*www.co.cobb.ga.us*
	Coweta	*www.coweta.ga.us*
	DeKalb	*www.co.dekalb.ga.us*
	Douglas	*www.co.douglas.ga.us*
	Fayette	*www.admin.co.fayette.ga.us*
	Forsyth	*www.co.forsyth.ga.us*
	Fulton	*www.co.fulton.ga.us*
	Gwinnett	*www.co.gwinnett.ga.us*
	Henry	*www.co.henry.ga.us*
	Newton	*www.co.newton.ga.us*
	Paulding	
	Pickens	
	Rockdale	*www.rockdalecounty.org/dale.cfm?pid=1*
	Spalding	*www.spaldingcounty.com*
	Walton	*www.waltoncountyga.org*

Metropolitan Planning
  Organization: Atlanta Regional
                  Commission   *www.atlantaregional.com*
                  (Serves Cherokee, Clayton, Cobb, DeKalb, Douglas, Fayette, Fulton, Gwinnett, Henry, and Rockdale counties, as well as the City of Atlanta.)

Largest Transit
  Agency: Metropolitan Atlanta
                  Rapid Transit
                  Authority (marta)   *www.itsmarta.com*

Largest Public School
  Districts: Atlanta City Schools   *www.atlanta.k12.ga.us*
                  DeKalb County
                  Schools   *www.dekalb.k12.ga.us*
                  Fulton County Schools   *www.fulton.k12.ga.us*
                  Gwinnett County
                  Public Schools   *www.gwinnett.k12.ga.us*

Metropolitan Public
  University: Georgia State
                  University   *www.gsu.edu*

Miami-Fort Lauderdale, FL CMSA

Population:	3,876	
Largest Cities:	Miami	*www.ci.miami.fl.us*
	Hialeah	*www.ci.hialeah.fl.us*
	Fort Lauderdale	*www.ci.ftlaud.fl.us*
	Hollywood	*www.hollywoodfl.org*
	Miami Beach	*ci.miami-beach.fl.us*

Counties: **Fort Lauderdale, FL PMSA**

        Broward   *www.co.broward.fl.us*

    Miami, FL, PMSA

        Miami-Dade   *miamidade.gov*

Metropolitan Planning
Organizations: Broward County
        Office of Planning   *www.broward.org/bcmpo*
        (Serves Broward county.)
    Metropolitan Planning
        Organization for
        the Miami Urbanized
        Area   *www.metro-dade.com/mpo*
        (Serves Miami-Dade county.)

Largest Transit
Agency: Miami-Dade Transit
        Agency   *www.co.miami-dade.fl.us/mdta*

Largest Public School
Districts: Broward County
        Public Schools   *browardschools.com*
    Miami-Dade County
        Public Schools   *dcps.dade.k12.fl.us*

Metropolitan Public
University: Florida International
        University   *www.fiu.edu*

Seattle-Tacoma-Bremerton, WA CMSA

Population:	3,554	
Largest Cities:	Seattle	*www.ci.seattle.wa.us*
	Tacoma	*www.cityoftacoma.org*
	Bellevue	*www.ci.bellevue.wa.us*
	Everett	*www.ci.everett.wa.us*
	Renton	*www.ci.renton.wa.us*

Counties: **Bremerton, WA PMSA**

        Kitsap   *www.wa.gov/kitsap*

    Olympia, WA PMSA

        Thurston   *www.co.thurston.wa.us*

    Seattle-Bellevue-Everett, WA PMSA

        Island   *www.islandcounty.net*
        King   *www.metrokc.gov*
        Snohomish   *www.co.snohomish.wa.us*

Tacoma, WA PMSA

Pierce   *www.co.pierce.wa.us*

Metropolitan Planning
  Organization: Puget Sound Regional
                 Council   *www.psrc.org*
                 (Serves King, Kitsap, Pierce and Snohomish counties.)

Largest Transit
  Agency: King County
                 Department of
                 Transportation-Metro
                 Transit Division
                 (Metro)   *transit.metrokc.gov*

Largest Public School
  District: Seattle Public Schools   *www.seattleschools.org*

Metropolitan Public
  University: University of
                 Washington   *www.washington.edu*

Phoenix-Mesa, AZ MSA

Population: 3,251

Largest Cities: Phoenix   *www.ci.phoenix.az.us*
                 Tucson   *www.ci.tucson.az.us*
                 Mesa   *www.ci.mesa.az.us/nsdefault.asp*
                 Glendale   *www.ci.glendale.az.us*
                 Tempe   *www.tempe.gov/default1.asp*

Counties: Maricopa   *www.maricopa.gov*
                 Pinal   *www.co.pinal.az.us*

Metropolitan Planning
  Organization: Maricopa
                 Association of
                 Governments   *www.mag.maricopa.gov*
                 (Serves Maricopa county.)

Largest Transit
  Agency: City of Phoenix
                 Public Transit   *www.valleymetro.maricopa.gov*

Largest Public
  School District: Mesa Public Schools   *www.mpsaz.org/main2*

Metropolitan Public
  University: Arizona Sate
                 University   *www.asu.edu*

Minneapolis-St. Paul, MN-WI, MSA

Population: 2,968

Largest Cities: Minneapolis, MN   *www.ci.mpls.mn.us*
                 St. Paul, MN   *www.stpaul.gov*
                 Bloomington, MN   *www.ci.bloomington.mn.us*
                 Brooklyn Park, MN   *www.ci.brooklyn-park.mn.us*
                 Coon Rapids, MN   *www.ci.coon-rapids.mn.us*

Counties:	Anoka, MN	*www.co.anoka.mn.us*
	Carver, MN	*www.co.carver.mn.us*
	Chisago, MN	*www.co.chisago.mn.us*
	Dakota, MN	*www.co.dakota.mn.us*
	Hennepin, MN	*www.co.hennepin.mn.us*
	Isanti, MN	
	Ramsey, MN	*www.co.ramsey.mn.us*
	Scott, MN	*www.co.scott.mn.us*
	Sherburne, MN	*www.co.sherburne.mn.us*
	Washington, MN	*www.co.washington.mn.us*
	Wright, MN	*www.co.wright.mn.us*
	Pierce, WI	*www.co.pierce.wi.us*
	St. Croix, WI	*www.co.saint-croix.wi.us*

Metropolitan Planning
  Organization: Metropolitan Council   *www.metrocouncil.org*
Largest Transit
  Agency: Minneapolis-St. Paul
      Metropolitan Council,
      Metro Transit
      Division (T)   *www.metrotransit.org*
Largest Public School
  Districts: Minneapolis Public
      Schools   *www.mpls.k12.mn.us*
      St. Paul Public
      Schools   *www.spps.org*
Metropolitan Public
  University: University of
      Minnesota-Twin
      Cities   *www1.umn.edu/twincities*

Cleveland-Akron, OH CMSA

Population: 2,945
Largest Cities: Cleveland   *www.cityofcleveland.org*
      Akron   *ci.akron.oh.us*
      Parma
      Lorain   *www.ci.lorain.oh.us*
      Lakewood   *www.lkwdpl.org/city*

Counties: **Akron, OH PMSA**
      Portage   *www.co.portage.oh.us*
      Summit   *www.co.summit.oh.us*

      Cleveland-Lorain-Elyria, OH PMSA
      Ashtabula   *www.co.ashtabula.oh.us*
      Cuyahoga   *www.cuyahoga.oh.us*
      Geauga   *www.co.geauga.oh.us*
      Lake   *www.lakecountyohio.org*
      Lorain
      Medina   *www.co.medina.oh.us*

Metropolitan Planning
  Organization: Akron Metropolitan
                      ATS Northeast
                      Ohio Areawide
                      Coordinating Agency *www.noaca.org*
                      (Serves Cuyahoga, Geauga, Lake, Lorain, and Medina counties.)

Largest Transit
  Agency: Greater Cleveland
                      Regional Transit
                      Authority (RTA)   *www.gcrta.org*

Largest Public School
  District: Cleveland Municipal
                      School District   *www.cleveland.k12.oh.us*

Metropolitan Public
  Universities: Cleveland State
                      University   *www.csuohio.edu*
                      University of Akron   *www.uakron.edu*

San Diego, CA MSA
Population: 2,813
Largest Cities: San Diego   *www.ci.san-diego.ca.us*
                      Chula Vista   *www.ci.chula-vista.ca.us/index.html*
                      Oceanside   *www.ci.oceanside.ca.us*
                      Escondido   *www.ci.escondido.ca.us*
                      El Cajon   *www.ci.el-cajon.ca.us*
Counties: San Diego   *www.co.san-diego.ca.us*
Metropolitan Planning
  Organization: San Diego Association
                      of Governments   *www.sandag.org*
Largest Transit
  Agency: San Diego
                      Trolley, Inc.
                      (The Trolley)   *www.sandag.cog.ca.us/sdmts/trolleypage.htm*
                      San Diego Transit
                      Corporation (MTS) *www.sdcommute.com*
Largest Public School
  District: San Diego City
                      Schools   *www.sdcs.k12.ca.us*
Metropolitan Public
  Universities: University of
                      California-San Diego *www.ucsd.edu*

St. Louis, MO-IL MSA
Population: 2,603
Largest Cities: St. Louis, MO   *stlouis.missouri.org*
                      St. Charles, MO   *www.stcharlescity.com*
                      Florissant, MO   *www.florissantmo.com*
                      St. Peters, MO   *www.ci.st-peters.mo.us*
                      Belleville, IL   *www.belleville.net*

Counties:	Clinton, IL	www.clintonco.org/index.html
	Jersey, IL	www.jerseycounty.org
	Madison, IL	www.co.madison.il.us
	Monroe, IL	
	St. Clair, IL	www.co.st-clair.il.us
	Franklin, MO	www.usmo.com/~franklin
	Jefferson, MO	www.jeffcomo.org
	Lincoln, MO	
	St. Charles, MO	www.win.org/county/sccg.htm
	St. Louis, MO	www.co.st-louis.mo.us
	Warren, MO	www.warrencountymo.net
	St. Louis city, MO	stlouis.missouri.org

Metropolitan Planning
  Organization: East-West Gateway
                      Coordinating Council www.ewgateway.org
                      (Serves the counties of Franklin, Jefferson, St. Charles, St. Louis
                      and St. Louis City, Missouri and Madison, Monroe and St. Clair
                      in Illinois.)

Largest Transit
  Agency: Bi-State Development
                      Agency   www.bi-state.org

Largest Public School
  District: St. Louis Public
                      Schools   www.slps.k12.mo.us

Metropolitan Public
  University: University of
                      Missouri-St. Louis www.umsl.edu

Denver-Boulder-Greeley, CO CMSA

Population: 2,581

Largest Cities:	Denver	www.denvergov.org
	Aurora	www.ci.aurora.co.us
	Lakewood	www.ci.lakewood.co.us
	Arvada	www.arvadainteractive.com
	Boulder	www.ci.boulder.co.us

Counties: **Boulder-Longmont, CO PMSA**

| | Boulder | www.co.boulder.co.us |

Denver, CO PMSA

	Adams	www.co.adams.co.us
	Arapahoe	www.co.arapahoe.co.us
	Denver	www.denvergov.org
	Douglas	www.douglas.co.us
	Jefferson	206.247.49.21/ext/index.htm

Greeley, CO PMSA

| | Weld | www.co.weld.co.us |

Metropolitan Planning
  Organization: Denver Regional
                      Council of
                      Governments   www.drcog.com

Largest Transit
  Agency: Regional Transportation
                           District (RTD)   *www.rtd-denver.com*
Largest Public School
  District: Denver Public Schools   *www.denver.k12.co.us*
Metropolitan Public
  University: University of
                           Colorado-Denver   *www.cudenver.edu*

Tampa-St. Petersburg-Clearwater, FL MSA
Population: 2,395
Largest Cities: Tampa   *www.ci.tampa.fl.us*
                           St. Petersburg   *www.ci.saint-petersburg.fl.us*
                           Clearwater   *www.clearwater-fl.com*
                           Lakeland   *government.lakeland.net*
                           Largo   *www.largo.com*
Counties: Hernando   *www.co.hernando.fl.us*
                                                   org/home.html
                           Hillsborough   *www.hillsboroughcounty.org*
                           Pasco   *pascocounty.com/govt*
                           Pinellas   *www.co.pcinellas.fl.us/bcc*
Metropolitan Planning
  Organizations: Hillsborough County
                           Metropolitan Planning
                           Organization   *www.hillsboroughmpo.org*
                           Pinellas County
                           Metropolitan Planning
                           Organization   *www.co.pinellas.fl.us/mpo*
Largest Transit
  Agency: Hillsborough Area
                           Regional Transit
                           Authority (HARTline)   *www.hartline.org*
                           Pinellas Suncoast
                           Transit Authority
                           (PSTA)   *www.psta.net*
Largest Public School
  District: Hillsborough County
                           Public Schools   *www.sdhc.k12.fl.us*
Metropolitan Public
  University: University of
                           South Florida   *www.usf.edu*

Pittsburgh, PA MSA
Population: 2,358
Largest Cities: Pittsburgh   *www.city.pittsburgh.pa.us*
                           McKeesport
                           Greensburg   *www.city.greensburg.pa.us/html/contact.html*
                           New Kensington
                           Washington   *www.cityofwashingtonpa.com*
Counties: Allegheny   *www.county.allegheny.pa.us*
                           Beaver   *www.co.beaver.pa.us*

	Butler	www.co.butler.pa.us
	Fayette	www.fforward.com
	Washington	www.co.washington.pa.us
	Westmoreland	www.co.westmoreland.pa.us

Metropolitan Planning Organization:	Southwestern Pennsylvania Regional Planning Commission	
Largest Transit Agency:	Port Authority of Allegheny County	www.ridegold.com
Largest Public School District:	Pittsburgh Public Schools	www.pps.pgh.pa.us
Metropolitan Public University:	University of Pittsburgh	www.pitt.edu

Portland-Salem, OR-WA CMSA

Population:	2,265	
Largest Cities:	Portland, OR	www.ci.portland.or.us
	Salem, OR	www.ci.salem.or.us
	Gresham, OR	www.ci.gresham.or.us
	Beaverton, OR	www.ci.beaverton.or.us
	Vancouver, WA	

Counties:	**Portland-Vancouver, OR-WA PMSA**	
	Clackamas, OR	www.co.clackamas.or.us
	Columbia, OR	www.co.columbia.or.us
	Multnomah, OR	www.multnomah.or.us
	Washington, OR	www.co.washington.or.us
	Yamhill, OR	www.co.yamhill.or.us
	Clark, WA	www.co.clark.wa.us
	Salem, OR PMSA	
	Marion, OR	www.open.org/~marion
	Polk, OR	www.co.polk.or.us

Metropolitan Planning Organizations:	Metro	www.metro-region.org
	(Serves Clackamas, Multnomah, and Washington counties.)	
	Mid-Willamette Valley Council of Governments	www.open.org/~cog/
Largest Transit Agency:	Tri-County Metropolitan Transportation District of Oregon (TRI-MET)	www.tri-met.org
Largest Public School District:	Portland Public Schools	www.pps.k12.or.us

Metropolitan Public
  University: Portland State
                            University   *www.pdx.edu*

Cincinnati-Hamilton, OH-KY-IN CMSA

Population:	1,979	
Largest Cities:	Cincinnati, OH	*www.rcc.org*
	Hamilton, OH	*www.hamilton-city.org*
	Middletown, OH	*www.ci.middletown.oh.us*
	Covington, KY	*www.covingtonky.com*
	Fairfield, OH	*www.fairfield-city.org*
Counties:	**Cincinnati, OH-KY-IN, PMSA**	
	Brown, OH	
	Clermont, OH	*www.co.clermont.oh.us*
	Hamilton, OH	*www.hamilton-co.org*
	Warren, OH	*www.co.warren.oh.us*
	Boone, KY	*www.boonecountyky.org*
	Campbell, KY	*www.campbellcountyky.org*
	Gallatin, KY	
	Grant, KY	*grantco.org*
	Kenton, KY	*www.kentoncounty.org*
	Pendleton, KY	
	Dearborn, IN	*www.dearborncounty.org*
	Ohio, IN	
	Hamilton-Middletown, OH PMSA	
	Butler, OH	*www.butlercountyohio.org*
Metropolitan Planning		
Organization:	Ohio, Kentucky,	
	Indiana Regional	
	Council of	
	Governments	*www.oki.org*
Largest Transit		
Agency:	Southwest Ohio	
	Regional Transit	
	Authority (Metro)	*www.sorta.com*
Largest Public School		
District:	Cincinnati Public	
	Schools	*www.cpsboe.k12.oh.us*
Metropolitan Public		
University:	University of Cincinnati	*www.uc.edu*

Sacramento-Yolo, CA CMSA

Population:	1,796	
Largest Cities:	Sacramento	*www.ci.sacramento.ca.us*
	Antioch	*www.ci.antioch.ca.us*
	Davis	*www.city.davis.ca.us*
	Roseville	*www.roseville.ca.us*
	Woodland	*www.ci.woodland.ca.us*

Counties:	**Sacramento, CA PMSA**	
	El Dorado	www.co.el-dorado.ca.us
	Placer	www.placer.ca.gov
	Sacramento	www.co.sacramento.ca.us
	Yolo, CA PMSA	
	Yolo	www.yolocounty.org
Metropolitan Planning Organization:	Sacramento Area Council of Governments	www.sacog.org
	(Serves El Dorado, Placer, Sacramento, Sutter, Yolo,Yuba counties.)	
Largest Transit Agency:	Sacramento Regional Transit District (RT)	www.sacrt.com
Largest Public School District:	Sacramento City Unified School District	www.scusd.edu
Metropolitan Public University:	University of California-Davis	www.ucdavis.edu

Kansas City, MO-KS MSA

Population:	1,776	
Largest Cities:	Kansas City, MO	www.kcmo.org/index.htm
	Kansas City, KS	
	Independence, MO	www.ci.independence.mo.us
	Overland Park, KS	www.opkansas.org
	Olathe, KS	www.olatheks.org
Counties:	Johnson, KS	www.jocoks.com
	Leavenworth, KS	www.lvarea.com/lvcounty.htm
	Miami, KS	
	Wyandotte, KS	www.wycokck.org
	Cass, MO	www.casscounty.com
	Clay, MO	
	Clinton, MO	
	Jackson, MO	www.co.jackson.mo.us
	Lafayette, MO	
	Platte, MO	co.platte.mo.us
	Ray, MO	
Metropolitan Planning Organization:	Mid-America Regional Council	www.marc.org/transportation
	(Serves Wyandotte, Johnson and Jackson counties, and portions of Leavenworth, Platte, Clay, and Cass counties.)	
Largest Transit Agency:	Kansas City Area Transit Authority (ATA)	www.kcata.org

Largest Public
    School District: Kansas City, Missouri
                                School District   www.kcmsd.k12.mo.us
Metropolitan Public
    University: University of
                                Missouri-Kansas City   www.umkc.edu

Milwaukee-Racine, WI CMSA
Population: 1,689
Largest Cities: Milwaukee   www.ci.mil.wi.us
                            Racine   www.cityofracine.org
                            West Allis   www.ci.west-allis.wi.us
                            Waukesha   www.ci.waukesha.wi.us
                            Wauwatosa   www.ci.wauwatosa.wi.us
Counties: **Milwaukee-Waukesha, WI PMSA**
                            Milwaukee   www.co.milwaukee.wi.us
                            Ozaukee   www.co.ozaukee.wi.us
                            Washington   www.co.washington.wi.us
                            Waukesha   www.co.waukesha.wi.us
                            Racine, WI PMSA
                            Racine   www.racinecounty.com
Metropolitan Planning
    Organization: Southeastern
                                Wisconsin Regional
                                Planning
                                Commission   www.wisrep.org/SEWRPC/sewrpc.html
Largest Transit
    Agency: Milwaukee County
                                Transit System   www.ridemcts.com
Largest Public School
    District: Milwaukee Public
                                Schools   www.milwaukee.k12.wi.us
Metropolitan Public
    University: University of Wisconsin
                                Milwaukee   www.uwm.edu

Orlando, FL MSA
Population: 1,644
Largest Cities: Orlando   www.cityoforlando.net
                            Altamonte Springs   www.altamonte.org
                            Sanford   www.ci.sanford.fl.us
                            Kissimmee   www.kissimmee.org
                            Winter Park   www.ci.winter-park.fl.us
Counties: Lake   www.lakegovernment.com
                            Orange   www.onetgov.net
                            Osceola   www.osceola.org
                            Seminole   www.co.seminole.fl.us/indexmu.html
Metropolitan Planning
    Organization: Metroplan Orlando   www.metroplanorlando.com
                            (Serves Orange, Osceola, and Seminole counties.)

Largest Transit Agency:	Central Florida Regional Transportation Authority (LYNX)	www.golynx.com
Largest Public School District:	Orange County Public Schools	www.ocps.k12.fl.us
Metropolitan Public Universities:	University of Central Florida	www.ucf.edu

Indianapolis, IN MSA

Population:	1,607	
Largest Cities:	Indianapolis	www.indygov.org
	Anderson	www.cityofanderson.com
	Lawrence	
	Greenwood	www.ci.greenwood.in.us
	Carmel	www.ci.carmel.in.us
Counties:	Boone	www.bccn.boone.in.us
	Hamilton	www.co.hamilton.in.us
	Hancock	www.co.hancock.in.us
	Hendricks	www.hendrickscounty.com
	Johnson	www.jccn.org
	Madison	www.indico.net/counties/MADISON/index.htm
	Marion	www.indygov.org
	Morgan	
	Shelby	www.co.shelby.tn.us
Metropolitan Planning Organizations:	Indianapolis	www.indygov.org/indympo/index.htm
	(Serves all of Indianapolis and Marion County and portions of the surrounding counties of Boone, Hamilton, Hancock, Hendricks and Johnson.)	
	Madison County Council of Governments	www.mccog.net
Largest Transit Agency:	Indianapolis Public Transportation Corporation (IndyGo)	www.indygo.net
Largest Public School District:	Indianapolis Public Schools	www.ips.k12.in.us
Metropolitan Public University:	Indiana University-Purdue University Indianapolis	www.iupui.edu

San Antonio, TX MSA

Population:	1,592	
Largest Cities:	San Antonio	*www.ci.sat.tx.us*
	New Braunfels	*www.ci.new-braunfels.tx.us*
	Seguin	*www.ci.seguin.tx.us*
	Universal City	
	Schertz	*www.ci.schertz.tx.us*
Counties:	Bexar	*www.co.bexar.tx.us*
	Comal	*www.co.comal.tx.us*
	Guadalupe	*www.co.guadalupe.tx.us*
	Wilson	
Metropolitan Planning Organization:	San Antonio-Bexar County Metropolitan Planning Organization	*www.sametroplan.org*
Largest Transit Agency:	VIA Metropolitan Transit (VIA)	*www.viainfo.net*
Largest Public School Districts:	North East Independent School District	*www.northeast.isd.tenet.edu*
	Northside Independent School District	*www.nisd.net*
	San Antonio Independent School District	*www.saisd.net*
Metropolitan Public University:	University of Texas-San Antonio	*www.utsa.edu*

Norfolk-Virginia Beach-Newport News, VA-NC MSA

Population:	1,569	
Largest Cities:	Virginia Beach, VA	*www.virginia-beach.va.us*
	Norfolk, VA	*www.norfolk.va.us/home.htm*
	Newport News, VA	*www.newport-news.va.us*
	Chesapeake, VA	*www.chesapeake.va.us*
	Hampton, VA	*www.hampton.va.us*
Counties:	Currituck, NC	*www.co.currituck.nc.us*
	Gloucester, VA	*www.co.gloucester.va.us*
	Isle of Wight, VA	*www.co.isle-of-wight.va.us*
	James City, VA	*www.james-city.va.us*
	Mathews, VA	*www.co.mathews.va.us*
	York, VA	*www.co.york.va.us*
	Chesapeake city, VA	*www.chesapeake.va.us*
	Hampton city, VA	*www.hampton.va.us*
	Newport News city, VA	*www.newport-news.va.us*
	Norfolk city, VA	*www.norfolk.va.us/home.htm*
	Poquoson city, VA	*www.ci.poquoson.va.us*
	Portsmouth city, VA	*www.ci.portsmouth.va.us*

	Suffolk city, VA	www.city.suffolk.va.us
	Virginia Beach city, VA	www.virginia-beach.va.us
	Williamsburg city, VA	www.ci.williamsburg.va.us

Metropolitan Planning
  Organization: Hampton Roads
              Metropolitan Planning
              Organization   www.hrpdc.org/transport/mpo.shtml

Largest Transit
  Agency: Hampton Roads
              Transit   www.hrtransit.org
              (formerly Tidewater Transportation District Commission)

Largest Public School
  District: Virginia Beach City
              Public Schools   www.vbcps.k12.va.us

Metropolitan Public
  University: Old Dominion
              University   www.odu.edu

Las Vegas, NV-AZ MSA

Population: 1,563

Largest Cities:	Las Vegas, NV	www.ci.las-vegas.nv.us
	Henderson, NV	www.ci.henderson.nv.us
	North Las Vegas, NV	www.ci.north-las-vegas.nv.us
	Lake Havasu City, AZ	www.lakehavasucity.com
	Bullhead City, AZ	www.bullheadcity.com
Counties:	Mohave, AZ	www.co.mohave.az.us
	Clark, NV	www.co.clark.nv.us
	Nye, NV	www.governet.net/NV/CO/NYE/home.cfm

Metropolitan Planning
  Organization: Regional Transportation
              Commission of
              Clark County   www.rtc.co.clark.nv.us
              (Serves Clark, Mohave, and Nye counties.)

Largest Transit
  Agency: ATC\VanCom

Largest Public School
  District: Clark County School
              District   www.ccsd.net

Metropolitan Public
  University: University of
              Nevada-Las Vegas www.unlv.edu

Columbus, OH MSA

Population: 1,540

Largest Cities:	Columbus	www.ci.columbus.oh.us
	Newark	www.ci.newark.oh.us
	Lancaster	www.ci.lancaster.oh.us
	Upper Arlington	www.ci.upper-arlington.oh.us
	Westerville	www.ci.westerville.oh.us

Counties:	Delaware	www.co.delaware.oh.us
	Fairfield	www.ci.westerville.oh.us
	Franklin	www.co.franklin.oh.us
	Licking	www.lcounty.com
	Madison	www.co.madison.oh.us
	Pickaway	

Metropolitan Planning
   Organizations: Mid-Ohio Regional
                          Planning
                          Commission   www.morpc.org/trans/morpcmpo/morpcmpo.htm
                       Newark-Heath
                          Metropolitan Planning
                          Organization   www.lcats.org

Largest Transit
   Agency: Central Ohio Transit
                          Authority (COTA)   www.cota.com

Largest Public School
   District: Columbus Public
                          Schools   www.columbus.k12.oh.us

Metropolitan Public
   University: Ohio State University   www.osu.edu

Charlotte-Gastonia-Rock Hill, NC-SC MSA

Population:	1,499	
Largest Cities:	Charlotte, NC	www.co.mecklenburg.nc.us/welcome.htm
	Gastonia, NC	www.cityofgastonia.com
	Rock Hill, SC	www.ci.rock-hill.sc.us
	Kannapolis, NC	www.ci.kannapolis.nc.us
	Concord, NC	www.ci.concord.nc.us
Counties:	Cabarrus, NC	www.co.cabarrus.nc.us
	Gaston, NC	www.co.gaston.nc.us
	Lincoln, NC	www.lincolncounty.org
	Mecklenburg, NC	www.co.mecklenburg.nc.us/welcome.htm
	Rowan, NC	www.co.rowan.nc.us
	Union, NC	www.co.union.nc.us
	York, SC	www.yorkcountygov.com

Metropolitan Planning
   Organizations: Cabarrus/South Rowan
                          Metropolitan Planning
                          Organization   www.ci.concord.nc.us/planning
                       Mecklenburg-Union
                          Metropolitan Planning
                          Organization
                       Gaston Urban Area
                          Metropolitan Planning
                          Organization   www.cityofgastonia.com/plantransmpo.htm
                       (Serves Belmont, Bessemer City, Cramerton, Dallas, Gaston County,
                       Gastonia, Lowell, McAdenville, Mount Holly, Ranlo, Spencer Mountain,
                       and Stanley.)

Largest Transit Agency:	Charlotte Department of Transportation (CTS)	*www.ridetransit.org*
Largest Public School District:	Charlotte-Mecklenburg Schools	*www.cms.k12.nc.us*
Metropolitan Public University:	University of North Carolina-Charlotte	*www.uncc.edu*

New Orleans, LA MSA

Population:	1,337	
Largest Cities:	New Orleans	*www2.new-orleans.la.us*
	Kenner	*www.kenner.la.us*
	Slidell	*www.slidell.la.us*
	Gretna	*www.gretnala.com*
	Westwego	
Counties:	Jefferson Parish	*www.jeffparish.net*
	Orleans Parish	
	Plaquemines Parish	
	St. Bernard Parish	*www.st-bernard.la.us*
	St. Charles Parish	*www.st-charles.la.us*
	St. James Parish	*www.stjamesla.com*
	St. John the Baptist Parish	*www.stjohnla.org*
	St. Tammany Parish	*stp.pa.st-tammany.la.us*
Metropolitan Planning Organization:	Regional Planning Commission	*www.norpc.org*
	(Serves Jefferson, Orleans, Plaquemines, St. Bernard, and St. Tammany Parishes.)	
Largest Transit Agency:	Regional Transit Authority (RTA)	*www.regionaltransit.org*
Largest Public School District:	New Orleans Public Schools	*nops.k12.la.us*
Metropolitan Public University:	University of New Orleans	*www.uno.edu*

Salt Lake City-Ogden, UT MSA

Population:	1,333	
Largest Cities:	Salt Lake City	*www.ci.slc.ut.us*
	West Valley City	*www.ci.west-valley.ut.us*
	Sandy	*www.sandy-city.net*
	Ogden	*www.ogdencity.com*
	West Jordan	*www.ci.west-jordan.ut.us*

Counties:	Davis	*www.co.davis.ut.us*
	Salt Lake	*www.co.slc.ut.us*
	Weber	*www.co.weber.ut.us*
Metropolitan Planning Organization:	Wasatch Front Regional Council	*www.wfrc.org*

(Serves municipalities within and the counties of Weber, Morgan, Davis, Salt Lake, and Tooele.)

Largest Transit Agency:	Utah Transit Authority	*www.rideuta.com*
Largest Public School District:	Salt Lake City School District	*www.slc.k12.ut.us*
Metropolitan Public University:	University of Utah	*www.utah.edu*

Greensboro-Winston-Salem-High Point, NC MSA

Population:	1,251	
Largest Cities:	Greensboro	*www.ci.greensboro.nc.us*
	Winston-Salem	*www.ci.winston-salem.nc.us*
	High Point	*www.high-point.net*
	Burlington	*www.ci.burlington.nc.us*
	Lexington	
Counties:	Alamance	*www.alamance-nc.com*
	Davidson	*www.co.davidson.nc.us*
	Davie	*www.co.davie.nc.us*
	Forsyth	*www.co.forsyth.nc.us*
	Guilford	*www.co.guilford.nc.us*
	Randolph	*www.co.randolph.nc.us*
	Stokes	*www.co.stokes.nc.us*
	Yadkin	*www.yadkin.com*
Metropolitan Planning Organizations:	Burlington-Graham Metropolitan Planning Organization	*www.mpo.burlington.nc.us*

(Serves ten municipalities: Burlington, Gibsonville, Graham, Green Level, Haw River, Mebane, Elon College, Whitsett, Saxapahaw, and the Village of Alamance and portions of Alamance, Guilford, and Orange Counties.)

	Greensboro Department of Transportation	*www.ci.greensboro.nc.us/gdot/planning/mpo/*

(Serves the Greensboro urban area that includes all of Guilford County except the Gibsonville, Whitsett, High Point, and Jamestown areas.)

	High Point Urban Area Transportation Metropolitan Planning Organization	*tocfs2.ci.high-point.nc.us/trplan/himpo.html*

(Serves the High Point urban area of High Point, Jamestown, Archdale, Thomasville, and portions of Guilford, Randolph and Davidson counties.)

	Winston-Salem/Forsyth County Urban Area Metropolitan Planning Organization	*www.cityofws.org/DOT/mpo_tac.html*
	(Serves all of Forsyth county.)	
Largest Transit Agency:	Winston-Salem Transit Authority-Trans-Aid of Forsyth County	*www.eos.ncsu.edu/eos/info/ce400_info/wsta.html*
Largest Public School District:	Guilford County Schools	*www.guilford.k12.nc.us*
Metropolitan Public University:	University of North Carolina-Greensboro	*www.uncg.edu*

Austin-San Marcos, TX MSA

Population:	1,249	
Largest Cities:	Austin	*www.ci.austin.tx.usdefaultfull.htm*
	Round Rock	*www.ci.round-rock.tx.us*
	San Marcos	*ci.san-marcos.tx.us*
	Georgetown	*georgetown.org/city/index.html*
	Taylor	*ci.taylor.tx.us/taylorcity/homepage.html*
Counties:	Bastrop	
	Caldwell	
	Hays	*www.co.hays.tx.us*
	Travis	*www.co.travis.tx.us*
	Williamson	*www.williamson-county.org*
Metropolitan Planning Organization:	Capital Area Metropolitan Planning Organization	*www.ci.austin.tx.us/campo/default.htm*
	(Serves Travis, Hays, and Williamson counties, and nineteen cities.)	
Largest Transit Agency:	Capital Metropolitan Transit Authority	*www.capmetro.austin.tx.us*
Largest Public School District:	Austin Independent School District	*www.austin.isd.tenet.edu*
Metropolitan Public University:	University of Texas at Austin	*www.utexas.edu*

Nashville, TN MSA

Population: 1,231
Largest Cities: Nashville-Davidson   www.nashville.org
                       Murfreesboro   ci.murfreesboro.tn.us
                       Hendersonville   www.hvilletn.org
                       Franklin   www.franklin-gov.com
                       Gallatin
Counties: Cheatham   www.cheathamcounty.net
                       Davidson   www.nashville.org
                       Dickson
                       Robertson
                       Rutherford   www.rc.state.tn.us
                       Sumner   www.sumnertn.org
                       Williamson   williamson-tn.org
                       Wilson   www.wilsoncountytn.com

Metropolitan Planning
  Organization: Nashville Area
                         Metropolitan Planning
                         Organization   www.nashville.org/mpc/trans/index.html
                       (Serves Davidson, Rutherford, Sumner, Wilson, and Williamson
                       counties.)

Largest Transit
  Agency: Metropolitan Transit
                         Authority   nashvillemta.org

Largest Public School
  District: Metropolitan Nashville
                         Davidson County
                         Public Schools   www.nashville-schools.davidson.k12.tn.us

Metropolitan Public
  University: Tennessee State
                         University   www.tnstate.edu

Raleigh-Durham-Chapel Hill, NC MSA

Population: 1,187
Largest Cities: Raleigh   www.raleigh-nc.org
                       Durham   www.ci.durham.nc.us
                       Cary (town)   www.townofcary.org
                       Chapel Hill (town)   www.ci.chapel-hill.nc.us
                       Garner (town)   www.ci.garner.nc.us
Counties: Chatham   www.co.chatham.nc.us
                       Durham   www.co.durham.nc.us
                       Franklin   www.co.franklin.nc.us
                       Johnston   www.co.johnston.nc.us
                       Orange   www.co.orange.nc.us
                       Wake   www.co.wake.nc.us

Metropolitan Planning
  Organization: Capital Area
                         Metropolitan Planning
                         Organization   www.raleigh-nc.org/campo

	Durham-Chapel Hill-Carrboro Metropolitan Planning Organization	
Largest Transit Agency:	Research Triangle Regional Public Transportation Authority	*www.ridetta.org*
Largest Public School District:	Wake County Public School System	*www.wcpss.net*
Metropolitan Public Universities:	University of North Carolina at Chapel Hill	*www.unc.edu*
	North Carolina State University	*www.ncsu.edu*

Hartford, CT NECMA

Population:	1,183	
Largest Cities:	Hartford	*ci.hartford.ct.us*
	New Britain	*www.new-britain.net*
	Bristol	*www.ci.bristol.ct.us*
	Meriden	*www.cityofmeriden.org*
	Middletown	*www.cityofmiddletown.com*
Counties:	Hartford	
	Middlesex	
	Tolland	
Metropolitan Planning Organization:	Capital Region Council of Governments	*www.crcog.org*

(Serves the City of Hartford and following 28 surrounding suburban and rural communities: Andover, Avon, Bolton, Bloomfield, Canton, East Granby, East Hartford, East Windsor, Ellington, Enfield, Farmington, Glastonbury, Granby, Hebron, Manchester, Marlborough, Newington, Rocky Hill, Simsbury, Somers, South Windsor, Suffield, Tolland, Vernon, West Hartford, Wethersfield, Windsor, and Windsor Locks.)

Largest Transit Agency:	Connecticut Transit-Hartford Division	*www.cttransit.com*
Largest Public School District:	Hartford Public Schools[3]	*ci.hartford.ct.us/Education/root*
Metropolitan Public University:	None	

Buffalo-Niagara Falls, NY MSA

Population:	1,170	
Largest Cities:	Buffalo	www.ci.buffalo.ny.us/city/index.html
	Niagara Falls	www.ci.niagara-falls.ny.us
	North Tonawanda	www.northtonawanda.org/default.htm
	Lockport	
	Lackawanna	
Counties:	Erie	www.erie.gov
	Niagara	www.niagaracounty.com
Metropolitan Planning Organization:	Greater Buffalo-Niagara Frontier Transportation Council	www.gbnrtc.org
	(Serves Erie and Niagara counties.)	
Largest Transit Agency:	Niagara Frontier Transit Metro System, Inc.	www.nfta.com
Largest Public School District:	Buffalo Public Schools	www.buffaloschools.org
Metropolitan Public University:	State University of New York at Buffalo	www.buffalo.edu

Memphis, TN-AR-MS MSA

Population:	1,135	
Largest Cities:	Memphis, TN	www.ci.memphis.tn.us
	Germantown, TN	www.ci.germantown.tn.us
	West Memphis, AR	http://www.ci.west-memphis.ar.us/index.html
	Southaven, MS	www.southaven.org
	Millington, TN	www.ci.millington.tn.us/index.html
Counties:	Fayette, TN	
	Shelby, TN	www.co.shelby.tn.us/index.htm
	Tipton, TN	
	Crittenden, AR	
	DeSoto, MS	
Metropolitan Planning Organization:	Memphis Metropolitan Planning Organization	
	(Serves Shelby and the western portion of Fayette County, Tennessee, and northern Desoto County, Mississippi.)	
Largest Transit Agency:	Memphis Area Transit Authority	www.matatransit.com
Largest Public School District:	Memphis City School District	www.memphis-schools.k12.tn.us

| Metropolitan Public University: | University of Memphis | www.memphis.edu |

West Palm Beach-Boca Raton, FL MSA

Population:	1,131	
Largest Cities:	West Palm Beach	www.excitingcity.com
	Boca Raton	www.ci.boca-raton.fl.us
	Delray Beach	www.delraybeach.com
	Deerfield Beach	www.deerfieldbch.com
	Boynton Beach	www.ci.boynton-beach.fl.us
Counties:	Palm Beach	www.co.palm-beach.fl.us or www.pbcgov.com
Metropolitan Planning Organization:	Metropolitan Planning Organization of Palm Beach County	www.pbcgov.com/MPO
Largest Transit Agency:	Palm Tran	www.co.palm-beach.fl.us/palmtran
Largest Public School District:	The School District of Palm Beach County	www.palmbeach.k12.fl.us
Metropolitan Public University:	Florida Atlantic University	www.fau.edu

Jacksonville, FL MSA

Population:	1,100	
Largest Cities:	Jacksonville Beach	www.jacksonvillebeach.org
	St. Augustine	www.ci.st-augustine.fl.us
	Atlantic Beach	ci.atlantic-beach.fl.us
	Fernandina Beach	www.fernandinabeachflorida.org/index.html
	Neptune Beach	CI.Neptune-Beach.FL.US
Counties:	Clay	www.co.clay.fl.us
	Duval	www.coj.net/tc
	Nassau	www.nassauclerk.com
	St. Johns	www.co.st-johns.fl.us
Metropolitan Planning Organization:	Jacksonville PDD	www.coj.net/planning
Largest Transit Agency:	Jacksonville Transportation Authority	www.jtaonthemove.com
Largest Public School District:	Duval County Public Schools	www.educationcentral.org
Metropolitan Public University:	University of North Florida	www.unf.edu

Rochester, NY MSA

Population:	1,098	
Largest Cities:	Rochester	*www.ci.rochester.ny.us*
	Batavia	*www.batavianewyork.com*
	Geneva	*www.geneva.ny.us*
	Canandaigua	*www.ci.canandaigua.ny.us*
Counties:	Genesee	*www.co.genesee.ny.us*
	Livingston	*www.co.livingston.state.ny.us*
	Monroe	*www.co.monroe.ny.us*
	Ontario	*www.co.ontario.ny.us*
	Orleans	*www.orleansny.com*
	Wayne	

Metropolitan Planning
   Organization: Genesee Transportation
                      Council   *www.gtcmpo.org*
                      (Serves Orleans, Monroe, Wayne, Genesee, Livingston, Ontario,
                      Seneca, Wyoming, Yates counties.)

Largest Transit
   Agency: Rochester-Genesee
                      Regional
                      Transportation
                      Authority   *www.rgrta.org*

Largest Public School
   District: Rochester City
                      School District   *www.rochester.k12.ny.us*

Metropolitan Public
   University: none

Grand Rapids-Muskegon-Holland, MI MSA

Population:	1,088	
Largest Cities:	Grand Rapids	*www.grand-rapids.mi.us*
	Wyoming	*www.ci.wyoming.mi.us*
	Muskegon	*www.ci.muskegon.mi.us*
	Kentwood	*www.ci.kentwood.mi.us/contact.htm*
	Holland	*www.ci.holland.mi.us*
Counties:	Allegan	*www.multimag.com/county/mi/allegan*
	Kent	*www.co.kent.mi.us*
	Muskegon	*co.muskegon.mi.us*
	Ottawa	*www.multimag.com/county/mi/ottawa*

Metropolitan Planning
   Organization: Grand Valley
                      Metropolitan Council *www.gvmc.org*

Largest Transit
   Agency: Grand Rapids Area
                      Transit Authority   *www.grata.org*

Largest Public School
   District: Grand Rapids Public
                      School District   *www.grps.k12.mi.us/homepage2.spml*

Metropolitan Public
   University: none

Oklahoma City, OK MSA

Population:	1,083	
Largest Cities:	Oklahoma City	*www.okc-cityhall.org*
	Norman	*www.ci.norman.ok.us*
	Edmond	*www.ci.edmond.ok.us*
	Midwest City	
	Moore	*www.ci.moore.ok.us*
Counties:	Canadian	*co.canadian.ok.us/government/county/index.htm*
	Cleveland	
	Logan	
	McClain	
	Oklahoma	*www.oklahomacounty.org*
	Pottawatomie	

Metropolitan Planning
   Organization: Association of
                Central
                Governments   *www.acogok.org*
                (Serves all of Oklahoma county and portions of Canadian, Cleveland,
                Grady, Logan, and McClain counties.)

Largest Transit
   Agency: Central Oklahoma
                Transportation and
                Parking Authority   *www.okc-cityhall.org*

Largest Public School
   District: Oklahoma City
                Public Schools   *www.okcps.k12.ok.us*

Metropolitan Public
   University: The University of
                Oklahoma   *www.ou.edu*

Louisville, KY-IN MSA

Population:	1,025	
Largest Cities:	Louisville, KY	*www.louky.org*
	New Albany, IN	
	Jeffersontown, KY	
	Jeffersonville, IN	*ci.jeffersonville.in.us*
	St. Matthews, KY	
Counties:	Clark, IN	*www.co.clark.in.us*
	Floyd, IN	*www.indico.net/counties/FLOYD*
	Harrison, IN	*www.indico.net/counties/HARRISON/*
		government.html
	Scott, IN	*www.scottcounty.org*
	Bullitt, KY	*www.ltadd.org:80/bullitt*
	Jefferson, KY	*www.co.jefferson.ky.us*
	Oldham, KY	*www.oldhamcounty.net/default.htm*

Metropolitan Planning
    Organization: Kentuckiana Regional
                             Planning and
                             Development Agency *www.kipda.org*
                             (Serves the counties of Clark and Floyd, Indiana and Trimble, Oldham,
                             Henry Jefferson, Shelby, Bullitt and Spencer, Kentucky.)
Largest Transit
    Agency: Transit Authority of
                             River City   *www.ridetarc.com* or *www.ridetarc.org*
Largest Public School
    District: Jefferson County
                             Public Schools   *www.jefferson.k12.ky.us*
Metropolitan Public
    University: University of
                             Louisville   *www.louisville.edu*

---

[1]Five PMSAs of the New York-Northern New Jersey-Long, NY-NJ-CT-PA CMSA are in Connecticut and therefore do not appear in this listing; also, the CMSA's population shown here reflects the absence of those PMSAs.
[2]Cities with a population of 25,000 or more as of 1990.
[3]Public school enrollment is monitored by towns as opposed to school districts.

Sources

All the Web, All the Time (Search engine). Accessed at *www.alltheweb.com* 2001.

Association of Metropolitan Planning Organizations. 2000. *Profiles of Metropolitan Planning Organizations.* Washington, DC: Association of Metropolitan Planning Organizations.

Connecticut State Department of Education.

Council of the Great City Schools. Member Districts. Accessed at *http://cgcs.org/members.cfm* March 2001.

Federal Transit Administration National Transit Database. Accessed at *http://www.ntdprogram.com/NTD/ntdhome.nsf/?Open* March 2001.

Geolytics, Inc. 1990. *CensusCD+Maps.* New Jersey. *www.geolytics.com.*

Google (Search engine). Accessed at *www.google.com* 2001.

National Association of Counties. Accessed at *www.naco.org* June 2001.

Piper Resources. Accessed at *www.piperinfo.com/index.cfm* June 2001.

U.S. Census Bureau, Population Division. 2000. *Ranking Tables for Metropolitan Areas: Population in 2000 and Population Change from 1990 to 2000 (PHTC-T-3).* Accessed at *http://census.gov.prod/www/statistical-abstract-us.htm* July 2001.

U.S. Census Bureau, Statistical Abstract of the United States. 2000. *Appendix II: Metropolitan Areas: Concepts, Components, and Population.* Accessed at *http://www.census.gov/prod/www/statistical-abstract-us.htm* June 2001.

Photo Credits

Index